SWAMP THING
regenesis

RICK VEITCH
ALFREDO ALCALA
BRETT EWINS

TATJANA WOOD
COLORIST

JOHN COSTANZA
LETTERER

RICK VEITCH
JOHN TOTLEBEN
TOM YEATES
ORIGINAL COVERS

SWAMP THING CREATED BY LEN WEIN & BERNI WRIGHTSON

KAREN BERGER — VP-EXECUTIVE EDITOR/EDITOR-ORIGINAL SERIES

SCOTT NYBAKKEN — EDITOR-COLLECTED EDITION

ROBBIN BROSTERMAN — SENIOR ART DIRECTOR

PAUL LEVITZ — PRESIDENT & PUBLISHER

GEORG BREWER — VP-DESIGN & RETAIL PRODUCT DEVELOPMENT

RICHARD BRUNING — SENIOR VP-CREATIVE DIRECTOR

PATRICK CALDON — SENIOR VP-FINANCE & OPERATIONS

CHRIS CARAMALIS — VP-FINANCE

TERRI CUNNINGHAM — VP-MANAGING EDITOR

DAN DIDIO — VP-EDITORIAL

ALISON GILL — VP-MANUFACTURING

RICH JOHNSON — VP-BOOK TRADE SALES

HANK KANALZ — VP-GENERAL MANAGER-WILDSTORM

LILLIAN LASERSON — SENIOR VP & GENERAL COUNSEL

JIM LEE — EDITORIAL DIRECTOR-WILDSTORM

DAVID MCKILLIPS — VP-ADVERTISING & CUSTOM PUBLISHING

JOHN NEE — VP-BUSINESS DEVELOPMENT

GREGORY NOVECK — SENIOR VP-CREATIVE AFFAIRS

CHERYL RUBIN — SENIOR VP-BRAND MANAGEMENT

BOB WAYNE — VP-SALES & MARKETING

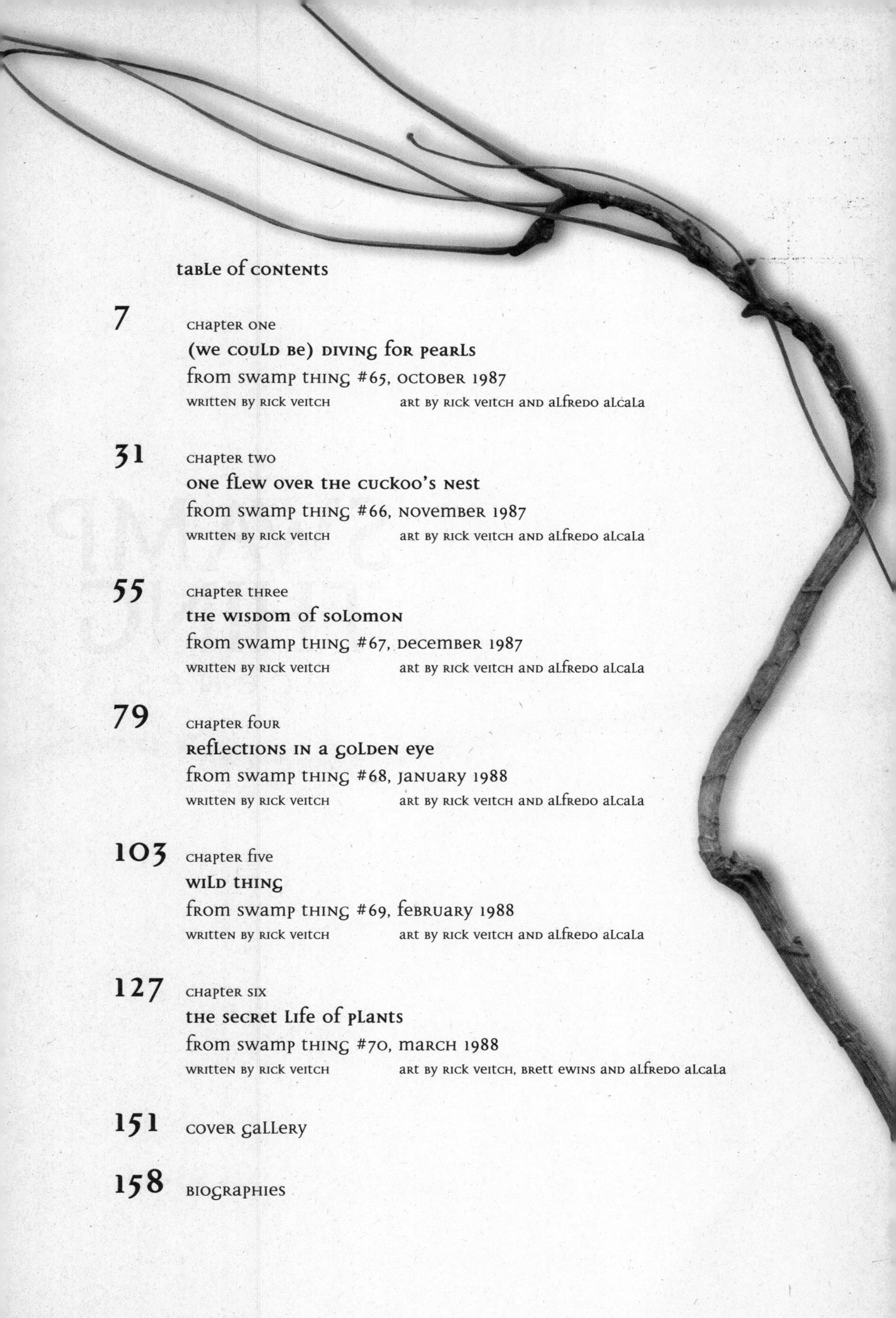

table of contents

SWAMP THING

regenesis

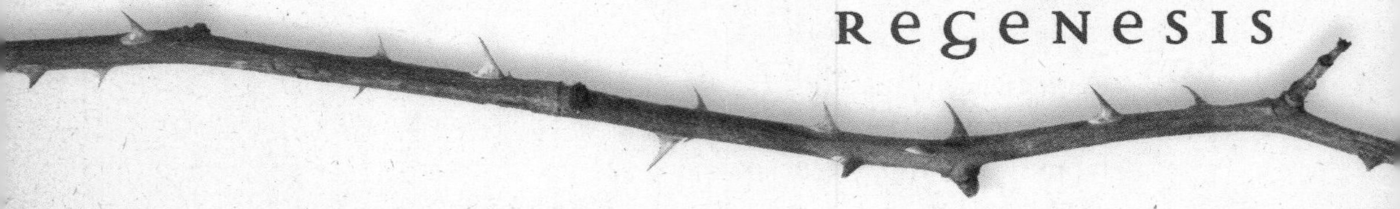

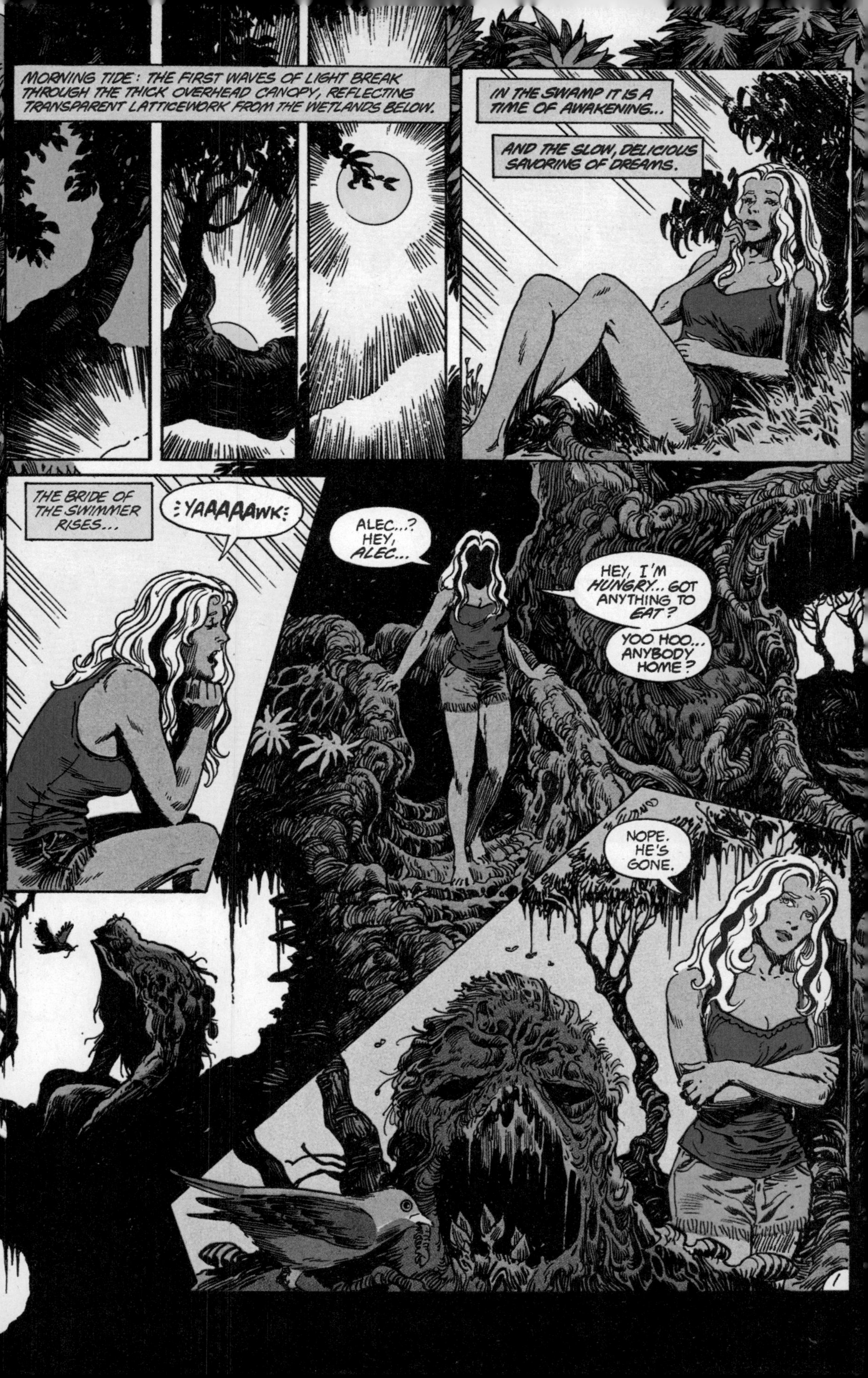
MORNING TIDE: THE FIRST WAVES OF LIGHT BREAK THROUGH THE THICK OVERHEAD CANOPY, REFLECTING TRANSPARENT LATTICEWORK FROM THE WETLANDS BELOW.
IN THE SWAMP IT IS A TIME OF AWAKENING...
AND THE SLOW, DELICIOUS SAVORING OF DREAMS.
THE BRIDE OF THE SWIMMER RISES...
YAAAAAWK
ALEC...? HEY, ALEC...
HEY, I'M HUNGRY... GOT ANYTHING TO EAT?
YOO HOO... ANYBODY HOME?
NOPE. HE'S GONE.
1

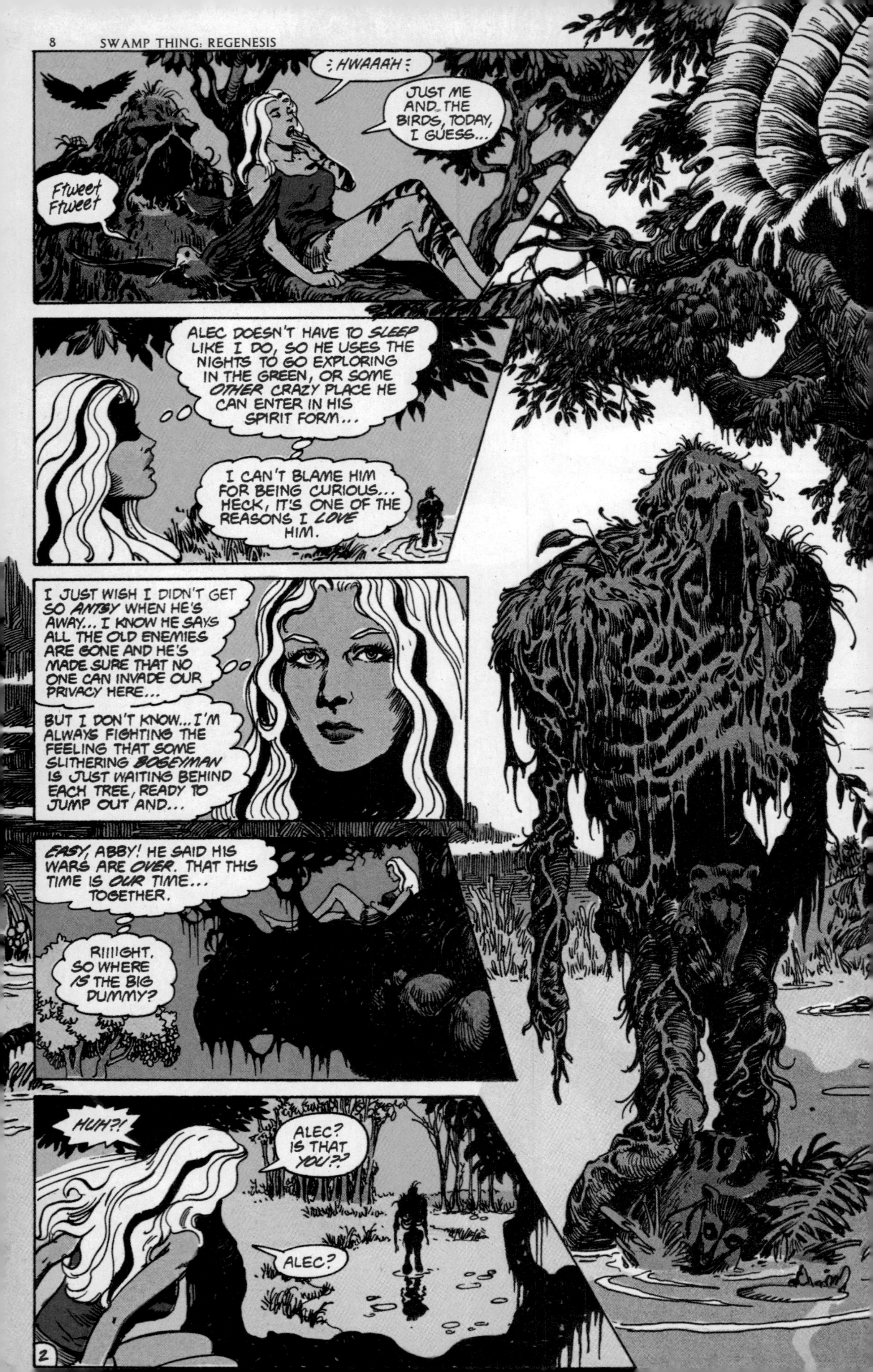
HWAAAH
JUST ME AND THE BIRDS, TODAY, I GUESS...
Ftweet Ftweet
ALEC DOESN'T HAVE TO SLEEP LIKE I DO, SO HE USES THE NIGHTS TO GO EXPLORING IN THE GREEN, OR SOME OTHER CRAZY PLACE HE CAN ENTER IN HIS SPIRIT FORM...
I CAN'T BLAME HIM FOR BEING CURIOUS... HECK, IT'S ONE OF THE REASONS I LOVE HIM.
I JUST WISH I DIDN'T GET SO ANTSY WHEN HE'S AWAY... I KNOW HE SAYS ALL THE OLD ENEMIES ARE GONE AND HE'S MADE SURE THAT NO ONE CAN INVADE OUR PRIVACY HERE...
BUT I DON'T KNOW... I'M ALWAYS FIGHTING THE FEELING THAT SOME SLITHERING BOGEYMAN IS JUST WAITING BEHIND EACH TREE, READY TO JUMP OUT AND...
EASY, ABBY! HE SAID HIS WARS ARE OVER. THAT THIS TIME IS OUR TIME... TOGETHER.
RIIIIGHT. SO WHERE IS THE BIG DUMMY?
HUH?!
ALEC? IS THAT YOU??
ALEC?
2

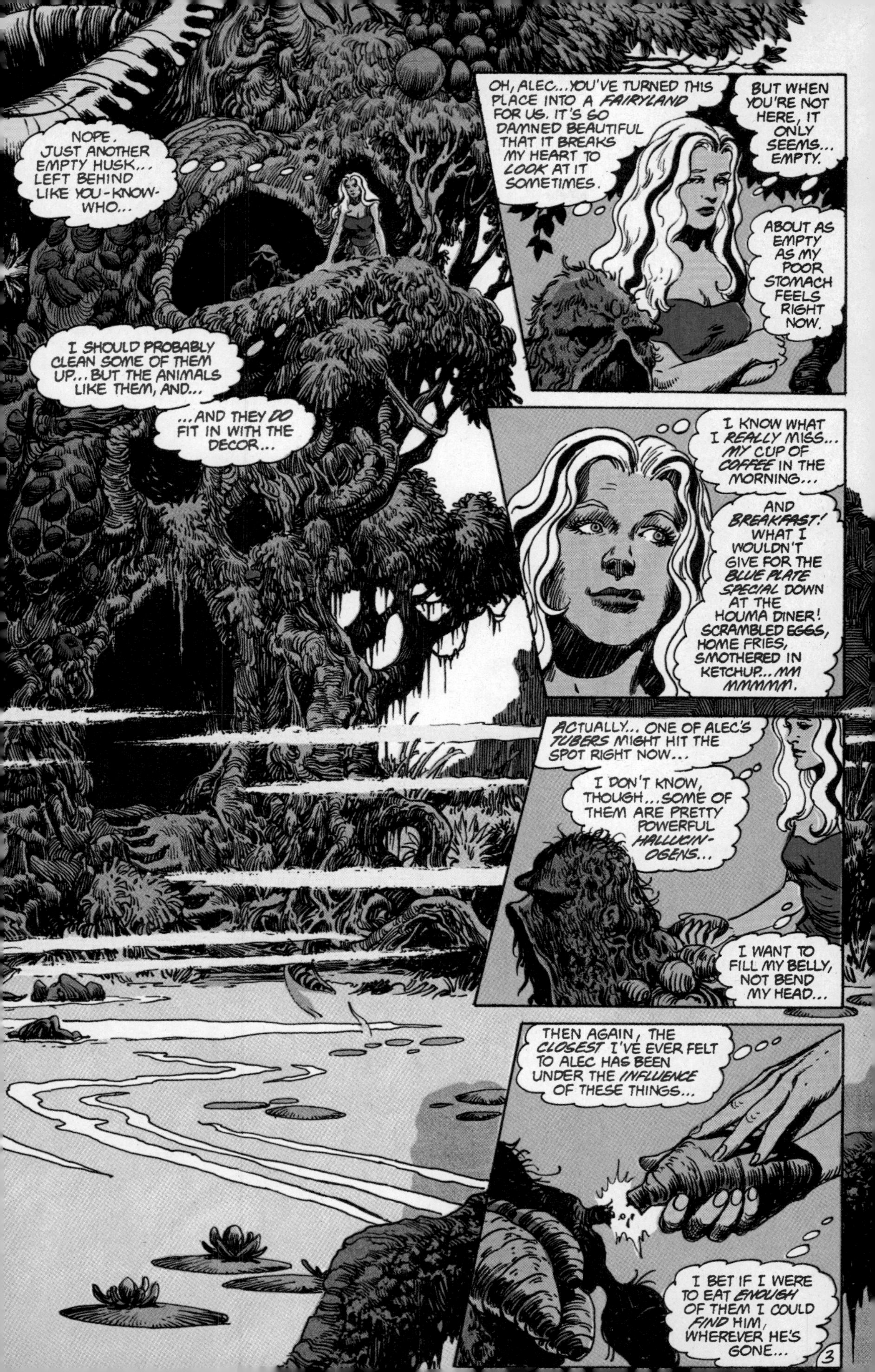
NOPE. JUST ANOTHER EMPTY HUSK... LEFT BEHIND LIKE YOU-KNOW-WHO...
I SHOULD PROBABLY CLEAN SOME OF THEM UP... BUT THE ANIMALS LIKE THEM, AND...
...AND THEY DO FIT IN WITH THE DECOR...
OH, ALEC... YOU'VE TURNED THIS PLACE INTO A FAIRYLAND FOR US. IT'S SO DAMNED BEAUTIFUL THAT IT BREAKS MY HEART TO LOOK AT IT SOMETIMES.
BUT WHEN YOU'RE NOT HERE, IT ONLY SEEMS... EMPTY.
ABOUT AS EMPTY AS MY POOR STOMACH FEELS RIGHT NOW.
I KNOW WHAT I REALLY MISS... MY CUP OF COFFEE IN THE MORNING...
AND BREAKFAST! WHAT I WOULDN'T GIVE FOR THE BLUE PLATE SPECIAL DOWN AT THE HOUMA DINER! SCRAMBLED EGGS, HOME FRIES, SMOTHERED IN KETCHUP... MM MMMMM.
ACTUALLY... ONE OF ALEC'S TUBERS MIGHT HIT THE SPOT RIGHT NOW...
I DON'T KNOW, THOUGH... SOME OF THEM ARE PRETTY POWERFUL HALLUCIN-OGENS...
I WANT TO FILL MY BELLY, NOT BEND MY HEAD...
THEN AGAIN, THE CLOSEST I'VE EVER FELT TO ALEC HAS BEEN UNDER THE INFLUENCE OF THESE THINGS...
I BET IF I WERE TO EAT ENOUGH OF THEM I COULD FIND HIM, WHEREVER HE'S GONE...
3

THE SWIMMER IN A SECRET SEA DESCENDS.
POWERFUL STROKES PROPEL HIM DEEP INTO THE DARKENING DEPTHS OF THE GREEN DIMENSION...
DEEP INTO THE REALM OF THE ROOTBOUND ELDERS...
DEEP INTO THE SOCIETY OF MIND...
(WE COULD BE)
SWAMP THING
4

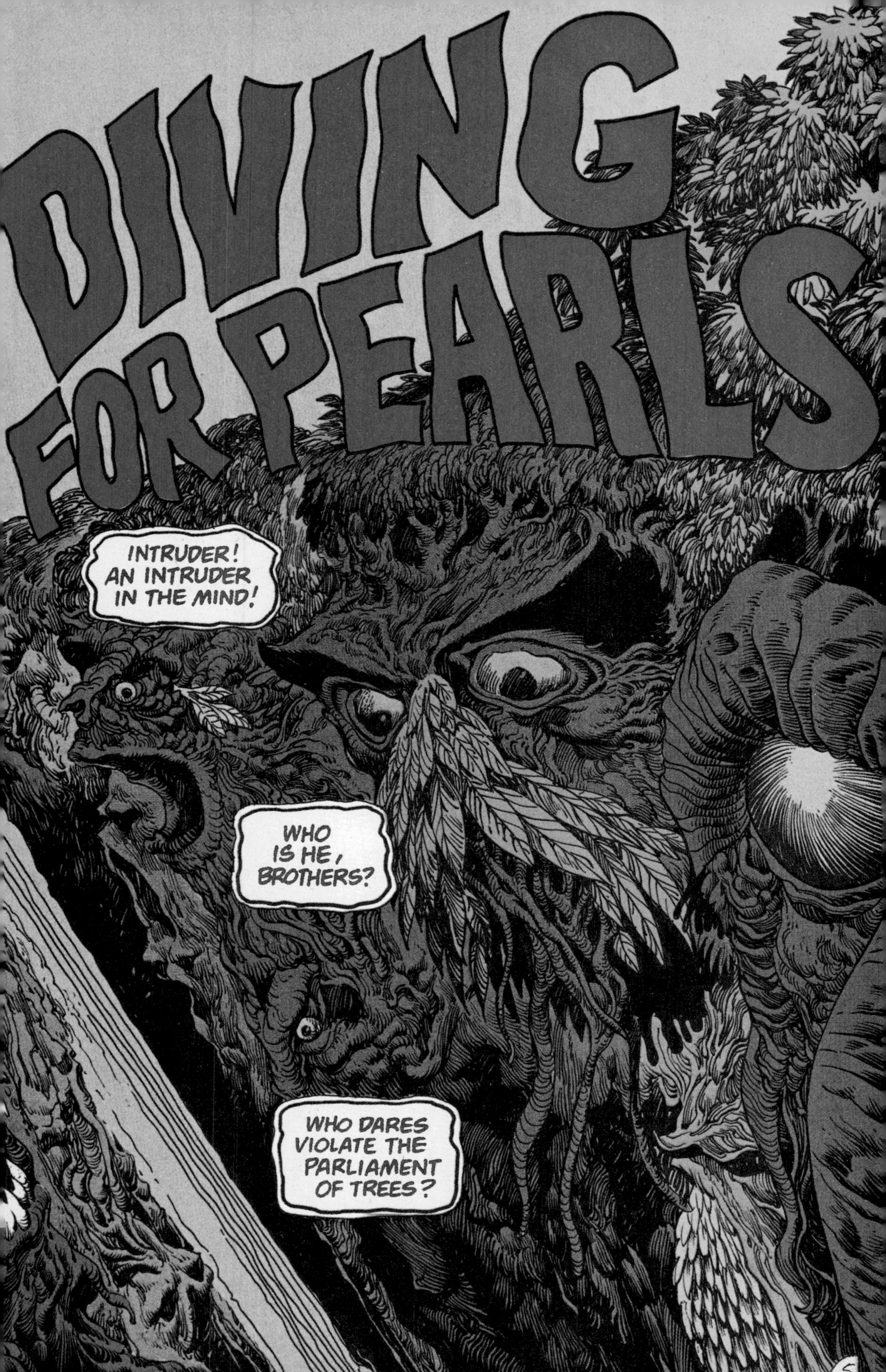
DIVING FOR PEARLS
INTRUDER! AN INTRUDER IN THE MIND!
WHO IS HE, BROTHERS?
WHO DARES VIOLATE THE PARLIAMENT OF TREES?

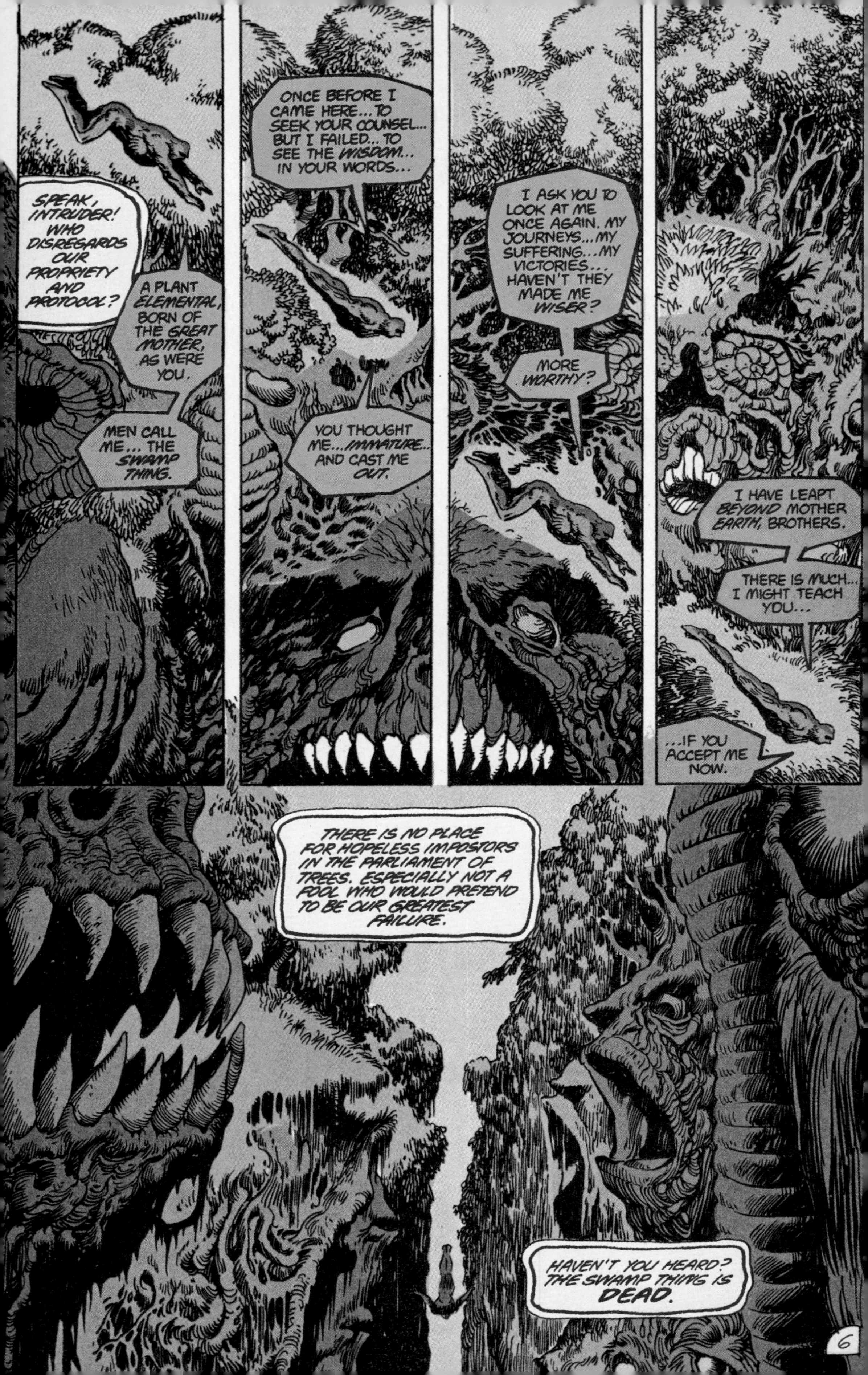
SPEAK, INTRUDER! WHO DISREGARDS OUR PROPRIETY AND PROTOCOL?
A PLANT ELEMENTAL, BORN OF THE GREAT MOTHER, AS WERE YOU.
MEN CALL ME... THE SWAMP THING.
ONCE BEFORE I CAME HERE... TO SEEK YOUR COUNSEL... BUT I FAILED... TO SEE THE WISDOM... IN YOUR WORDS...
YOU THOUGHT ME... IMMATURE... AND CAST ME OUT.
I ASK YOU TO LOOK AT ME ONCE AGAIN. MY JOURNEYS... MY SUFFERING... MY VICTORIES... HAVEN'T THEY MADE ME WISER?
MORE WORTHY?
I HAVE LEAPT BEYOND MOTHER EARTH, BROTHERS.
THERE IS MUCH... I MIGHT TEACH YOU...
...IF YOU ACCEPT ME NOW.
THERE IS NO PLACE FOR HOPELESS IMPOSTORS IN THE PARLIAMENT OF TREES. ESPECIALLY NOT A FOOL WHO WOULD PRETEND TO BE OUR GREATEST FAILURE.
HAVEN'T YOU HEARD? THE SWAMP THING IS DEAD.
6

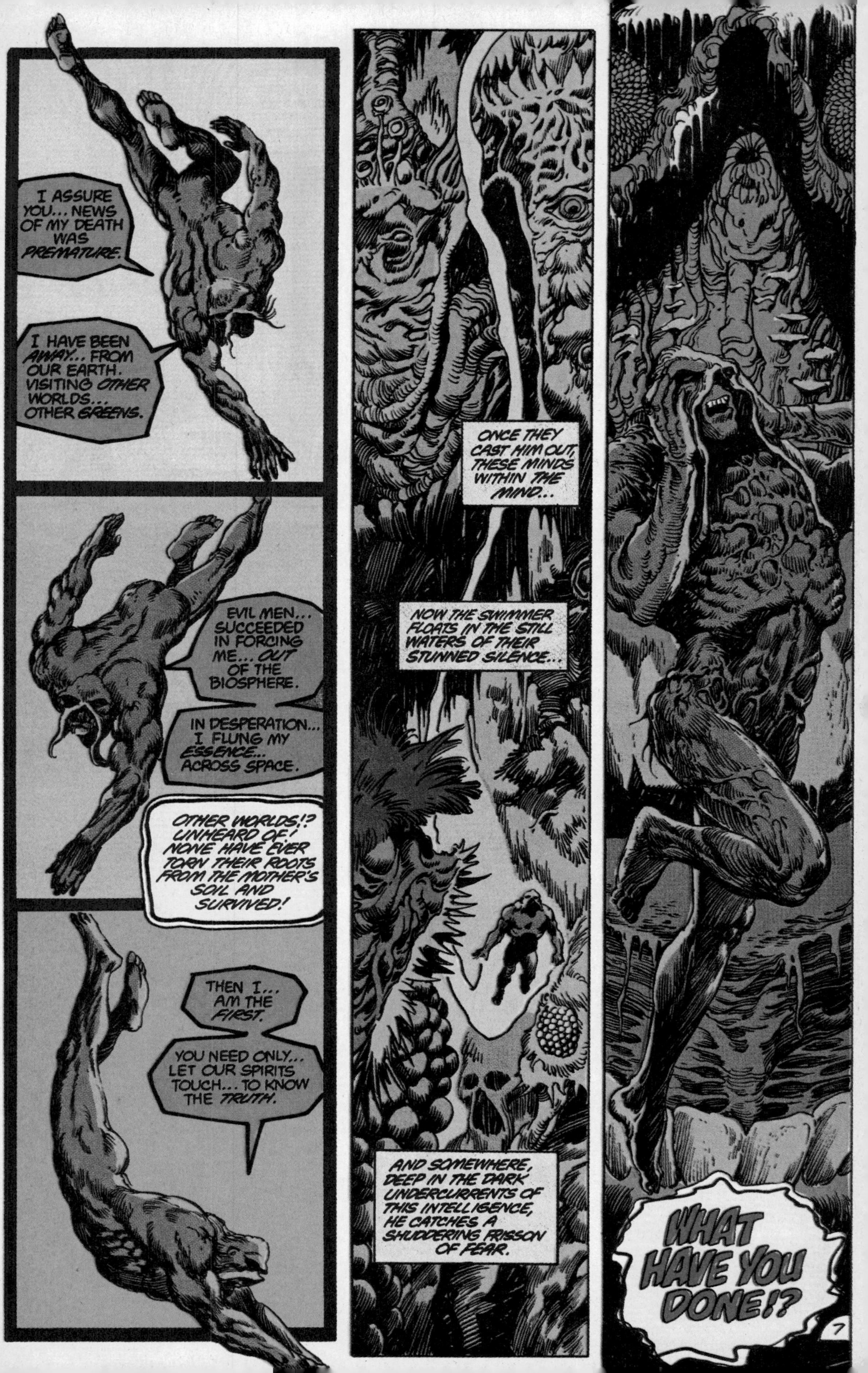

I ASSURE YOU... NEWS OF MY DEATH WAS PREMATURE.
I HAVE BEEN AWAY... FROM OUR EARTH. VISITING OTHER WORLDS... OTHER GREENS.
EVIL MEN... SUCCEEDED IN FORCING ME... OUT OF THE BIOSPHERE.
IN DESPERATION... I FLUNG MY ESSENCE... ACROSS SPACE.
OTHER WORLDS!? UNHEARD OF! NONE HAVE EVER TORN THEIR ROOTS FROM THE MOTHER'S SOIL AND SURVIVED!
THEN I... AM THE FIRST.
YOU NEED ONLY... LET OUR SPIRITS TOUCH... TO KNOW THE TRUTH.
ONCE THEY CAST HIM OUT, THESE MINDS WITHIN THE MIND...
NOW THE SWIMMER FLOATS IN THE STILL WATERS OF THEIR STUNNED SILENCE...
AND SOMEWHERE, DEEP IN THE DARK UNDERCURRENTS OF THIS INTELLIGENCE, HE CATCHES A SHUDDERING FRISSON OF FEAR.
WHAT HAVE YOU DONE!?
7

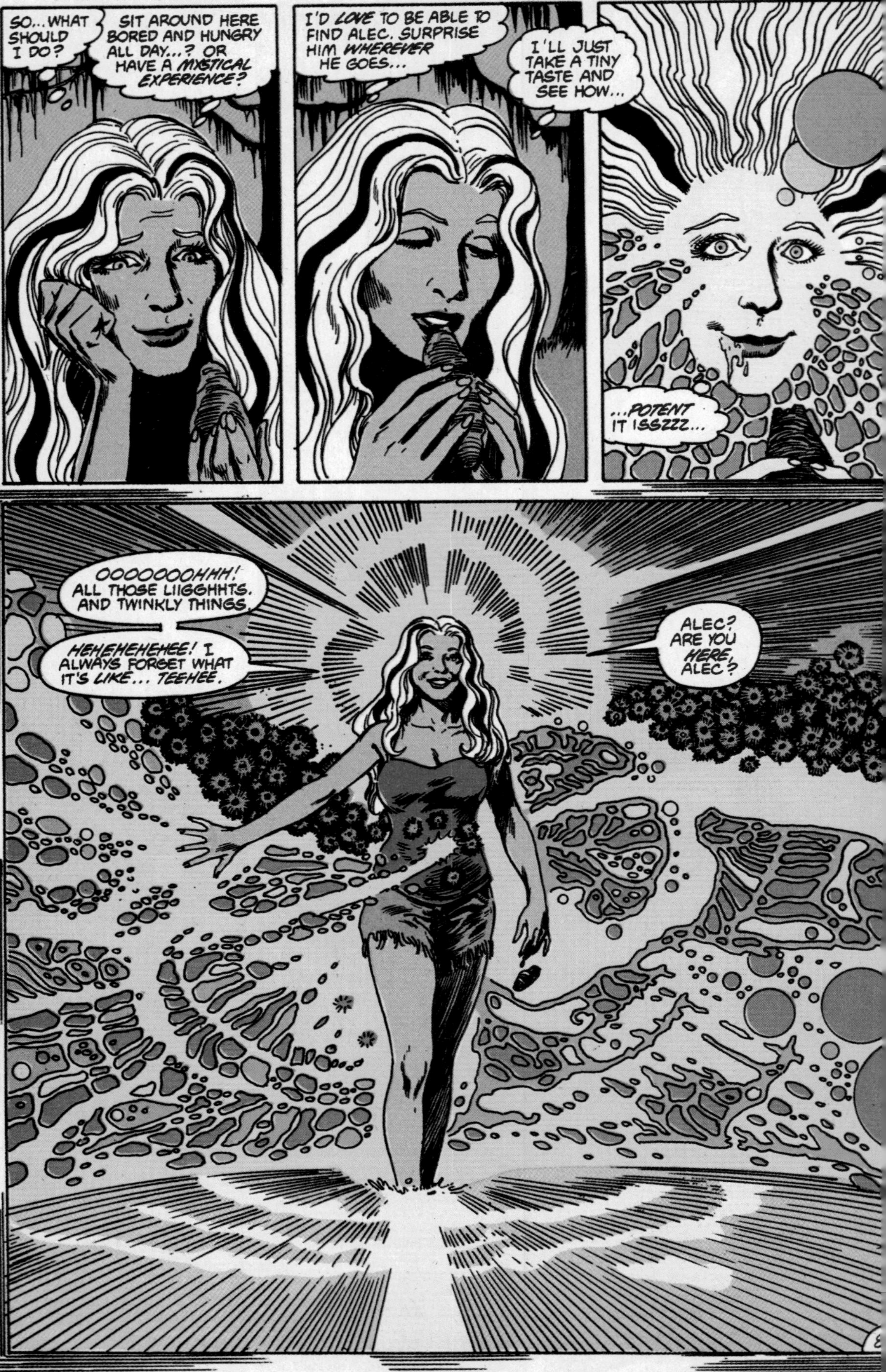
SO... WHAT SHOULD I DO?
SIT AROUND HERE BORED AND HUNGRY ALL DAY...? OR HAVE A MYSTICAL EXPERIENCE?
I'D LOVE TO BE ABLE TO FIND ALEC. SURPRISE HIM WHEREVER HE GOES...
I'LL JUST TAKE A TINY TASTE AND SEE HOW...
...POTENT IT ISSZZZ...
OOOOOOOOHHH! ALL THOSE LIIGGHHTS. AND TWINKLY THINGS.
HEHEHEHEHEE! I ALWAYS FORGET WHAT IT'S LIKE... TEEHEE.
ALEC? ARE YOU HERE, ALEC?

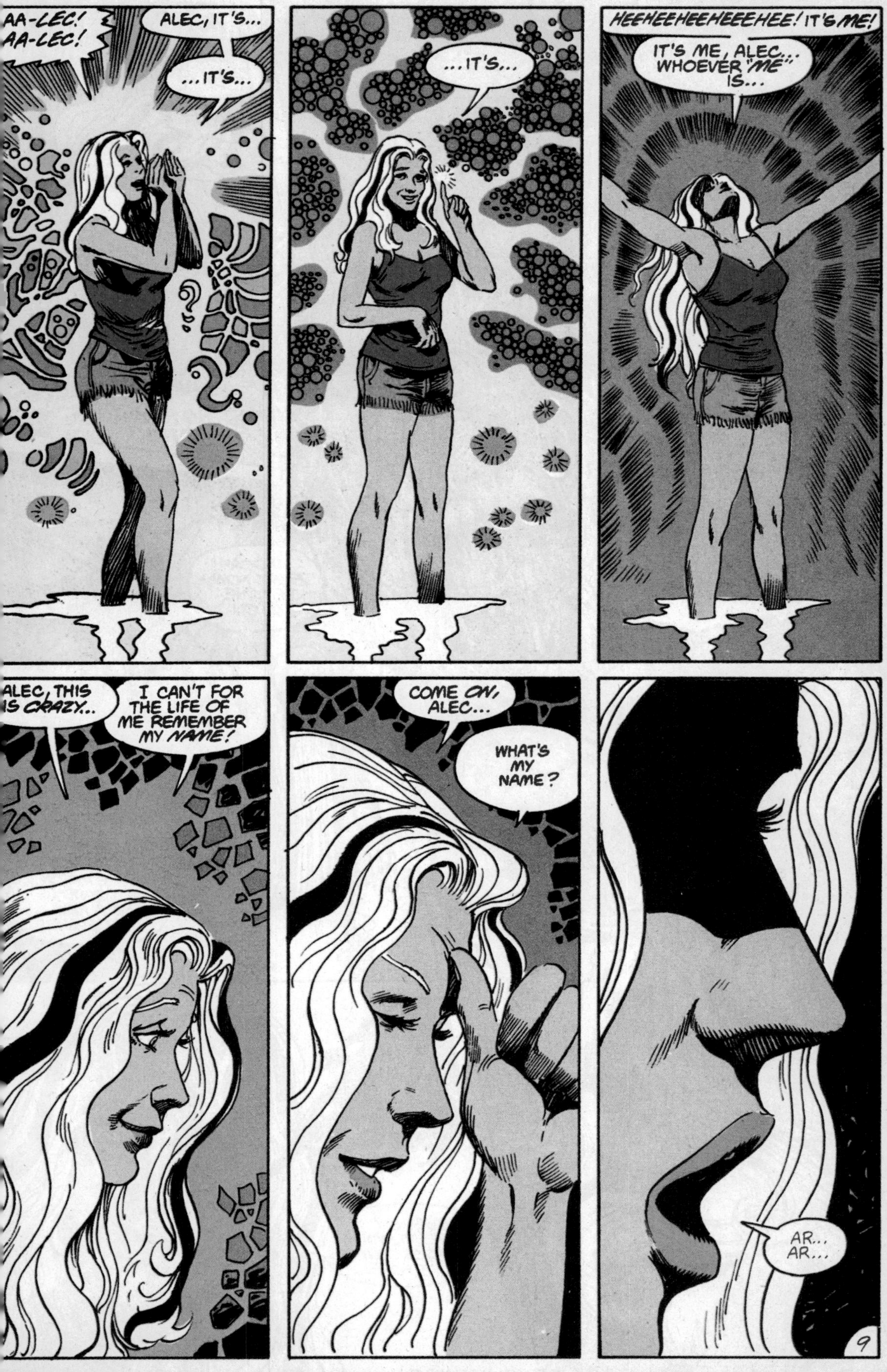

AA-LEC! AA-LEC!
ALEC, IT'S...
...IT'S...
...IT'S,...
HEEHEEHEEHEEEHEE! IT'S ME!
IT'S ME, ALEC... WHOEVER "ME" IS...
ALEC, THIS IS CRAZY...
I CAN'T FOR THE LIFE OF ME REMEMBER MY NAME!
COME ON, ALEC...
WHAT'S MY NAME?
AR... AR...
9

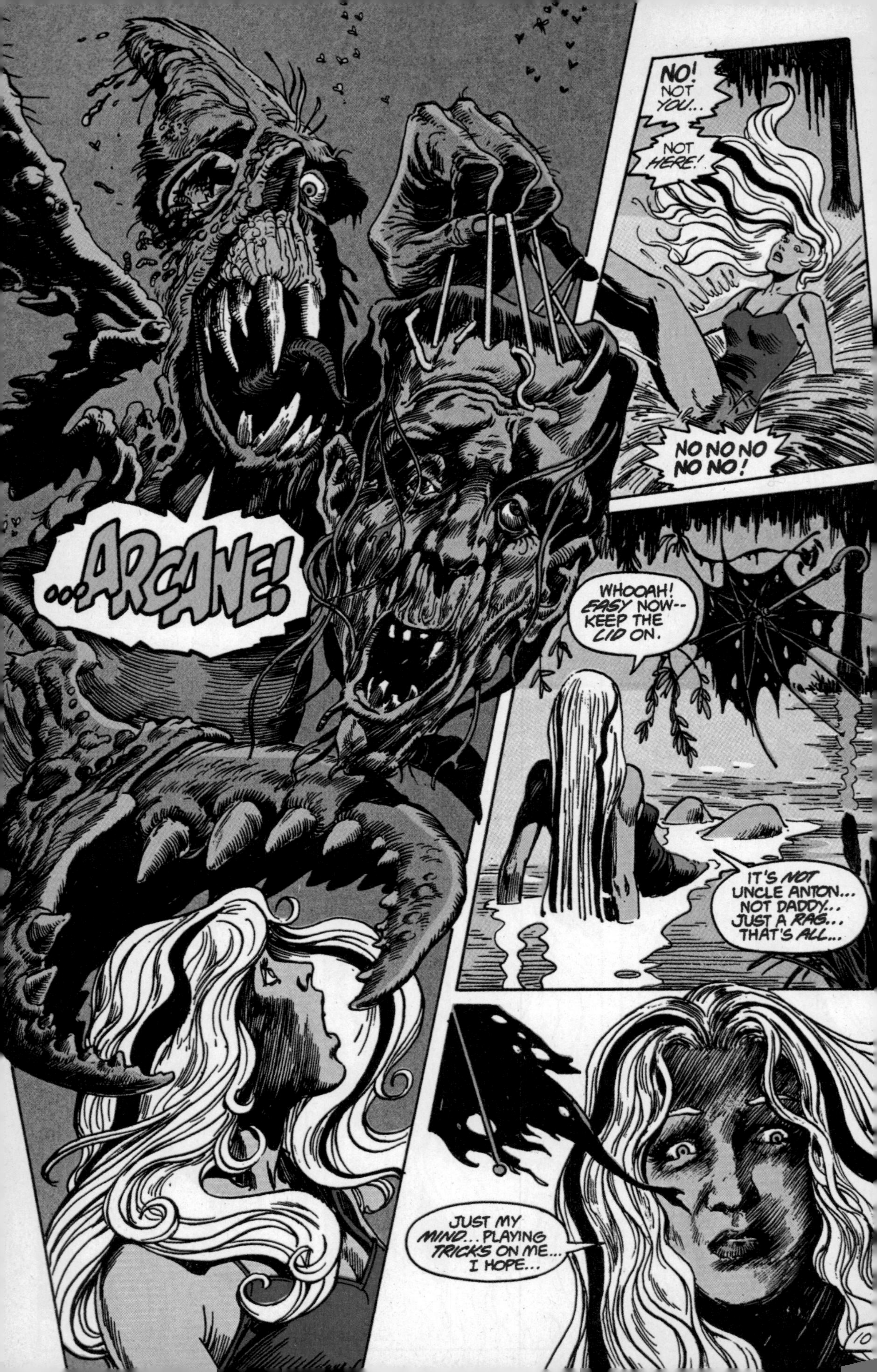
...ARCANE!
NO! NOT YOU...
NOT HERE!
NO NO NO NO NO!
WHOOAH! EASY NOW-- KEEP THE LID ON.
IT'S NOT UNCLE ANTON... NOT DADDY... JUST A RAG... THAT'S ALL...
JUST MY MIND... PLAYING TRICKS ON ME... I HOPE...
10

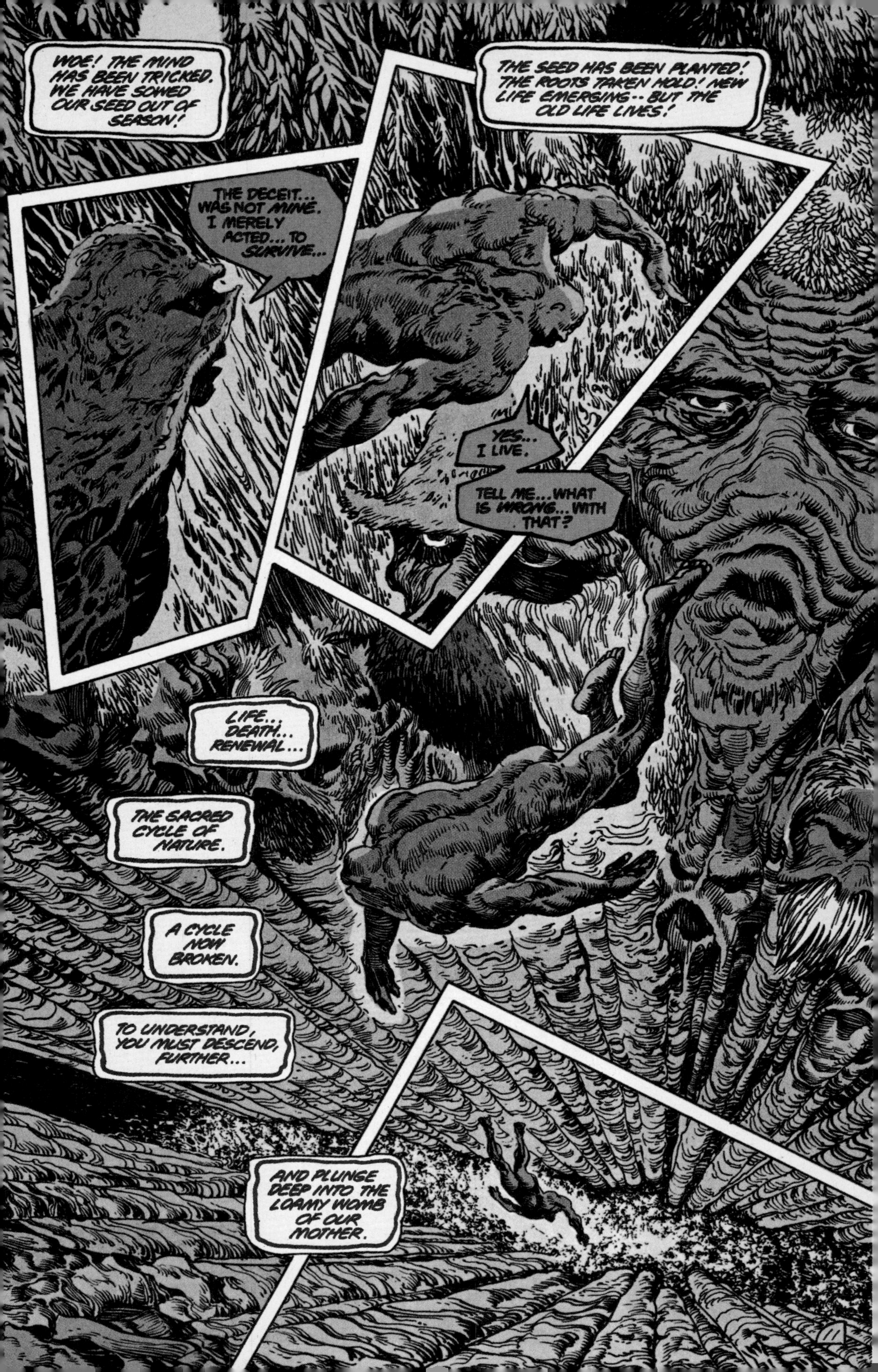
WOE! THE MIND HAS BEEN TRICKED. WE HAVE SOWED OUR SEED OUT OF SEASON!
THE SEED HAS BEEN PLANTED! THE ROOTS TAKEN HOLD! NEW LIFE EMERGING-- BUT THE OLD LIFE LIVES!
THE DECEIT... WAS NOT MINE. I MERELY ACTED... TO SURVIVE...
YES... I LIVE.
TELL ME... WHAT IS WRONG... WITH THAT?
LIFE... DEATH... RENEWAL...
THE SACRED CYCLE OF NATURE.
A CYCLE NOW BROKEN.
TO UNDERSTAND, YOU MUST DESCEND, FURTHER...
AND PLUNGE DEEP INTO THE LOAMY WOMB OF OUR MOTHER.

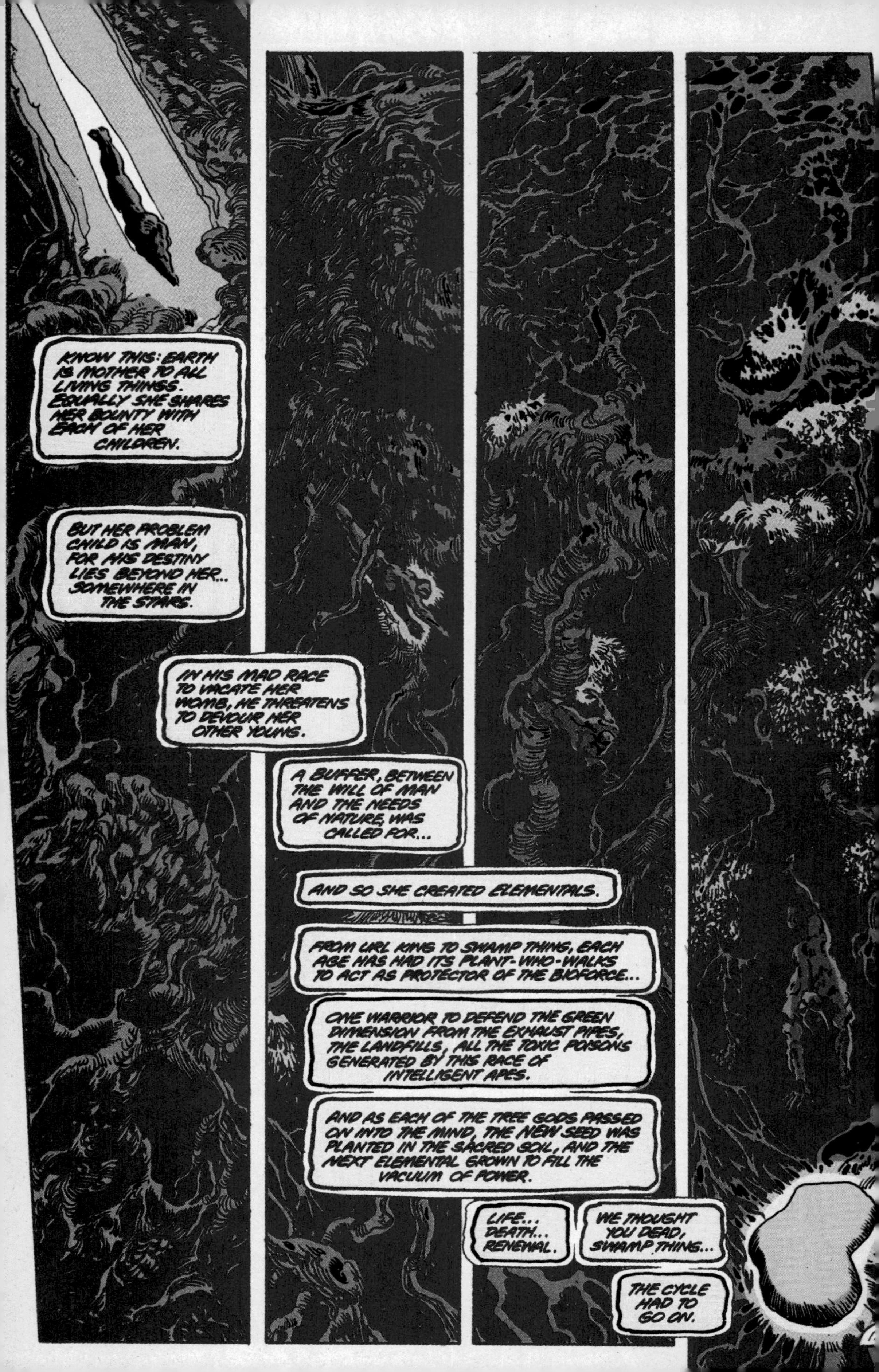
KNOW THIS: EARTH IS MOTHER TO ALL LIVING THINGS. EQUALLY SHE SHARES HER BOUNTY WITH EACH OF HER CHILDREN.
BUT HER PROBLEM CHILD IS MAN, FOR HIS DESTINY LIES BEYOND HER... SOMEWHERE IN THE STARS.
IN HIS MAD RACE TO VACATE HER WOMB, HE THREATENS TO DEVOUR HER OTHER YOUNG.
A BUFFER, BETWEEN THE WILL OF MAN AND THE NEEDS OF NATURE, WAS CALLED FOR...
AND SO SHE CREATED ELEMENTALS.
FROM URL KING TO SWAMP THING, EACH AGE HAS HAD ITS PLANT-WHO-WALKS TO ACT AS PROTECTOR OF THE BIOFORCE...
ONE WARRIOR TO DEFEND THE GREEN DIMENSION FROM THE EXHAUST PIPES, THE LANDFILLS, ALL THE TOXIC POISONS GENERATED BY THIS RACE OF INTELLIGENT APES.
AND AS EACH OF THE TREE GODS PASSED ON INTO THE MIND, THE NEW SEED WAS PLANTED IN THE SACRED SOIL, AND THE NEXT ELEMENTAL GROWN TO FILL THE VACUUM OF POWER.
LIFE... DEATH... RENEWAL.
WE THOUGHT YOU DEAD, SWAMP THING...
THE CYCLE HAD TO GO ON.

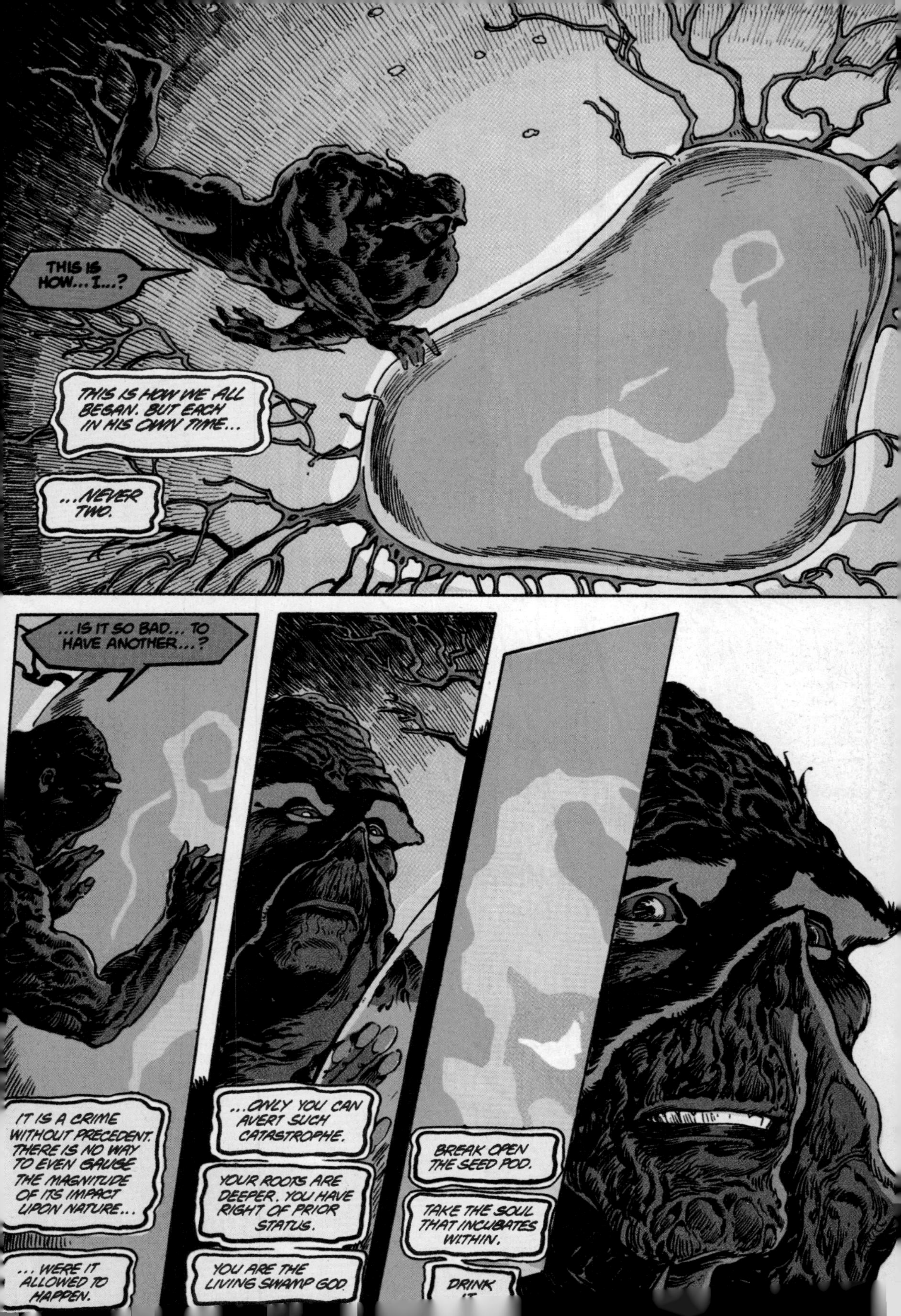
THIS IS HOW... I...?
THIS IS HOW WE ALL BEGAN. BUT EACH IN HIS OWN TIME...
...NEVER TWO.
...IS IT SO BAD... TO HAVE ANOTHER...?
IT IS A CRIME WITHOUT PRECEDENT. THERE IS NO WAY TO EVEN GAUGE THE MAGNITUDE OF ITS IMPACT UPON NATURE...
...WERE IT ALLOWED TO HAPPEN.
...ONLY YOU CAN AVERT SUCH CATASTROPHE.
YOUR ROOTS ARE DEEPER. YOU HAVE RIGHT OF PRIOR STATUS.
YOU ARE THE LIVING SWAMP GOD.
BREAK OPEN THE SEED POD.
TAKE THE SOUL THAT INCUBATES WITHIN.
DRINK

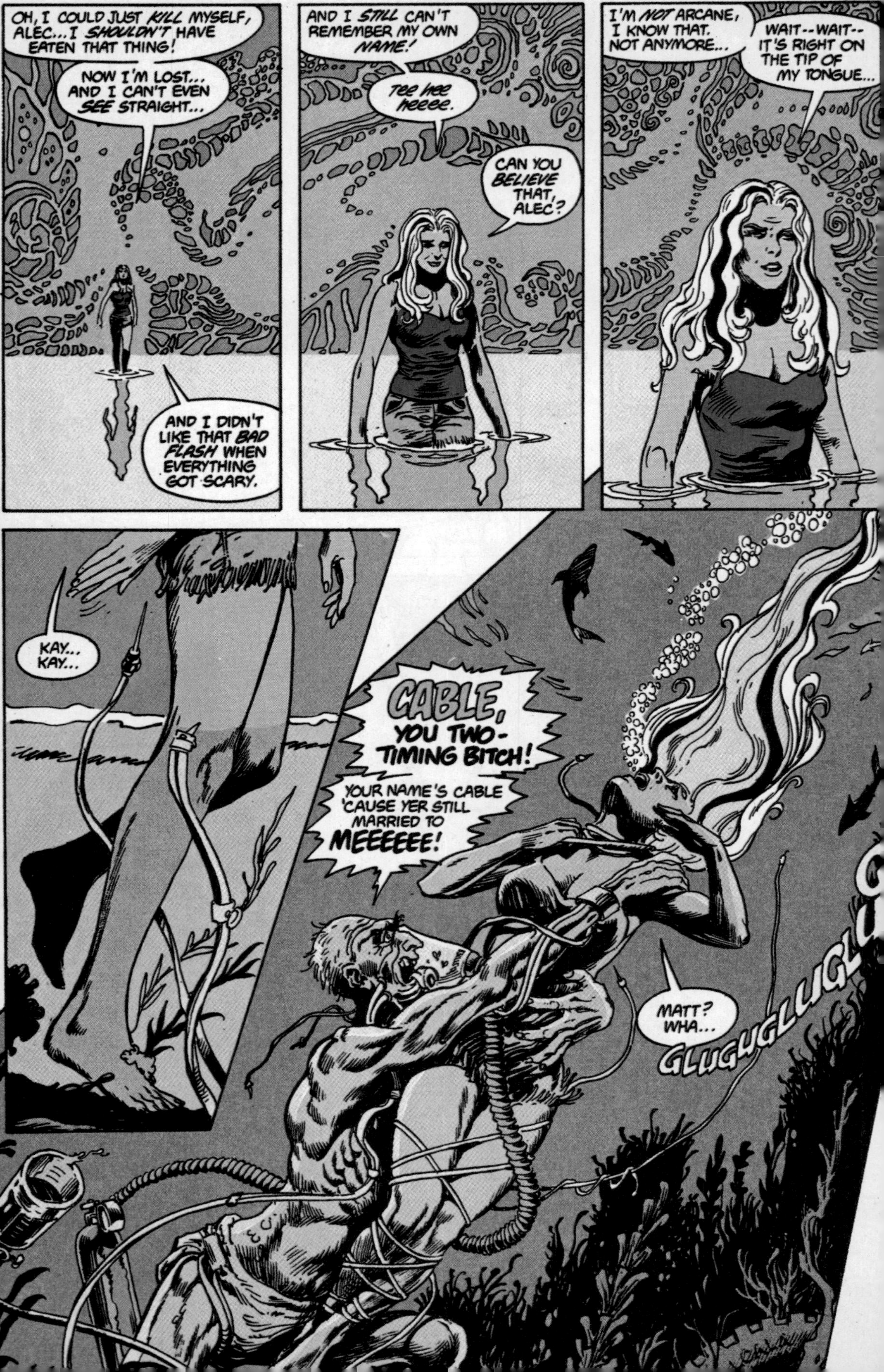
OH, I COULD JUST KILL MYSELF, ALEC...I SHOULDN'T HAVE EATEN THAT THING!
NOW I'M LOST... AND I CAN'T EVEN SEE STRAIGHT...
AND I DIDN'T LIKE THAT BAD FLASH WHEN EVERYTHING GOT SCARY.
AND I STILL CAN'T REMEMBER MY OWN NAME!
Tee hee heeee.
CAN YOU BELIEVE THAT, ALEC?
I'M NOT ARCANE, I KNOW THAT. NOT ANYMORE...
WAIT--WAIT-- IT'S RIGHT ON THE TIP OF MY TONGUE...
KAY... KAY...
CABLE, YOU TWO-TIMING BITCH!
YOUR NAME'S CABLE 'CAUSE YER STILL MARRIED TO MEEEEEE!
MATT? WHA...
GLUGUGLUGL

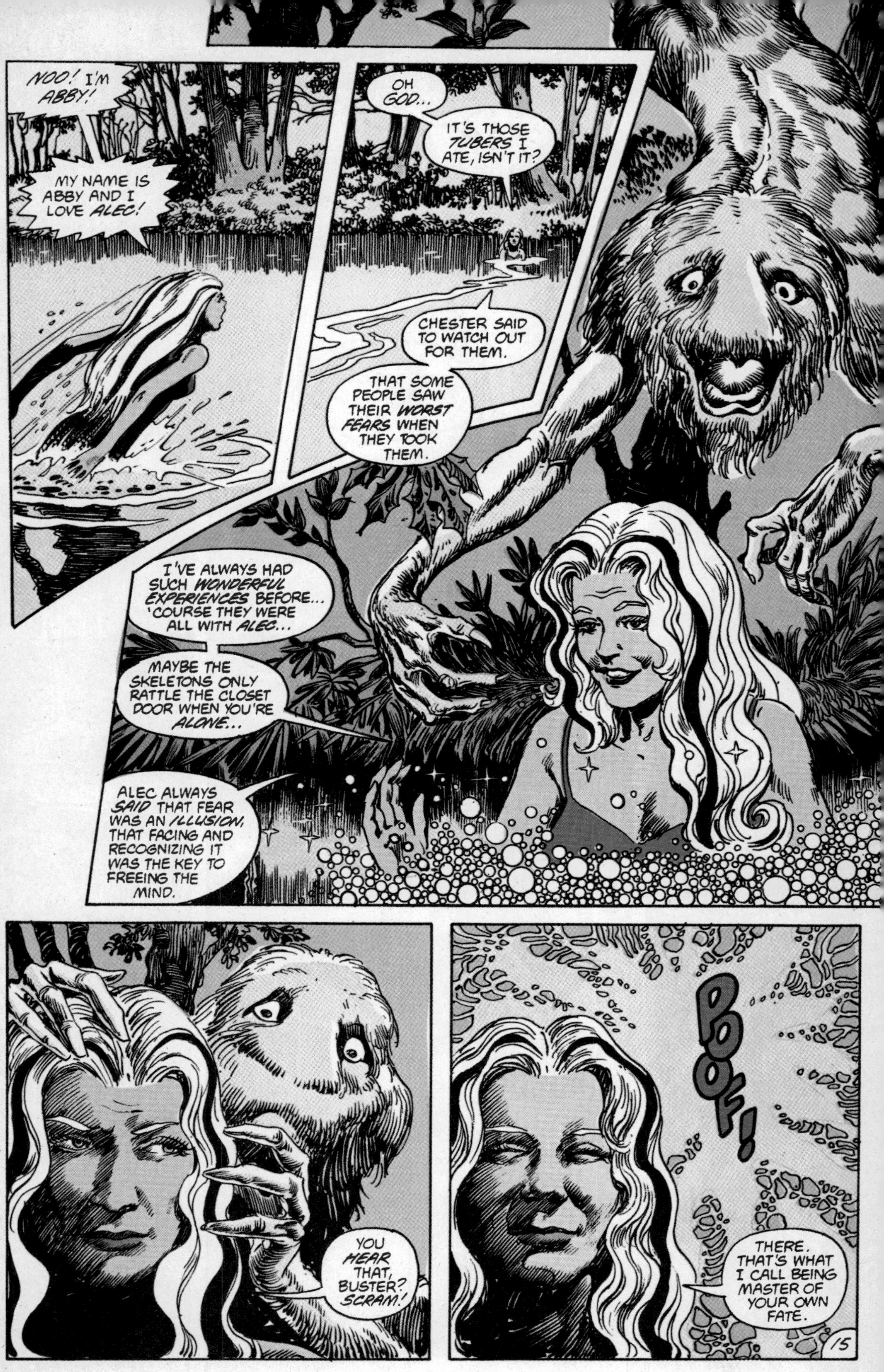
NOO! I'M ABBY!
MY NAME IS ABBY AND I LOVE ALEC!
OH GOD...
IT'S THOSE TUBERS I ATE, ISN'T IT?
CHESTER SAID TO WATCH OUT FOR THEM.
THAT SOME PEOPLE SAW THEIR WORST FEARS WHEN THEY TOOK THEM.
I'VE ALWAYS HAD SUCH WONDERFUL EXPERIENCES BEFORE... 'COURSE THEY WERE ALL WITH ALEC...
MAYBE THE SKELETONS ONLY RATTLE THE CLOSET DOOR WHEN YOU'RE ALONE...
ALEC ALWAYS SAID THAT FEAR WAS AN ILLUSION, THAT FACING AND RECOGNIZING IT WAS THE KEY TO FREEING THE MIND.
YOU HEAR THAT, BUSTER? SCRAM!
POOF!
THERE. THAT'S WHAT I CALL BEING MASTER OF YOUR OWN FATE.

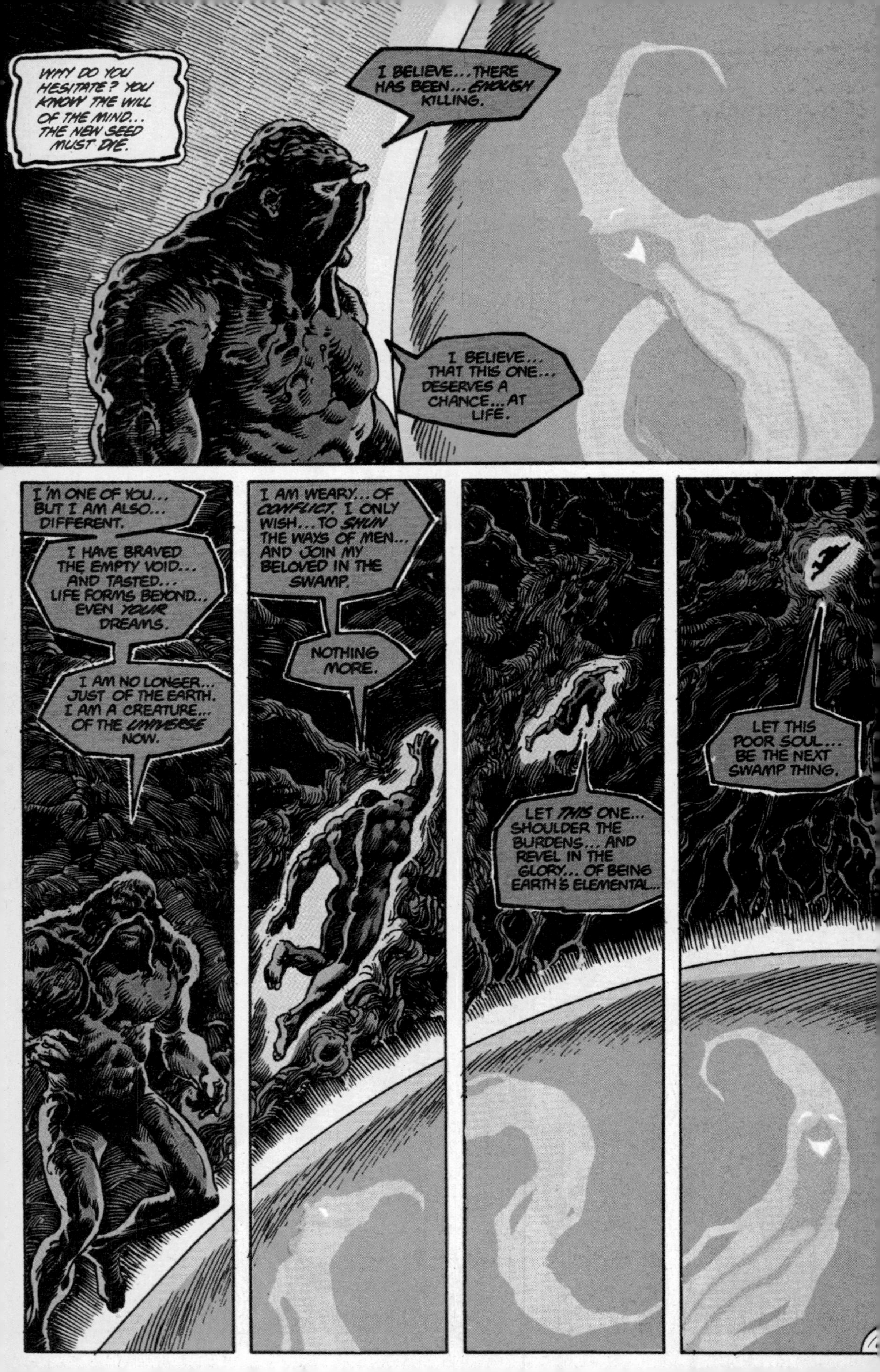
WHY DO YOU HESITATE? YOU KNOW THE WILL OF THE MIND... THE NEW SEED MUST DIE.
I BELIEVE... THERE HAS BEEN... ENOUGH KILLING.
I BELIEVE... THAT THIS ONE... DESERVES A CHANCE... AT LIFE.
I'M ONE OF YOU... BUT I AM ALSO... DIFFERENT.
I HAVE BRAVED THE EMPTY VOID... AND TASTED... LIFE FORMS BEYOND... EVEN YOUR DREAMS.
I AM NO LONGER... JUST OF THE EARTH. I AM A CREATURE... OF THE UNIVERSE NOW.
I AM WEARY... OF CONFLICT. I ONLY WISH... TO SHUN THE WAYS OF MEN... AND JOIN MY BELOVED IN THE SWAMP.
NOTHING MORE.
LET THIS ONE... SHOULDER THE BURDENS... AND REVEL IN THE GLORY... OF BEING EARTH'S ELEMENTAL...
LET THIS POOR SOUL... BE THE NEXT SWAMP THING.

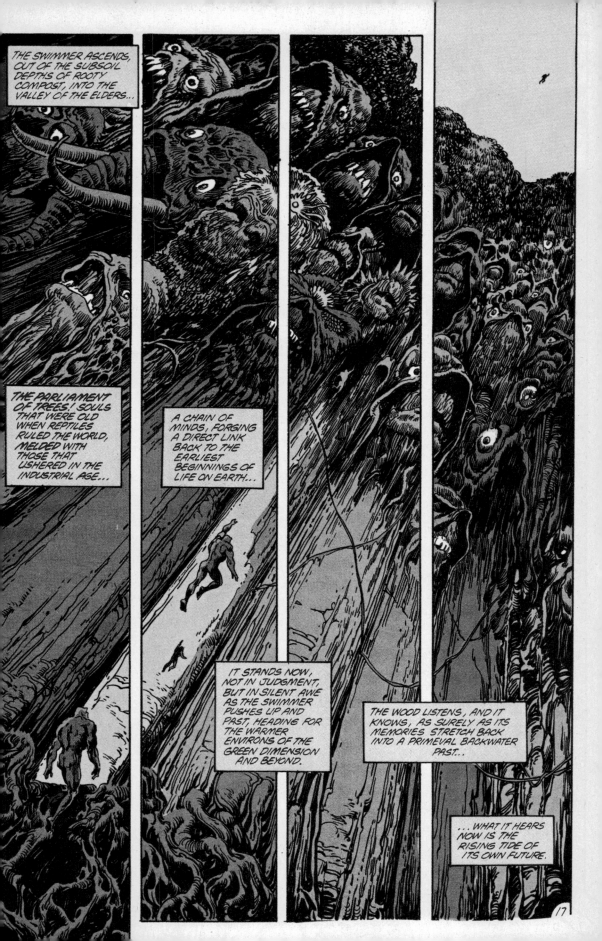

THE SWIMMER ASCENDS, OUT OF THE SUBSOIL DEPTHS OF ROOTY COMPOST, INTO THE VALLEY OF THE ELDERS...

THE PARLIAMENT OF TREES! SOULS THAT WERE OLD WHEN REPTILES RULED THE WORLD, MELDED WITH THOSE THAT USHERED IN THE INDUSTRIAL AGE...

A CHAIN OF MINDS, FORGING A DIRECT LINK BACK TO THE EARLIEST BEGINNINGS OF LIFE ON EARTH...

IT STANDS NOW, NOT IN JUDGMENT, BUT IN SILENT AWE AS THE SWIMMER PUSHES UP AND PAST, HEADING FOR THE WARMER ENVIRONS OF THE GREEN DIMENSION AND BEYOND.

THE WOOD LISTENS, AND IT KNOWS, AS SURELY AS ITS MEMORIES STRETCH BACK INTO A PRIMEVAL BACKWATER PAST...

...WHAT IT HEARS NOW IS THE RISING TIDE OF ITS OWN FUTURE.

17

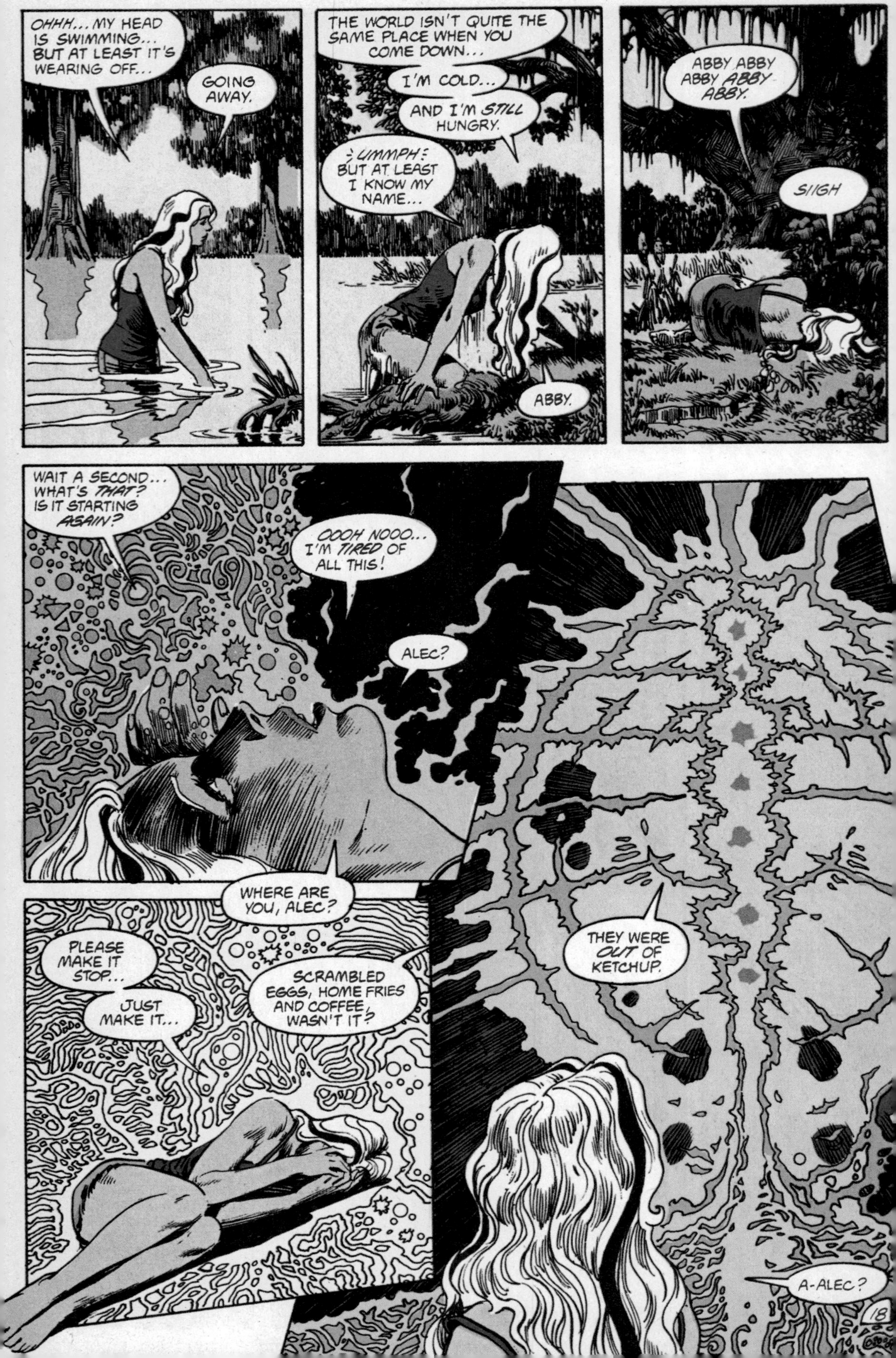
OHHH... MY HEAD IS SWIMMING... BUT AT LEAST IT'S WEARING OFF...
GOING AWAY.
THE WORLD ISN'T QUITE THE SAME PLACE WHEN YOU COME DOWN...
I'M COLD...
AND I'M STILL HUNGRY.
UMMPH BUT AT LEAST I KNOW MY NAME...
ABBY.
ABBY ABBY ABBY ABBY ABBY.
SIIGH
WAIT A SECOND... WHAT'S THAT? IS IT STARTING AGAIN?
OOOH NOOO... I'M TIRED OF ALL THIS!
ALEC?
WHERE ARE YOU, ALEC?
PLEASE MAKE IT STOP...
JUST MAKE IT...
SCRAMBLED EGGS, HOME FRIES AND COFFEE, WASN'T IT?
THEY WERE OUT OF KETCHUP.
A-ALEC?
18

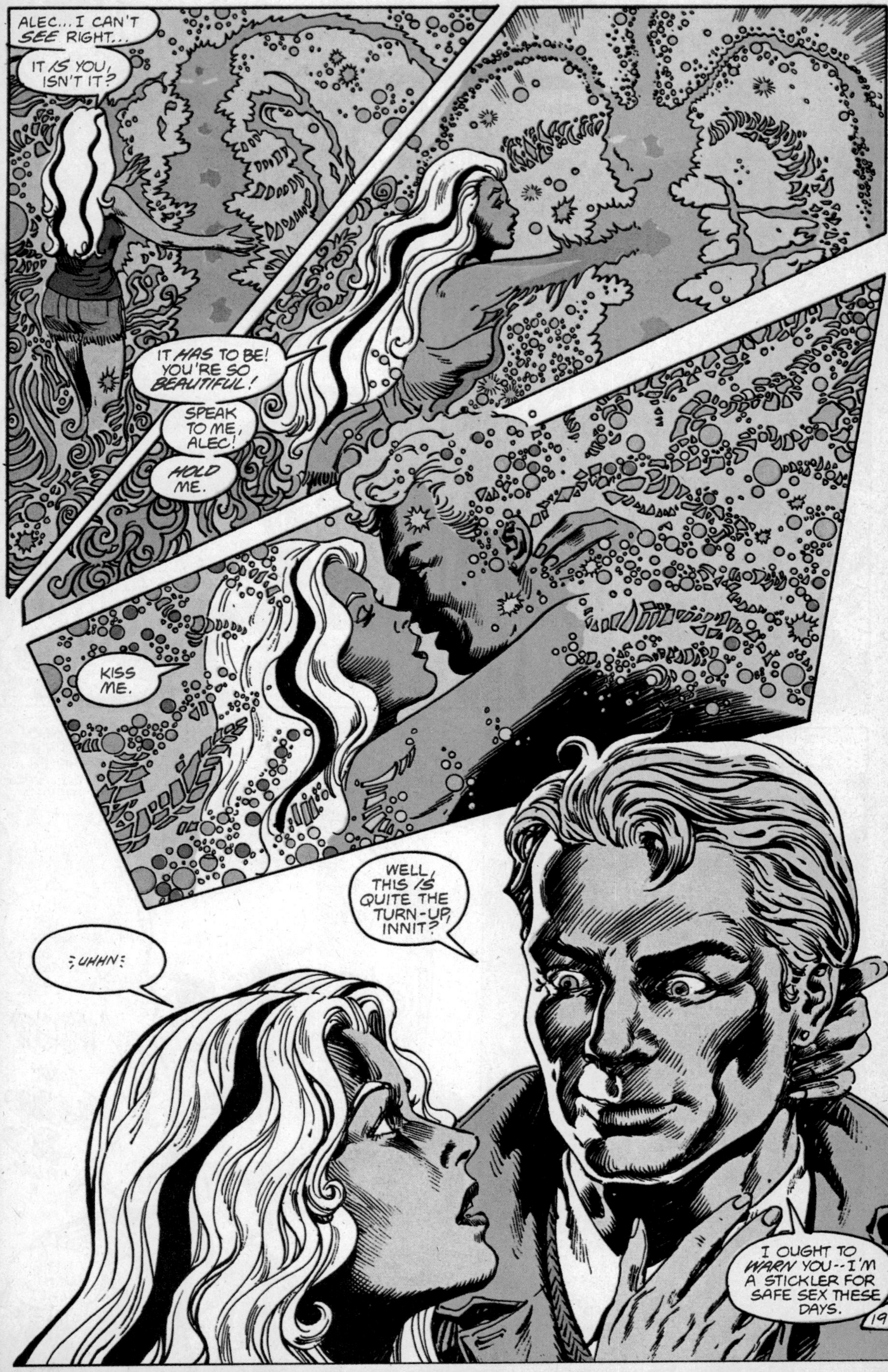
ALEC... I CAN'T SEE RIGHT...
IT IS YOU, ISN'T IT?
IT HAS TO BE! YOU'RE SO BEAUTIFUL!
SPEAK TO ME, ALEC!
HOLD ME.
KISS ME.
WELL, THIS IS QUITE THE TURN-UP, INNIT?
UHHN
I OUGHT TO WARN YOU--I'M A STICKLER FOR SAFE SEX THESE DAYS.
19

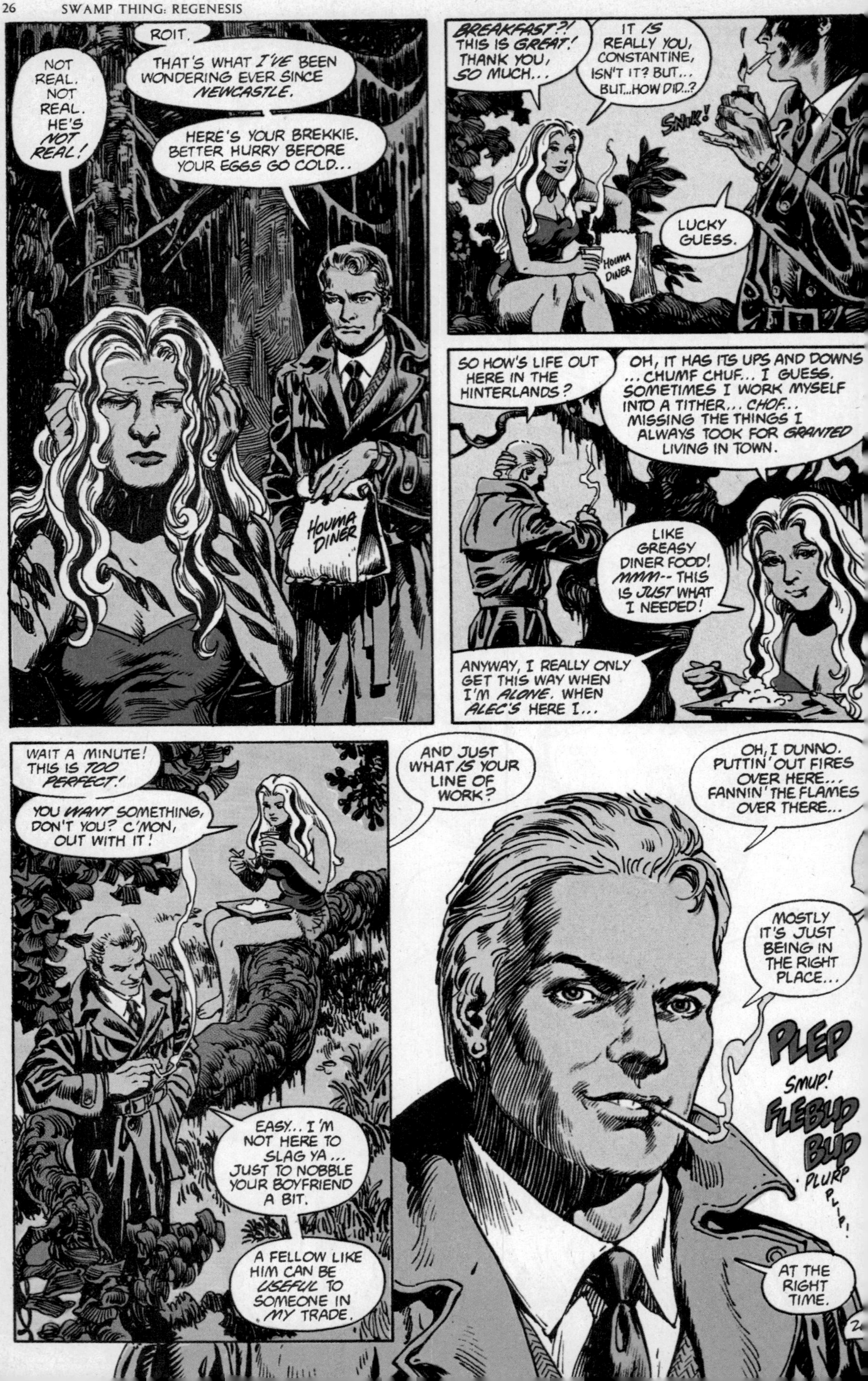
ROIT.
NOT REAL. NOT REAL. HE'S NOT REAL!
THAT'S WHAT I'VE BEEN WONDERING EVER SINCE NEWCASTLE.
HERE'S YOUR BREKKIE. BETTER HURRY BEFORE YOUR EGGS GO COLD...
HOUMA DINER
BREAKFAST?! THIS IS GREAT! THANK YOU, SO MUCH...
IT IS REALLY YOU, CONSTANTINE, ISN'T IT? BUT... BUT...HOW DID..?
SNIK!
LUCKY GUESS.
HOUMA DINER
SO HOW'S LIFE OUT HERE IN THE HINTERLANDS?
OH, IT HAS ITS UPS AND DOWNS ...CHUMF CHUF... I GUESS. SOMETIMES I WORK MYSELF INTO A TITHER... CHOF... MISSING THE THINGS I ALWAYS TOOK FOR GRANTED LIVING IN TOWN.
LIKE GREASY DINER FOOD! MMM-- THIS IS JUST WHAT I NEEDED!
ANYWAY, I REALLY ONLY GET THIS WAY WHEN I'M ALONE. WHEN ALEC'S HERE I...
WAIT A MINUTE! THIS IS TOO PERFECT!
YOU WANT SOMETHING, DON'T YOU? C'MON, OUT WITH IT!
AND JUST WHAT IS YOUR LINE OF WORK?
EASY... I'M NOT HERE TO SLAG YA... JUST TO NOBBLE YOUR BOYFRIEND A BIT.
A FELLOW LIKE HIM CAN BE USEFUL TO SOMEONE IN MY TRADE.
OH, I DUNNO. PUTTIN' OUT FIRES OVER HERE... FANNIN' THE FLAMES OVER THERE...
MOSTLY IT'S JUST BEING IN THE RIGHT PLACE...
PLEP
SMUP!
FLEBUP
BUP
PLURP
PVIP!
AT THE RIGHT TIME.

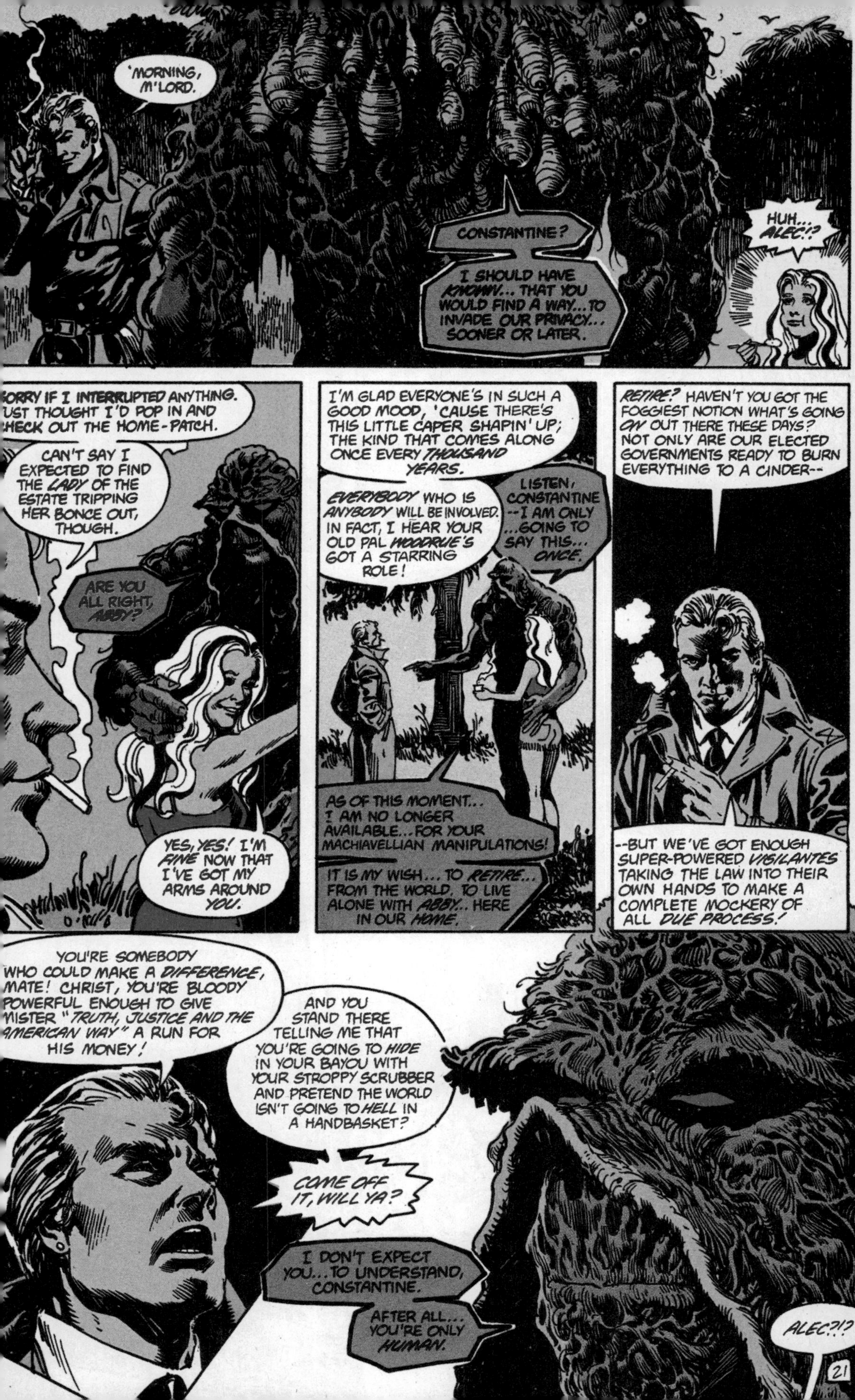

'MORNING, M'LORD.
CONSTANTINE?
I SHOULD HAVE KNOWN... THAT YOU WOULD FIND A WAY... TO INVADE OUR PRIVACY... SOONER OR LATER.
HUH... ALEC!?
SORRY IF I INTERRUPTED ANYTHING. JUST THOUGHT I'D POP IN AND CHECK OUT THE HOME-PATCH.
CAN'T SAY I EXPECTED TO FIND THE LADY OF THE ESTATE TRIPPING HER BONCE OUT, THOUGH.
ARE YOU ALL RIGHT, ABBY?
YES, YES! I'M FINE NOW THAT I'VE GOT MY ARMS AROUND YOU.
I'M GLAD EVERYONE'S IN SUCH A GOOD MOOD, 'CAUSE THERE'S THIS LITTLE CAPER SHAPIN' UP; THE KIND THAT COMES ALONG ONCE EVERY THOUSAND YEARS.
EVERYBODY WHO IS ANYBODY WILL BE INVOLVED. IN FACT, I HEAR YOUR OLD PAL WOODRUE'S GOT A STARRING ROLE!
LISTEN, CONSTANTINE --I AM ONLY ...GOING TO SAY THIS... ONCE.
AS OF THIS MOMENT... I AM NO LONGER AVAILABLE...FOR YOUR MACHIAVELLIAN MANIPULATIONS!
IT IS MY WISH... TO RETIRE... FROM THE WORLD, TO LIVE ALONE WITH ABBY... HERE IN OUR HOME.
RETIRE? HAVEN'T YOU GOT THE FOGGIEST NOTION WHAT'S GOING ON OUT THERE THESE DAYS? NOT ONLY ARE OUR ELECTED GOVERNMENTS READY TO BURN EVERYTHING TO A CINDER--
--BUT WE'VE GOT ENOUGH SUPER-POWERED VIGILANTES TAKING THE LAW INTO THEIR OWN HANDS TO MAKE A COMPLETE MOCKERY OF ALL DUE PROCESS!
YOU'RE SOMEBODY WHO COULD MAKE A DIFFERENCE, MATE! CHRIST, YOU'RE BLOODY POWERFUL ENOUGH TO GIVE MISTER "TRUTH, JUSTICE AND THE AMERICAN WAY" A RUN FOR HIS MONEY!
AND YOU STAND THERE TELLING ME THAT YOU'RE GOING TO HIDE IN YOUR BAYOU WITH YOUR STROPPY SCRUBBER AND PRETEND THE WORLD ISN'T GOING TO HELL IN A HANDBASKET?
COME OFF IT, WILL YA?
I DON'T EXPECT YOU... TO UNDERSTAND, CONSTANTINE.
AFTER ALL... YOU'RE ONLY HUMAN.
ALEC?!?

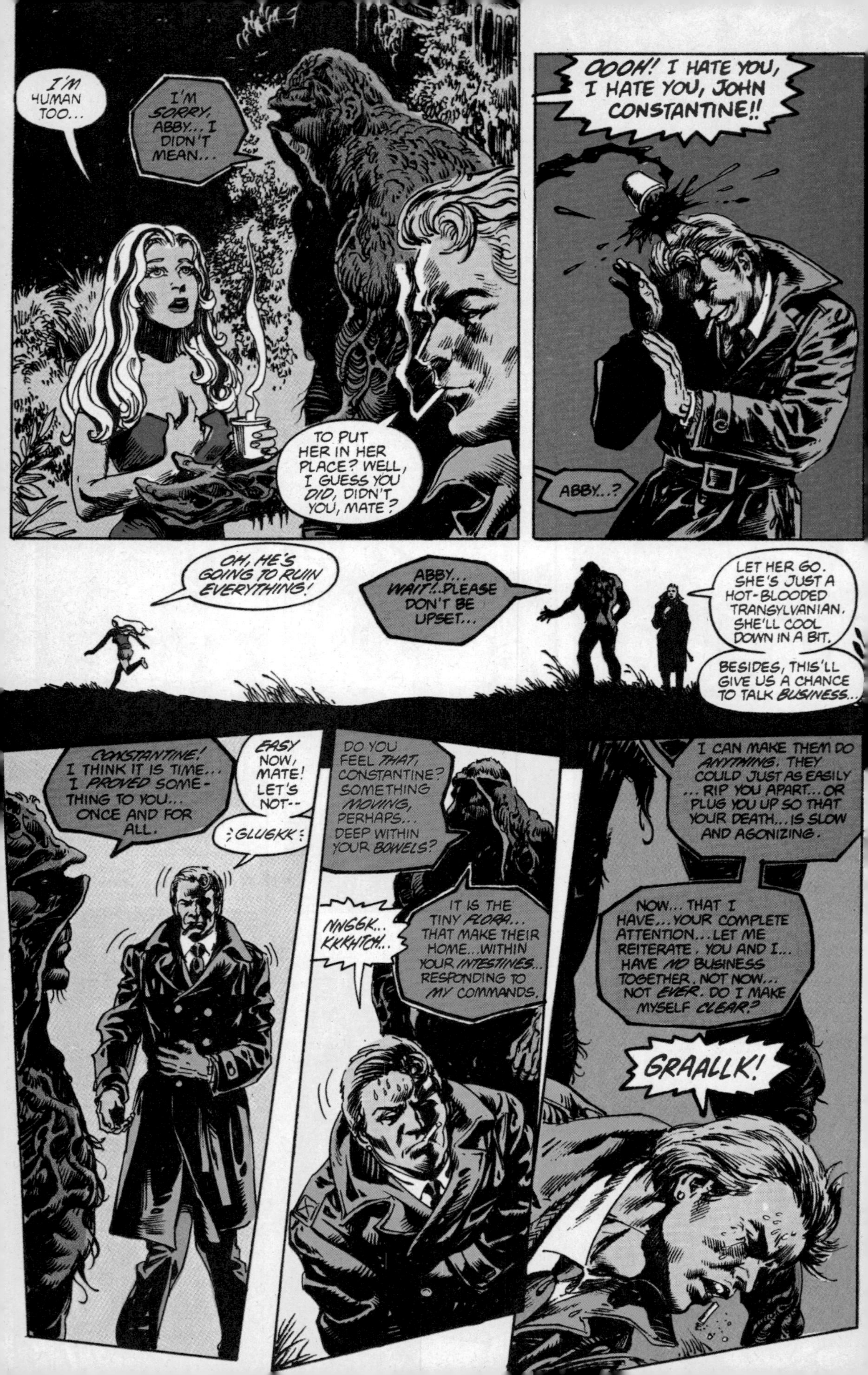
I'M HUMAN TOO...
I'M SORRY, ABBY... I DIDN'T MEAN...
TO PUT HER IN HER PLACE? WELL, I GUESS YOU DID, DIDN'T YOU, MATE?
OOOH! I HATE YOU, I HATE YOU, JOHN CONSTANTINE!!
ABBY...?
OH, HE'S GOING TO RUIN EVERYTHING!
ABBY... WAIT!..PLEASE DON'T BE UPSET...
LET HER GO. SHE'S JUST A HOT-BLOODED TRANSYLVANIAN. SHE'LL COOL DOWN IN A BIT.
BESIDES, THIS'LL GIVE US A CHANCE TO TALK BUSINESS...
CONSTANTINE! I THINK IT IS TIME... I PROVED SOME-THING TO YOU... ONCE AND FOR ALL.
EASY NOW, MATE! LET'S NOT--
GLUGKK
DO YOU FEEL THAT, CONSTANTINE? SOMETHING MOVING, PERHAPS... DEEP WITHIN YOUR BOWELS?
NNGGK... KKKHTCH...
IT IS THE TINY FLORA... THAT MAKE THEIR HOME... WITHIN YOUR INTESTINES... RESPONDING TO MY COMMANDS.
I CAN MAKE THEM DO ANYTHING. THEY COULD JUST AS EASILY ... RIP YOU APART... OR PLUG YOU UP SO THAT YOUR DEATH... IS SLOW AND AGONIZING.
NOW... THAT I HAVE... YOUR COMPLETE ATTENTION... LET ME REITERATE. YOU AND I... HAVE NO BUSINESS TOGETHER. NOT NOW... NOT EVER. DO I MAKE MYSELF CLEAR?
GRAALLK!

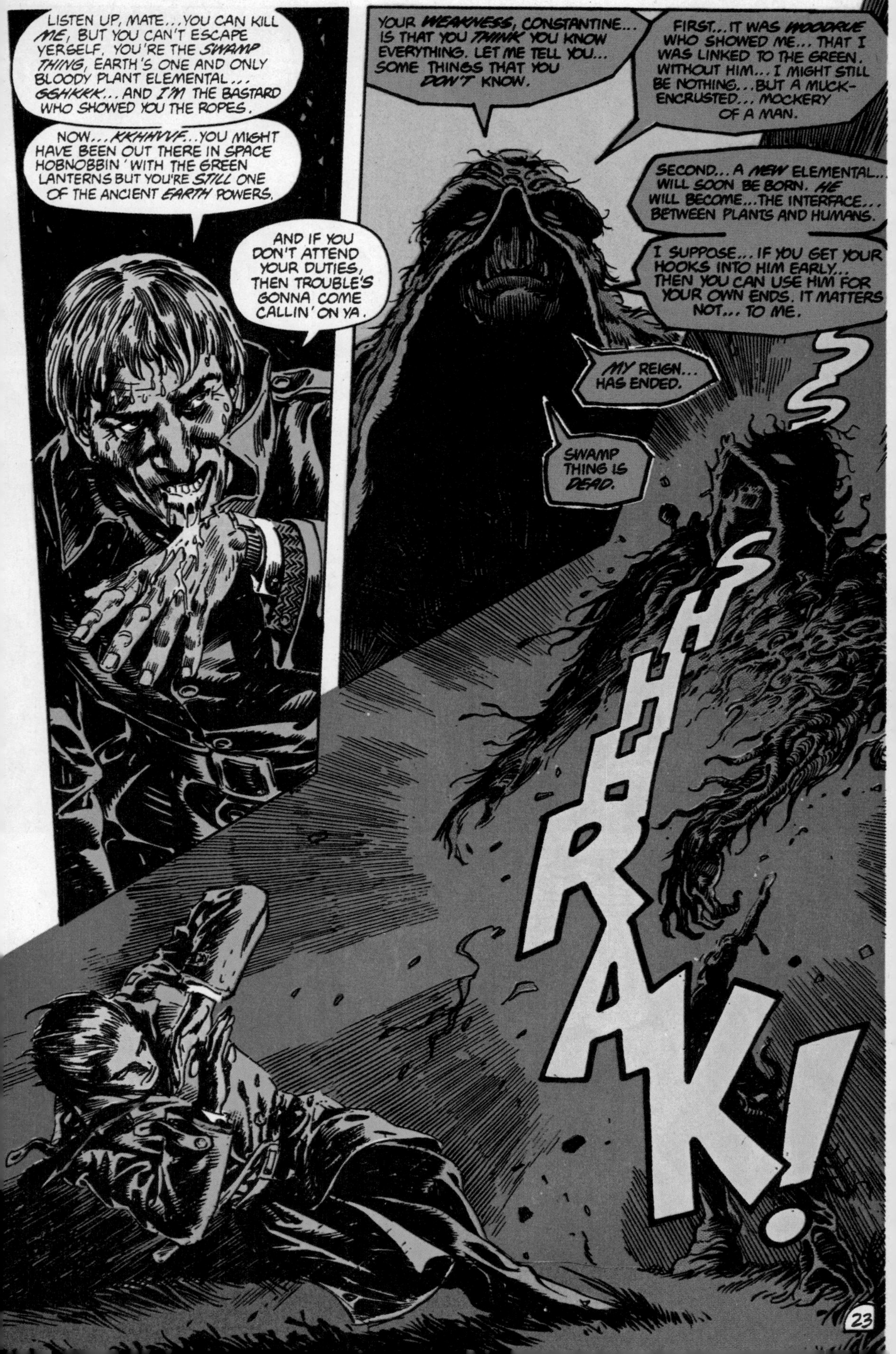
LISTEN UP, MATE...YOU CAN KILL *ME*, BUT YOU CAN'T ESCAPE YERSELF. YOU'RE THE *SWAMP THING*, EARTH'S ONE AND ONLY BLOODY PLANT ELEMENTAL... *GGHKKK*... AND *I'M* THE BASTARD WHO SHOWED YOU THE ROPES.
NOW... *KKHHVVF*... YOU MIGHT HAVE BEEN OUT THERE IN SPACE HOBNOBBIN' WITH THE GREEN LANTERNS BUT YOU'RE *STILL* ONE OF THE ANCIENT *EARTH* POWERS.
AND IF YOU DON'T ATTEND YOUR DUTIES, THEN TROUBLE'S GONNA COME CALLIN' ON YA.
YOUR *WEAKNESS*, CONSTANTINE... IS THAT YOU *THINK* YOU KNOW EVERYTHING. LET ME TELL YOU... SOME THINGS THAT YOU *DON'T* KNOW.
FIRST... IT WAS *WOODRUE* WHO SHOWED ME... THAT I WAS LINKED TO THE GREEN. WITHOUT HIM... I MIGHT STILL BE NOTHING... BUT A MUCK-ENCRUSTED... MOCKERY OF A MAN.
SECOND... A *NEW* ELEMENTAL... WILL SOON BE BORN. *HE* WILL BECOME... THE INTERFACE... BETWEEN PLANTS AND HUMANS.
I SUPPOSE... IF YOU GET YOUR HOOKS INTO HIM EARLY... THEN YOU CAN USE HIM FOR YOUR OWN ENDS. IT MATTERS NOT... TO ME.
MY REIGN... HAS ENDED.
SWAMP THING IS *DEAD*.
SHHHRRAK!
23

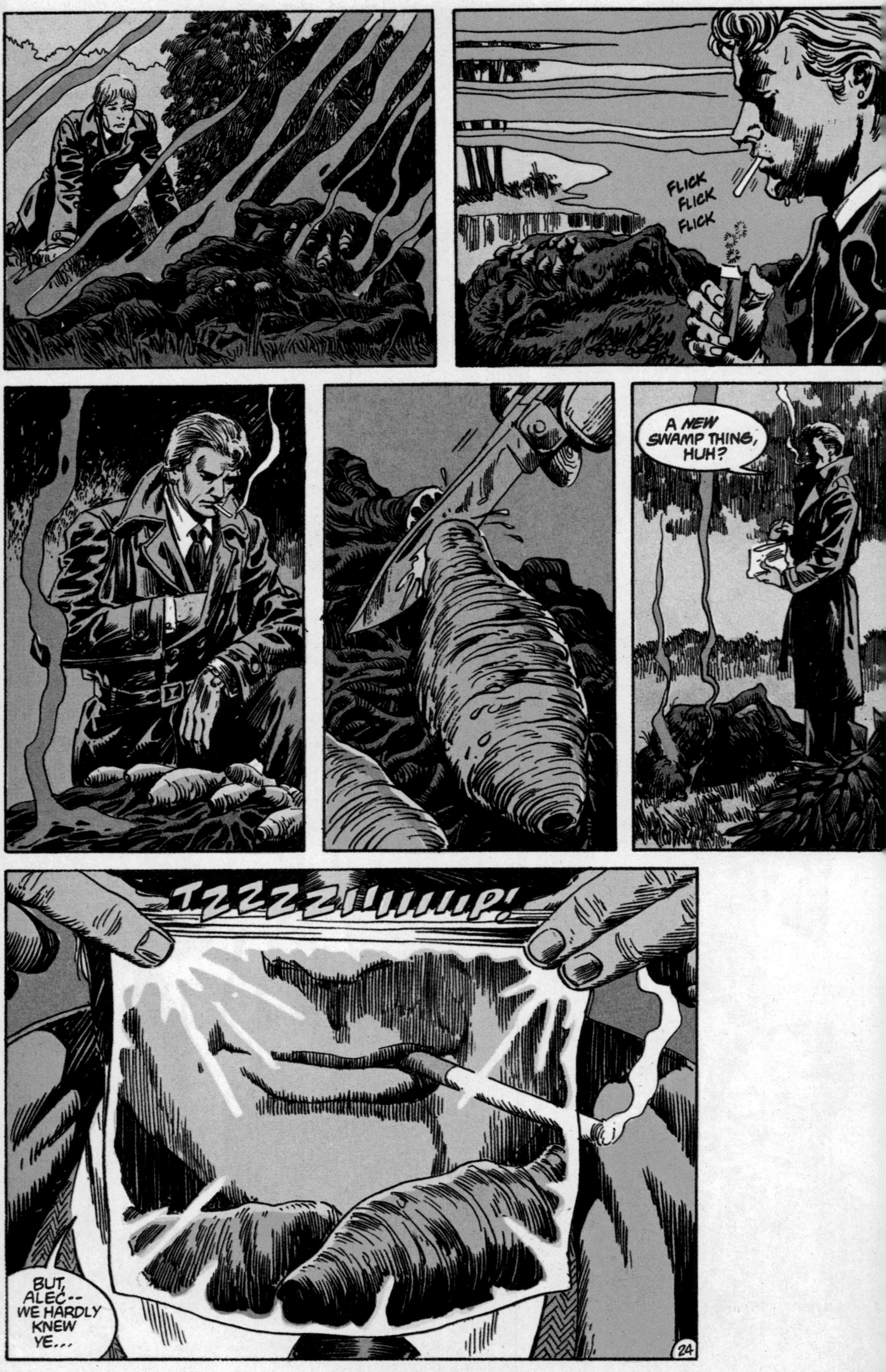
FLICK
FLICK
FLICK
A NEW SWAMP THING, HUH?
TZZZZZIIIIIIP!
BUT, ALEC-- WE HARDLY KNEW YE...
24

Chapter 2

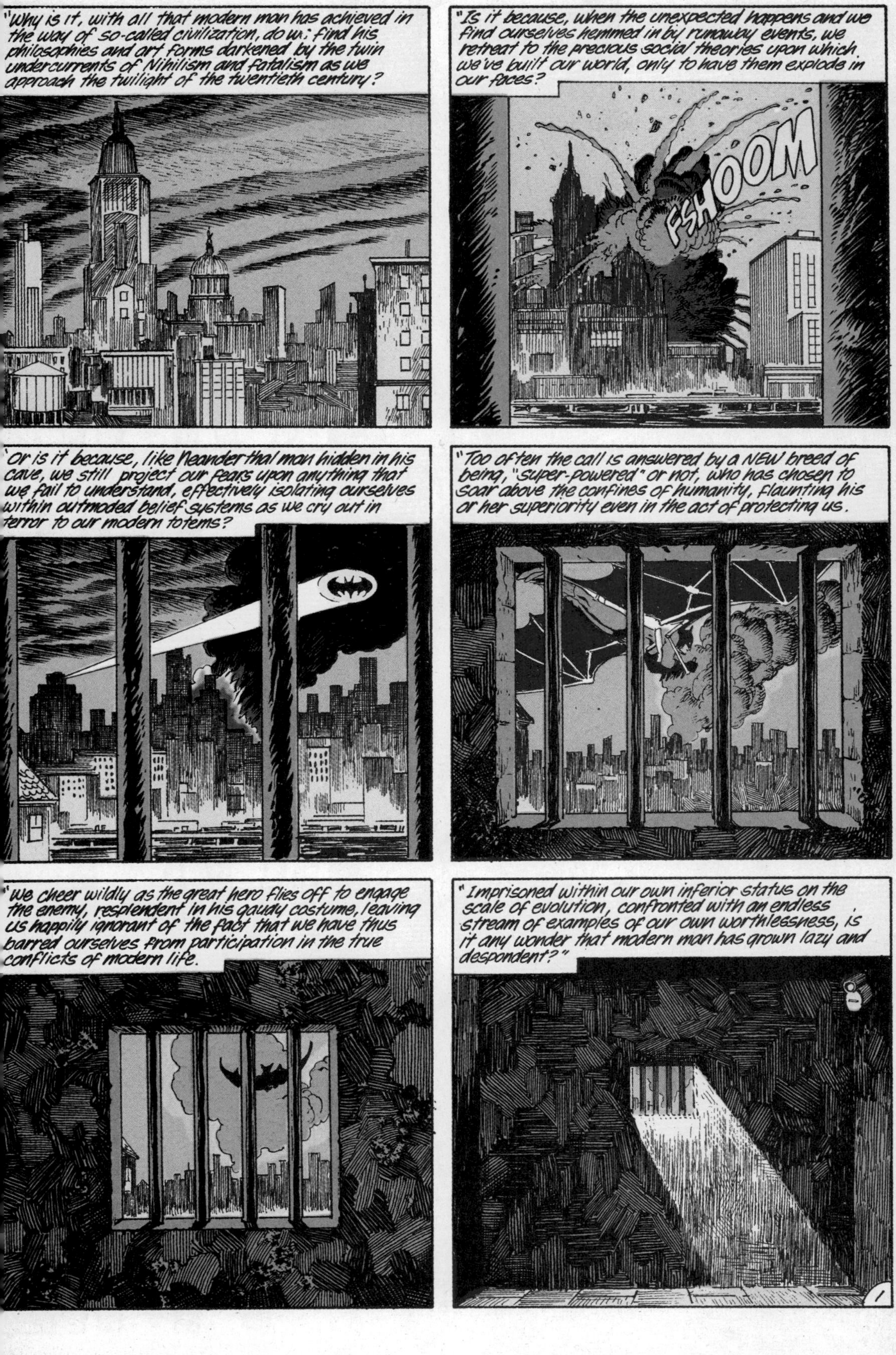
"Why is it, with all that modern man has achieved in the way of so-called civilization, do we find his philosophies and art forms darkened by the twin undercurrents of Nihilism and fatalism as we approach the twilight of the twentieth century?
"Is it because, when the unexpected happens and we find ourselves hemmed in by runaway events, we retreat to the precious social theories upon which we've built our world, only to have them explode in our faces?
FSHOOM
"Or is it because, like Neanderthal man hidden in his cave, we still project our fears upon anything that we fail to understand, effectively isolating ourselves within outmoded belief systems as we cry out in terror to our modern totems?
"Too often the call is answered by a NEW breed of being, "super-powered" or not, who has chosen to soar above the confines of humanity, flaunting his or her superiority even in the act of protecting us.
"We cheer wildly as the great hero flies off to engage the enemy, resplendent in his gaudy costume, leaving us happily ignorant of the fact that we have thus barred ourselves from participation in the true conflicts of modern life.
"Imprisoned within our own inferior status on the scale of evolution, confronted with an endless stream of examples of our own worthlessness, is it any wonder that modern man has grown lazy and despondent?"
1

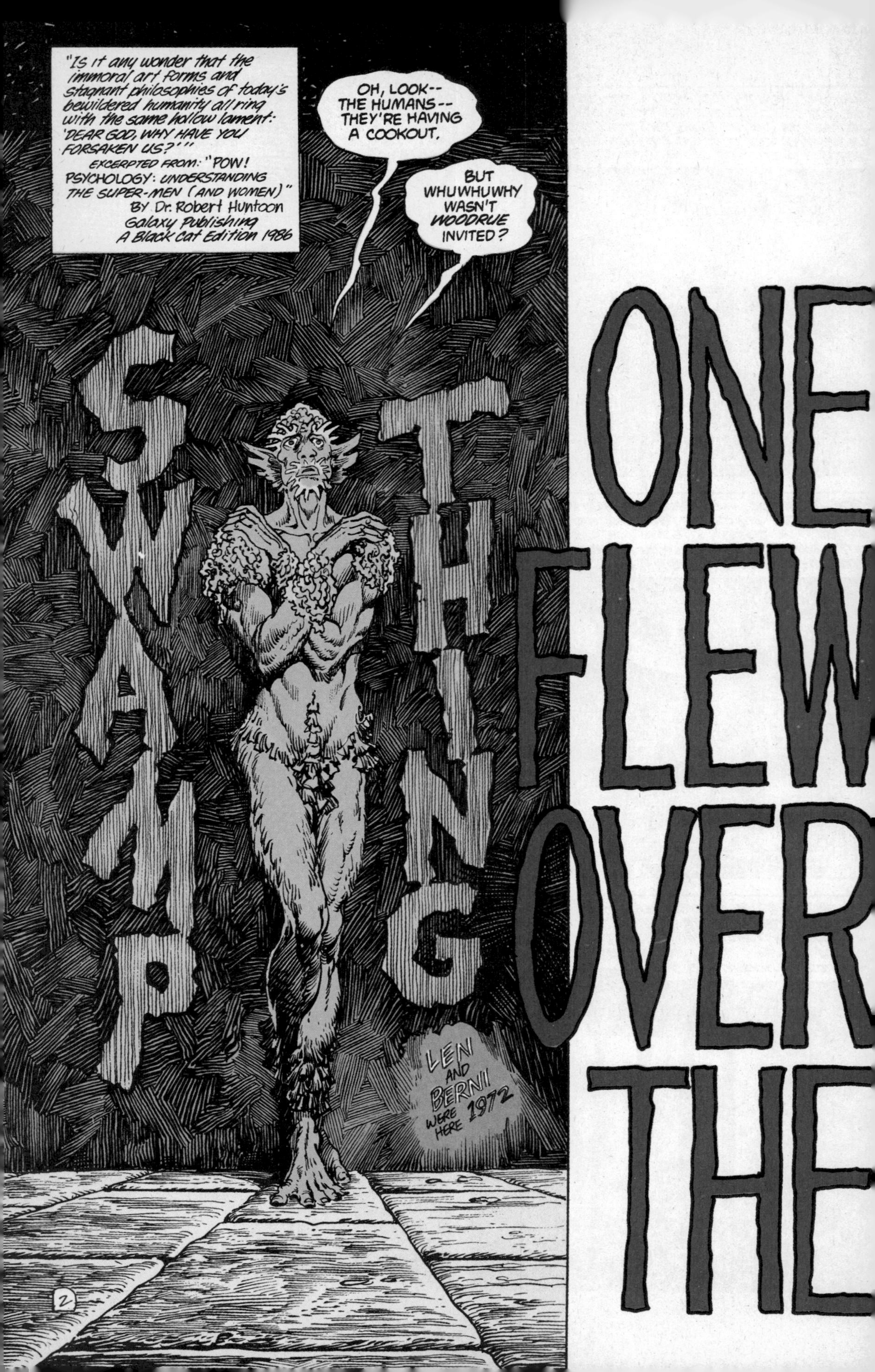
"Is it any wonder that the immoral art forms and stagnant philosophies of today's bewildered humanity all ring with the same hollow lament: 'DEAR GOD, WHY HAVE YOU FORSAKEN US?'"
EXCERPTED FROM: "POW! PSYCHOLOGY: UNDERSTANDING THE SUPER-MEN (AND WOMEN)" BY Dr. Robert Huntoon Galaxy Publishing A Black Cat Edition 1986
OH, LOOK-- THE HUMANS-- THEY'RE HAVING A COOKOUT.
BUT WHUWHUWHY WASN'T WOODRUE INVITED?
SWAMP THING
LEN AND BERNII WERE HERE 1972
2
ONE FLEW OVER THE

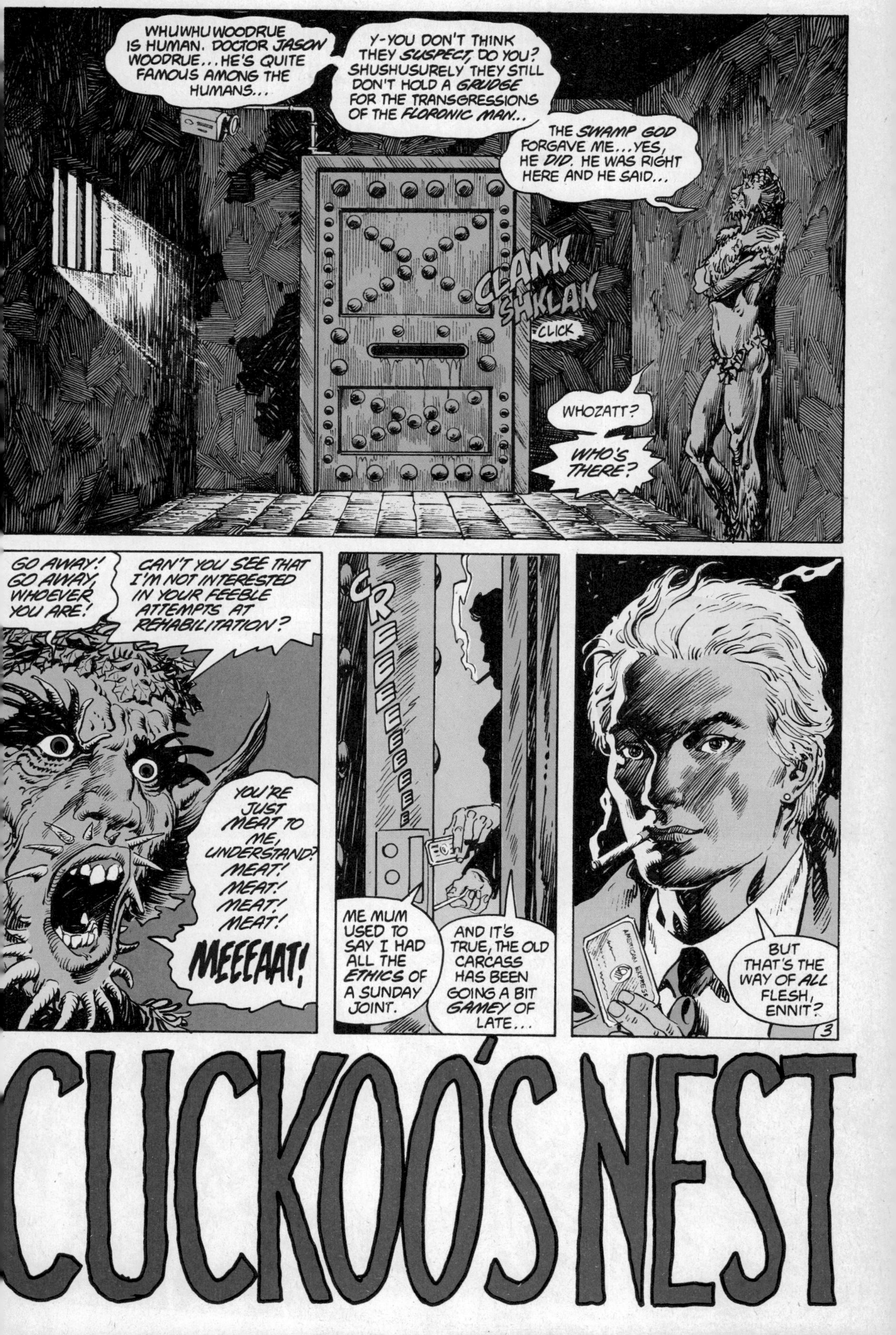
WHUWHU WOODRUE IS HUMAN. DOCTOR JASON WOODRUE... HE'S QUITE FAMOUS AMONG THE HUMANS...
Y-YOU DON'T THINK THEY SUSPECT, DO YOU? SHUSHUSURELY THEY STILL DON'T HOLD A GRUDGE FOR THE TRANSGRESSIONS OF THE FLORONIC MAN...
THE SWAMP GOD FORGAVE ME... YES, HE DID. HE WAS RIGHT HERE AND HE SAID...
CLANK
SHKLAK
CLICK
WHOZATT?
WHO'S THERE?
GO AWAY! GO AWAY, WHOEVER YOU ARE!
CAN'T YOU SEE THAT I'M NOT INTERESTED IN YOUR FEEBLE ATTEMPTS AT REHABILITATION?
YOU'RE JUST MEAT TO ME, UNDERSTAND? MEAT! MEAT! MEAT! MEAT!
MEEEAAT!
CREEEEEEEEEE
ME MUM USED TO SAY I HAD ALL THE ETHICS OF A SUNDAY JOINT.
AND IT'S TRUE, THE OLD CARCASS HAS BEEN GOING A BIT GAMEY OF LATE...
BUT THAT'S THE WAY OF ALL FLESH, ENNIT?
3
CUCKOO'S NEST

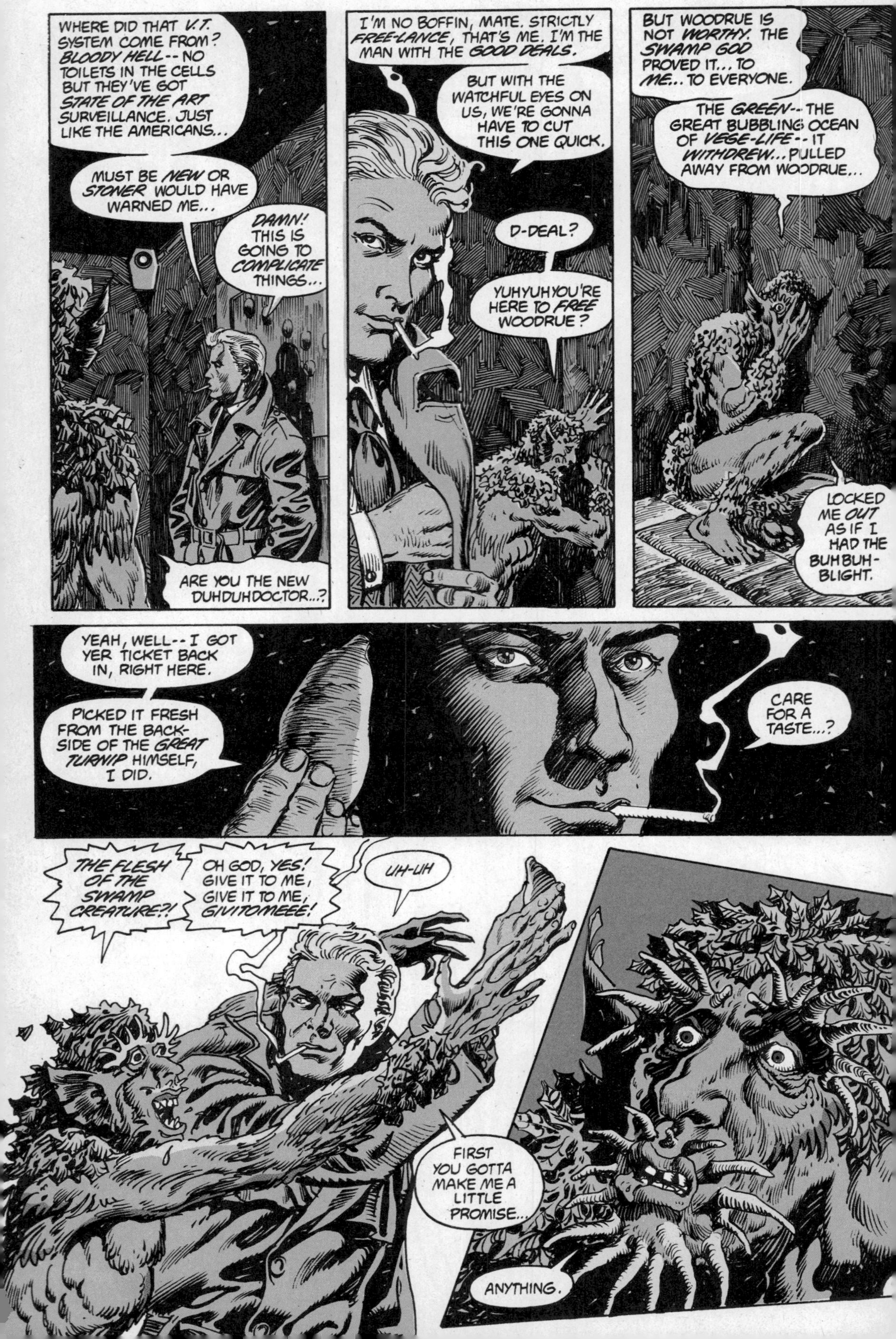
WHERE DID THAT V.T. SYSTEM COME FROM? BLOODY HELL -- NO TOILETS IN THE CELLS BUT THEY'VE GOT STATE OF THE ART SURVEILLANCE. JUST LIKE THE AMERICANS...
MUST BE NEW OR STONER WOULD HAVE WARNED ME...
DAMN! THIS IS GOING TO COMPLICATE THINGS...
ARE YOU THE NEW DUHDUHDOCTOR...?
I'M NO BOFFIN, MATE. STRICTLY FREE-LANCE, THAT'S ME. I'M THE MAN WITH THE GOOD DEALS.
BUT WITH THE WATCHFUL EYES ON US, WE'RE GONNA HAVE TO CUT THIS ONE QUICK.
D-DEAL?
YUHYUHYOU'RE HERE TO FREE WOODRUE?
BUT WOODRUE IS NOT WORTHY. THE SWAMP GOD PROVED IT... TO ME... TO EVERYONE.
THE GREEN -- THE GREAT BUBBLING OCEAN OF VEGE-LIFE -- IT WITHDREW... PULLED AWAY FROM WOODRUE...
LOCKED ME OUT AS IF I HAD THE BUHBUH-BLIGHT.
YEAH, WELL -- I GOT YER TICKET BACK IN, RIGHT HERE.
PICKED IT FRESH FROM THE BACK-SIDE OF THE GREAT TURNIP HIMSELF, I DID.
CARE FOR A TASTE...?
THE FLESH OF THE SWAMP CREATURE?!
OH GOD, YES! GIVE IT TO ME, GIVE IT TO ME, GIVITOMEEE!
UH-UH
FIRST YOU GOTTA MAKE ME A LITTLE PROMISE...
ANYTHING.

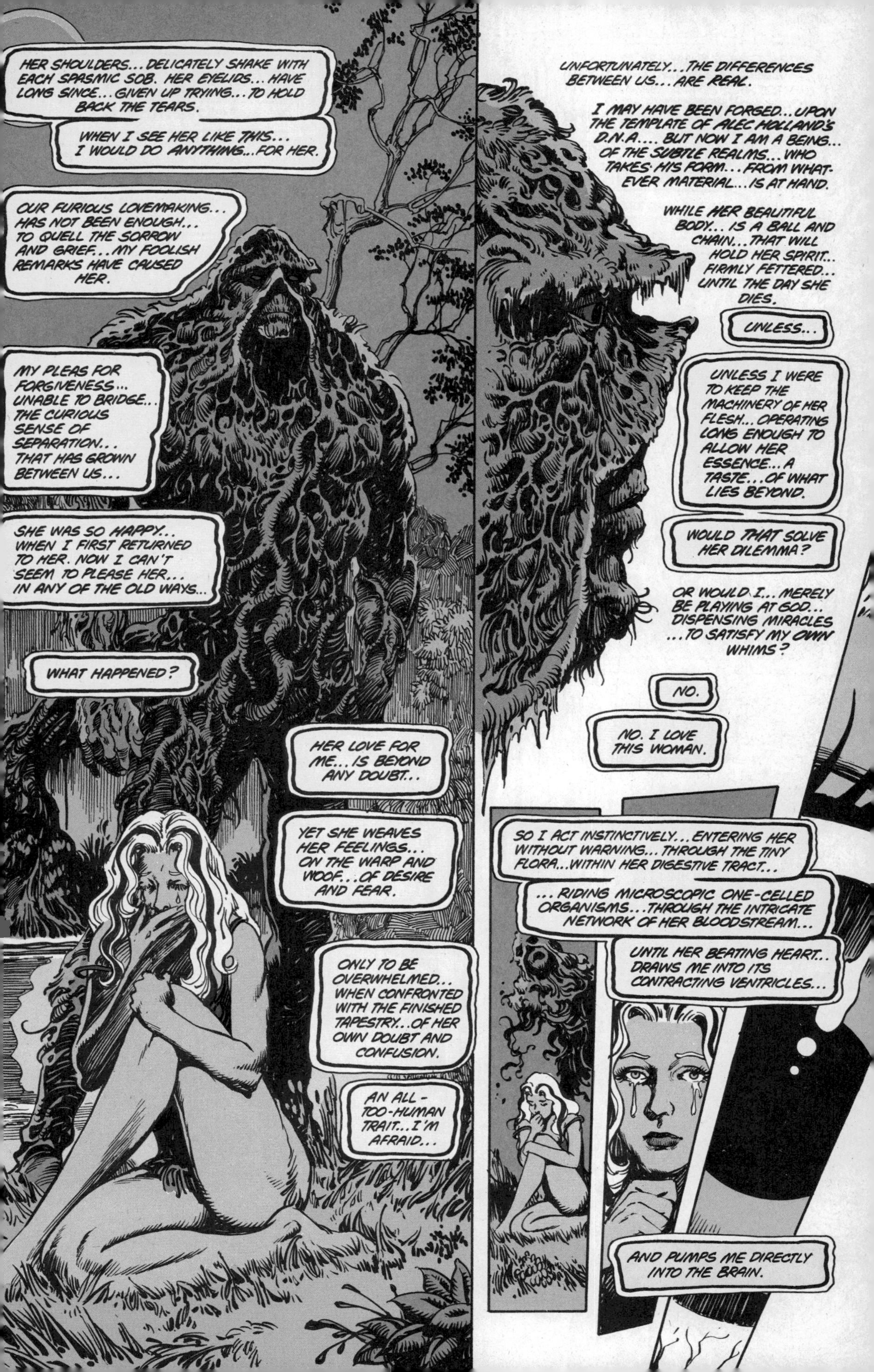
HER SHOULDERS... DELICATELY SHAKE WITH EACH SPASMIC SOB. HER EYELIDS... HAVE LONG SINCE... GIVEN UP TRYING... TO HOLD BACK THE TEARS.
WHEN I SEE HER LIKE THIS... I WOULD DO ANYTHING... FOR HER.
OUR FURIOUS LOVEMAKING... HAS NOT BEEN ENOUGH... TO QUELL THE SORROW AND GRIEF... MY FOOLISH REMARKS HAVE CAUSED HER.
MY PLEAS FOR FORGIVENESS... UNABLE TO BRIDGE... THE CURIOUS SENSE OF SEPARATION... THAT HAS GROWN BETWEEN US...
SHE WAS SO HAPPY... WHEN I FIRST RETURNED TO HER. NOW I CAN'T SEEM TO PLEASE HER... IN ANY OF THE OLD WAYS...
WHAT HAPPENED?
HER LOVE FOR ME... IS BEYOND ANY DOUBT...
YET SHE WEAVES HER FEELINGS... ON THE WARP AND WOOF... OF DESIRE AND FEAR.
ONLY TO BE OVERWHELMED... WHEN CONFRONTED WITH THE FINISHED TAPESTRY... OF HER OWN DOUBT AND CONFUSION.
AN ALL-TOO-HUMAN TRAIT... I'M AFRAID...
UNFORTUNATELY... THE DIFFERENCES BETWEEN US... ARE REAL.
I MAY HAVE BEEN FORGED... UPON THE TEMPLATE OF ALEC HOLLAND'S D.N.A.... BUT NOW I AM A BEING... OF THE SUBTLE REALMS... WHO TAKES HIS FORM... FROM WHATEVER MATERIAL... IS AT HAND.
WHILE HER BEAUTIFUL BODY... IS A BALL AND CHAIN... THAT WILL HOLD HER SPIRIT... FIRMLY FETTERED... UNTIL THE DAY SHE DIES.
UNLESS...
UNLESS I WERE TO KEEP THE MACHINERY OF HER FLESH... OPERATING LONG ENOUGH TO ALLOW HER ESSENCE... A TASTE... OF WHAT LIES BEYOND.
WOULD THAT SOLVE HER DILEMMA?
OR WOULD I... MERELY BE PLAYING AT GOD... DISPENSING MIRACLES ...TO SATISFY MY OWN WHIMS?
NO.
NO. I LOVE THIS WOMAN.
SO I ACT INSTINCTIVELY... ENTERING HER WITHOUT WARNING... THROUGH THE TINY FLORA... WITHIN HER DIGESTIVE TRACT...
... RIDING MICROSCOPIC ONE-CELLED ORGANISMS... THROUGH THE INTRICATE NETWORK OF HER BLOODSTREAM...
UNTIL HER BEATING HEART... DRAWS ME INTO ITS CONTRACTING VENTRICLES...
AND PUMPS ME DIRECTLY INTO THE BRAIN.

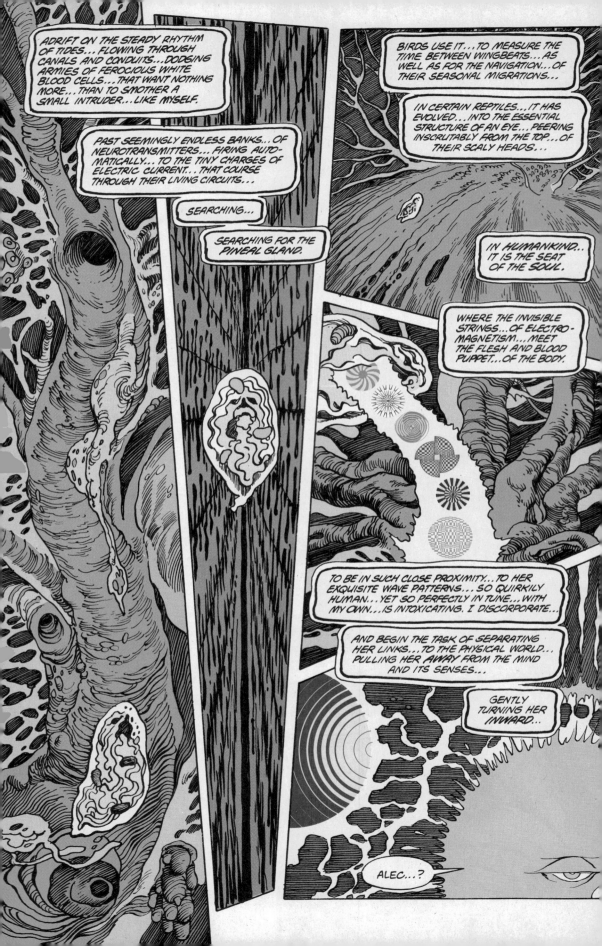

ADRIFT ON THE STEADY RHYTHM OF TIDES... FLOWING THROUGH CANALS AND CONDUITS... DODGING ARMIES OF FEROCIOUS WHITE BLOOD CELLS... THAT WANT NOTHING MORE... THAN TO SMOTHER A SMALL INTRUDER... LIKE MYSELF.

PAST SEEMINGLY ENDLESS BANKS... OF NEUROTRANSMITTERS... FIRING AUTO-MATICALLY... TO THE TINY CHARGES OF ELECTRIC CURRENT... THAT COURSE THROUGH THEIR LIVING CIRCUITS...

SEARCHING...

SEARCHING FOR THE PINEAL GLAND.

BIRDS USE IT... TO MEASURE THE TIME BETWEEN WINGBEATS... AS WELL AS FOR THE NAVIGATION... OF THEIR SEASONAL MIGRATIONS...

IN CERTAIN REPTILES... IT HAS EVOLVED... INTO THE ESSENTIAL STRUCTURE OF AN EYE... PEERING INSCRUTABLY FROM THE TOP... OF THEIR SCALY HEADS...

IN HUMANKIND... IT IS THE SEAT OF THE SOUL.

WHERE THE INVISIBLE STRINGS... OF ELECTRO-MAGNETISM... MEET THE FLESH AND BLOOD PUPPET... OF THE BODY.

TO BE IN SUCH CLOSE PROXIMITY... TO HER EXQUISITE WAVE PATTERNS... SO QUIRKILY HUMAN... YET SO PERFECTLY IN TUNE... WITH MY OWN... IS INTOXICATING. I DISCORPORATE...

AND BEGIN THE TASK OF SEPARATING HER LINKS... TO THE PHYSICAL WORLD... PULLING HER AWAY FROM THE MIND AND ITS SENSES...

GENTLY TURNING HER INWARD...

ALEC...?

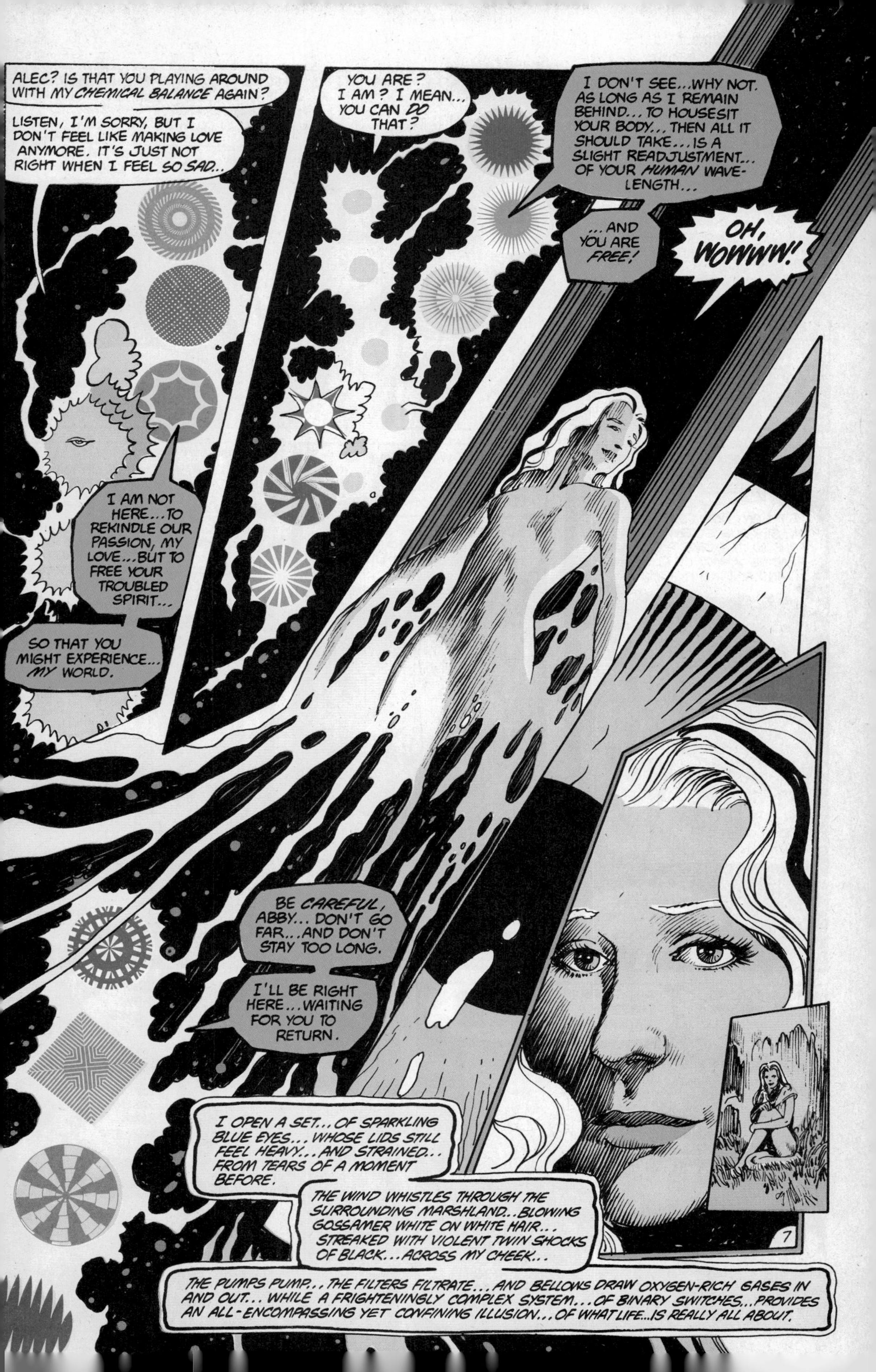
ALEC? IS THAT YOU PLAYING AROUND WITH MY CHEMICAL BALANCE AGAIN?
LISTEN, I'M SORRY, BUT I DON'T FEEL LIKE MAKING LOVE ANYMORE. IT'S JUST NOT RIGHT WHEN I FEEL SO SAD...
I AM NOT HERE...TO REKINDLE OUR PASSION, MY LOVE...BUT TO FREE YOUR TROUBLED SPIRIT...
SO THAT YOU MIGHT EXPERIENCE... MY WORLD.
YOU ARE? I AM? I MEAN... YOU CAN DO THAT?
I DON'T SEE...WHY NOT. AS LONG AS I REMAIN BEHIND...TO HOUSESIT YOUR BODY...THEN ALL IT SHOULD TAKE...IS A SLIGHT READJUSTMENT... OF YOUR HUMAN WAVE-LENGTH...
...AND YOU ARE FREE!
OH, WOWWW!
BE CAREFUL, ABBY... DON'T GO FAR...AND DON'T STAY TOO LONG.
I'LL BE RIGHT HERE...WAITING FOR YOU TO RETURN.
I OPEN A SET... OF SPARKLING BLUE EYES... WHOSE LIDS STILL FEEL HEAVY... AND STRAINED... FROM TEARS OF A MOMENT BEFORE.
THE WIND WHISTLES THROUGH THE SURROUNDING MARSHLAND...BLOWING GOSSAMER WHITE ON WHITE HAIR... STREAKED WITH VIOLENT TWIN SHOCKS OF BLACK...ACROSS MY CHEEK...
7
THE PUMPS PUMP... THE FILTERS FILTRATE... AND BELLOWS DRAW OXYGEN-RICH GASES IN AND OUT... WHILE A FRIGHTENINGLY COMPLEX SYSTEM... OF BINARY SWITCHES...PROVIDES AN ALL-ENCOMPASSING YET CONFINING ILLUSION... OF WHAT LIFE...IS REALLY ALL ABOUT.

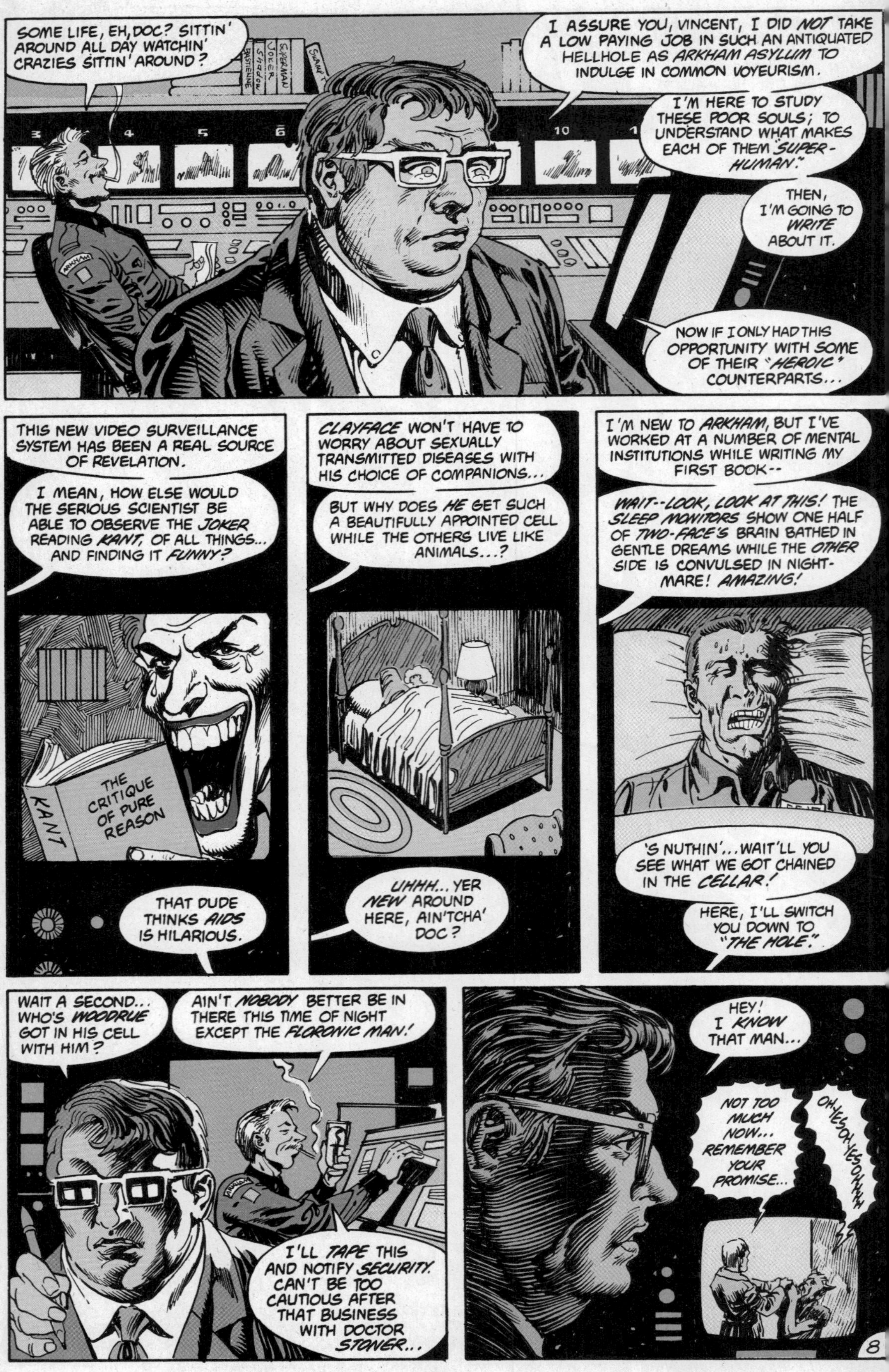
SOME LIFE, EH, DOC? SITTIN' AROUND ALL DAY WATCHIN' CRAZIES SITTIN' AROUND?
I ASSURE YOU, VINCENT, I DID NOT TAKE A LOW PAYING JOB IN SUCH AN ANTIQUATED HELLHOLE AS ARKHAM ASYLUM TO INDULGE IN COMMON VOYEURISM.
I'M HERE TO STUDY THESE POOR SOULS; TO UNDERSTAND WHAT MAKES EACH OF THEM "SUPER-HUMAN."
THEN, I'M GOING TO WRITE ABOUT IT.
NOW IF I ONLY HAD THIS OPPORTUNITY WITH SOME OF THEIR "HEROIC" COUNTERPARTS...
THIS NEW VIDEO SURVEILLANCE SYSTEM HAS BEEN A REAL SOURCE OF REVELATION.
I MEAN, HOW ELSE WOULD THE SERIOUS SCIENTIST BE ABLE TO OBSERVE THE JOKER READING KANT, OF ALL THINGS... AND FINDING IT FUNNY?
KANT
THE CRITIQUE OF PURE REASON
THAT DUDE THINKS AIDS IS HILARIOUS.
CLAYFACE WON'T HAVE TO WORRY ABOUT SEXUALLY TRANSMITTED DISEASES WITH HIS CHOICE OF COMPANIONS...
BUT WHY DOES HE GET SUCH A BEAUTIFULLY APPOINTED CELL WHILE THE OTHERS LIVE LIKE ANIMALS...?
UHHH... YER NEW AROUND HERE, AIN'TCHA' DOC?
I'M NEW TO ARKHAM, BUT I'VE WORKED AT A NUMBER OF MENTAL INSTITUTIONS WHILE WRITING MY FIRST BOOK--
WAIT--LOOK, LOOK AT THIS! THE SLEEP MONITORS SHOW ONE HALF OF TWO-FACE'S BRAIN BATHED IN GENTLE DREAMS WHILE THE OTHER SIDE IS CONVULSED IN NIGHT-MARE! AMAZING!
'S NUTHIN'... WAIT'LL YOU SEE WHAT WE GOT CHAINED IN THE CELLAR!
HERE, I'LL SWITCH YOU DOWN TO "THE HOLE."
WAIT A SECOND... WHO'S WOODRUE GOT IN HIS CELL WITH HIM?
AIN'T NOBODY BETTER BE IN THERE THIS TIME OF NIGHT EXCEPT THE FLORONIC MAN!
I'LL TAPE THIS AND NOTIFY SECURITY. CAN'T BE TOO CAUTIOUS AFTER THAT BUSINESS WITH DOCTOR STONER...
HEY! I KNOW THAT MAN...
NOT TOO MUCH NOW... REMEMBER YOUR PROMISE...
OHYESOHYESOHHHH
8

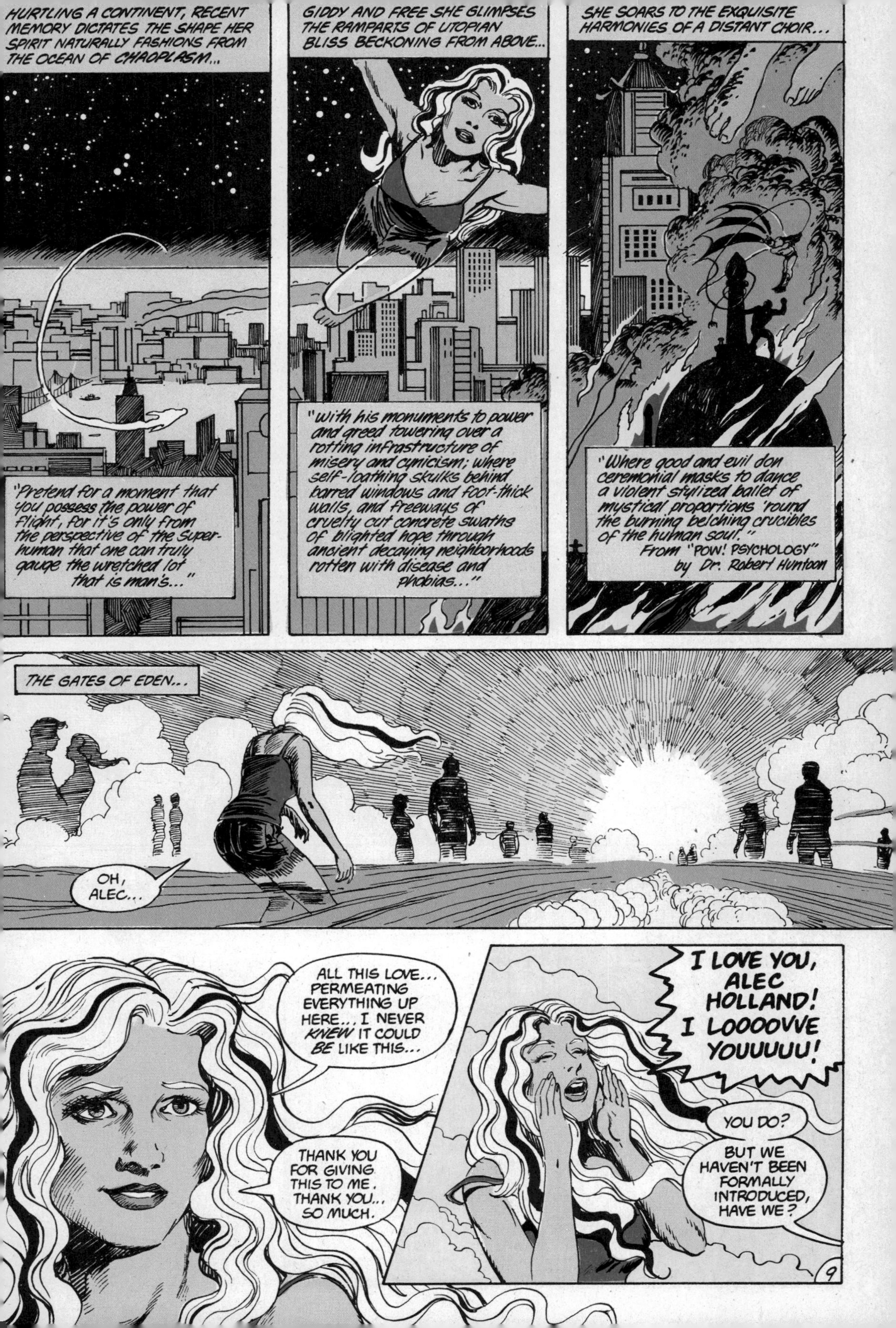
HURTLING A CONTINENT, RECENT MEMORY DICTATES THE SHAPE HER SPIRIT NATURALLY FASHIONS FROM THE OCEAN OF CHAOPLASM...
"Pretend for a moment that you possess the power of flight, for it's only from the perspective of the Super-human that one can truly gauge the wretched lot that is man's..."
GIDDY AND FREE SHE GLIMPSES THE RAMPARTS OF UTOPIAN BLISS BECKONING FROM ABOVE...
"With his monuments to power and greed towering over a rotting infrastructure of misery and cynicism; where self-loathing skulks behind barred windows and foot-thick walls, and freeways of cruelty cut concrete swaths of blighted hope through ancient decaying neighborhoods rotten with disease and phobias..."
SHE SOARS TO THE EXQUISITE HARMONIES OF A DISTANT CHOIR...
"Where good and evil don ceremonial masks to dance a violent stylized ballet of mystical proportions 'round the burning belching crucibles of the human soul."
From "POW! PSYCHOLOGY" by Dr. Robert Huntoon
THE GATES OF EDEN...
OH, ALEC...
ALL THIS LOVE... PERMEATING EVERYTHING UP HERE... I NEVER KNEW IT COULD BE LIKE THIS...
THANK YOU FOR GIVING THIS TO ME. THANK YOU... SO MUCH.
I LOVE YOU, ALEC HOLLAND! I LOOOOVVE YOUUUUU!
YOU DO?
BUT WE HAVEN'T BEEN FORMALLY INTRODUCED, HAVE WE?
9

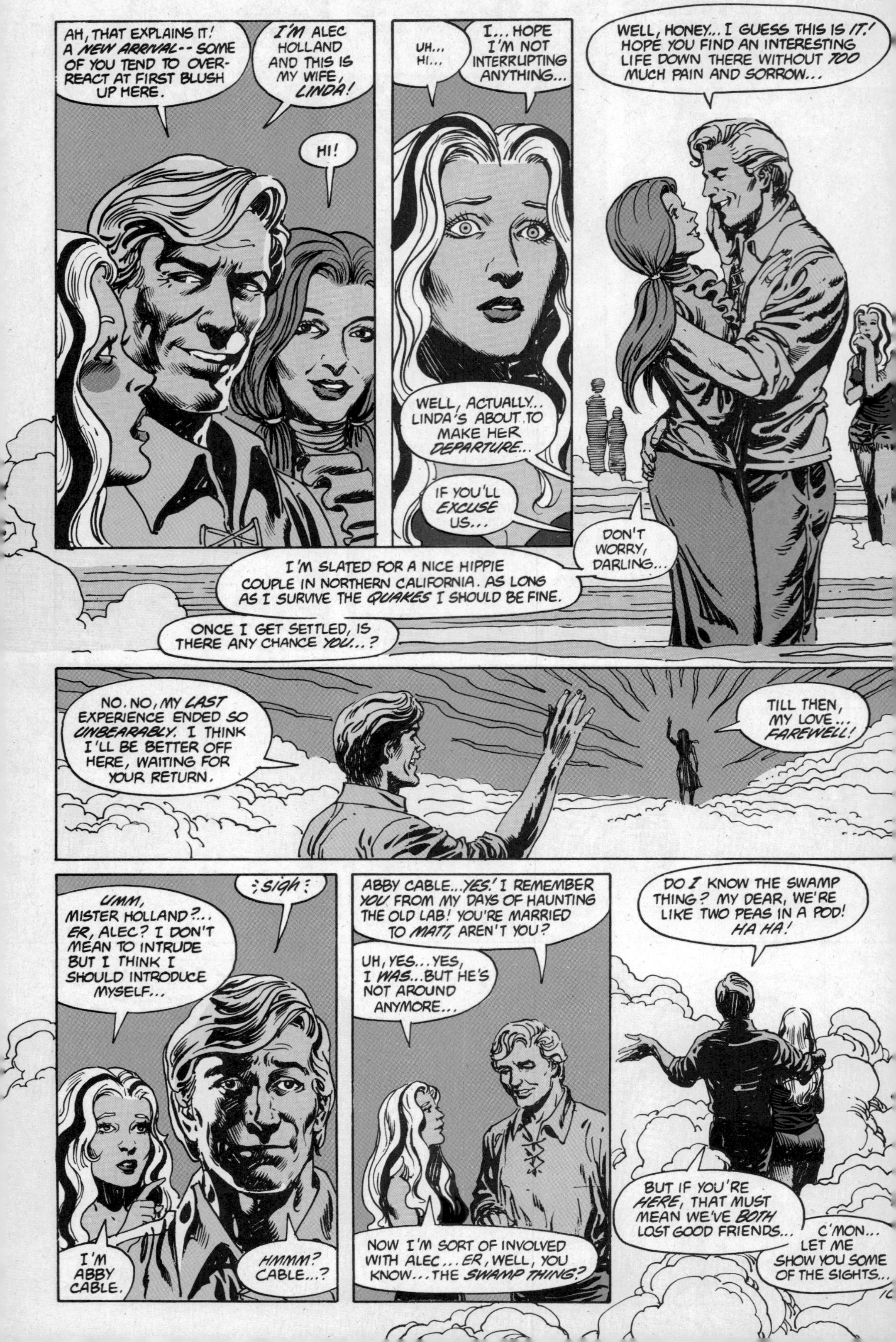
AH, THAT EXPLAINS IT! A NEW ARRIVAL-- SOME OF YOU TEND TO OVER-REACT AT FIRST BLUSH UP HERE.
I'M ALEC HOLLAND AND THIS IS MY WIFE, LINDA!
HI!
UH... HI...
I... HOPE I'M NOT INTERRUPTING ANYTHING...
WELL, ACTUALLY... LINDA'S ABOUT TO MAKE HER DEPARTURE...
IF YOU'LL EXCUSE US...
WELL, HONEY... I GUESS THIS IS IT! HOPE YOU FIND AN INTERESTING LIFE DOWN THERE WITHOUT TOO MUCH PAIN AND SORROW...
DON'T WORRY, DARLING...
I'M SLATED FOR A NICE HIPPIE COUPLE IN NORTHERN CALIFORNIA. AS LONG AS I SURVIVE THE QUAKES I SHOULD BE FINE.
ONCE I GET SETTLED, IS THERE ANY CHANCE YOU...?
NO. NO, MY LAST EXPERIENCE ENDED SO UNBEARABLY. I THINK I'LL BE BETTER OFF HERE, WAITING FOR YOUR RETURN.
TILL THEN, MY LOVE... FAREWELL!
UMM, MISTER HOLLAND?... ER, ALEC? I DON'T MEAN TO INTRUDE BUT I THINK I SHOULD INTRODUCE MYSELF...
:sigh:
I'M ABBY CABLE.
HMMM? CABLE...?
ABBY CABLE... YES! I REMEMBER YOU FROM MY DAYS OF HAUNTING THE OLD LAB! YOU'RE MARRIED TO MATT, AREN'T YOU?
UH, YES... YES, I WAS... BUT HE'S NOT AROUND ANYMORE...
NOW I'M SORT OF INVOLVED WITH ALEC... ER, WELL, YOU KNOW... THE SWAMP THING?
DO I KNOW THE SWAMP THING? MY DEAR, WE'RE LIKE TWO PEAS IN A POD! HA HA!
BUT IF YOU'RE HERE, THAT MUST MEAN WE'VE BOTH LOST GOOD FRIENDS...
C'MON... LET ME SHOW YOU SOME OF THE SIGHTS...
10

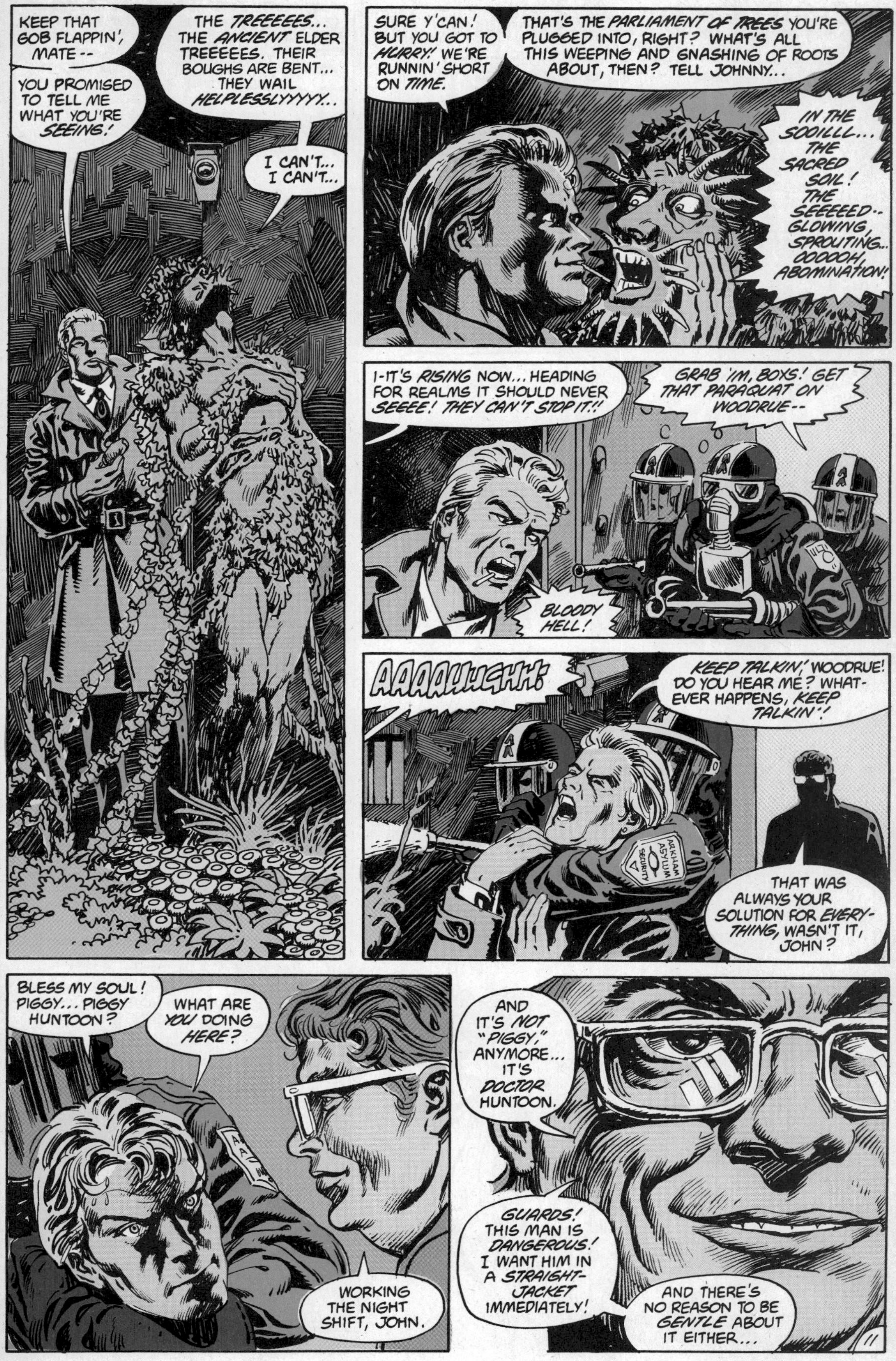
KEEP THAT GOB FLAPPIN', MATE --
YOU PROMISED TO TELL ME WHAT YOU'RE SEEING!
THE TREEEEES... THE ANCIENT ELDER TREEEEES. THEIR BOUGHS ARE BENT... THEY WAIL HELPLESSLYYYYY...
I CAN'T... I CAN'T...
SURE Y'CAN! BUT YOU GOT TO HURRY! WE'RE RUNNIN' SHORT ON TIME.
THAT'S THE PARLIAMENT OF TREES YOU'RE PLUGGED INTO, RIGHT? WHAT'S ALL THIS WEEPING AND GNASHING OF ROOTS ABOUT, THEN? TELL JOHNNY...
IN THE SOOILLL... THE SACRED SOIL! THE SEEEEED.. GLOWING, SPROUTING.. OOOOOH, ABOMINATION!
I-IT'S RISING NOW... HEADING FOR REALMS IT SHOULD NEVER SEEEE! THEY CAN'T STOP IT!!
GRAB 'IM, BOYS! GET THAT PARAQUAT ON WOODRUE--
BLOODY HELL!
AAAAUUGHH!
KEEP TALKIN', WOODRUE! DO YOU HEAR ME? WHATEVER HAPPENS, KEEP TALKIN'!
ARKHAM ASYLUM SECURITY
THAT WAS ALWAYS YOUR SOLUTION FOR EVERYTHING, WASN'T IT, JOHN?
BLESS MY SOUL! PIGGY... PIGGY HUNTOON?
WHAT ARE YOU DOING HERE?
WORKING THE NIGHT SHIFT, JOHN.
AND IT'S NOT "PIGGY," ANYMORE... IT'S DOCTOR HUNTOON.
GUARDS! THIS MAN IS DANGEROUS! I WANT HIM IN A STRAIGHT-JACKET IMMEDIATELY!
AND THERE'S NO REASON TO BE GENTLE ABOUT IT EITHER...
11

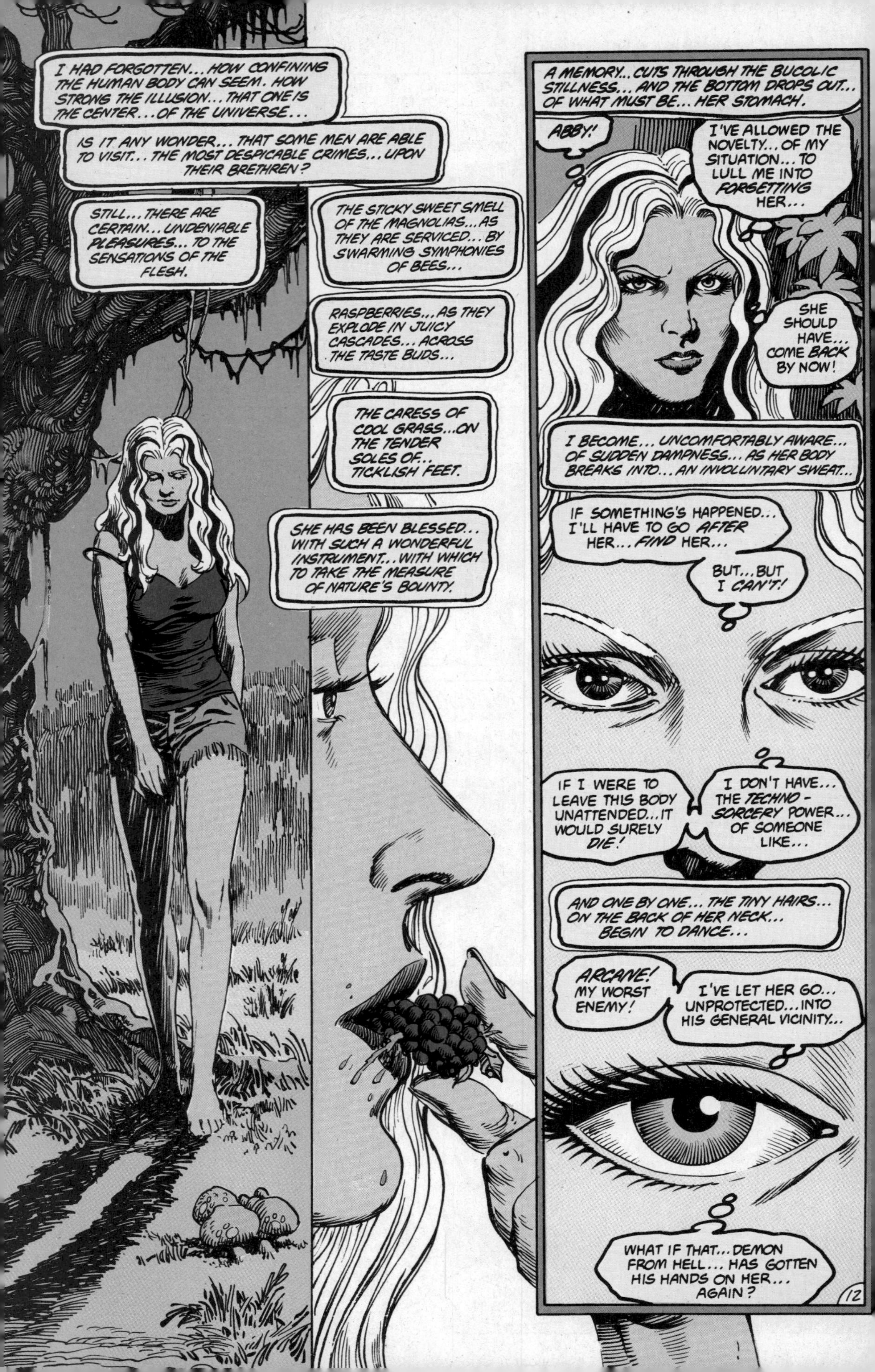

I HAD FORGOTTEN... HOW CONFINING THE HUMAN BODY CAN SEEM. HOW STRONG THE ILLUSION... THAT ONE IS THE CENTER... OF THE UNIVERSE...
IS IT ANY WONDER... THAT SOME MEN ARE ABLE TO VISIT... THE MOST DESPICABLE CRIMES... UPON THEIR BRETHREN?
STILL... THERE ARE CERTAIN... UNDENIABLE PLEASURES... TO THE SENSATIONS OF THE FLESH.
THE STICKY SWEET SMELL OF THE MAGNOLIAS... AS THEY ARE SERVICED... BY SWARMING SYMPHONIES OF BEES...
RASPBERRIES... AS THEY EXPLODE IN JUICY CASCADES... ACROSS THE TASTE BUDS...
THE CARESS OF COOL GRASS... ON THE TENDER SOLES OF... TICKLISH FEET.
SHE HAS BEEN BLESSED... WITH SUCH A WONDERFUL INSTRUMENT... WITH WHICH TO TAKE THE MEASURE OF NATURE'S BOUNTY.
A MEMORY... CUTS THROUGH THE BUCOLIC STILLNESS... AND THE BOTTOM DROPS OUT... OF WHAT MUST BE... HER STOMACH.
ABBY!
I'VE ALLOWED THE NOVELTY... OF MY SITUATION... TO LULL ME INTO FORGETTING HER...
SHE SHOULD HAVE... COME BACK BY NOW!
I BECOME... UNCOMFORTABLY AWARE... OF SUDDEN DAMPNESS... AS HER BODY BREAKS INTO... AN INVOLUNTARY SWEAT...
IF SOMETHING'S HAPPENED... I'LL HAVE TO GO AFTER HER... FIND HER...
BUT... BUT I CAN'T!
IF I WERE TO LEAVE THIS BODY UNATTENDED... IT WOULD SURELY DIE!
I DON'T HAVE... THE TECHNO-SORCERY POWER... OF SOMEONE LIKE...
AND ONE BY ONE... THE TINY HAIRS... ON THE BACK OF HER NECK... BEGIN TO DANCE...
ARCANE! MY WORST ENEMY!
I'VE LET HER GO... UNPROTECTED... INTO HIS GENERAL VICINITY...
WHAT IF THAT... DEMON FROM HELL... HAS GOTTEN HIS HANDS ON HER... AGAIN?
12

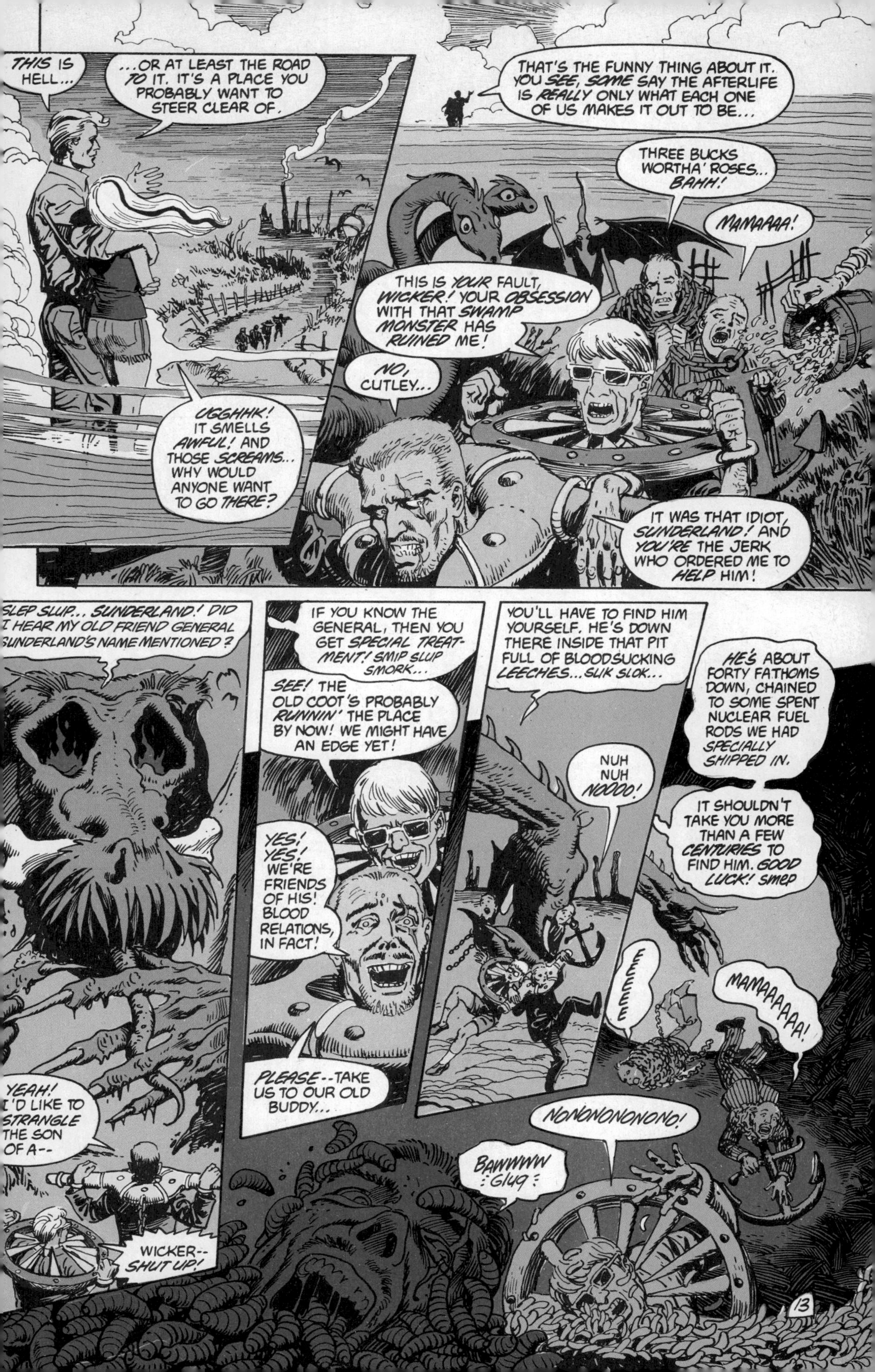

THIS IS HELL...
...OR AT LEAST THE ROAD TO IT. IT'S A PLACE YOU PROBABLY WANT TO STEER CLEAR OF.
UGGHHK! IT SMELLS AWFUL! AND THOSE SCREAMS... WHY WOULD ANYONE WANT TO GO THERE?
THAT'S THE FUNNY THING ABOUT IT. YOU SEE, SOME SAY THE AFTERLIFE IS REALLY ONLY WHAT EACH ONE OF US MAKES IT OUT TO BE...
THREE BUCKS WORTHA' ROSES... BAHH!
MAMAAAA!
THIS IS YOUR FAULT, WICKER! YOUR OBSESSION WITH THAT SWAMP MONSTER HAS RUINED ME!
NO, CUTLEY...
IT WAS THAT IDIOT, SUNDERLAND! AND YOU'RE THE JERK WHO ORDERED ME TO HELP HIM!
SLEP SLUP... SUNDERLAND! DID I HEAR MY OLD FRIEND GENERAL SUNDERLAND'S NAME MENTIONED?
YEAH! I'D LIKE TO STRANGLE THE SON OF A--
WICKER-- SHUT UP!
IF YOU KNOW THE GENERAL, THEN YOU GET SPECIAL TREATMENT! SMIP SLUP SMORK...
SEE! THE OLD COOT'S PROBABLY RUNNIN' THE PLACE BY NOW! WE MIGHT HAVE AN EDGE YET!
YES! YES! WE'RE FRIENDS OF HIS! BLOOD RELATIONS, IN FACT!
PLEASE--TAKE US TO OUR OLD BUDDY...
YOU'LL HAVE TO FIND HIM YOURSELF. HE'S DOWN THERE INSIDE THAT PIT FULL OF BLOODSUCKING LEECHES... SLIK SLOK...
NUH NUH NOOOO!
EEEEE
HE'S ABOUT FORTY FATHOMS DOWN, CHAINED TO SOME SPENT NUCLEAR FUEL RODS WE HAD SPECIALLY SHIPPED IN.
IT SHOULDN'T TAKE YOU MORE THAN A FEW CENTURIES TO FIND HIM. GOOD LUCK! smep
MAMAAAAAA!
NONONONONONONO!
BAWWWW Glug
13

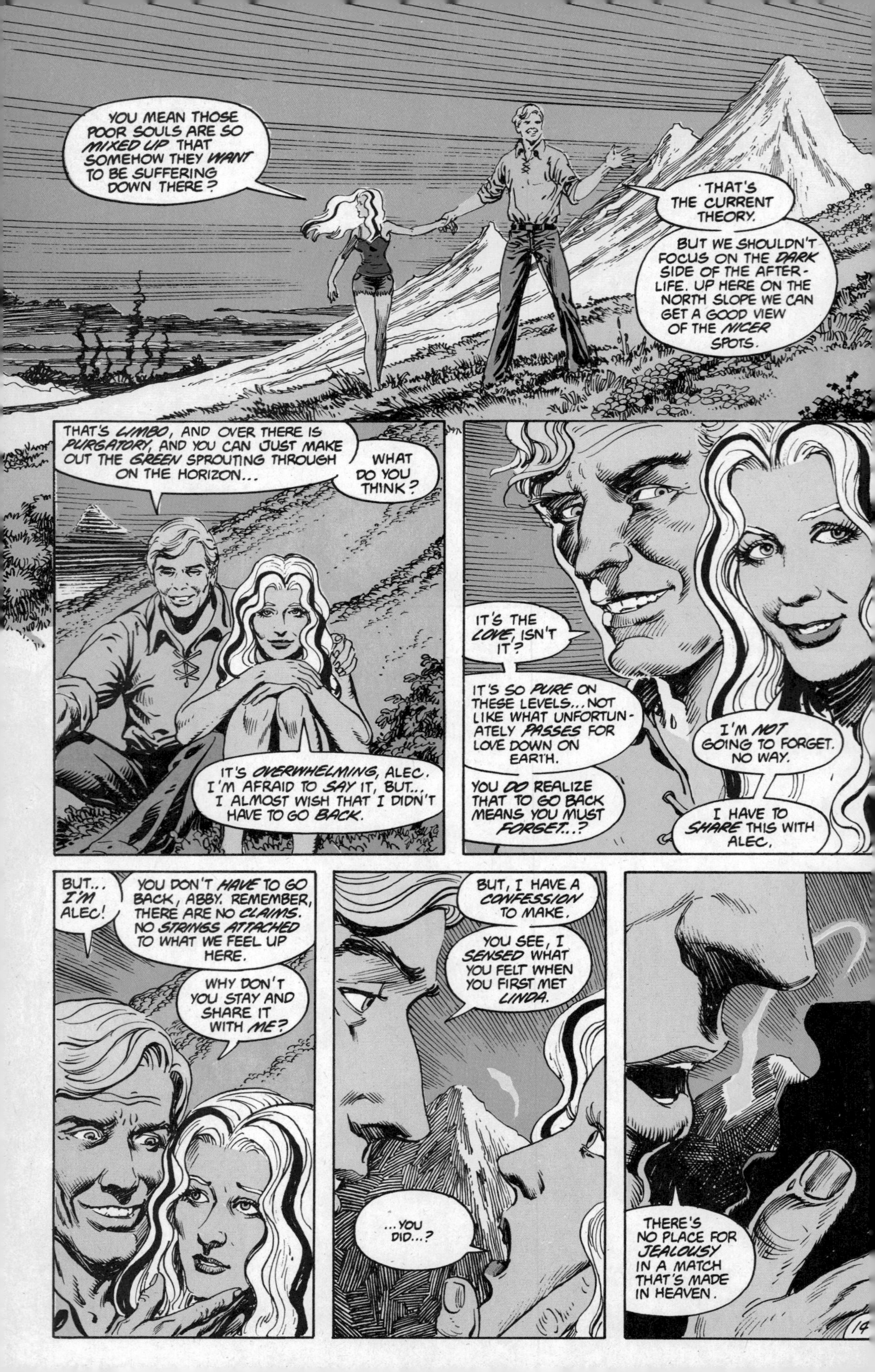
YOU MEAN THOSE POOR SOULS ARE SO MIXED UP THAT SOMEHOW THEY WANT TO BE SUFFERING DOWN THERE?
THAT'S THE CURRENT THEORY.
BUT WE SHOULDN'T FOCUS ON THE DARK SIDE OF THE AFTER-LIFE. UP HERE ON THE NORTH SLOPE WE CAN GET A GOOD VIEW OF THE NICER SPOTS.
THAT'S LIMBO, AND OVER THERE IS PURGATORY, AND YOU CAN JUST MAKE OUT THE GREEN SPROUTING THROUGH ON THE HORIZON...
WHAT DO YOU THINK?
IT'S OVERWHELMING, ALEC. I'M AFRAID TO SAY IT, BUT... I ALMOST WISH THAT I DIDN'T HAVE TO GO BACK.
IT'S THE LOVE, ISN'T IT?
IT'S SO PURE ON THESE LEVELS... NOT LIKE WHAT UNFORTUN-ATELY PASSES FOR LOVE DOWN ON EARTH.
YOU DO REALIZE THAT TO GO BACK MEANS YOU MUST FORGET...?
I'M NOT GOING TO FORGET. NO WAY.
I HAVE TO SHARE THIS WITH ALEC.
BUT... I'M ALEC!
YOU DON'T HAVE TO GO BACK, ABBY. REMEMBER, THERE ARE NO CLAIMS. NO STRINGS ATTACHED TO WHAT WE FEEL UP HERE.
WHY DON'T YOU STAY AND SHARE IT WITH ME?
BUT, I HAVE A CONFESSION TO MAKE.
YOU SEE, I SENSED WHAT YOU FELT WHEN YOU FIRST MET LINDA.
...YOU DID...?
THERE'S NO PLACE FOR JEALOUSY IN A MATCH THAT'S MADE IN HEAVEN.
14

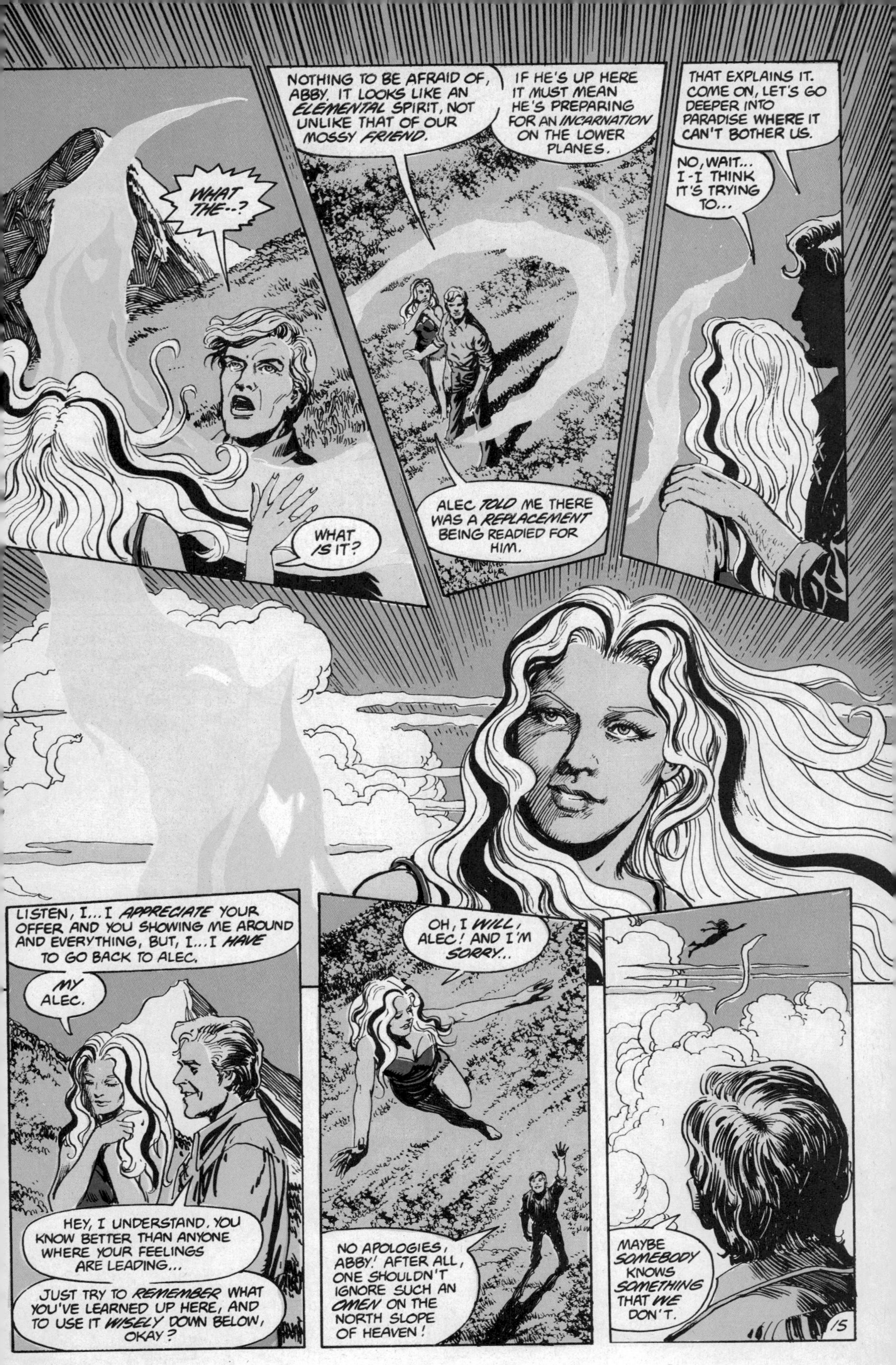
WHAT THE--?
WHAT IS IT?
NOTHING TO BE AFRAID OF, ABBY. IT LOOKS LIKE AN ELEMENTAL SPIRIT, NOT UNLIKE THAT OF OUR MOSSY FRIEND.
IF HE'S UP HERE IT MUST MEAN HE'S PREPARING FOR AN INCARNATION ON THE LOWER PLANES.
ALEC TOLD ME THERE WAS A REPLACEMENT BEING READIED FOR HIM.
THAT EXPLAINS IT. COME ON, LET'S GO DEEPER INTO PARADISE WHERE IT CAN'T BOTHER US.
NO, WAIT... I-I THINK IT'S TRYING TO...
LISTEN, I... I APPRECIATE YOUR OFFER AND YOU SHOWING ME AROUND AND EVERYTHING, BUT, I... I HAVE TO GO BACK TO ALEC.
MY ALEC.
HEY, I UNDERSTAND. YOU KNOW BETTER THAN ANYONE WHERE YOUR FEELINGS ARE LEADING...
JUST TRY TO REMEMBER WHAT YOU'VE LEARNED UP HERE, AND TO USE IT WISELY DOWN BELOW, OKAY?
OH, I WILL, ALEC! AND I'M SORRY...
NO APOLOGIES, ABBY! AFTER ALL, ONE SHOULDN'T IGNORE SUCH AN OMEN ON THE NORTH SLOPE OF HEAVEN!
MAYBE SOMEBODY KNOWS SOMETHING THAT WE DON'T.
15

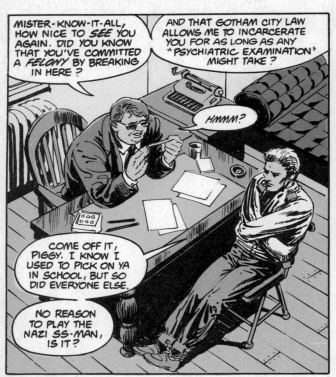

MISTER-KNOW-IT-ALL, HOW NICE TO *SEE* YOU AGAIN. DID YOU KNOW THAT YOU'VE COMMITTED A *FELONY* BY BREAKING IN HERE?

AND THAT GOTHAM CITY LAW ALLOWS ME TO INCARCERATE YOU FOR AS LONG AS ANY "PSYCHIATRIC EXAMINATION" MIGHT TAKE?

HMMM?

COME OFF IT, PIGGY. I KNOW I USED TO PICK ON YA IN SCHOOL, BUT SO DID EVERYONE ELSE.

NO REASON TO PLAY THE NAZI SS-MAN, IS IT?

NO REASON? HOW ABOUT *DIANE*?

OR DID YOU *FORGET* ABOUT HER AS SOON AS YOU WERE *DONE* WITH HER?

Dr. HUNTOON

THAT WAS *FIFTEEN YEARS AGO*, MATE! DON'T TELL ME YER *STILL* STUCK ON THAT TART?

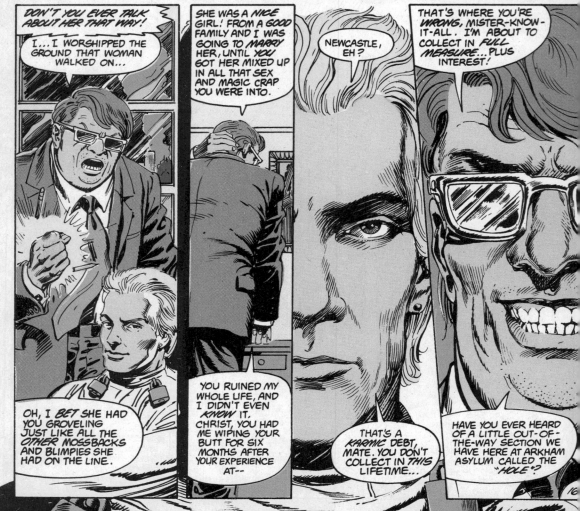

DON'T YOU *EVER* TALK ABOUT HER THAT WAY!

I... I WORSHIPPED THE GROUND THAT WOMAN WALKED ON...

SHE WAS A *NICE* GIRL! FROM A *GOOD* FAMILY AND I WAS GOING TO *MARRY* HER, UNTIL *YOU* GOT HER MIXED UP IN ALL THAT SEX AND MAGIC CRAP YOU WERE INTO.

NEWCASTLE, EH?

THAT'S WHERE YOU'RE *WRONG*, MISTER-KNOW-IT-ALL. I'M ABOUT TO COLLECT IN *FULL MEASURE*... PLUS INTEREST!

OH, I *BET* SHE HAD YOU GROVELING JUST LIKE ALL THE *OTHER* MOSSBACKS AND BLIMPIES SHE HAD ON THE LINE.

YOU RUINED MY WHOLE LIFE, AND I DIDN'T EVEN *KNOW* IT. CHRIST, YOU HAD ME WIPING YOUR BUTT FOR SIX MONTHS AFTER YOUR EXPERIENCE AT--

THAT'S A *KARMIC* DEBT, MATE. YOU DON'T COLLECT IN *THIS* LIFETIME...

HAVE YOU EVER HEARD OF A LITTLE OUT-OF-THE-WAY SECTION WE HAVE HERE AT ARKHAM ASYLUM CALLED THE "HOLE"?

16

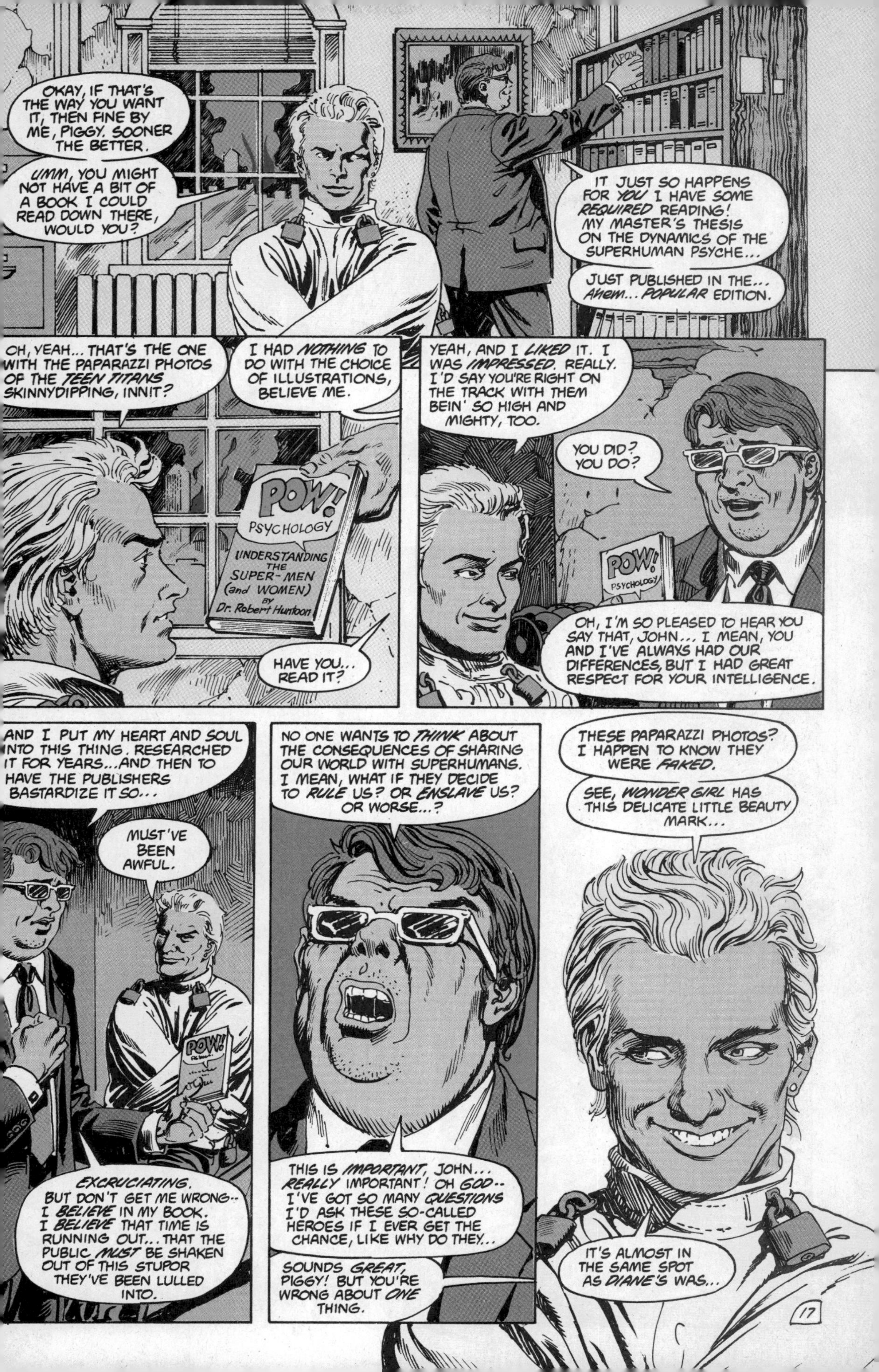
OKAY, IF THAT'S THE WAY YOU WANT IT, THEN FINE BY ME, PIGGY. SOONER THE BETTER.
UMM, YOU MIGHT NOT HAVE A BIT OF A BOOK I COULD READ DOWN THERE, WOULD YOU?
IT JUST SO HAPPENS FOR YOU I HAVE SOME REQUIRED READING! MY MASTER'S THESIS ON THE DYNAMICS OF THE SUPERHUMAN PSYCHE...
JUST PUBLISHED IN THE... AHEM... POPULAR EDITION.
POW
OH, YEAH... THAT'S THE ONE WITH THE PAPARAZZI PHOTOS OF THE TEEN TITANS SKINNYDIPPING, INNIT?
I HAD NOTHING TO DO WITH THE CHOICE OF ILLUSTRATIONS, BELIEVE ME.
POW! PSYCHOLOGY
UNDERSTANDING THE SUPER-MEN (and WOMEN) BY Dr. Robert Huntoon
HAVE YOU... READ IT?
YEAH, AND I LIKED IT. I WAS IMPRESSED. REALLY. I'D SAY YOU'RE RIGHT ON THE TRACK WITH THEM BEIN' SO HIGH AND MIGHTY, TOO.
YOU DID? YOU DO?
POW! PSYCHOLOGY
OH, I'M SO PLEASED TO HEAR YOU SAY THAT, JOHN... I MEAN, YOU AND I'VE ALWAYS HAD OUR DIFFERENCES, BUT I HAD GREAT RESPECT FOR YOUR INTELLIGENCE.
AND I PUT MY HEART AND SOUL INTO THIS THING. RESEARCHED IT FOR YEARS...AND THEN TO HAVE THE PUBLISHERS BASTARDIZE IT SO...
MUST'VE BEEN AWFUL.
POW!
EXCRUCIATING. BUT DON'T GET ME WRONG-- I BELIEVE IN MY BOOK. I BELIEVE THAT TIME IS RUNNING OUT... THAT THE PUBLIC MUST BE SHAKEN OUT OF THIS STUPOR THEY'VE BEEN LULLED INTO.
NO ONE WANTS TO THINK ABOUT THE CONSEQUENCES OF SHARING OUR WORLD WITH SUPERHUMANS. I MEAN, WHAT IF THEY DECIDE TO RULE US? OR ENSLAVE US? OR WORSE...?
THIS IS IMPORTANT, JOHN... REALLY IMPORTANT! OH GOD-- I'VE GOT SO MANY QUESTIONS I'D ASK THESE SO-CALLED HEROES IF I EVER GET THE CHANCE, LIKE WHY DO THEY...
SOUNDS GREAT, PIGGY! BUT YOU'RE WRONG ABOUT ONE THING.
THESE PAPARAZZI PHOTOS? I HAPPEN TO KNOW THEY WERE FAKED.
SEE, WONDER GIRL HAS THIS DELICATE LITTLE BEAUTY MARK...
IT'S ALMOST IN THE SAME SPOT AS DIANE'S WAS...

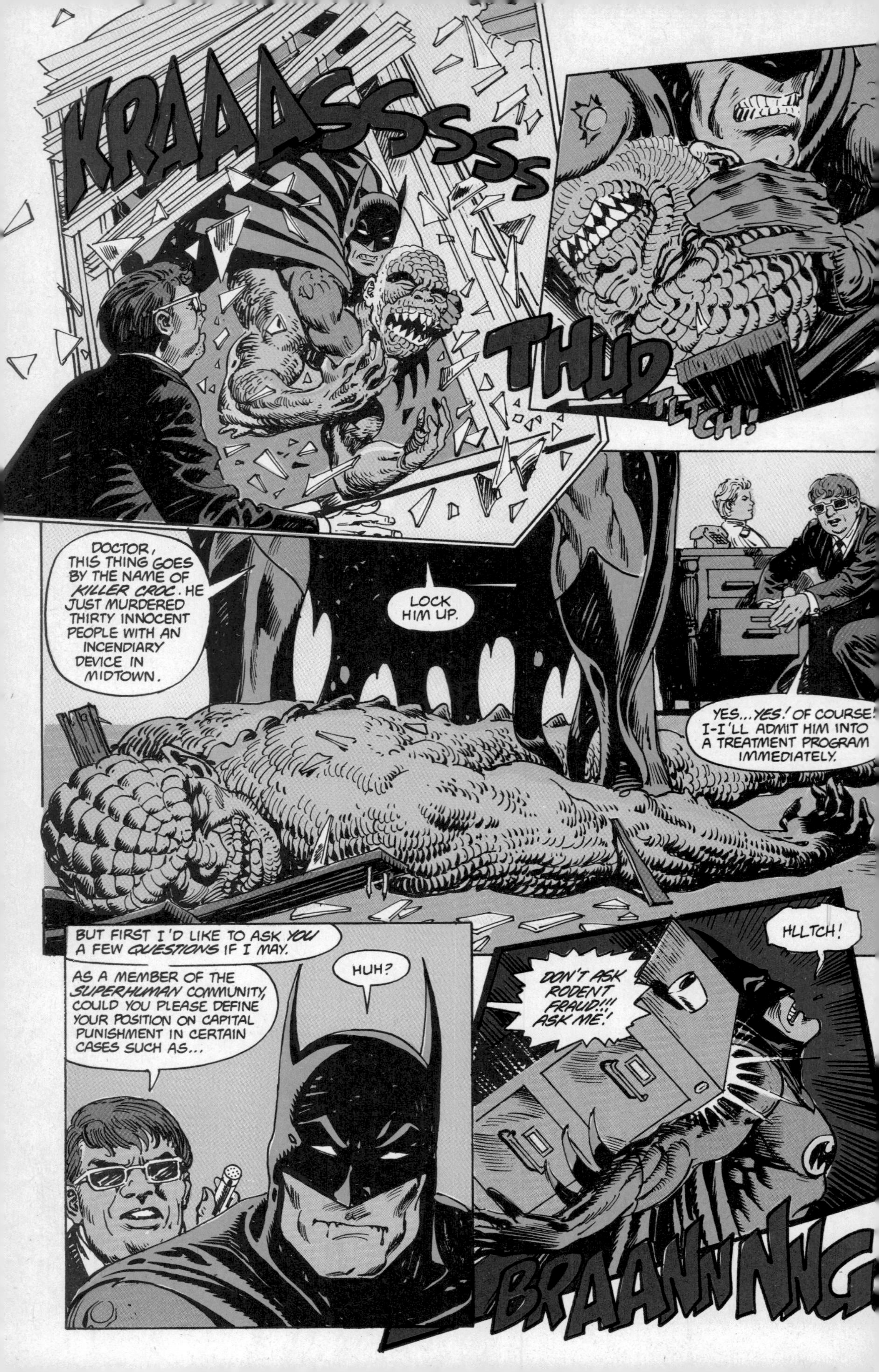
KRAAASSSSSS
THUD
TLLTCH!
DOCTOR, THIS THING GOES BY THE NAME OF KILLER CROC. HE JUST MURDERED THIRTY INNOCENT PEOPLE WITH AN INCENDIARY DEVICE IN MIDTOWN.
LOCK HIM UP.
YES... YES! OF COURSE! I-I'LL ADMIT HIM INTO A TREATMENT PROGRAM IMMEDIATELY.
BUT FIRST I'D LIKE TO ASK YOU A FEW QUESTIONS IF I MAY.
AS A MEMBER OF THE SUPERHUMAN COMMUNITY, COULD YOU PLEASE DEFINE YOUR POSITION ON CAPITAL PUNISHMENT IN CERTAIN CASES SUCH AS...
HUH?
DON'T ASK RODENT FRAUD!!! ASK ME!
HLLTCH!
BRAANNNNG

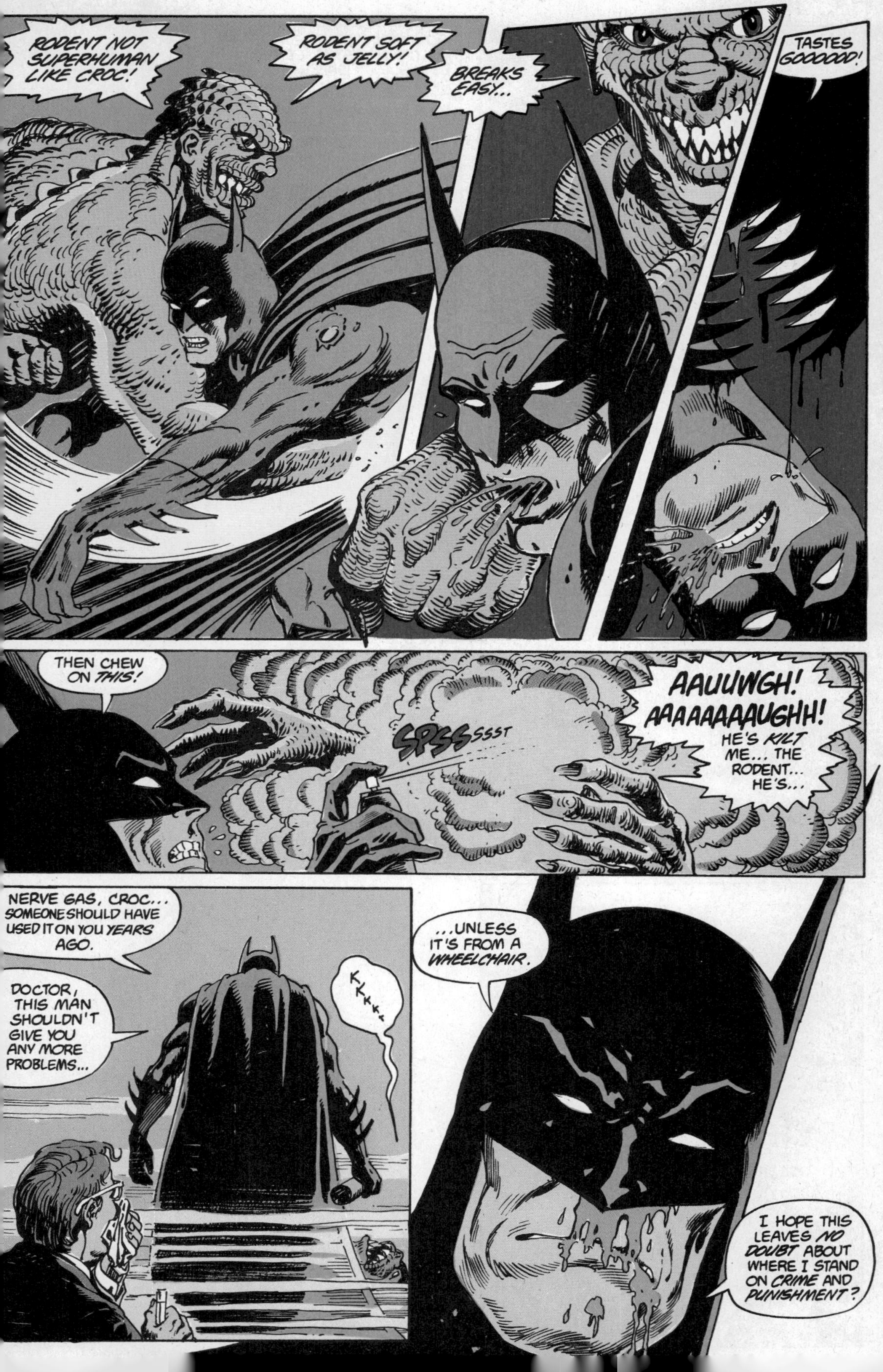
RODENT NOT SUPERHUMAN LIKE CROC!
RODENT SOFT AS JELLY!
BREAKS EASY...
TASTES GOOOOOD!
THEN CHEW ON THIS!
SPSSSSST
AAUUWGH! AAAAAAAAUGHH!
HE'S KILT ME... THE RODENT... HE'S...
NERVE GAS, CROC... SOMEONE SHOULD HAVE USED IT ON YOU YEARS AGO.
DOCTOR, THIS MAN SHOULDN'T GIVE YOU ANY MORE PROBLEMS...
...UNLESS IT'S FROM A WHEELCHAIR.
I HOPE THIS LEAVES NO DOUBT ABOUT WHERE I STAND ON CRIME AND PUNISHMENT?

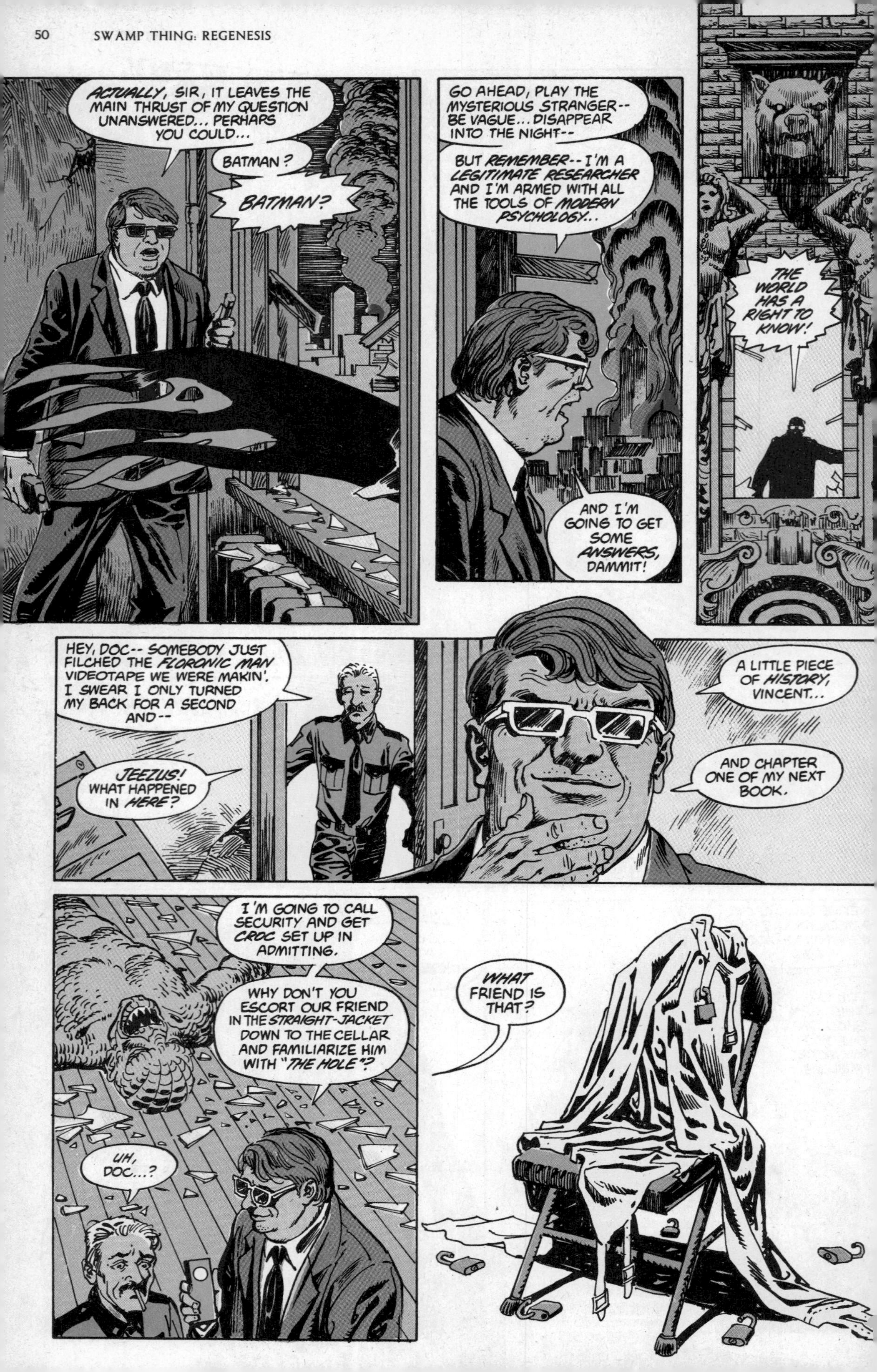
ACTUALLY, SIR, IT LEAVES THE MAIN THRUST OF MY QUESTION UNANSWERED... PERHAPS YOU COULD...
BATMAN?
BATMAN?
GO AHEAD, PLAY THE MYSTERIOUS STRANGER-- BE VAGUE... DISAPPEAR INTO THE NIGHT--
BUT REMEMBER-- I'M A LEGITIMATE RESEARCHER AND I'M ARMED WITH ALL THE TOOLS OF MODERN PSYCHOLOGY...
AND I'M GOING TO GET SOME ANSWERS, DAMMIT!
THE WORLD HAS A RIGHT TO KNOW!
HEY, DOC-- SOMEBODY JUST FILCHED THE FLORONIC MAN VIDEOTAPE WE WERE MAKIN'. I SWEAR I ONLY TURNED MY BACK FOR A SECOND AND--
JEEZUS! WHAT HAPPENED IN HERE?
A LITTLE PIECE OF HISTORY, VINCENT...
AND CHAPTER ONE OF MY NEXT BOOK.
I'M GOING TO CALL SECURITY AND GET CROC SET UP IN ADMITTING.
WHY DON'T YOU ESCORT OUR FRIEND IN THE STRAIGHT-JACKET DOWN TO THE CELLAR AND FAMILIARIZE HIM WITH "THE HOLE"?
UH, DOC...?
WHAT FRIEND IS THAT?

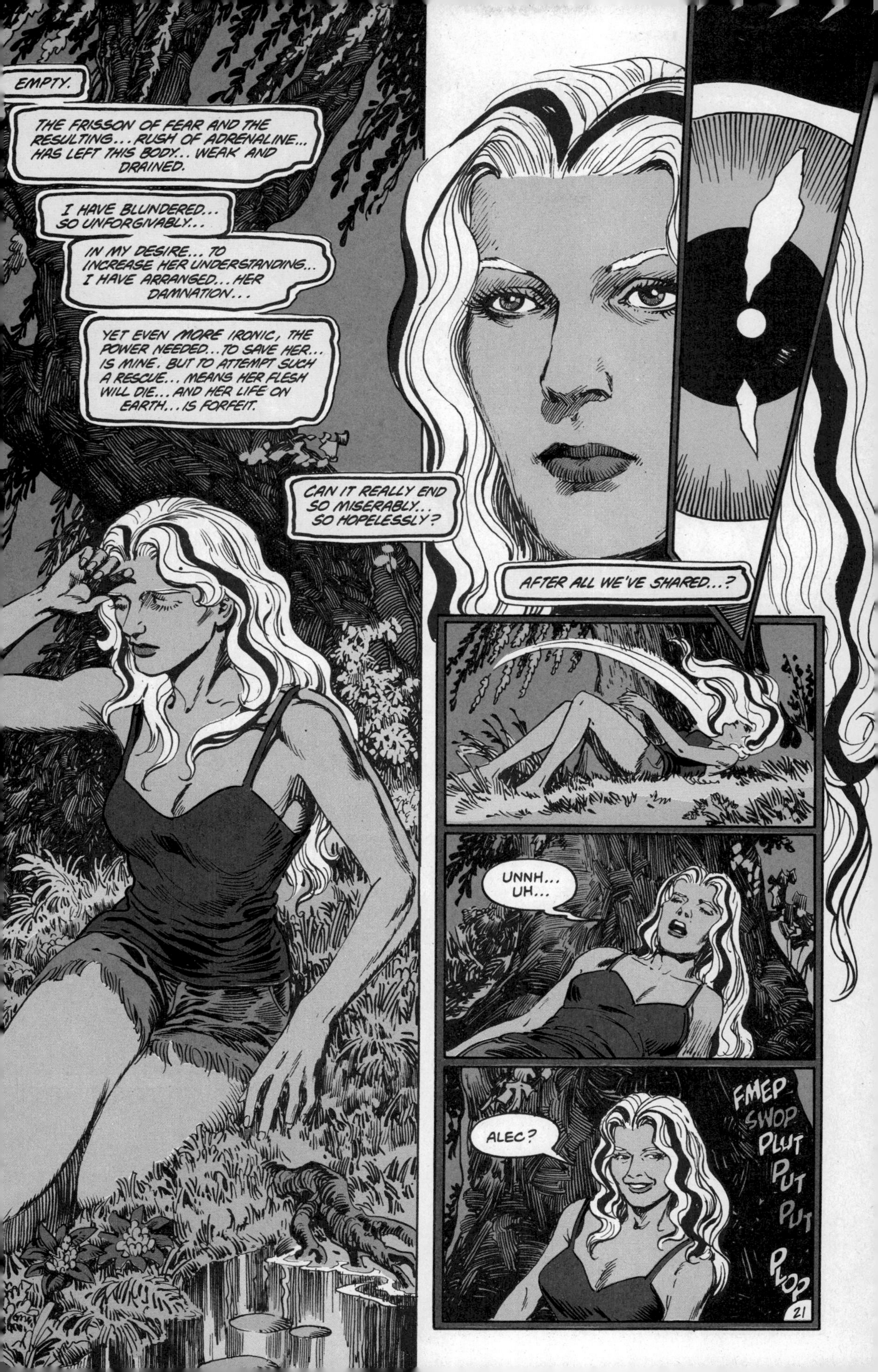

EMPTY.
THE FRISSON OF FEAR AND THE RESULTING... RUSH OF ADRENALINE... HAS LEFT THIS BODY... WEAK AND DRAINED.
I HAVE BLUNDERED... SO UNFORGIVABLY...
IN MY DESIRE... TO INCREASE HER UNDERSTANDING... I HAVE ARRANGED... HER DAMNATION...
YET EVEN MORE IRONIC, THE POWER NEEDED... TO SAVE HER... IS MINE. BUT TO ATTEMPT SUCH A RESCUE... MEANS HER FLESH WILL DIE... AND HER LIFE ON EARTH... IS FORFEIT.
CAN IT REALLY END SO MISERABLY... SO HOPELESSLY?
AFTER ALL WE'VE SHARED...?
UNNH... UH...
ALEC?
FMEP
SWOP
PLUT
PUT
PUT
PLOP
21

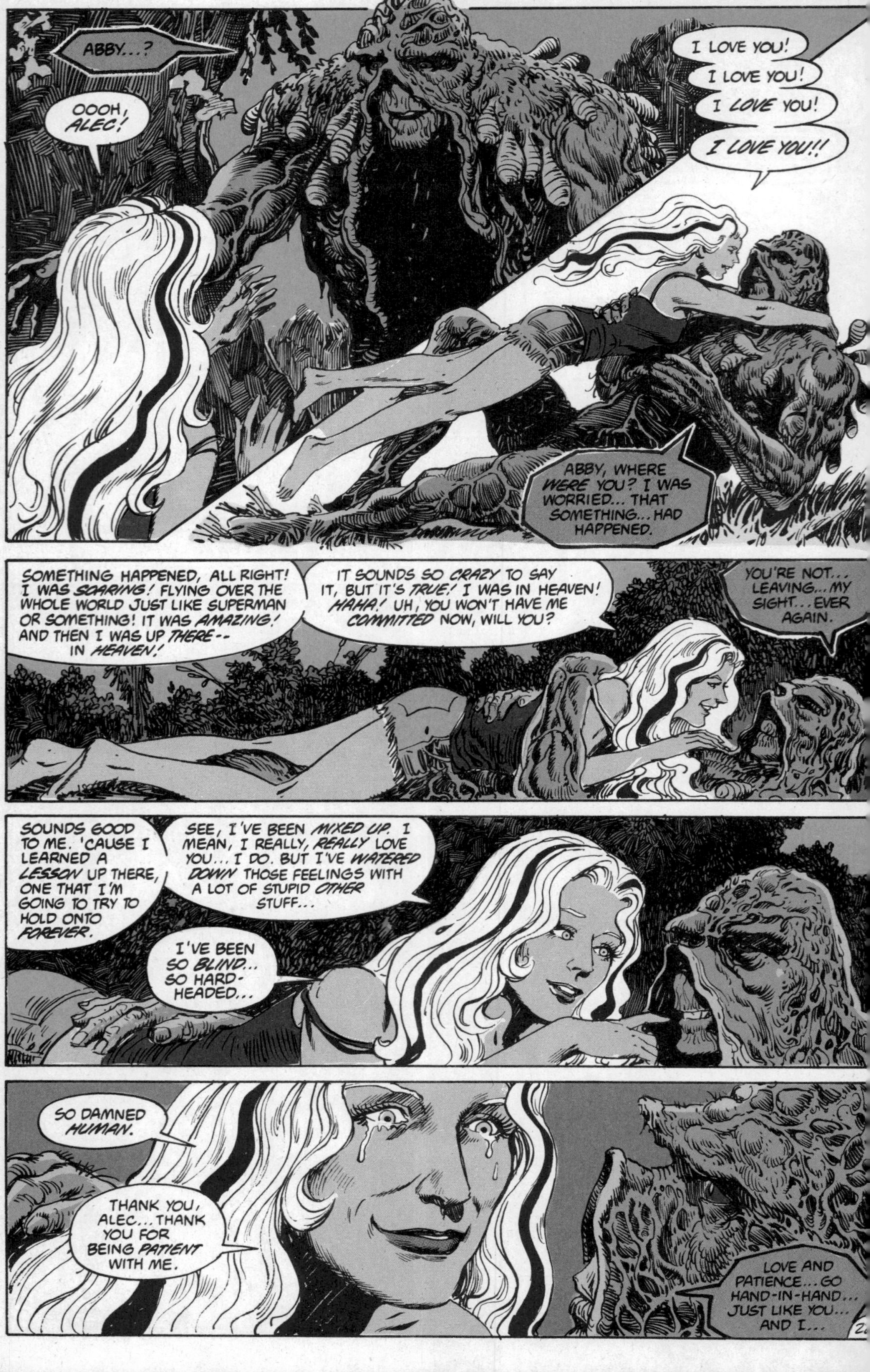
ABBY...?
OOOH, ALEC!
I LOVE YOU!
I LOVE YOU!
I LOVE YOU!
I LOVE YOU!!!
ABBY, WHERE WERE YOU? I WAS WORRIED... THAT SOMETHING... HAD HAPPENED.
SOMETHING HAPPENED, ALL RIGHT! I WAS SOARING! FLYING OVER THE WHOLE WORLD JUST LIKE SUPERMAN OR SOMETHING! IT WAS AMAZING! AND THEN I WAS UP THERE-- IN HEAVEN!
IT SOUNDS SO CRAZY TO SAY IT, BUT IT'S TRUE! I WAS IN HEAVEN! HAHA! UH, YOU WON'T HAVE ME COMMITTED NOW, WILL YOU?
YOU'RE NOT... LEAVING... MY SIGHT... EVER AGAIN.
SOUNDS GOOD TO ME. 'CAUSE I LEARNED A LESSON UP THERE, ONE THAT I'M GOING TO TRY TO HOLD ONTO FOREVER.
SEE, I'VE BEEN MIXED UP. I MEAN, I REALLY, REALLY LOVE YOU... I DO. BUT I'VE WATERED DOWN THOSE FEELINGS WITH A LOT OF STUPID OTHER STUFF...
I'VE BEEN SO BLIND... SO HARD-HEADED...
SO DAMNED HUMAN.
THANK YOU, ALEC... THANK YOU FOR BEING PATIENT WITH ME.
LOVE AND PATIENCE... GO HAND-IN-HAND... JUST LIKE YOU... AND I...

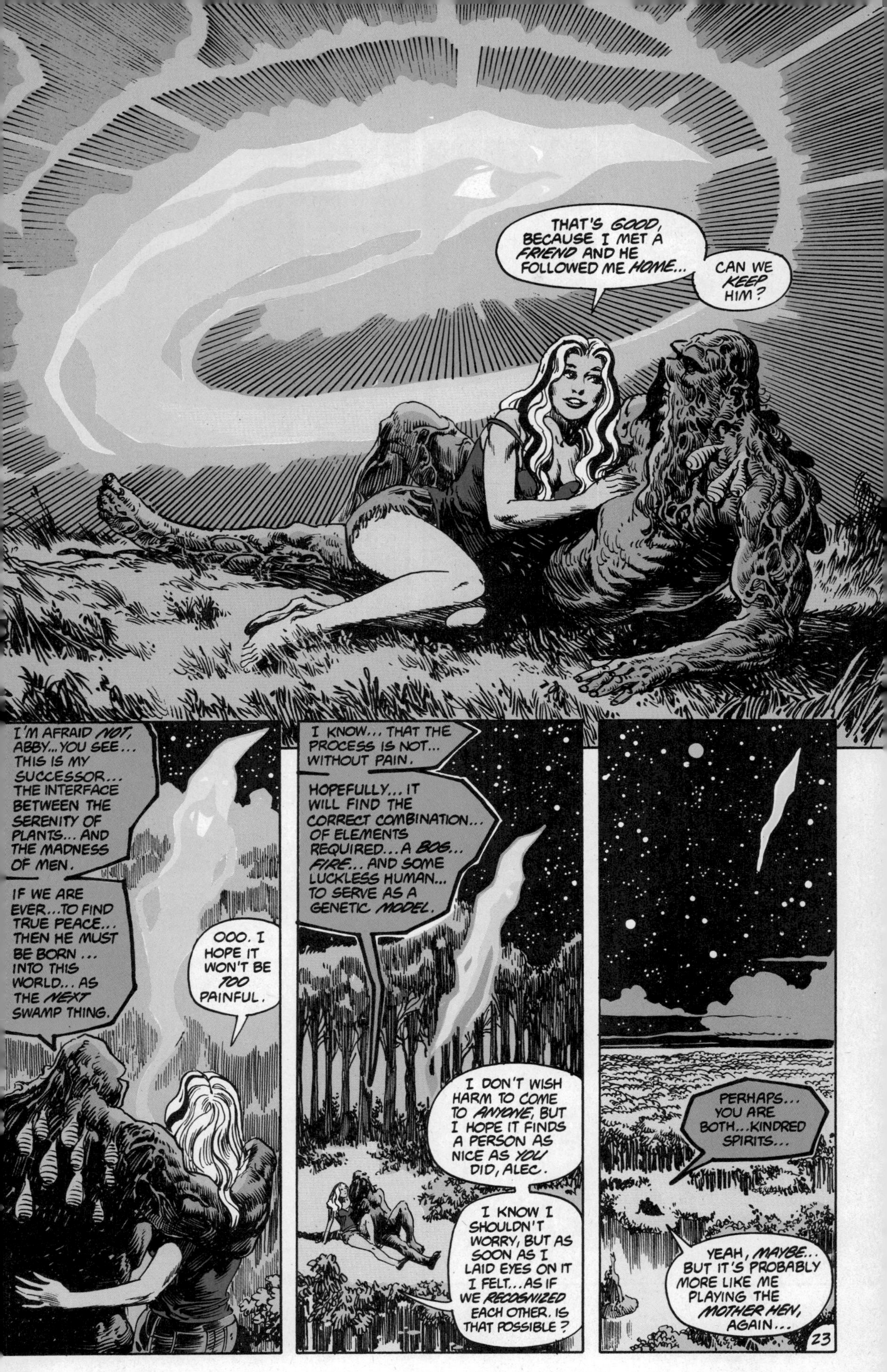

THAT'S GOOD, BECAUSE I MET A FRIEND AND HE FOLLOWED ME HOME...
CAN WE KEEP HIM?
I'M AFRAID NOT, ABBY... YOU SEE... THIS IS MY SUCCESSOR... THE INTERFACE BETWEEN THE SERENITY OF PLANTS... AND THE MADNESS OF MEN.
IF WE ARE EVER... TO FIND TRUE PEACE... THEN HE MUST BE BORN... INTO THIS WORLD... AS THE NEXT SWAMP THING.
OOO. I HOPE IT WON'T BE TOO PAINFUL.
I KNOW... THAT THE PROCESS IS NOT... WITHOUT PAIN.
HOPEFULLY... IT WILL FIND THE CORRECT COMBINATION... OF ELEMENTS REQUIRED... A BOG... FIRE... AND SOME LUCKLESS HUMAN... TO SERVE AS A GENETIC MODEL.
I DON'T WISH HARM TO COME TO ANYONE, BUT I HOPE IT FINDS A PERSON AS NICE AS YOU DID, ALEC.
I KNOW I SHOULDN'T WORRY, BUT AS SOON AS I LAID EYES ON IT I FELT... AS IF WE RECOGNIZED EACH OTHER. IS THAT POSSIBLE?
PERHAPS... YOU ARE BOTH... KINDRED SPIRITS...
YEAH, MAYBE... BUT IT'S PROBABLY MORE LIKE ME PLAYING THE MOTHER HEN, AGAIN...

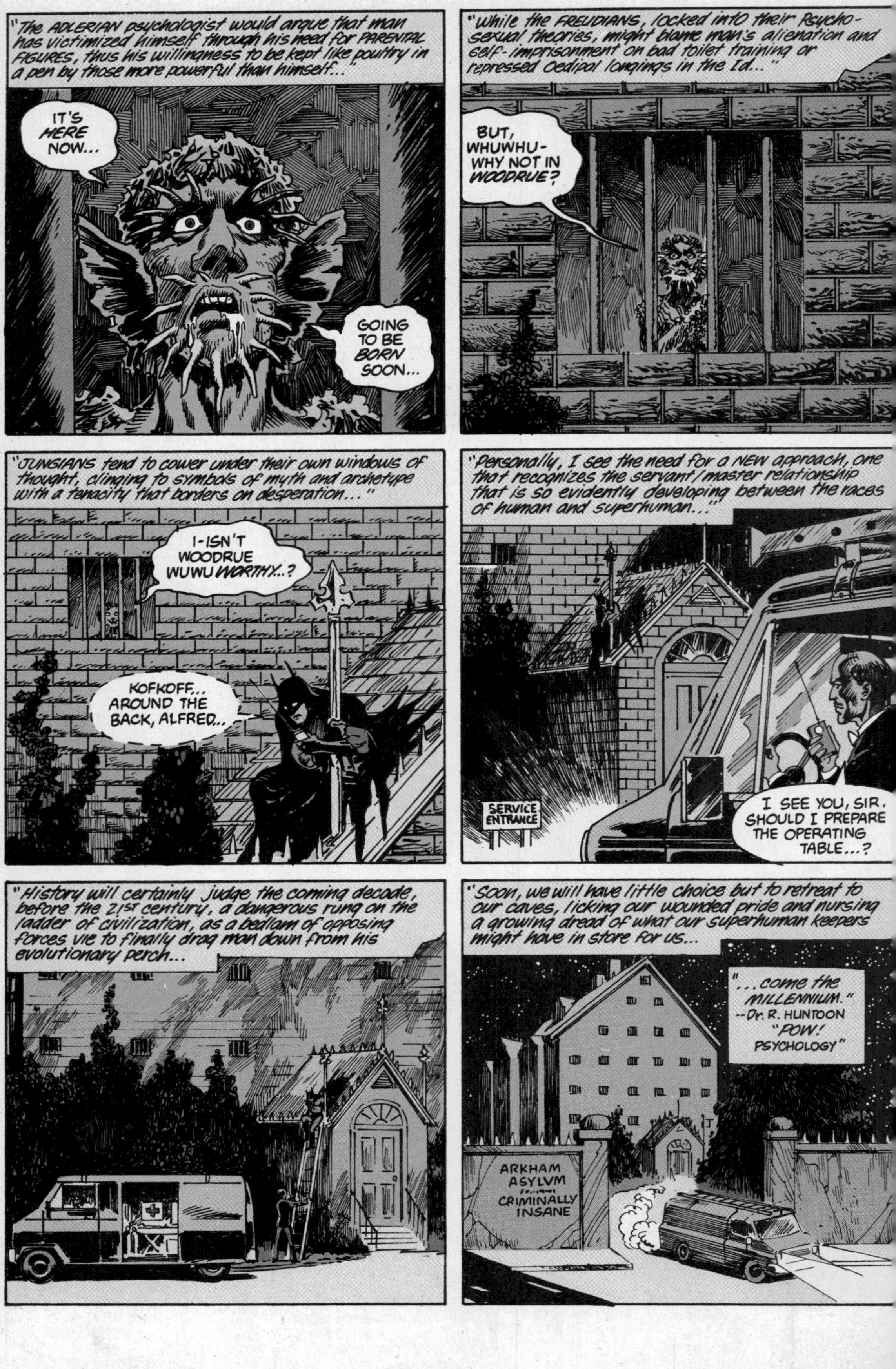
"The ADLERIAN psychologist would argue that man has victimized himself through his need for PARENTAL FIGURES, thus his willingness to be kept like poultry in a pen by those more powerful than himself..."
IT'S HERE NOW...
GOING TO BE BORN SOON...
"While the FREUDIANS, locked into their Psycho-sexual theories, might blame man's alienation and self-imprisonment on bad toilet training or repressed Oedipal longings in the Id..."
BUT, WHUWHU-WHY NOT IN WOODRUE?
"JUNGIANS tend to cower under their own windows of thought, clinging to symbols of myth and archetype with a tenacity that borders on desperation..."
I-ISN'T WOODRUE WUWU WORTHY..?
KOFKOFF... AROUND THE BACK, ALFRED...
"Personally, I see the need for a NEW approach, one that recognizes the servant/master relationship that is so evidently developing between the races of human and superhuman..."
SERVICE ENTRANCE
I SEE YOU, SIR. SHOULD I PREPARE THE OPERATING TABLE...?
"History will certainly judge the coming decade, before the 21st century, a dangerous rung on the ladder of civilization, as a bedlam of opposing forces vie to finally drag man down from his evolutionary perch...
"Soon, we will have little choice but to retreat to our caves, licking our wounded pride and nursing a growing dread of what our superhuman keepers might have in store for us...
"...come the MILLENNIUM." --Dr. R. HUNTOON "POW! PSYCHOLOGY"
ARKHAM ASYLUM CRIMINALLY INSANE

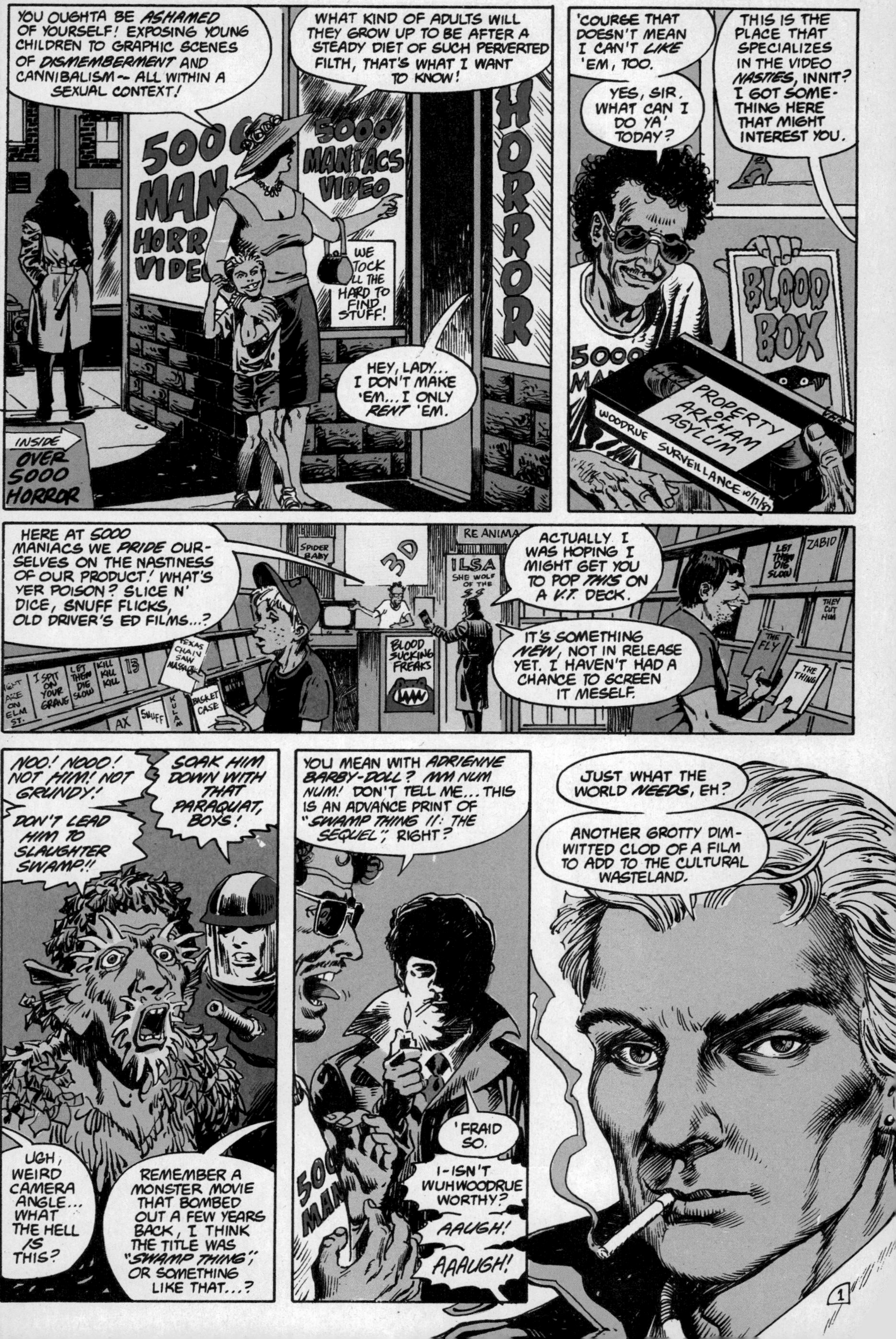
YOU OUGHTA BE ASHAMED OF YOURSELF! EXPOSING YOUNG CHILDREN TO GRAPHIC SCENES OF DISMEMBERMENT AND CANNIBALISM-- ALL WITHIN A SEXUAL CONTEXT!
WHAT KIND OF ADULTS WILL THEY GROW UP TO BE AFTER A STEADY DIET OF SUCH PERVERTED FILTH, THAT'S WHAT I WANT TO KNOW!
5000 MANIACS VIDEO
HORROR
WE STOCK ALL THE HARD TO FIND STUFF!
INSIDE OVER 5000 HORROR
HEY, LADY... I DON'T MAKE 'EM... I ONLY RENT 'EM.
'COURSE THAT DOESN'T MEAN I CAN'T LIKE 'EM, TOO.
YES, SIR. WHAT CAN I DO YA' TODAY?
THIS IS THE PLACE THAT SPECIALIZES IN THE VIDEO NASTIES, INNIT? I GOT SOME-THING HERE THAT MIGHT INTEREST YOU.
BLOOD BOX
PROPERTY OF ARKHAM ASYLUM
WOODRUE SURVEILLANCE 10/11/8?
HERE AT 5000 MANIACS WE PRIDE OUR-SELVES ON THE NASTINESS OF OUR PRODUCT! WHAT'S YER POISON? SLICE N' DICE, SNUFF FLICKS, OLD DRIVER'S ED FILMS...?
SPIDER BABY
3D
RE ANIMA
ILSA SHE WOLF OF THE SS
TEXAS CHAIN SAW MASSACRE
I SPIT ON YOUR GRAVE
LET THEM DIE SLOW
KILL KILL KILL
13
AX
SNUFF
BASKET CASE
BLOOD SUCKING FREAKS
ACTUALLY, I WAS HOPING I MIGHT GET YOU TO POP THIS ON A V.T. DECK.
IT'S SOMETHING NEW, NOT IN RELEASE YET. I HAVEN'T HAD A CHANCE TO SCREEN IT MESELF.
LET THEM DIE SLOW
ZABID
THEY CUT HIM
THE FLY
THE THING
NOO! NOOO! NOT HIM! NOT GRUNDY!
DON'T LEAD HIM TO SLAUGHTER SWAMP!!
SOAK HIM DOWN WITH THAT PARAQUAT, BOYS!
UGH, WEIRD CAMERA ANGLE... WHAT THE HELL IS THIS?
REMEMBER A MONSTER MOVIE THAT BOMBED OUT A FEW YEARS BACK, I THINK THE TITLE WAS "SWAMP THING", OR SOMETHING LIKE THAT...?
YOU MEAN WITH ADRIENNE BARBY-DOLL? MM NUM NUM! DON'T TELL ME... THIS IS AN ADVANCE PRINT OF "SWAMP THING II: THE SEQUEL", RIGHT?
'FRAID SO.
I-ISN'T WUHWOODRUE WORTHY?
AAUGH!
AAAUGH!
JUST WHAT THE WORLD NEEDS, EH?
ANOTHER GROTTY DIM-WITTED CLOD OF A FILM TO ADD TO THE CULTURAL WASTELAND.
1

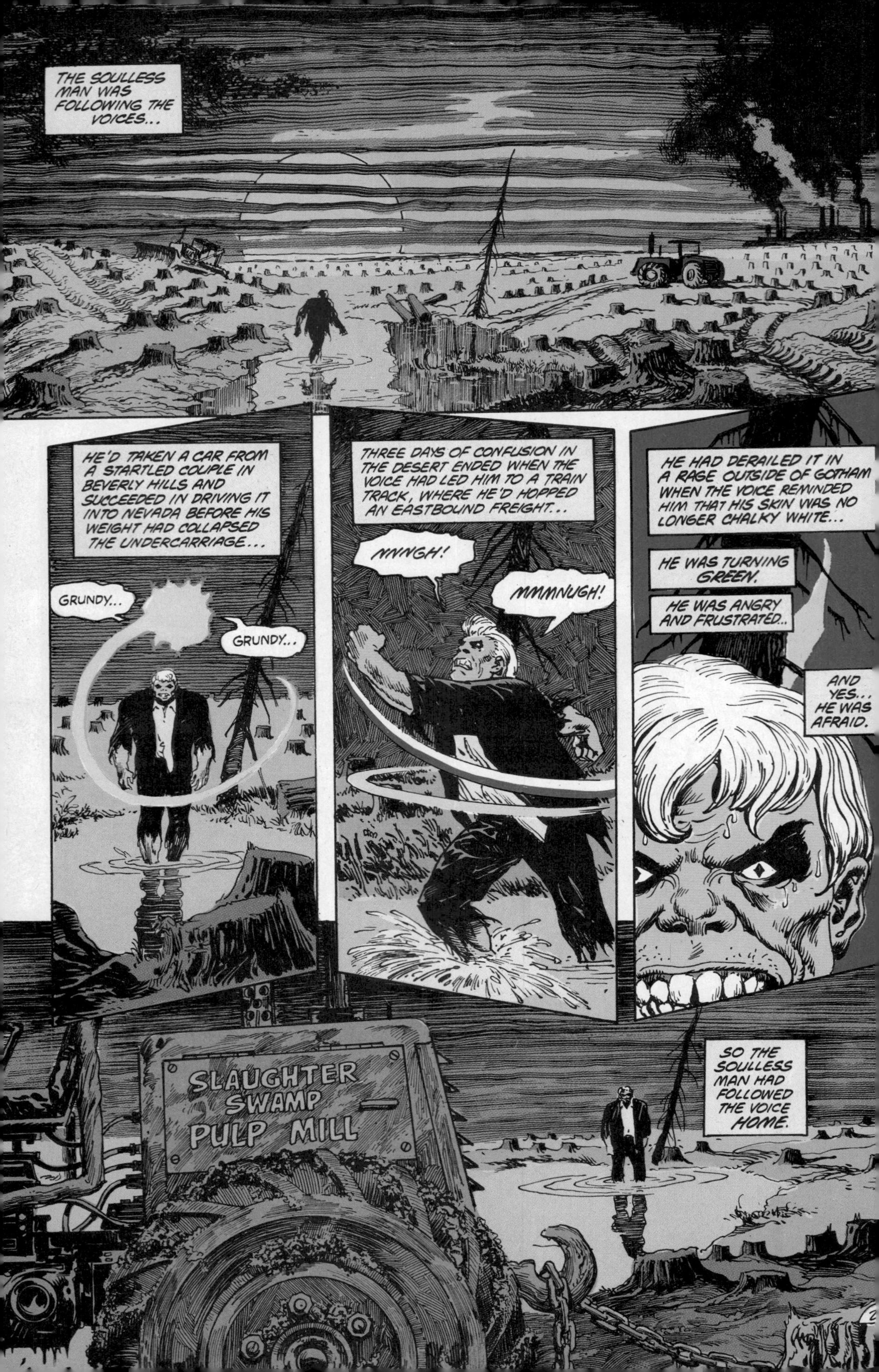
THE SOULLESS MAN WAS FOLLOWING THE VOICES...
HE'D TAKEN A CAR FROM A STARTLED COUPLE IN BEVERLY HILLS AND SUCCEEDED IN DRIVING IT INTO NEVADA BEFORE HIS WEIGHT HAD COLLAPSED THE UNDERCARRIAGE...
GRUNDY...
GRUNDY...
THREE DAYS OF CONFUSION IN THE DESERT ENDED WHEN THE VOICE HAD LED HIM TO A TRAIN TRACK, WHERE HE'D HOPPED AN EASTBOUND FREIGHT...
NNNGH!
MMMNUGH!
HE HAD DERAILED IT IN A RAGE OUTSIDE OF GOTHAM WHEN THE VOICE REMINDED HIM THAT HIS SKIN WAS NO LONGER CHALKY WHITE...
HE WAS TURNING GREEN.
HE WAS ANGRY AND FRUSTRATED...
AND YES... HE WAS AFRAID.
SLAUGHTER SWAMP PULP MILL
SO THE SOULLESS MAN HAD FOLLOWED THE VOICE HOME.

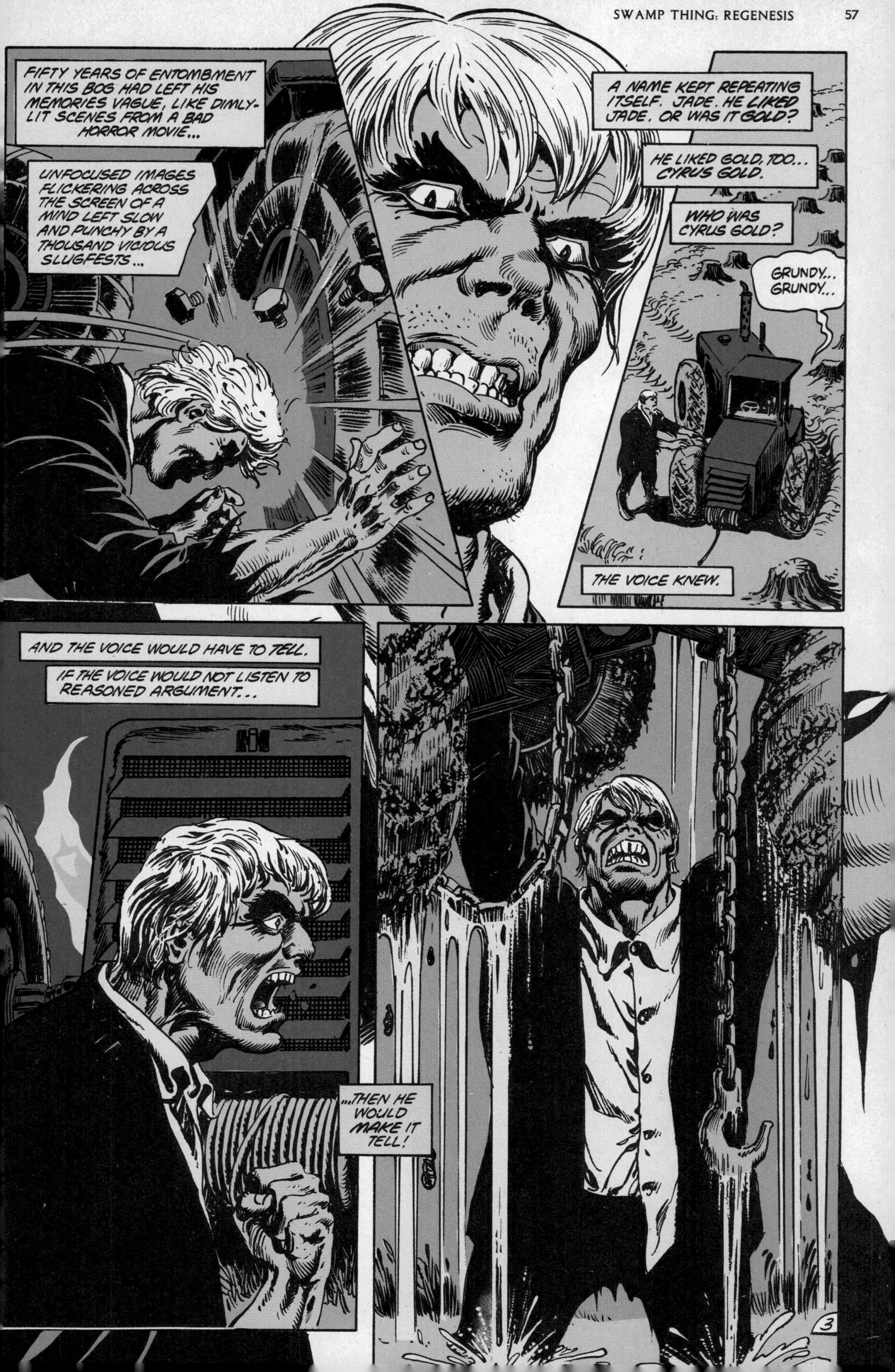
FIFTY YEARS OF ENTOMBMENT IN THIS BOG HAD LEFT HIS MEMORIES VAGUE, LIKE DIMLY-LIT SCENES FROM A BAD HORROR MOVIE...
UNFOCUSED IMAGES FLICKERING ACROSS THE SCREEN OF A MIND LEFT SLOW AND PUNCHY BY A THOUSAND VICIOUS SLUGFESTS...
A NAME KEPT REPEATING ITSELF. JADE. HE LIKED JADE. OR WAS IT GOLD?
HE LIKED GOLD, TOO... CYRUS GOLD.
WHO WAS CYRUS GOLD?
GRUNDY... GRUNDY...
THE VOICE KNEW.
AND THE VOICE WOULD HAVE TO TELL.
IF THE VOICE WOULD NOT LISTEN TO REASONED ARGUMENT...
...THEN HE WOULD MAKE IT TELL!
3

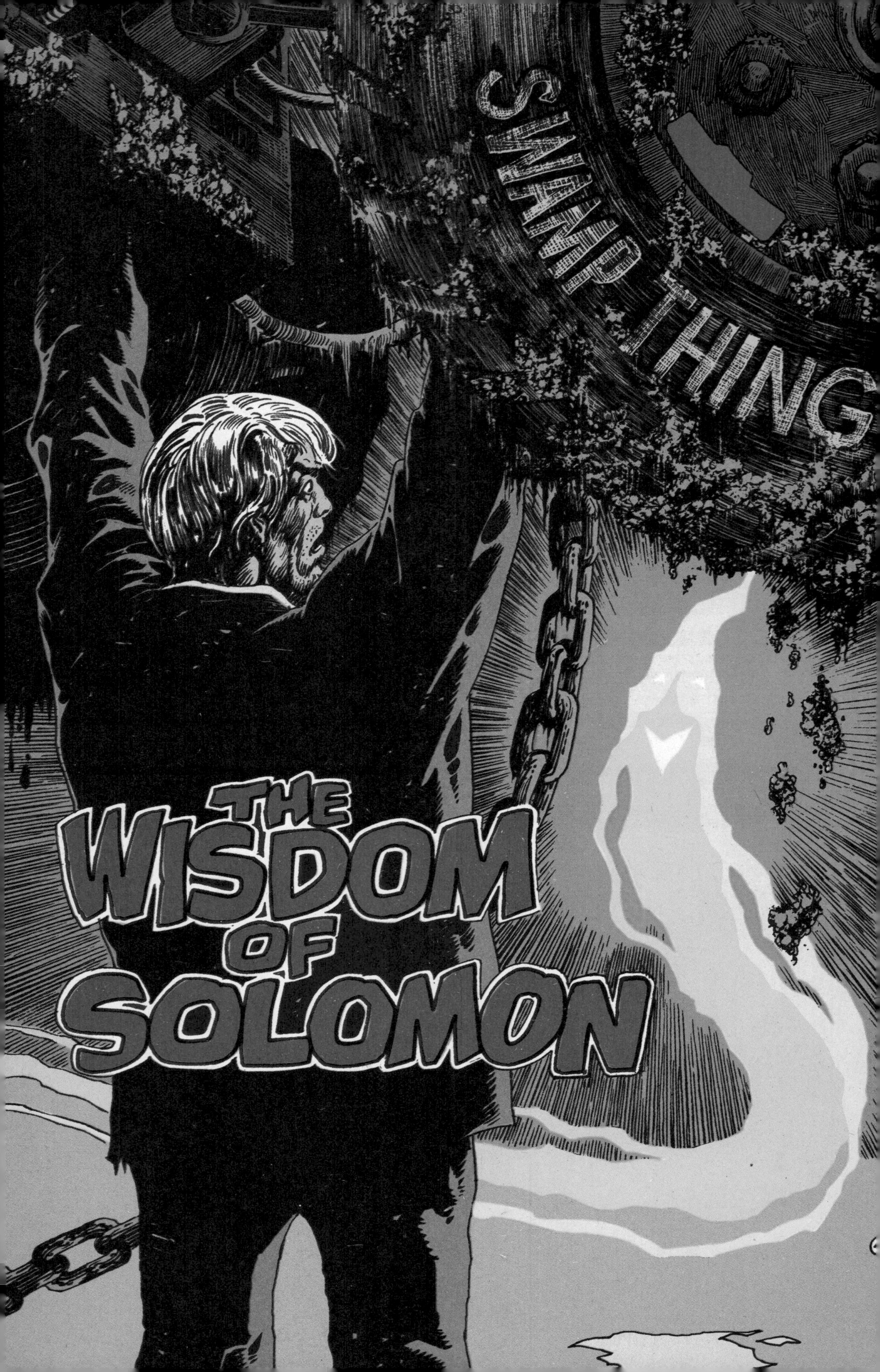
SWAMP THING
THE WISDOM OF SOLOMON

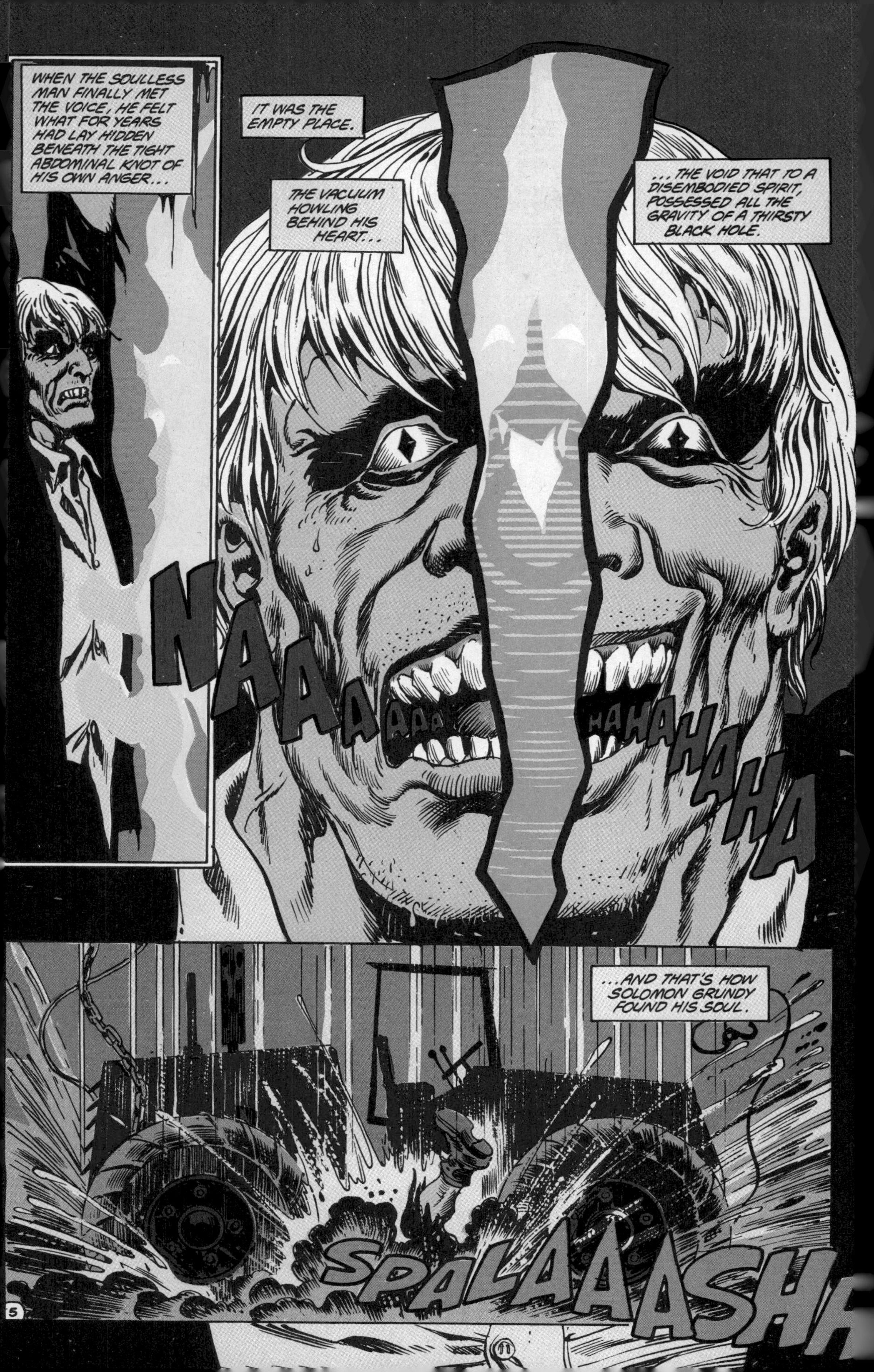

WHEN THE SOULLESS MAN FINALLY MET THE VOICE, HE FELT WHAT FOR YEARS HAD LAY HIDDEN BENEATH THE TIGHT ABDOMINAL KNOT OF HIS OWN ANGER...
IT WAS THE EMPTY PLACE.
THE VACUUM HOWLING BEHIND HIS HEART...
...THE VOID THAT TO A DISEMBODIED SPIRIT, POSSESSED ALL THE GRAVITY OF A THIRSTY BLACK HOLE.
NAAAAAA
HAHAHAHAHA
...AND THAT'S HOW SOLOMON GRUNDY FOUND HIS SOUL.
SPALAAASHH

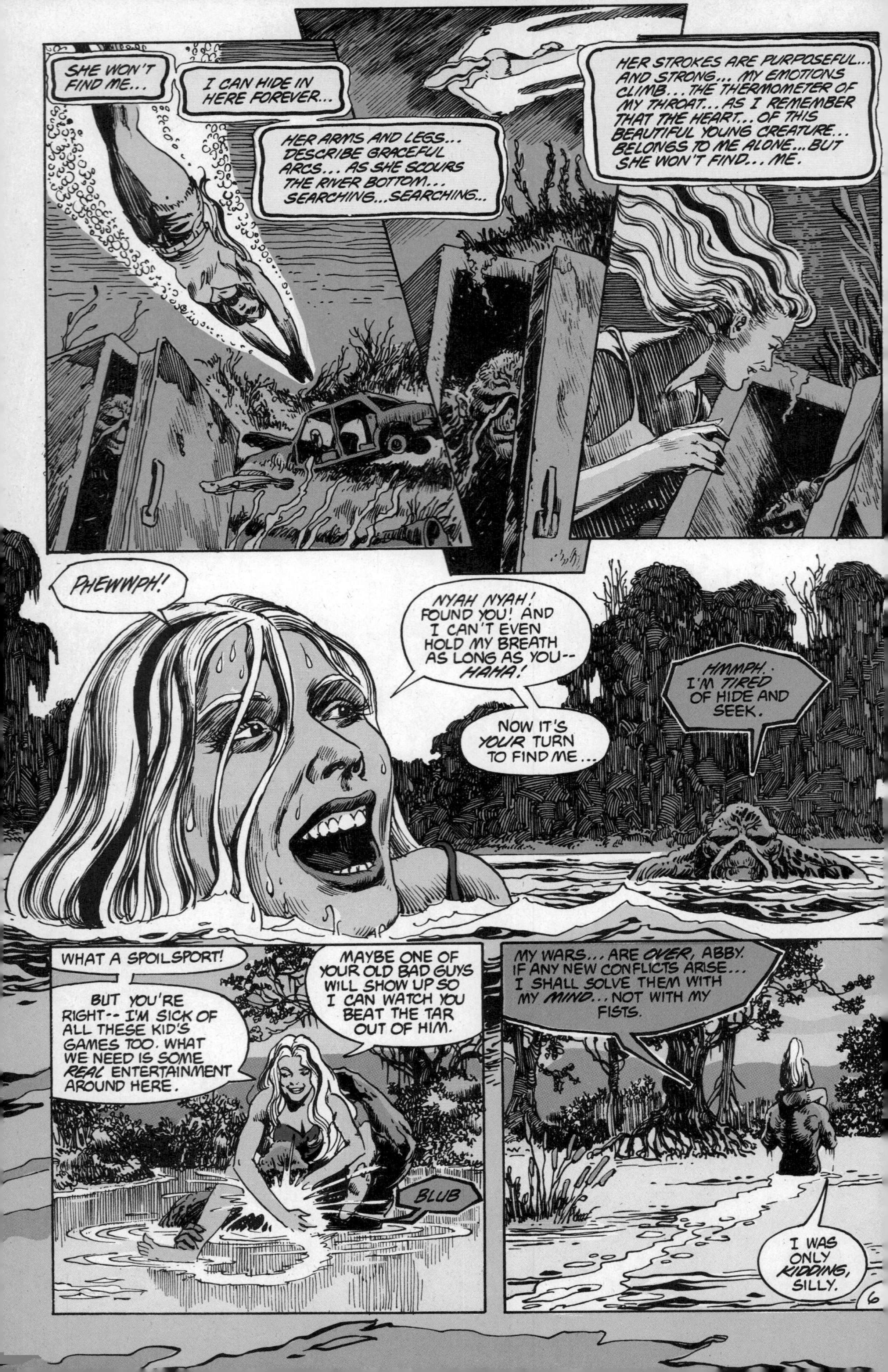
SHE WON'T FIND ME...
I CAN HIDE IN HERE FOREVER...
HER ARMS AND LEGS... DESCRIBE GRACEFUL ARCS... AS SHE SCOURS THE RIVER BOTTOM... SEARCHING...SEARCHING...
HER STROKES ARE PURPOSEFUL... AND STRONG... MY EMOTIONS CLIMB... THE THERMOMETER OF MY THROAT... AS I REMEMBER THAT THE HEART... OF THIS BEAUTIFUL YOUNG CREATURE... BELONGS TO ME ALONE... BUT SHE WON'T FIND... ME.
PHEWWPH!
NYAH NYAH! FOUND YOU! AND I CAN'T EVEN HOLD MY BREATH AS LONG AS YOU-- HAHA!
NOW IT'S YOUR TURN TO FIND ME...
HMMPH. I'M TIRED OF HIDE AND SEEK.
WHAT A SPOILSPORT!
BUT YOU'RE RIGHT-- I'M SICK OF ALL THESE KID'S GAMES TOO. WHAT WE NEED IS SOME REAL ENTERTAINMENT AROUND HERE.
MAYBE ONE OF YOUR OLD BAD GUYS WILL SHOW UP SO I CAN WATCH YOU BEAT THE TAR OUT OF HIM.
BLUB
MY WARS... ARE OVER, ABBY. IF ANY NEW CONFLICTS ARISE... I SHALL SOLVE THEM WITH MY MIND... NOT WITH MY FISTS.
I WAS ONLY KIDDING, SILLY.
6

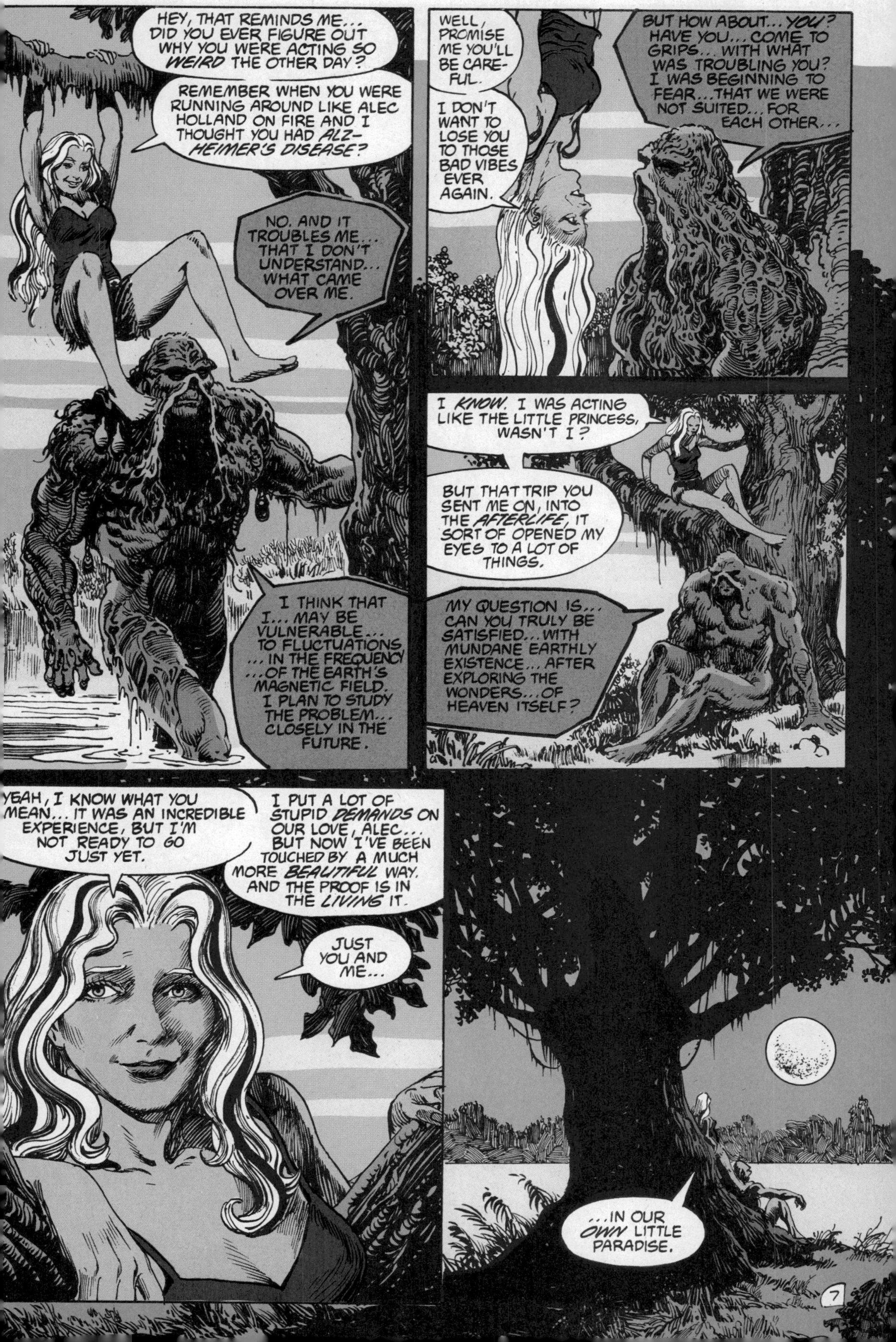
HEY, THAT REMINDS ME... DID YOU EVER FIGURE OUT WHY YOU WERE ACTING SO WEIRD THE OTHER DAY?
REMEMBER WHEN YOU WERE RUNNING AROUND LIKE ALEC HOLLAND ON FIRE AND I THOUGHT YOU HAD ALZ-HEIMER'S DISEASE?
NO. AND IT TROUBLES ME... THAT I DON'T UNDERSTAND... WHAT CAME OVER ME.
I THINK THAT I... MAY BE VULNERABLE... TO FLUCTUATIONS ...IN THE FREQUENCY ...OF THE EARTH'S MAGNETIC FIELD. I PLAN TO STUDY THE PROBLEM... CLOSELY IN THE FUTURE.
BUT HOW ABOUT... YOU? HAVE YOU... COME TO GRIPS... WITH WHAT WAS TROUBLING YOU? I WAS BEGINNING TO FEAR... THAT WE WERE NOT SUITED... FOR EACH OTHER...
WELL, PROMISE ME YOU'LL BE CARE-FUL.
I DON'T WANT TO LOSE YOU TO THOSE BAD VIBES EVER AGAIN.
I KNOW. I WAS ACTING LIKE THE LITTLE PRINCESS, WASN'T I?
BUT THAT TRIP YOU SENT ME ON, INTO THE AFTERLIFE, IT SORT OF OPENED MY EYES TO A LOT OF THINGS.
MY QUESTION IS... CAN YOU TRULY BE SATISFIED... WITH MUNDANE EARTHLY EXISTENCE... AFTER EXPLORING THE WONDERS... OF HEAVEN ITSELF?
YEAH, I KNOW WHAT YOU MEAN... IT WAS AN INCREDIBLE EXPERIENCE, BUT I'M NOT READY TO GO JUST YET.
I PUT A LOT OF STUPID DEMANDS ON OUR LOVE, ALEC... BUT NOW I'VE BEEN TOUCHED BY A MUCH MORE BEAUTIFUL WAY, AND THE PROOF IS IN THE LIVING IT.
JUST YOU AND ME...
...IN OUR OWN LITTLE PARADISE.
7

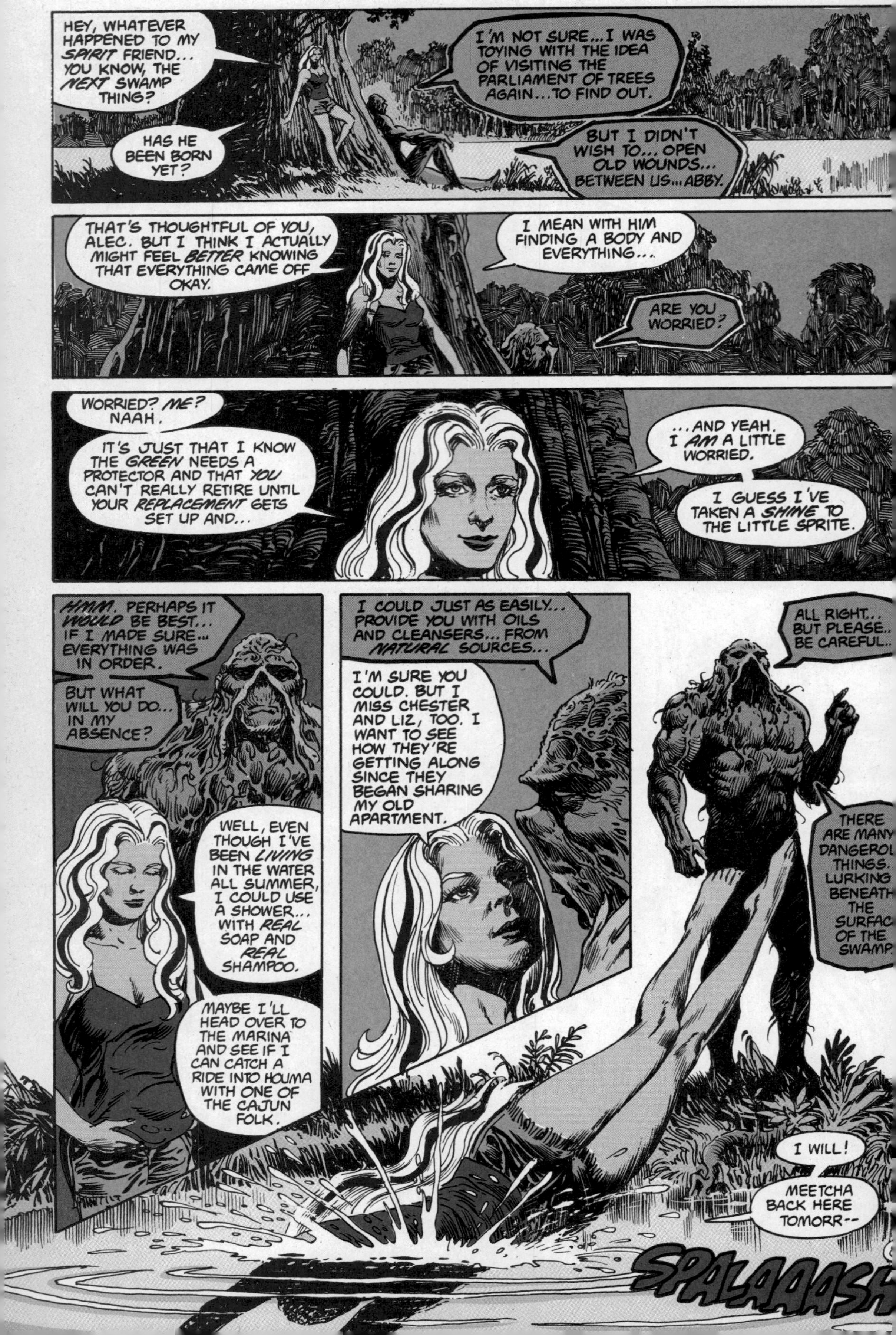
HEY, WHATEVER HAPPENED TO MY SPIRIT FRIEND... YOU KNOW, THE NEXT SWAMP THING?
HAS HE BEEN BORN YET?
I'M NOT SURE...I WAS TOYING WITH THE IDEA OF VISITING THE PARLIAMENT OF TREES AGAIN...TO FIND OUT.
BUT I DIDN'T WISH TO... OPEN OLD WOUNDS... BETWEEN US...ABBY.
THAT'S THOUGHTFUL OF YOU, ALEC. BUT I THINK I ACTUALLY MIGHT FEEL BETTER KNOWING THAT EVERYTHING CAME OFF OKAY.
I MEAN WITH HIM FINDING A BODY AND EVERYTHING...
ARE YOU WORRIED?
WORRIED? ME? NAAH.
IT'S JUST THAT I KNOW THE GREEN NEEDS A PROTECTOR AND THAT YOU CAN'T REALLY RETIRE UNTIL YOUR REPLACEMENT GETS SET UP AND...
...AND YEAH. I AM A LITTLE WORRIED.
I GUESS I'VE TAKEN A SHINE TO THE LITTLE SPRITE.
HMM. PERHAPS IT WOULD BE BEST... IF I MADE SURE... EVERYTHING WAS IN ORDER.
BUT WHAT WILL YOU DO... IN MY ABSENCE?
WELL, EVEN THOUGH I'VE BEEN LIVING IN THE WATER ALL SUMMER, I COULD USE A SHOWER... WITH REAL SOAP AND REAL SHAMPOO.
MAYBE I'LL HEAD OVER TO THE MARINA AND SEE IF I CAN CATCH A RIDE INTO HOUMA WITH ONE OF THE CAJUN FOLK.
I COULD JUST AS EASILY... PROVIDE YOU WITH OILS AND CLEANSERS... FROM NATURAL SOURCES...
I'M SURE YOU COULD. BUT I MISS CHESTER AND LIZ, TOO. I WANT TO SEE HOW THEY'RE GETTING ALONG SINCE THEY BEGAN SHARING MY OLD APARTMENT.
ALL RIGHT... BUT PLEASE... BE CAREFUL...
I WILL!
MEETCHA BACK HERE TOMORR--
SPALAAASH

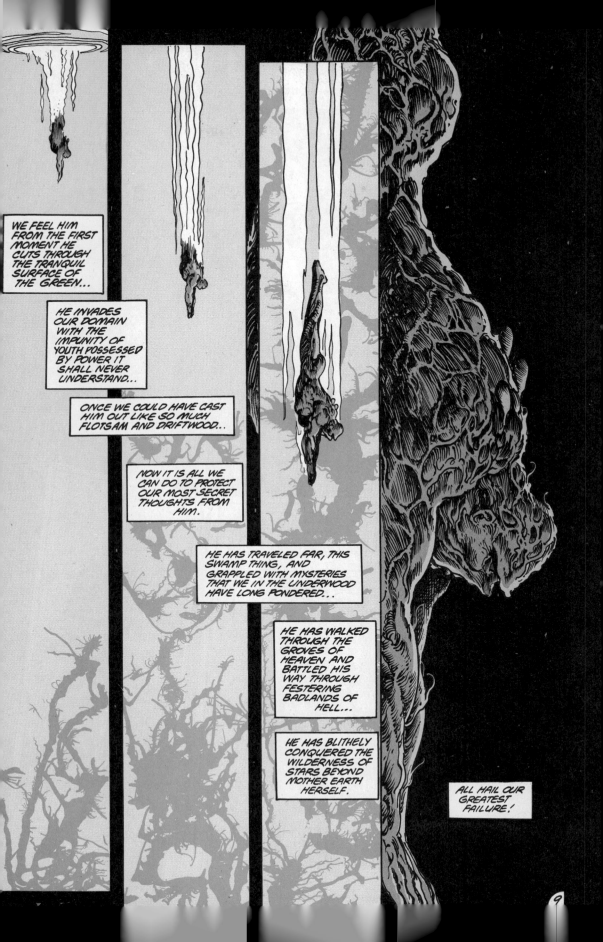

WE FEEL HIM FROM THE FIRST MOMENT HE CUTS THROUGH THE TRANQUIL SURFACE OF THE GREEN...

HE INVADES OUR DOMAIN WITH THE IMPUNITY OF YOUTH POSSESSED BY POWER IT SHALL NEVER UNDERSTAND...

ONCE WE COULD HAVE CAST HIM OUT LIKE SO MUCH FLOTSAM AND DRIFTWOOD...

NOW IT IS ALL WE CAN DO TO PROTECT OUR MOST SECRET THOUGHTS FROM HIM.

HE HAS TRAVELED FAR, THIS SWAMP THING, AND GRAPPLED WITH MYSTERIES THAT WE IN THE UNDERWOOD HAVE LONG PONDERED...

HE HAS WALKED THROUGH THE GROVES OF HEAVEN AND BATTLED HIS WAY THROUGH FESTERING BADLANDS OF HELL...

HE HAS BLITHELY CONQUERED THE WILDERNESS OF STARS BEYOND MOTHER EARTH HERSELF.

ALL HAIL OUR GREATEST FAILURE!

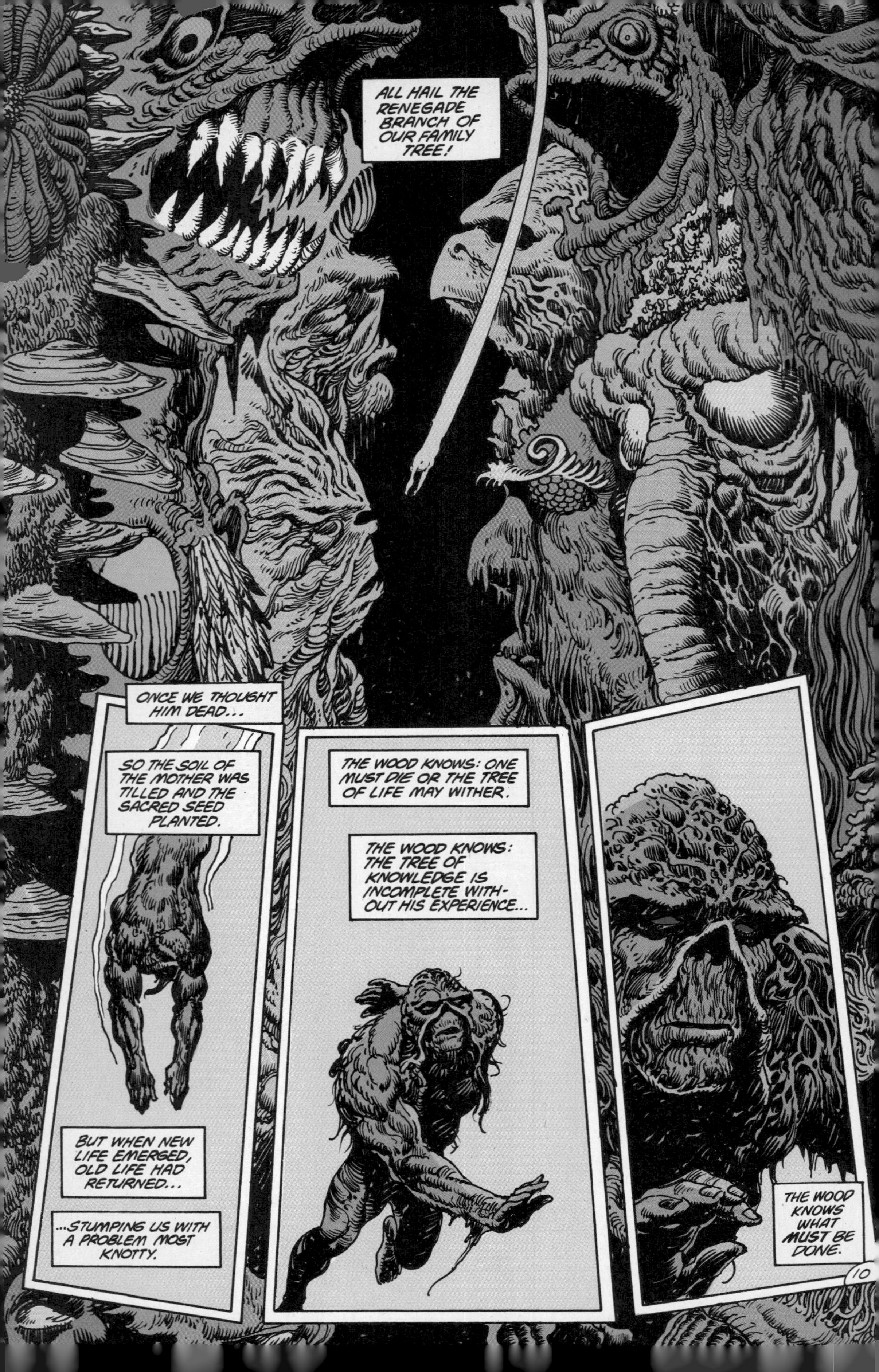
ALL HAIL THE RENEGADE BRANCH OF OUR FAMILY TREE!
ONCE WE THOUGHT HIM DEAD...
SO THE SOIL OF THE MOTHER WAS TILLED AND THE SACRED SEED PLANTED.
BUT WHEN NEW LIFE EMERGED, OLD LIFE HAD RETURNED...
...STUMPING US WITH A PROBLEM MOST KNOTTY.
THE WOOD KNOWS: ONE MUST DIE OR THE TREE OF LIFE MAY WITHER.
THE WOOD KNOWS: THE TREE OF KNOWLEDGE IS INCOMPLETE WITHOUT HIS EXPERIENCE...
THE WOOD KNOWS WHAT MUST BE DONE.
10

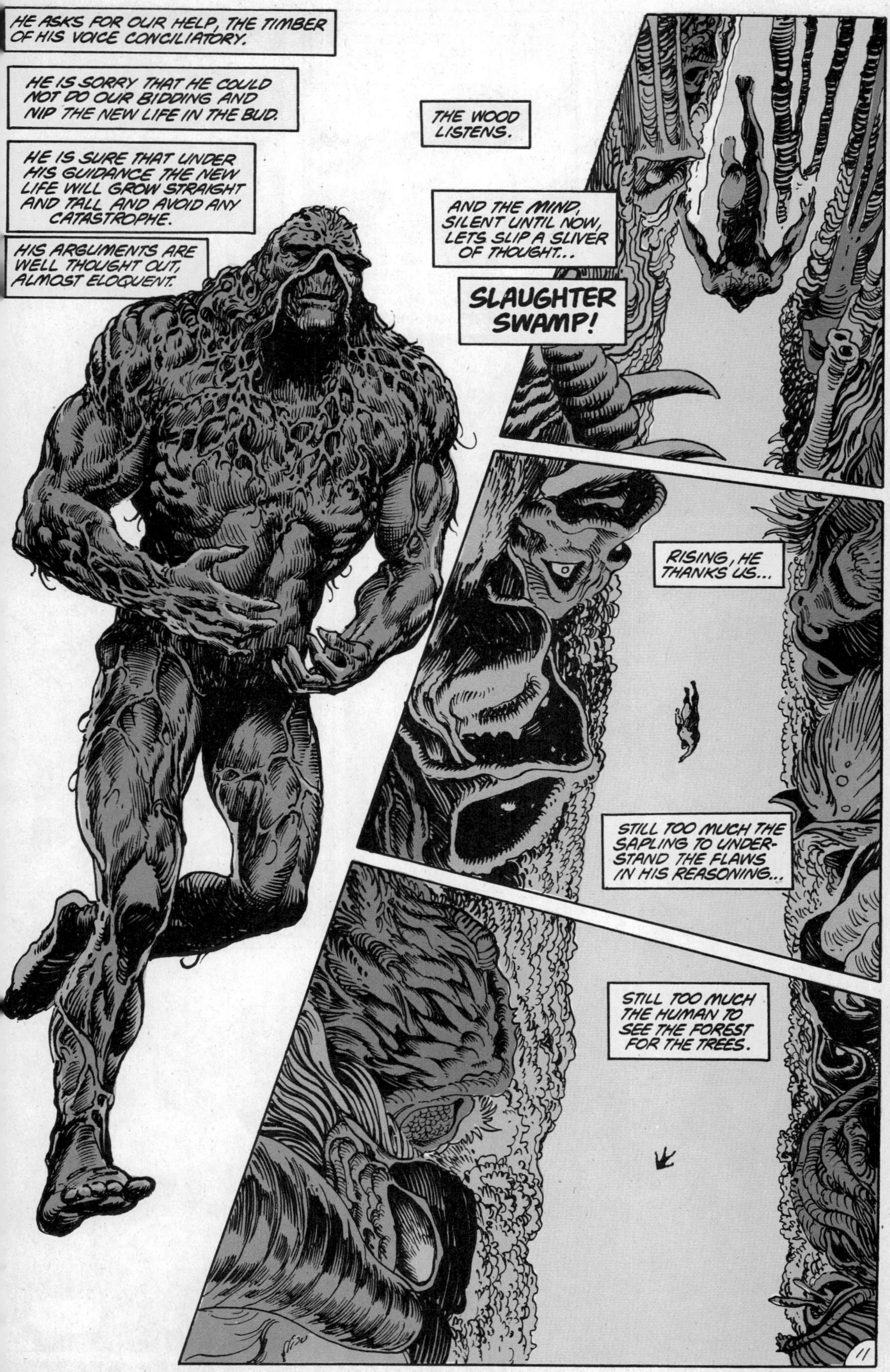
HE ASKS FOR OUR HELP, THE TIMBER OF HIS VOICE CONCILIATORY.
HE IS SORRY THAT HE COULD NOT DO OUR BIDDING AND NIP THE NEW LIFE IN THE BUD.
HE IS SURE THAT UNDER HIS GUIDANCE THE NEW LIFE WILL GROW STRAIGHT AND TALL AND AVOID ANY CATASTROPHE.
HIS ARGUMENTS ARE WELL THOUGHT OUT, ALMOST ELOQUENT.
THE WOOD LISTENS.
AND THE MIND, SILENT UNTIL NOW, LETS SLIP A SLIVER OF THOUGHT...
SLAUGHTER SWAMP!
RISING, HE THANKS US...
STILL TOO MUCH THE SAPLING TO UNDERSTAND THE FLAWS IN HIS REASONING...
STILL TOO MUCH THE HUMAN TO SEE THE FOREST FOR THE TREES.
11

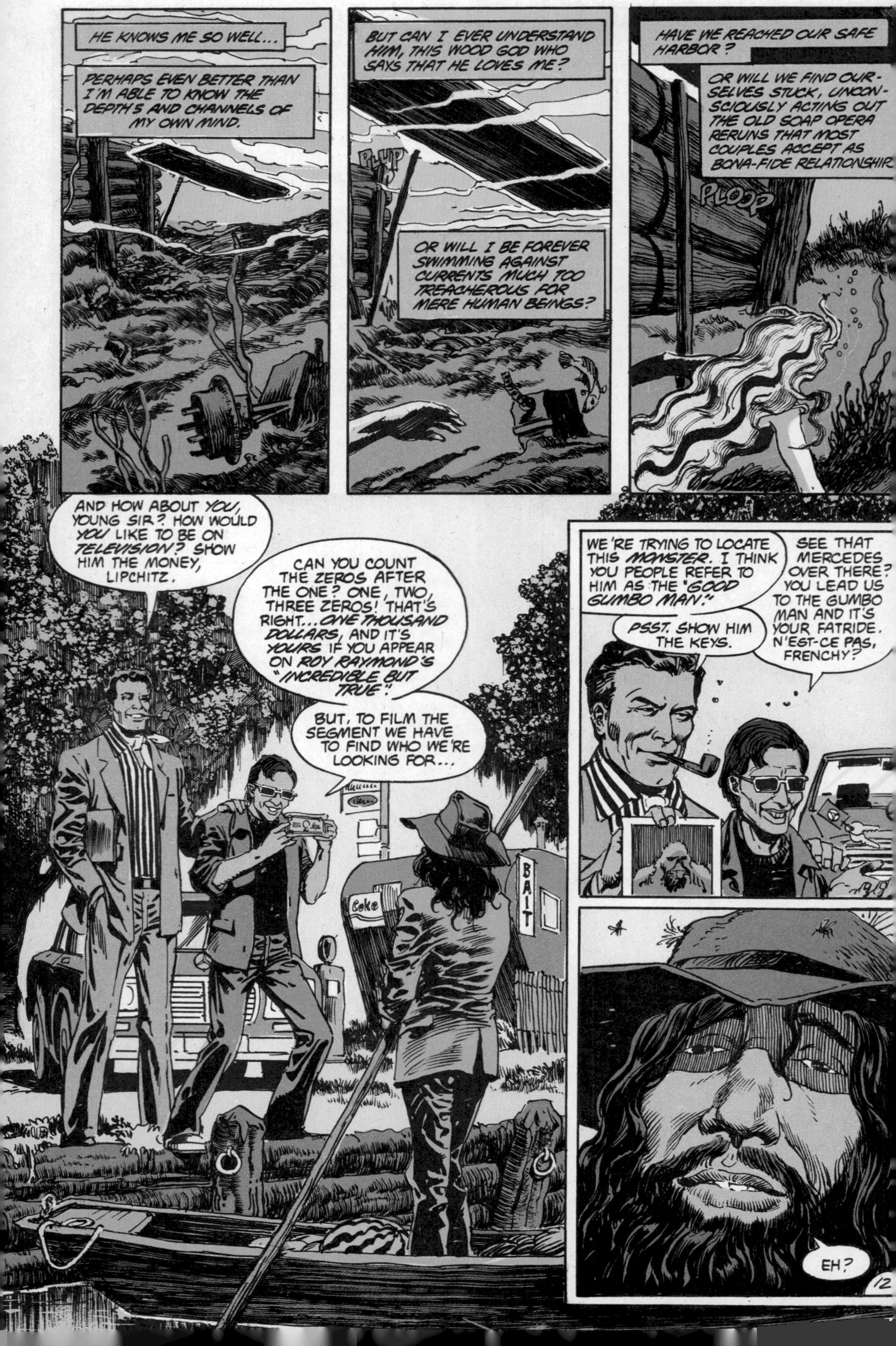
HE KNOWS ME SO WELL...
PERHAPS EVEN BETTER THAN I'M ABLE TO KNOW THE DEPTHS AND CHANNELS OF MY OWN MIND.
BUT CAN I EVER UNDERSTAND HIM, THIS WOOD GOD WHO SAYS THAT HE LOVES ME?
PLUP
OR WILL I BE FOREVER SWIMMING AGAINST CURRENTS MUCH TOO TREACHEROUS FOR MERE HUMAN BEINGS?
HAVE WE REACHED OUR SAFE HARBOR?
OR WILL WE FIND OURSELVES STUCK, UNCONSCIOUSLY ACTING OUT THE OLD SOAP OPERA RERUNS THAT MOST COUPLES ACCEPT AS BONA-FIDE RELATIONSHIP
PLOOP
AND HOW ABOUT YOU, YOUNG SIR? HOW WOULD YOU LIKE TO BE ON TELEVISION? SHOW HIM THE MONEY, LIPCHITZ.
CAN YOU COUNT THE ZEROS AFTER THE ONE? ONE, TWO, THREE ZEROS! THAT'S RIGHT... ONE THOUSAND DOLLARS, AND IT'S YOURS IF YOU APPEAR ON ROY RAYMOND'S "INCREDIBLE BUT TRUE".
BUT, TO FILM THE SEGMENT WE HAVE TO FIND WHO WE'RE LOOKING FOR...
BAIT
Coke
WE'RE TRYING TO LOCATE THIS MONSTER. I THINK YOU PEOPLE REFER TO HIM AS THE "GOOD GUMBO MAN."
PSST. SHOW HIM THE KEYS.
SEE THAT MERCEDES OVER THERE? YOU LEAD US TO THE GUMBO MAN AND IT'S YOUR FATRIDE. N'EST-CE PAS, FRENCHY?
EH?
12

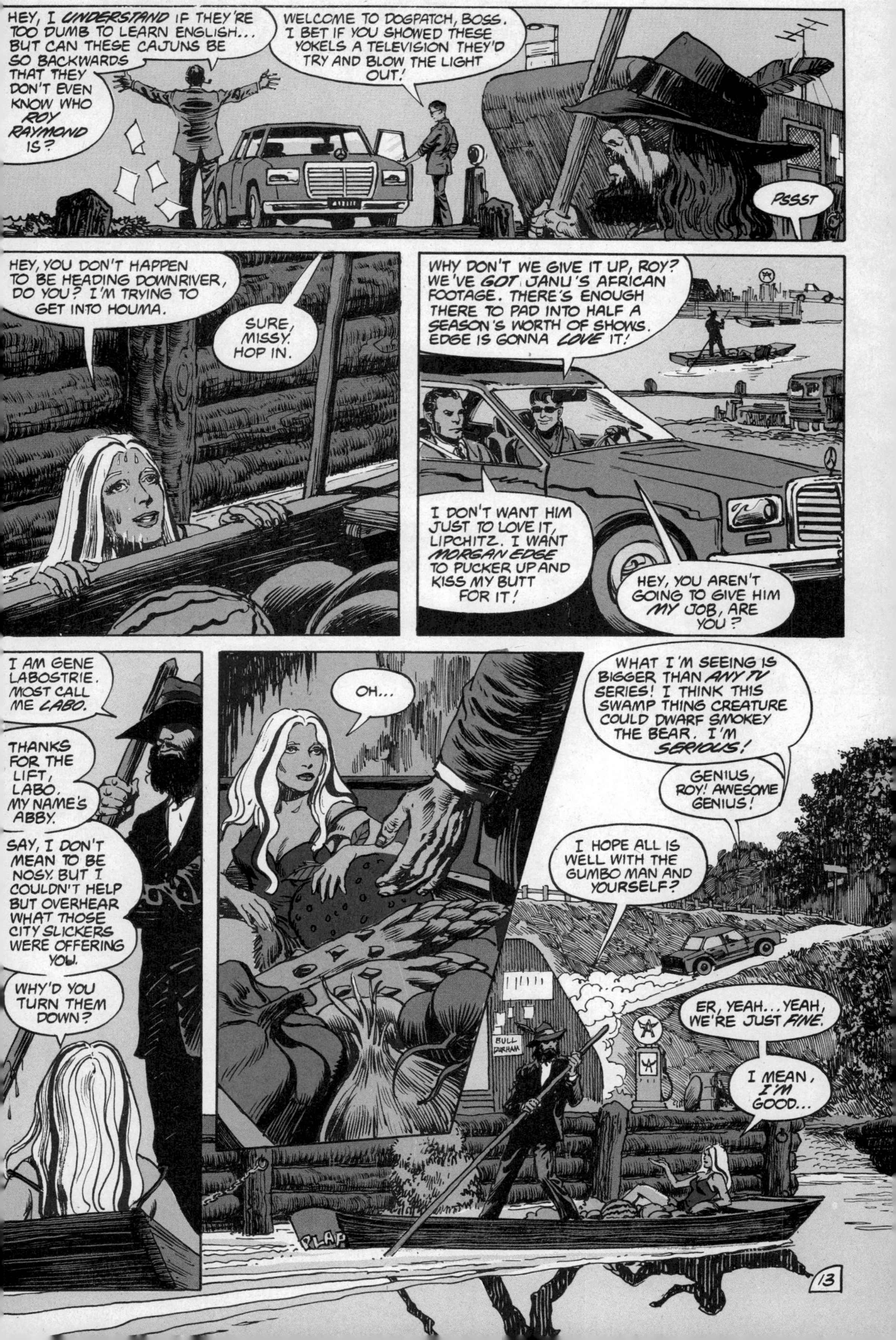
HEY, I UNDERSTAND IF THEY'RE TOO DUMB TO LEARN ENGLISH... BUT CAN THESE CAJUNS BE SO BACKWARDS THAT THEY DON'T EVEN KNOW WHO ROY RAYMOND IS?
WELCOME TO DOGPATCH, BOSS. I BET IF YOU SHOWED THESE YOKELS A TELEVISION THEY'D TRY AND BLOW THE LIGHT OUT!
PSSST
HEY, YOU DON'T HAPPEN TO BE HEADING DOWNRIVER, DO YOU? I'M TRYING TO GET INTO HOUMA.
SURE, MISSY. HOP IN.
WHY DON'T WE GIVE IT UP, ROY? WE'VE GOT JANU'S AFRICAN FOOTAGE. THERE'S ENOUGH THERE TO PAD INTO HALF A SEASON'S WORTH OF SHOWS. EDGE IS GONNA LOVE IT!
I DON'T WANT HIM JUST TO LOVE IT, LIPCHITZ. I WANT MORGAN EDGE TO PUCKER UP AND KISS MY BUTT FOR IT!
HEY, YOU AREN'T GOING TO GIVE HIM MY JOB, ARE YOU?
I AM GENE LABOSTRIE. MOST CALL ME LABO.
THANKS FOR THE LIFT, LABO. MY NAME'S ABBY.
SAY, I DON'T MEAN TO BE NOSY. BUT I COULDN'T HELP BUT OVERHEAR WHAT THOSE CITY SLICKERS WERE OFFERING YOU.
WHY'D YOU TURN THEM DOWN?
OH...
WHAT I'M SEEING IS BIGGER THAN ANY TV SERIES! I THINK THIS SWAMP THING CREATURE COULD DWARF SMOKEY THE BEAR. I'M SERIOUS!
GENIUS, ROY! AWESOME GENIUS!
I HOPE ALL IS WELL WITH THE GUMBO MAN AND YOURSELF?
ER, YEAH... YEAH, WE'RE JUST FINE.
I MEAN, I'M GOOD...
BULL DURHAM
PLAP
13

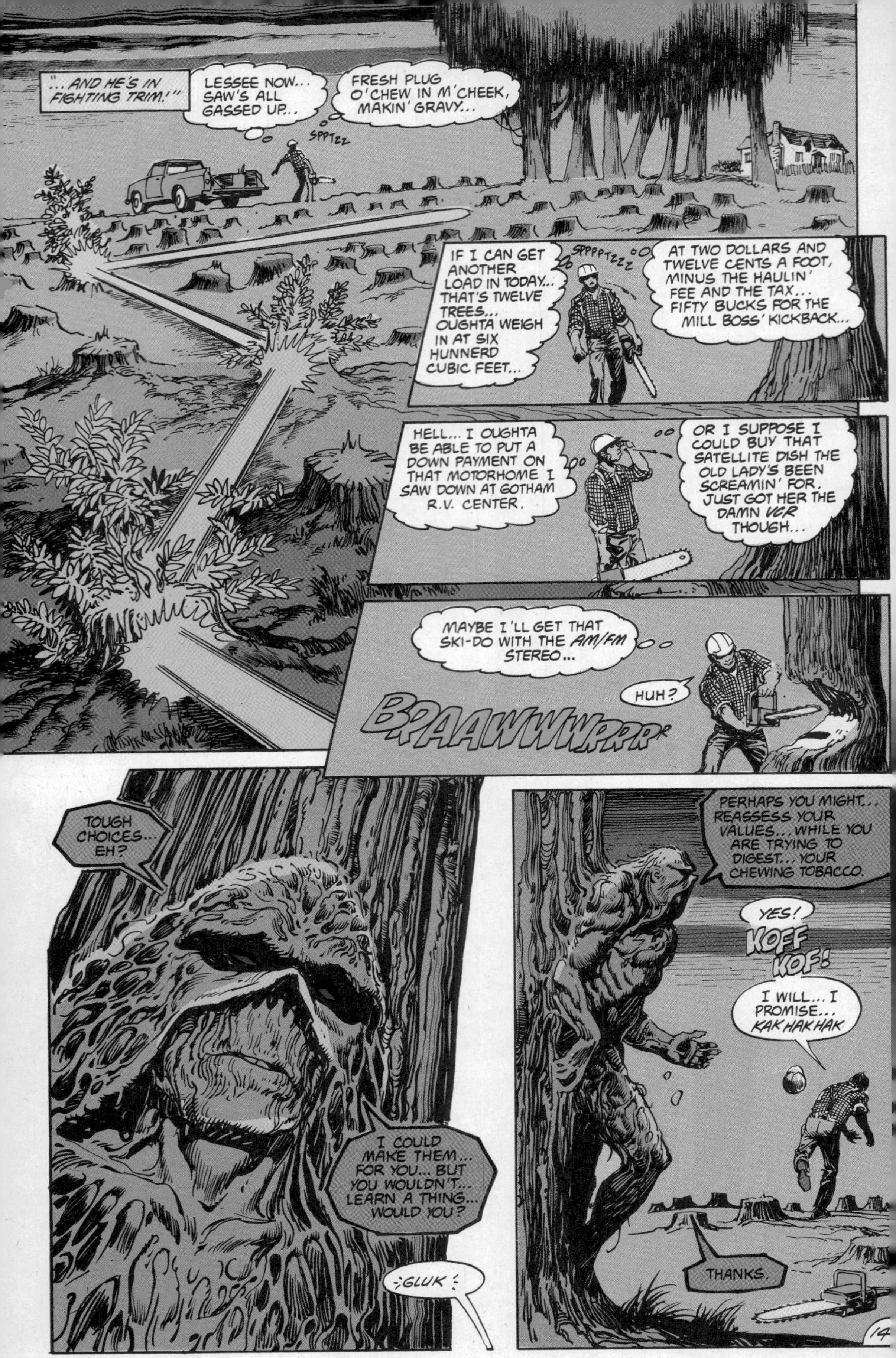

"...AND HE'S IN FIGHTING TRIM!"
LESSEE NOW... SAW'S ALL GASSED UP...
FRESH PLUG O'CHEW IN M'CHEEK, MAKIN' GRAVY...
SPPTzz
IF I CAN GET ANOTHER LOAD IN TODAY... THAT'S TWELVE TREES... OUGHTA WEIGH IN AT SIX HUNNERD CUBIC FEET...
SPPPPTzzz
AT TWO DOLLARS AND TWELVE CENTS A FOOT, MINUS THE HAULIN' FEE AND THE TAX... FIFTY BUCKS FOR THE MILL BOSS' KICKBACK...
HELL... I OUGHTA BE ABLE TO PUT A DOWN PAYMENT ON THAT MOTORHOME I SAW DOWN AT GOTHAM R.V. CENTER.
OR I SUPPOSE I COULD BUY THAT SATELLITE DISH THE OLD LADY'S BEEN SCREAMIN' FOR. JUST GOT HER THE DAMN VCR THOUGH...
MAYBE I'LL GET THAT SKI-DO WITH THE AM/FM STEREO...
HUH?
BRAAWWWRRRR
TOUGH CHOICES... EH?
I COULD MAKE THEM... FOR YOU... BUT YOU WOULDN'T... LEARN A THING... WOULD YOU?
GLUK
PERHAPS YOU MIGHT... REASSESS YOUR VALUES... WHILE YOU ARE TRYING TO DIGEST... YOUR CHEWING TOBACCO.
YES! KOFF KOF!
I WILL... I PROMISE... KAKHAKHAK
THANKS.
14

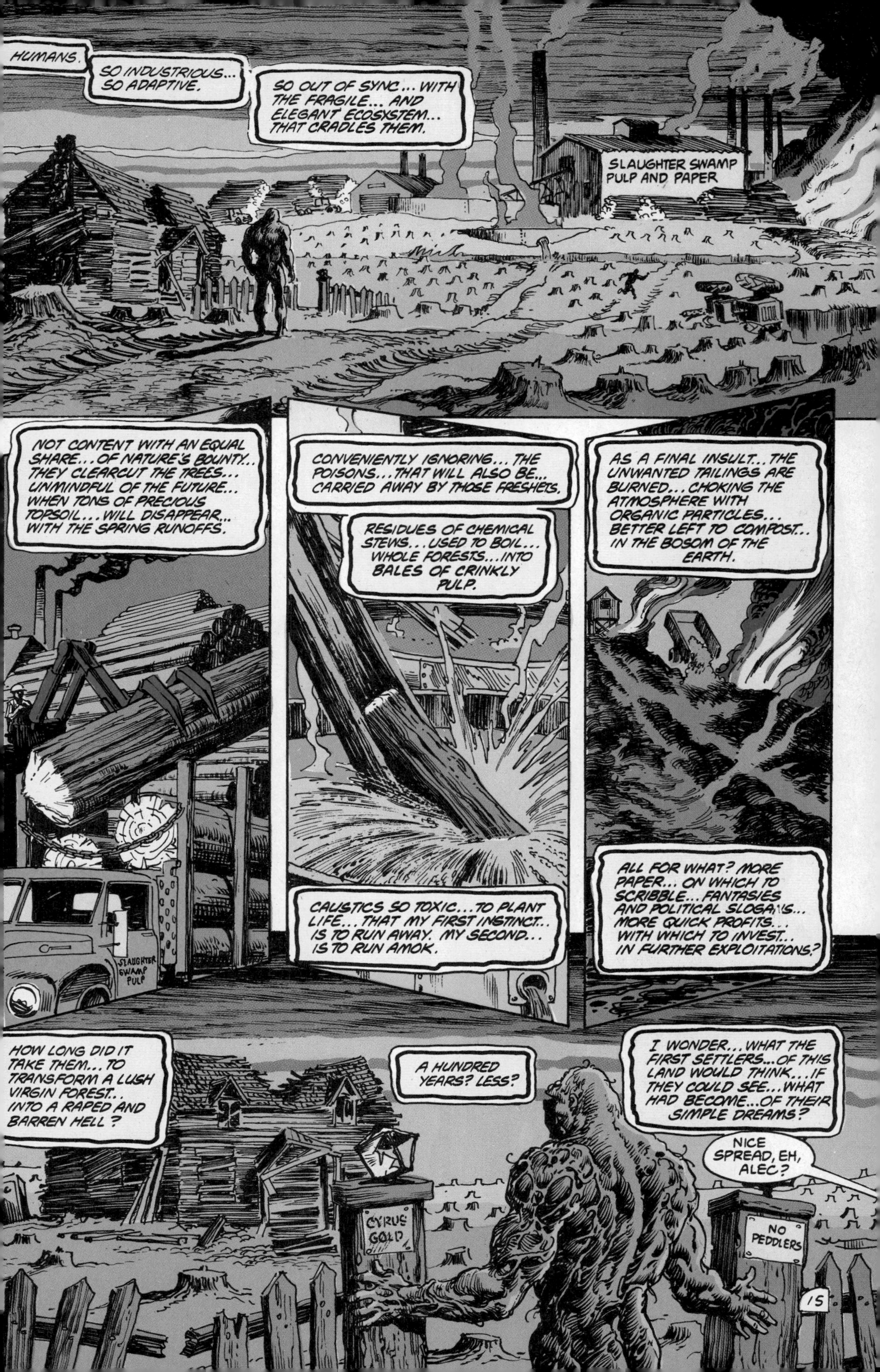
HUMANS.
SO INDUSTRIOUS... SO ADAPTIVE.
SO OUT OF SYNC... WITH THE FRAGILE... AND ELEGANT ECOSYSTEM... THAT CRADLES THEM.
SLAUGHTER SWAMP PULP AND PAPER
NOT CONTENT WITH AN EQUAL SHARE... OF NATURE'S BOUNTY... THEY CLEARCUT THE TREES... UNMINDFUL OF THE FUTURE... WHEN TONS OF PRECIOUS TOPSOIL... WILL DISAPPEAR... WITH THE SPRING RUNOFFS.
SLAUGHTER SWAMP PULP
CONVENIENTLY IGNORING... THE POISONS... THAT WILL ALSO BE... CARRIED AWAY BY THOSE FRESHETS.
RESIDUES OF CHEMICAL STEWS... USED TO BOIL... WHOLE FORESTS... INTO BALES OF CRINKLY PULP.
CAUSTICS SO TOXIC... TO PLANT LIFE... THAT MY FIRST INSTINCT... IS TO RUN AWAY. MY SECOND... IS TO RUN AMOK.
AS A FINAL INSULT... THE UNWANTED TAILINGS ARE BURNED... CHOKING THE ATMOSPHERE WITH ORGANIC PARTICLES... BETTER LEFT TO COMPOST... IN THE BOSOM OF THE EARTH.
ALL FOR WHAT? MORE PAPER... ON WHICH TO SCRIBBLE... FANTASIES AND POLITICAL SLOGANS... MORE QUICK PROFITS... WITH WHICH TO INVEST... IN FURTHER EXPLOITATIONS?
HOW LONG DID IT TAKE THEM... TO TRANSFORM A LUSH VIRGIN FOREST... INTO A RAPED AND BARREN HELL?
A HUNDRED YEARS? LESS?
I WONDER... WHAT THE FIRST SETTLERS... OF THIS LAND WOULD THINK... IF THEY COULD SEE... WHAT HAD BECOME... OF THEIR SIMPLE DREAMS?
NICE SPREAD, EH, ALEC?
CYRUS GOLD
NO PEDDLERS
15

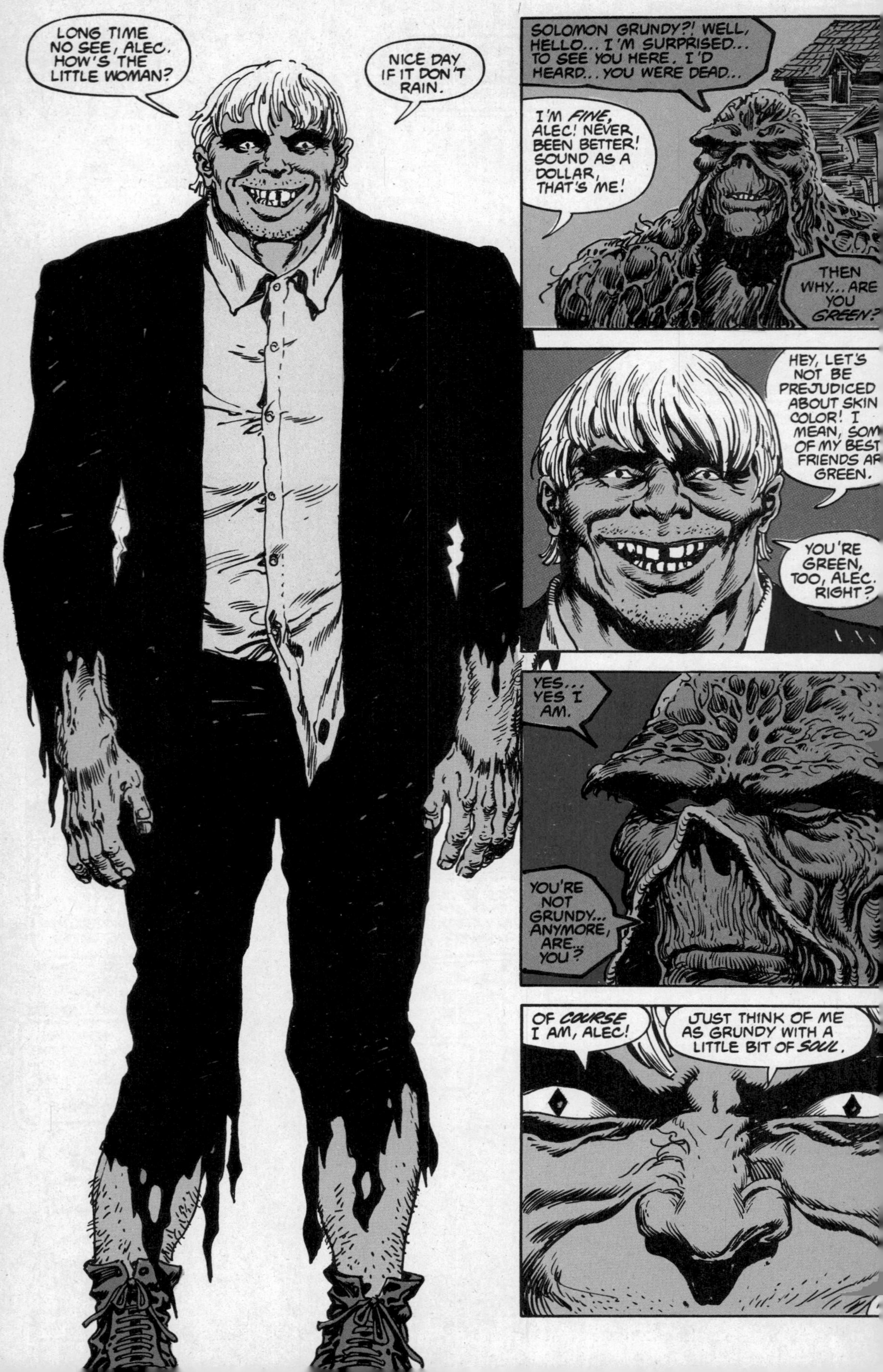
LONG TIME NO SEE, ALEC. HOW'S THE LITTLE WOMAN?
NICE DAY IF IT DON'T RAIN.
SOLOMON GRUNDY?! WELL, HELLO... I'M SURPRISED... TO SEE YOU HERE. I'D HEARD... YOU WERE DEAD...
I'M FINE, ALEC! NEVER BEEN BETTER! SOUND AS A DOLLAR, THAT'S ME!
THEN WHY... ARE YOU GREEN?
HEY, LET'S NOT BE PREJUDICED ABOUT SKIN COLOR! I MEAN, SOM OF MY BEST FRIENDS AR GREEN.
YOU'RE GREEN, TOO, ALEC. RIGHT?
YES... YES I AM.
YOU'RE NOT GRUNDY... ANYMORE, ARE... YOU?
OF COURSE I AM, ALEC!
JUST THINK OF ME AS GRUNDY WITH A LITTLE BIT OF SOUL.

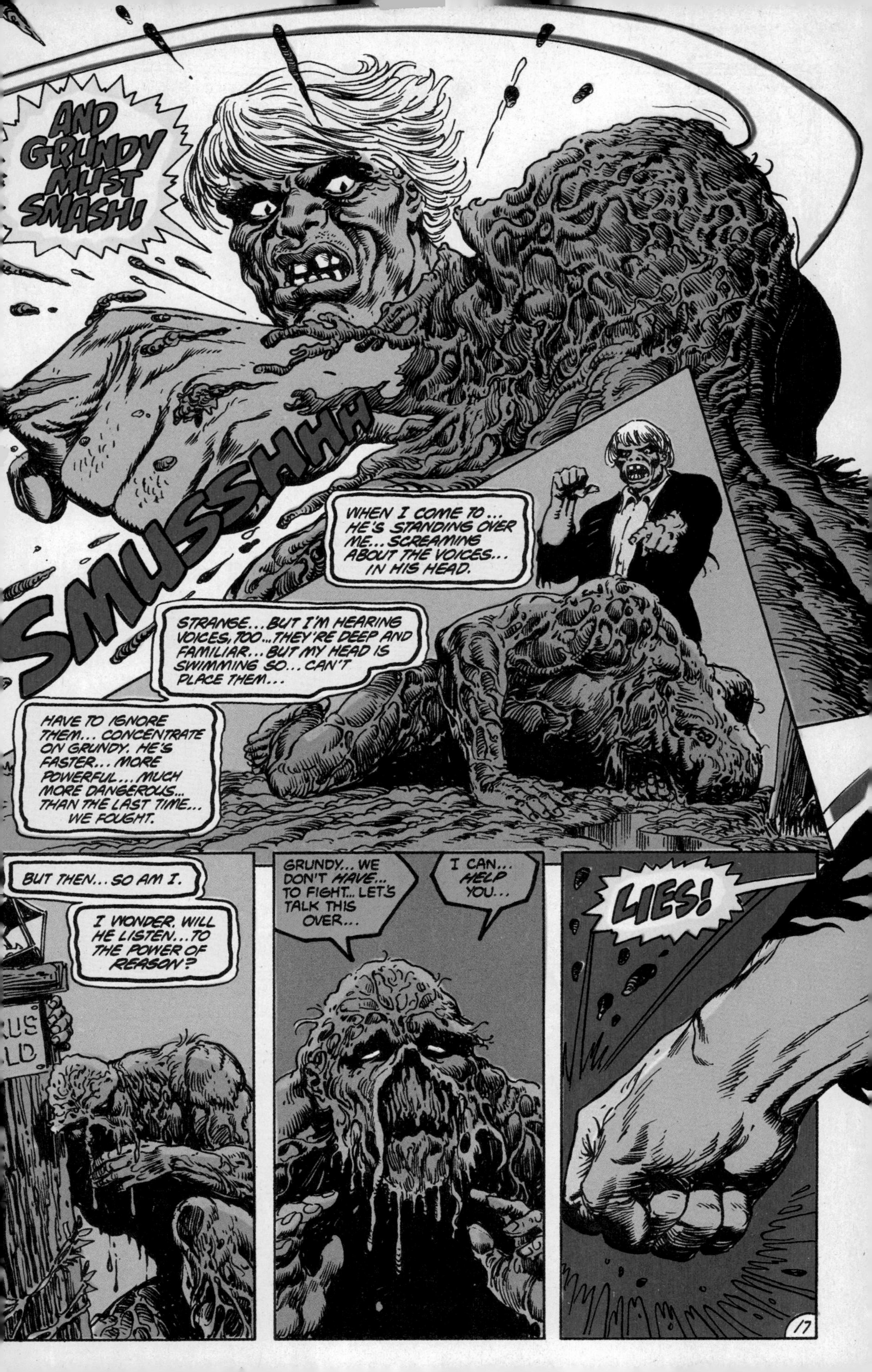
AND GRUNDY MUST SMASH!
SMUSSHHH
WHEN I COME TO... HE'S STANDING OVER ME... SCREAMING ABOUT THE VOICES... IN HIS HEAD.
STRANGE... BUT I'M HEARING VOICES, TOO... THEY'RE DEEP AND FAMILIAR... BUT MY HEAD IS SWIMMING SO... CAN'T PLACE THEM...
HAVE TO IGNORE THEM... CONCENTRATE ON GRUNDY. HE'S FASTER... MORE POWERFUL... MUCH MORE DANGEROUS... THAN THE LAST TIME... WE FOUGHT.
BUT THEN... SO AM I.
I WONDER. WILL HE LISTEN... TO THE POWER OF REASON?
GRUNDY... WE DON'T *HAVE*... TO FIGHT... LET'S TALK THIS OVER...
I CAN... *HELP* YOU...
LIES!

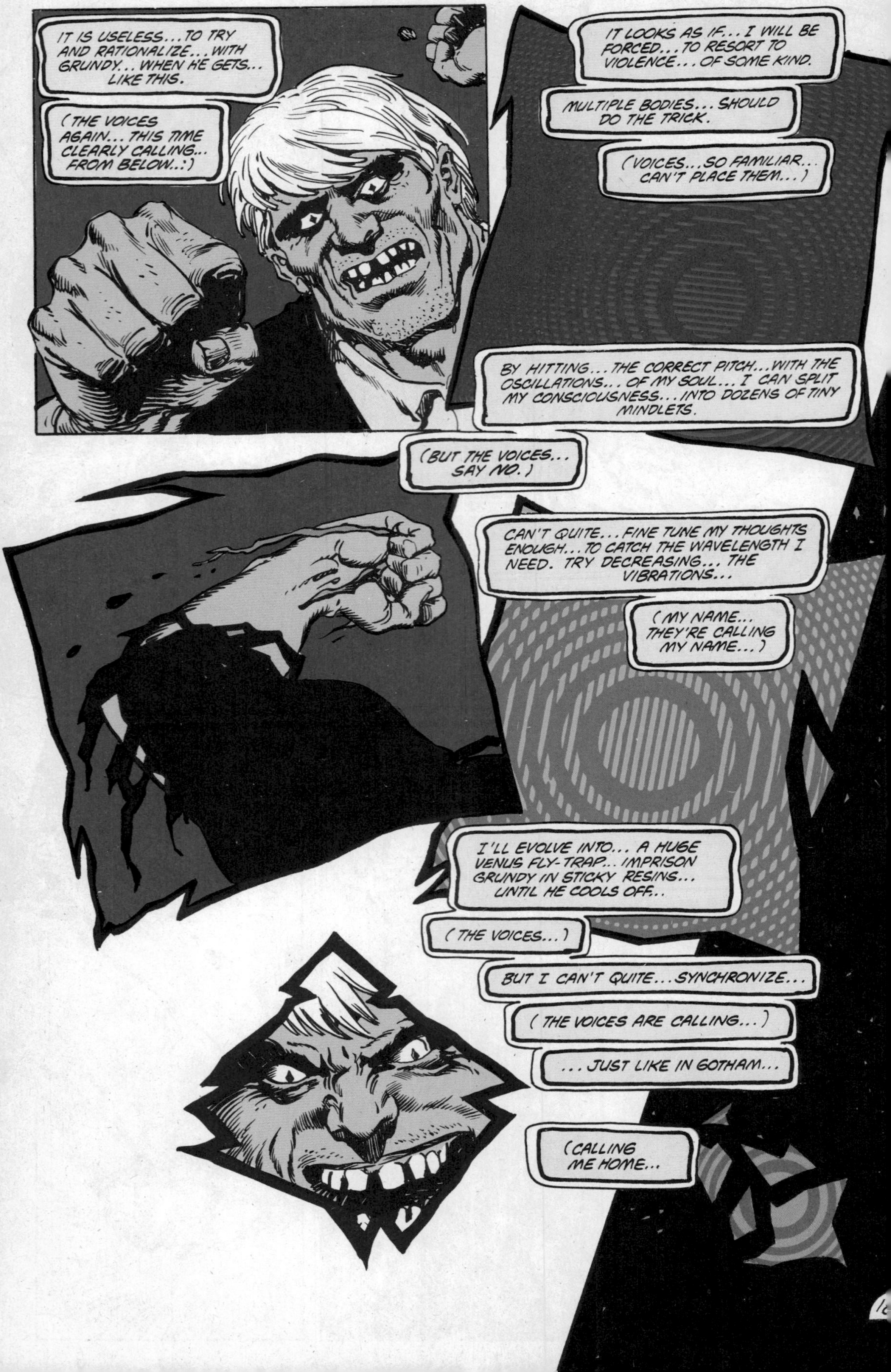
IT IS USELESS...TO TRY AND RATIONALIZE...WITH GRUNDY...WHEN HE GETS... LIKE THIS.
(THE VOICES AGAIN...THIS TIME CLEARLY CALLING... FROM BELOW..:)
IT LOOKS AS IF...I WILL BE FORCED...TO RESORT TO VIOLENCE...OF SOME KIND.
MULTIPLE BODIES...SHOULD DO THE TRICK.
(VOICES...SO FAMILIAR... CAN'T PLACE THEM...)
BY HITTING...THE CORRECT PITCH...WITH THE OSCILLATIONS...OF MY SOUL...I CAN SPLIT MY CONSCIOUSNESS...INTO DOZENS OF TINY MINDLETS.
(BUT THE VOICES... SAY NO.)
CAN'T QUITE...FINE TUNE MY THOUGHTS ENOUGH...TO CATCH THE WAVELENGTH I NEED. TRY DECREASING...THE VIBRATIONS...
(MY NAME... THEY'RE CALLING MY NAME...)
I'LL EVOLVE INTO... A HUGE VENUS FLY-TRAP...IMPRISON GRUNDY IN STICKY RESINS... UNTIL HE COOLS OFF...
(THE VOICES...)
BUT I CAN'T QUITE...SYNCHRONIZE...
(THE VOICES ARE CALLING...)
...JUST LIKE IN GOTHAM...
(CALLING ME HOME...

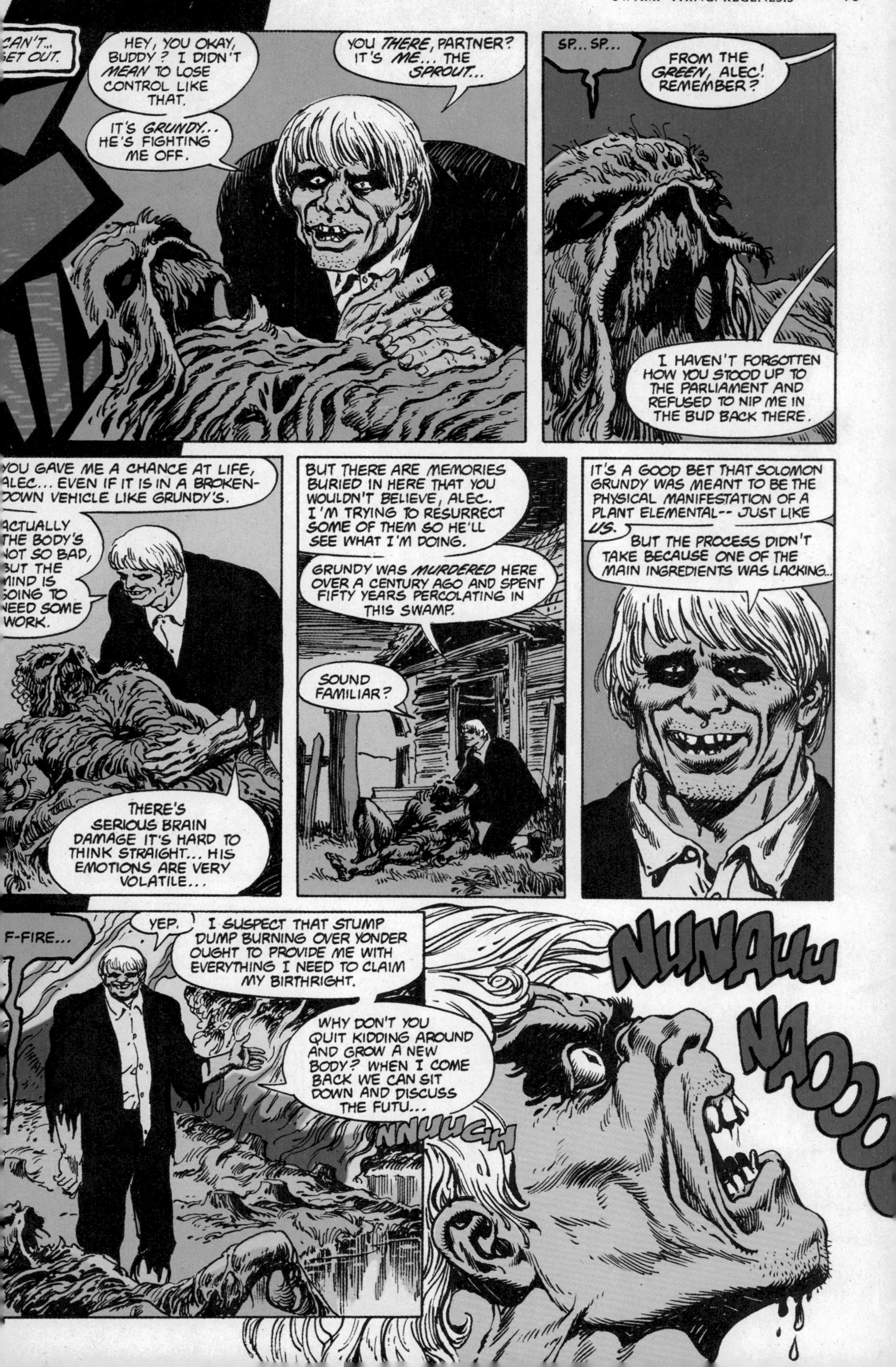
CAN'T... GET OUT.
HEY, YOU OKAY, BUDDY? I DIDN'T MEAN TO LOSE CONTROL LIKE THAT.
IT'S GRUNDY... HE'S FIGHTING ME OFF.
YOU THERE, PARTNER? IT'S ME... THE SPROUT...
SP... SP...
FROM THE GREEN, ALEC! REMEMBER?
I HAVEN'T FORGOTTEN HOW YOU STOOD UP TO THE PARLIAMENT AND REFUSED TO NIP ME IN THE BUD BACK THERE.
YOU GAVE ME A CHANCE AT LIFE, ALEC... EVEN IF IT IS IN A BROKEN-DOWN VEHICLE LIKE GRUNDY'S.
ACTUALLY THE BODY'S NOT SO BAD, BUT THE MIND IS GOING TO NEED SOME WORK.
THERE'S SERIOUS BRAIN DAMAGE IT'S HARD TO THINK STRAIGHT... HIS EMOTIONS ARE VERY VOLATILE...
BUT THERE ARE MEMORIES BURIED IN HERE THAT YOU WOULDN'T BELIEVE, ALEC. I'M TRYING TO RESURRECT SOME OF THEM SO HE'LL SEE WHAT I'M DOING.
GRUNDY WAS MURDERED HERE OVER A CENTURY AGO AND SPENT FIFTY YEARS PERCOLATING IN THIS SWAMP.
SOUND FAMILIAR?
IT'S A GOOD BET THAT SOLOMON GRUNDY WAS MEANT TO BE THE PHYSICAL MANIFESTATION OF A PLANT ELEMENTAL-- JUST LIKE US.
BUT THE PROCESS DIDN'T TAKE BECAUSE ONE OF THE MAIN INGREDIENTS WAS LACKING...
F-FIRE...
YEP.
I SUSPECT THAT STUMP DUMP BURNING OVER YONDER OUGHT TO PROVIDE ME WITH EVERYTHING I NEED TO CLAIM MY BIRTHRIGHT.
WHY DON'T YOU QUIT KIDDING AROUND AND GROW A NEW BODY? WHEN I COME BACK WE CAN SIT DOWN AND DISCUSS THE FUTU...
NNUUCH
NUNAuu
NAOOOO

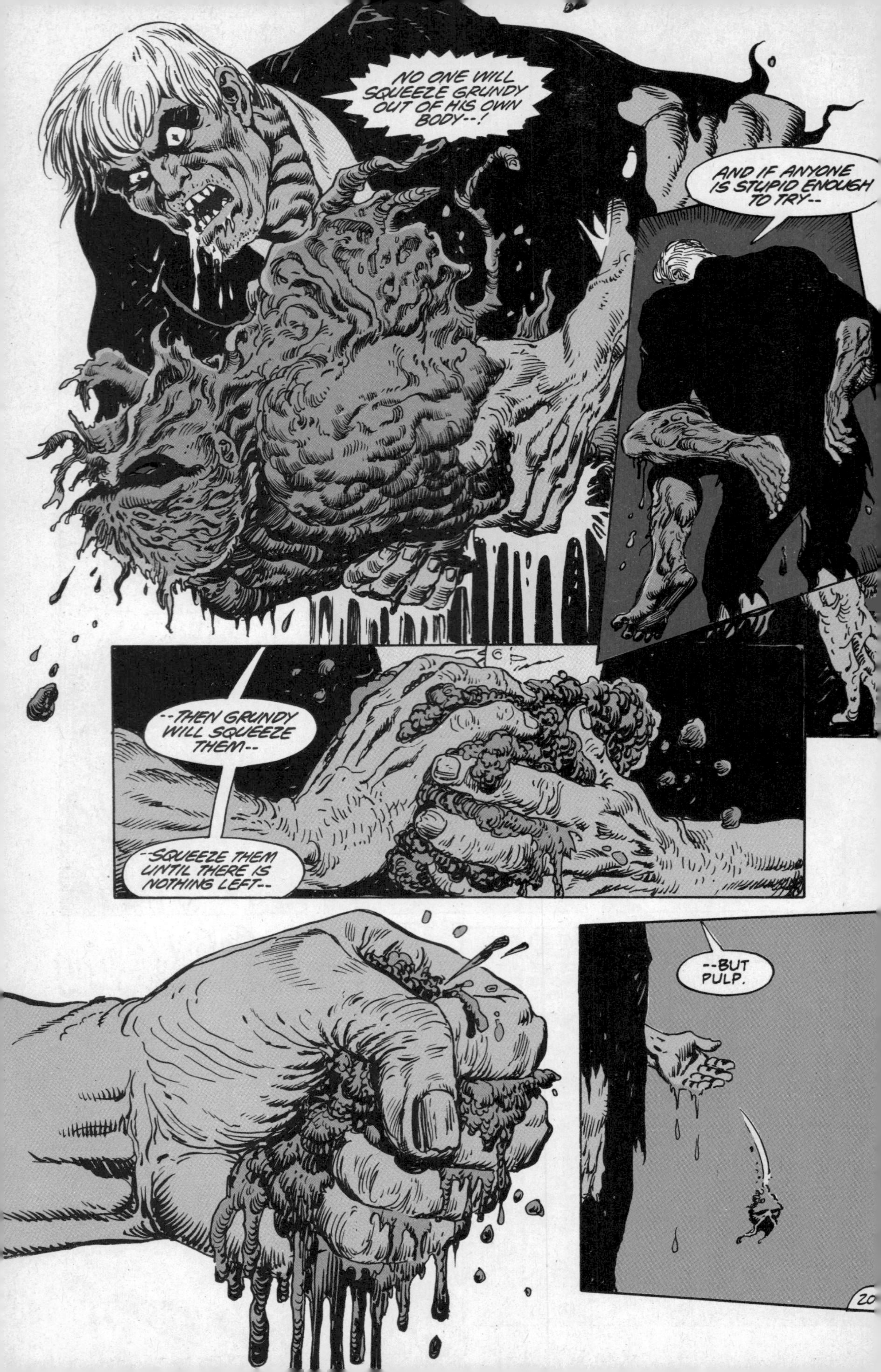
NO ONE WILL SQUEEZE GRUNDY OUT OF HIS OWN BODY--!
AND IF ANYONE IS STUPID ENOUGH TO TRY--
--THEN GRUNDY WILL SQUEEZE THEM--
--SQUEEZE THEM UNTIL THERE IS NOTHING LEFT--
--BUT PULP.

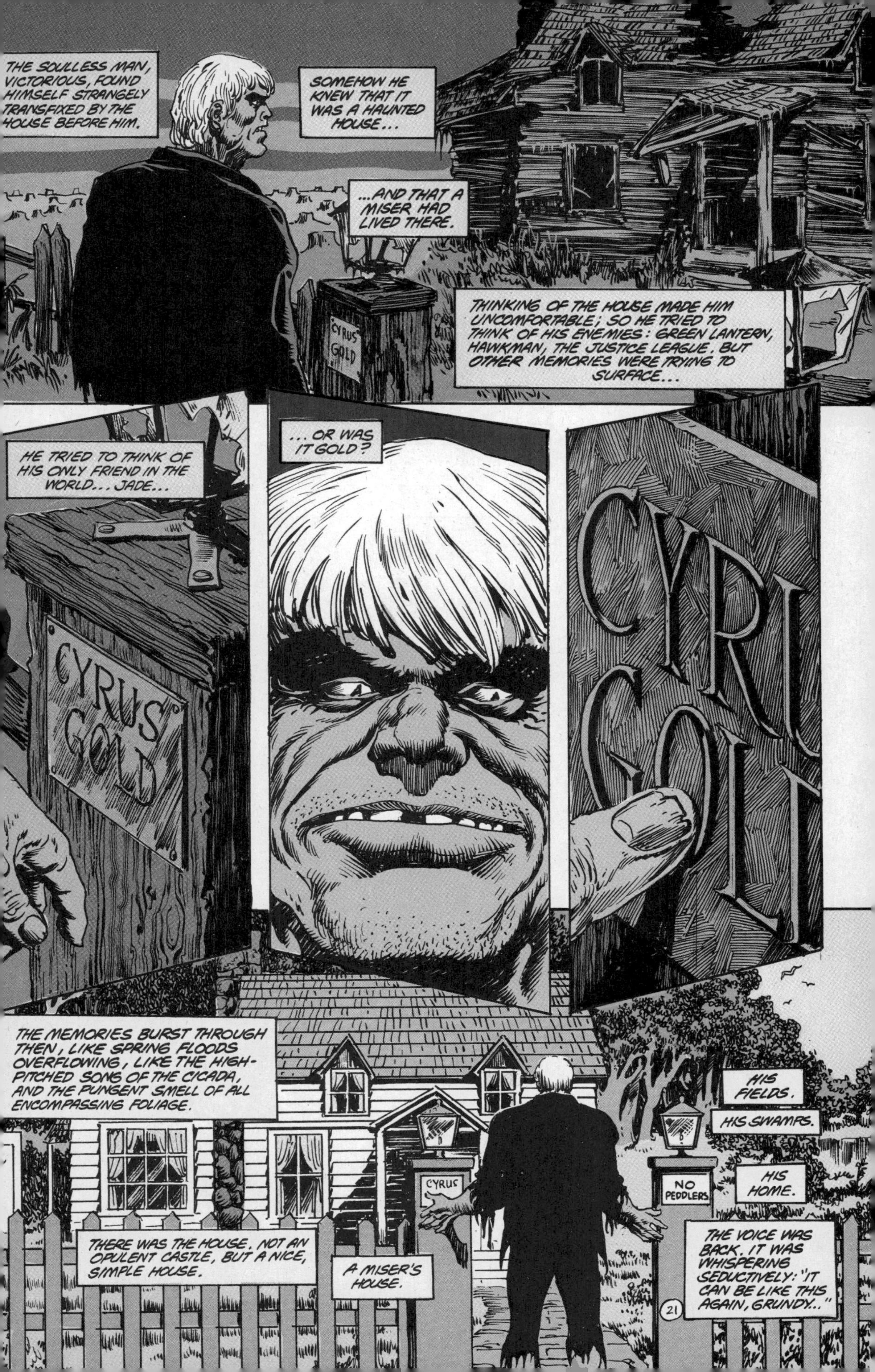
THE SOULLESS MAN, VICTORIOUS, FOUND HIMSELF STRANGELY TRANSFIXED BY THE HOUSE BEFORE HIM.
SOMEHOW HE KNEW THAT IT WAS A HAUNTED HOUSE...
...AND THAT A MISER HAD LIVED THERE.
CYRUS GOLD
THINKING OF THE HOUSE MADE HIM UNCOMFORTABLE; SO HE TRIED TO THINK OF HIS ENEMIES: GREEN LANTERN, HAWKMAN, THE JUSTICE LEAGUE. BUT OTHER MEMORIES WERE TRYING TO SURFACE...
HE TRIED TO THINK OF HIS ONLY FRIEND IN THE WORLD... JADE...
CYRUS GOLD
...OR WAS IT GOLD?
THE MEMORIES BURST THROUGH THEN, LIKE SPRING FLOODS OVERFLOWING, LIKE THE HIGH-PITCHED SONG OF THE CICADA, AND THE PUNGENT SMELL OF ALL ENCOMPASSING FOLIAGE.
HIS FIELDS.
HIS SWAMPS.
CYRUS
NO PEDDLERS
HIS HOME.
THERE WAS THE HOUSE. NOT AN OPULENT CASTLE, BUT A NICE, SIMPLE HOUSE.
A MISER'S HOUSE.
THE VOICE WAS BACK. IT WAS WHISPERING SEDUCTIVELY: "IT CAN BE LIKE THIS AGAIN, GRUNDY..."

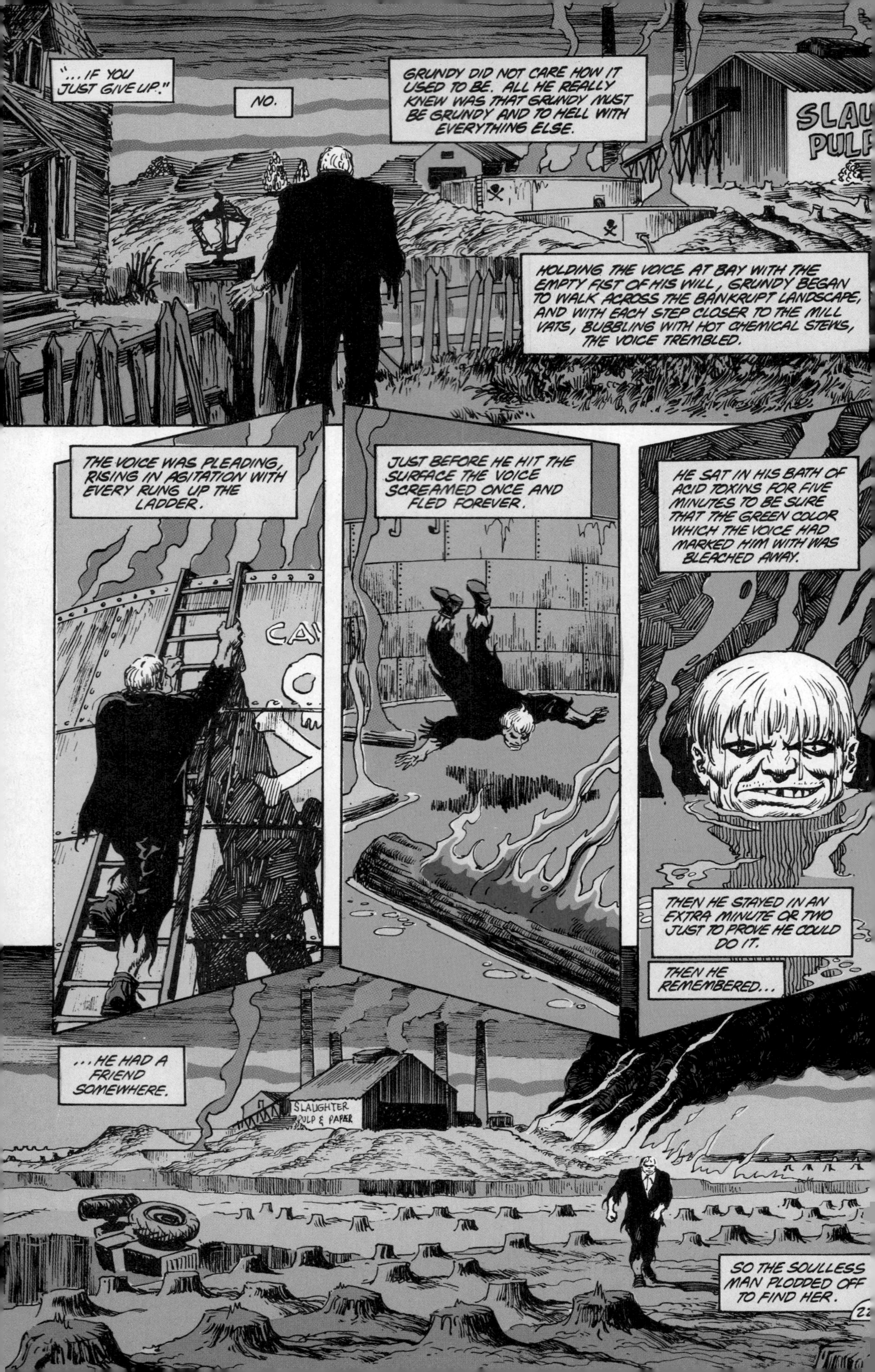
"...IF YOU JUST GIVE UP."
NO.
GRUNDY DID NOT CARE HOW IT USED TO BE. ALL HE REALLY KNEW WAS THAT GRUNDY MUST BE GRUNDY AND TO HELL WITH EVERYTHING ELSE.
SLAU PULP
HOLDING THE VOICE AT BAY WITH THE EMPTY FIST OF HIS WILL, GRUNDY BEGAN TO WALK ACROSS THE BANKRUPT LANDSCAPE, AND WITH EACH STEP CLOSER TO THE MILL VATS, BUBBLING WITH HOT CHEMICAL STEWS, THE VOICE TREMBLED.
THE VOICE WAS PLEADING, RISING IN AGITATION WITH EVERY RUNG UP THE LADDER.
JUST BEFORE HE HIT THE SURFACE THE VOICE SCREAMED ONCE AND FLED FOREVER.
HE SAT IN HIS BATH OF ACID TOXINS FOR FIVE MINUTES TO BE SURE THAT THE GREEN COLOR WHICH THE VOICE HAD MARKED HIM WITH WAS BLEACHED AWAY.
THEN HE STAYED IN AN EXTRA MINUTE OR TWO JUST TO PROVE HE COULD DO IT.
THEN HE REMEMBERED...
...HE HAD A FRIEND SOMEWHERE.
SLAUGHTER PULP & PAPER
SO THE SOULLESS MAN PLODDED OFF TO FIND HER.
22

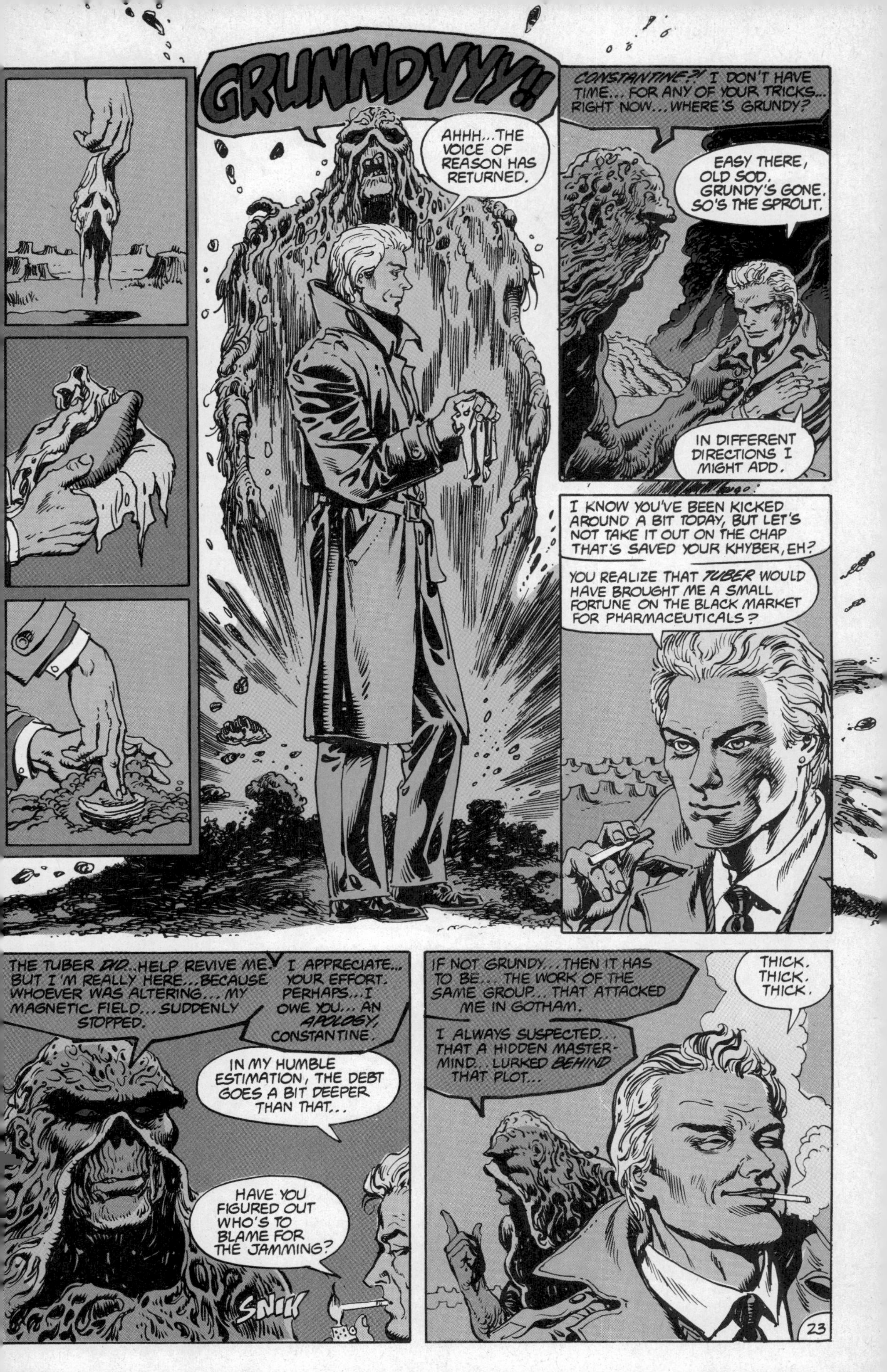
GRUNNDYYY!!
AHHH...THE VOICE OF REASON HAS RETURNED.
CONSTANTINE?! I DON'T HAVE TIME... FOR ANY OF YOUR TRICKS... RIGHT NOW... WHERE'S GRUNDY?
EASY THERE, OLD SOD. GRUNDY'S GONE. SO'S THE SPROUT.
IN DIFFERENT DIRECTIONS I MIGHT ADD.
I KNOW YOU'VE BEEN KICKED AROUND A BIT TODAY, BUT LET'S NOT TAKE IT OUT ON THE CHAP THAT'S SAVED YOUR KHYBER, EH?
YOU REALIZE THAT TUBER WOULD HAVE BROUGHT ME A SMALL FORTUNE ON THE BLACK MARKET FOR PHARMACEUTICALS?
THE TUBER DID...HELP REVIVE ME. BUT I'M REALLY HERE...BECAUSE WHOEVER WAS ALTERING... MY MAGNETIC FIELD... SUDDENLY STOPPED.
I APPRECIATE... YOUR EFFORT. PERHAPS...I OWE YOU... AN APOLOGY, CONSTANTINE.
IN MY HUMBLE ESTIMATION, THE DEBT GOES A BIT DEEPER THAN THAT...
HAVE YOU FIGURED OUT WHO'S TO BLAME FOR THE JAMMING?
SNIK
IF NOT GRUNDY... THEN IT HAS TO BE... THE WORK OF THE SAME GROUP... THAT ATTACKED ME IN GOTHAM.
I ALWAYS SUSPECTED... THAT A HIDDEN MASTER-MIND... LURKED BEHIND THAT PLOT...
THICK. THICK. THICK.

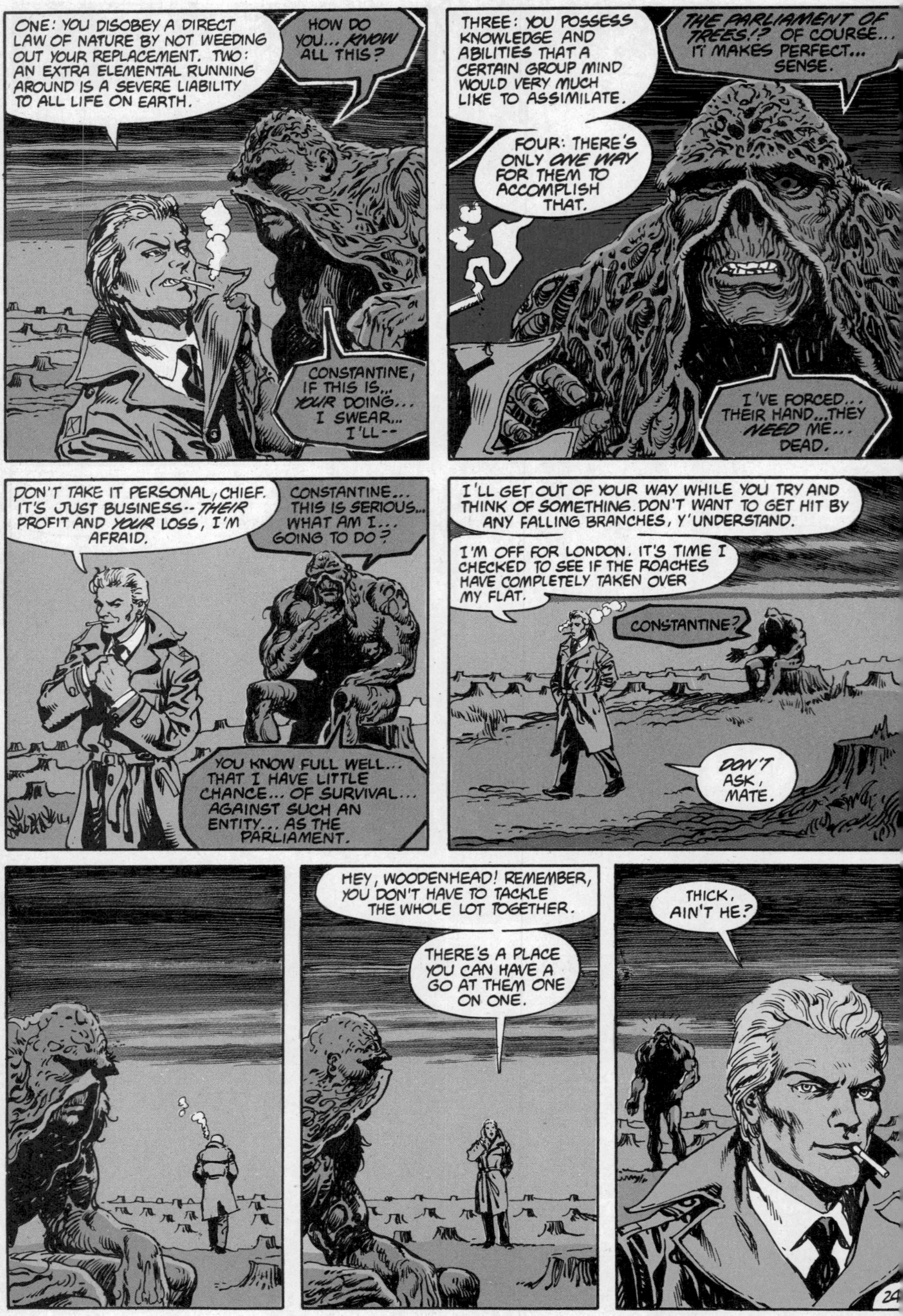
ONE: YOU DISOBEY A DIRECT LAW OF NATURE BY NOT WEEDING OUT YOUR REPLACEMENT. TWO: AN EXTRA ELEMENTAL RUNNING AROUND IS A SEVERE LIABILITY TO ALL LIFE ON EARTH.
HOW DO YOU... KNOW ALL THIS?
CONSTANTINE, IF THIS IS... YOUR DOING... I SWEAR... I'LL--
THREE: YOU POSSESS KNOWLEDGE AND ABILITIES THAT A CERTAIN GROUP MIND WOULD VERY MUCH LIKE TO ASSIMILATE.
THE PARLIAMENT OF TREES!? OF COURSE... IT MAKES PERFECT... SENSE.
FOUR: THERE'S ONLY ONE WAY FOR THEM TO ACCOMPLISH THAT.
I'VE FORCED... THEIR HAND... THEY NEED ME... DEAD.
DON'T TAKE IT PERSONAL, CHIEF. IT'S JUST BUSINESS-- THEIR PROFIT AND YOUR LOSS, I'M AFRAID.
CONSTANTINE... THIS IS SERIOUS... WHAT AM I... GOING TO DO?
YOU KNOW FULL WELL... THAT I HAVE LITTLE CHANCE... OF SURVIVAL... AGAINST SUCH AN ENTITY... AS THE PARLIAMENT.
I'LL GET OUT OF YOUR WAY WHILE YOU TRY AND THINK OF SOMETHING. DON'T WANT TO GET HIT BY ANY FALLING BRANCHES, Y'UNDERSTAND.
I'M OFF FOR LONDON. IT'S TIME I CHECKED TO SEE IF THE ROACHES HAVE COMPLETELY TAKEN OVER MY FLAT.
CONSTANTINE?
DON'T ASK, MATE.
HEY, WOODENHEAD! REMEMBER, YOU DON'T HAVE TO TACKLE THE WHOLE LOT TOGETHER.
THERE'S A PLACE YOU CAN HAVE A GO AT THEM ONE ON ONE.
THICK, AIN'T HE?
24

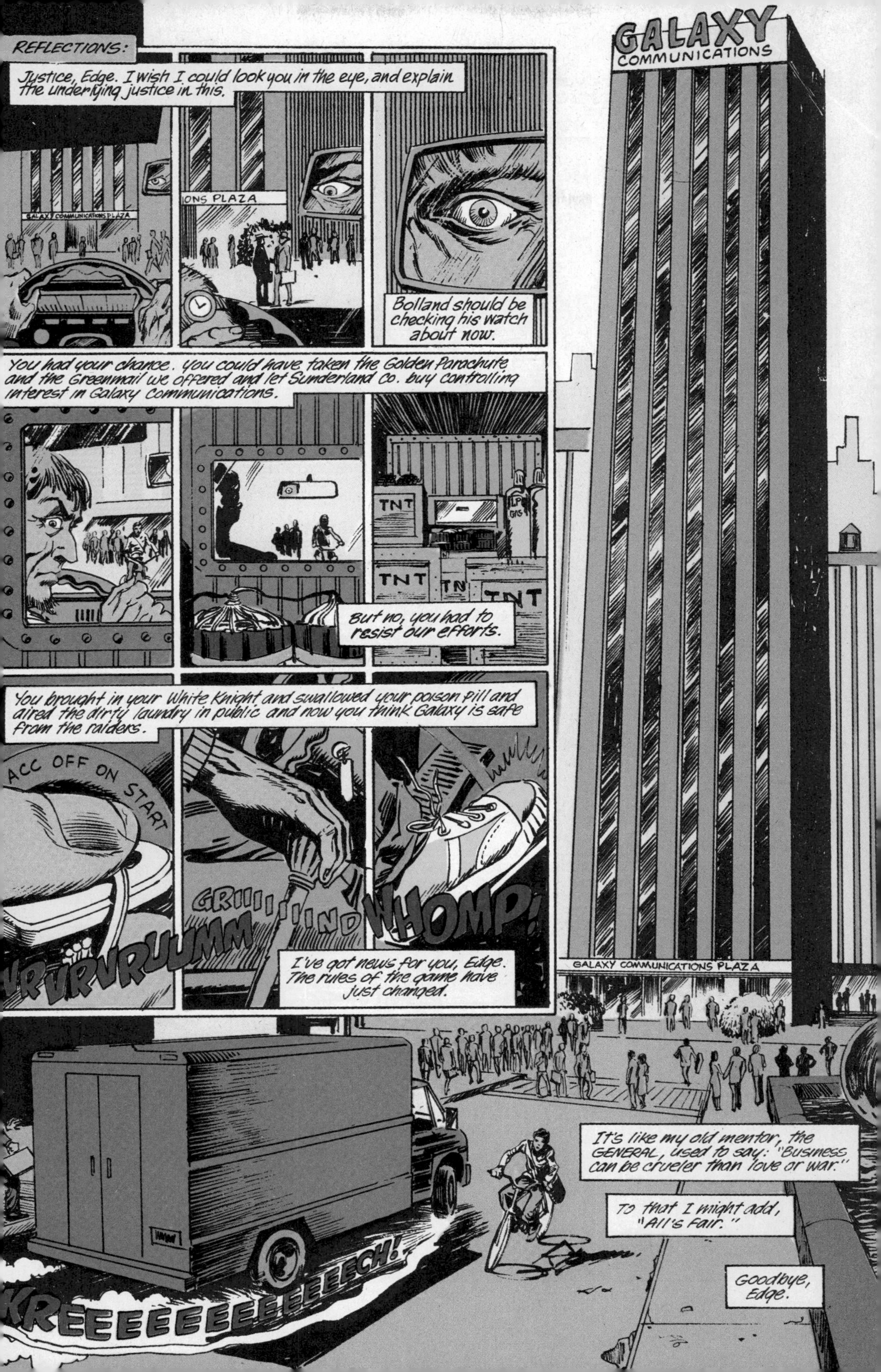
GALAXY COMMUNICATIONS
REFLECTIONS:
Justice, Edge. I wish I could look you in the eye, and explain the underlying justice in this.
GALAXY COMMUNICATIONS PLAZA
IONS PLAZA
Bolland should be checking his watch about now.
You had your chance. You could have taken the Golden Parachute and the Greenmail we offered and let Sunderland Co. buy controlling interest in Galaxy Communications.
TNT
LP GAS
TNT
TN
TNT
But no, you had to resist our efforts.
You brought in your White Knight and swallowed your poison pill and aired the dirty laundry in public and now you think Galaxy is safe from the raiders.
ACC OFF ON START
VRVRVRUUMM
GRIIIIIIIND
WHOMP!
I've got news for you, Edge. The rules of the game have just changed.
GALAXY COMMUNICATIONS PLAZA
It's like my old mentor, the GENERAL, used to say: "Business can be crueler than love or war."
To that I might add, "All's fair."
Goodbye, Edge.
KREEEEEEEEEEEEECH!

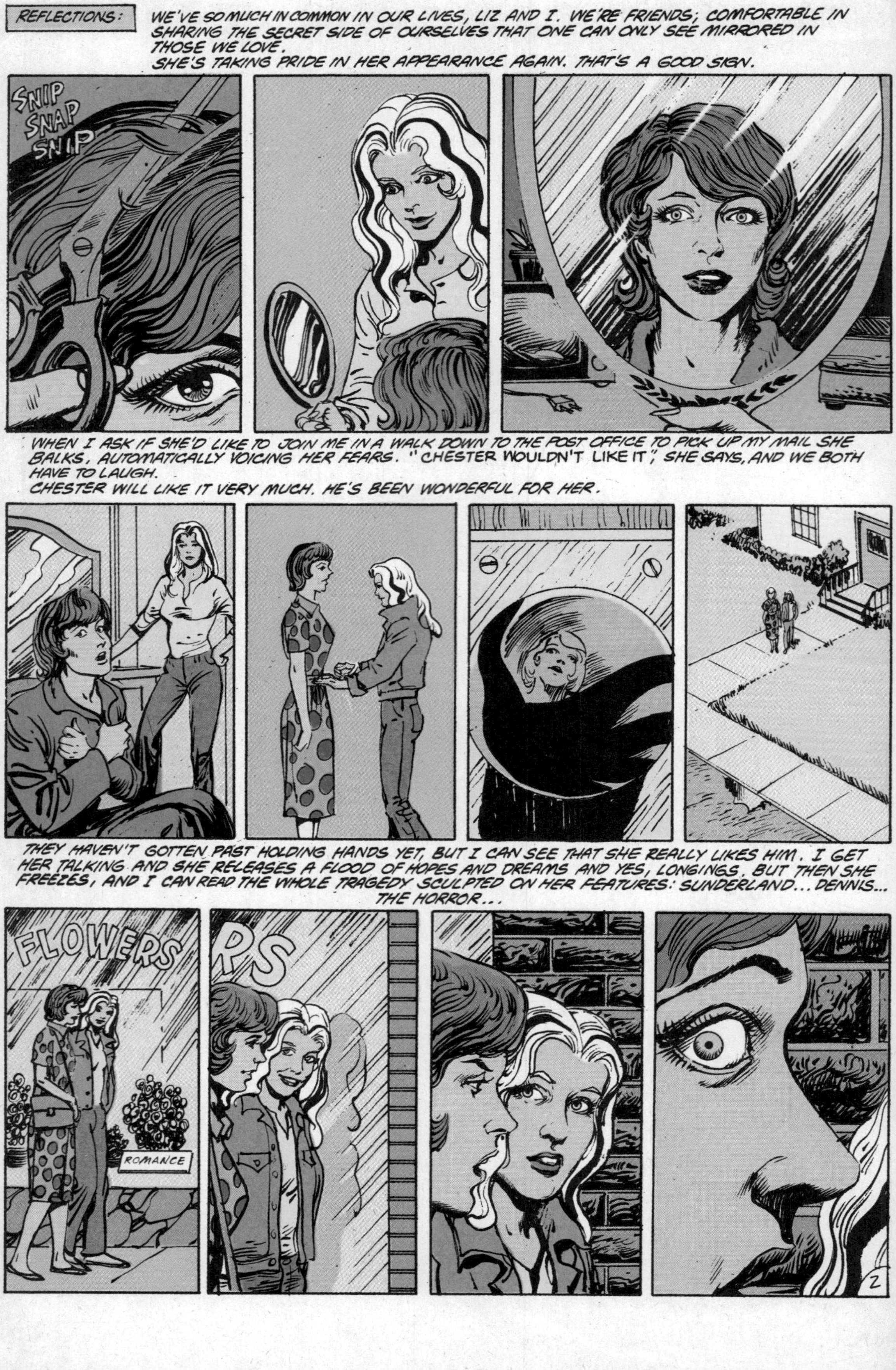
REFLECTIONS:
WE'VE SO MUCH IN COMMON IN OUR LIVES, LIZ AND I. WE'RE FRIENDS; COMFORTABLE IN SHARING THE SECRET SIDE OF OURSELVES THAT ONE CAN ONLY SEE MIRRORED IN THOSE WE LOVE.
SHE'S TAKING PRIDE IN HER APPEARANCE AGAIN. THAT'S A GOOD SIGN.
SNIP SNAP SNIP
WHEN I ASK IF SHE'D LIKE TO JOIN ME IN A WALK DOWN TO THE POST OFFICE TO PICK UP MY MAIL SHE BALKS, AUTOMATICALLY VOICING HER FEARS. "CHESTER WOULDN'T LIKE IT", SHE SAYS, AND WE BOTH HAVE TO LAUGH.
CHESTER WILL LIKE IT VERY MUCH. HE'S BEEN WONDERFUL FOR HER.
THEY HAVEN'T GOTTEN PAST HOLDING HANDS YET, BUT I CAN SEE THAT SHE REALLY LIKES HIM. I GET HER TALKING AND SHE RELEASES A FLOOD OF HOPES AND DREAMS AND YES, LONGINGS. BUT THEN SHE FREEZES, AND I CAN READ THE WHOLE TRAGEDY SCULPTED ON HER FEATURES: SUNDERLAND... DENNIS... THE HORROR...
FLOWERS
ROMANCE
RS
2

REFLECTIONS:

I SHOULD BE JOB-HUNTING BUT INSTEAD I'M DOWN AT THE NEWS-STAND SCANNING THE RACKS FOR ANYTHING THAT MIGHT FIT INTO MY SURE-FIRE FORMULA FOR UNDER-STANDING CURRENT EVENTS.

$$\frac{\text{REAGAN'S AMERIKA}}{\text{POPULAR CULTURE}^2} = \frac{\text{SOME SEMBLANCE}}{\text{OF REALITY}}$$

PICTURE NEWS

THE WHISPER
PRINCESS DIANA: SUPERMAN'S SECRET LOVER

GALA GIRL

VENTURE

SHINY BEAST

POW PSYCHOLOGY

UNDERSTANDING THE SUPERMEN (AND WOMEN)
DR. ROGER HUNTOON

POW! PSYCHOLOGY

ARE THESE TITANS TEEN INSIDE

THIS AIN'T TH' LIBRARY,

FREE HUEY DEWEY LOUIE

UNEMPLOYMENT BENNIES RAN OUT AND MY DEALING CAPITAL WENT FOR THE ECO-GROUP. IF I'M GONNA MAKE THE RENT THIS MONTH IT'S BACK-TO-WORK.

UNNH.

JOB: MINDLESS WORK
INSANE BOSS
REGULAR HOURS
NO TIME TO THINK

HEY, CHESTER!

LONG TIME NO SEE, M'MAN!

UHH..., HI, DO I KNOW YOU?

HOUMA NEWS

KNOW ME? DON'T TELL ME YOU'VE FORGOTTEN WOODSTOCK!? SHEESH, I INTRODUCED YOU TO MY SISTER THERE, BRO!

BACK THEN THEY USED TO CALL ME THE "COSMIC YO-YO." BUT THESE DAYS I'M JUST "LIPPY."

I DON'T REMEMBER MUCH OF WHAT HAPPENED AT WOODSTOCK. IT WAS KIND OF A LOST WEEKEND FOR ME.

BUT IF YOU SAY YOU KNEW ME, I'LL TAKE YOUR WORD FOR IT.

LOTTA BRAIN CELLS OVER THE DAM, EH, BUDDY? LISTEN, I GOT SOME BITCHIN' REEFER...

WHY DON'T WE BOOGIE OVER TO THE PARK AND SEE IF WE CAN JOG SOME OF THOSE MEMORIES LOOSE?

WHERE'D YOU FIND THE SMOKE? WE'VE BEEN DRY EVER SINCE THE CONTRA SCANDALS BROKE.

FRIENDS IN HIGH PLACES, CHESTER, I WORK FOR THIS DUDE WHOSE NAME IS-- GET THIS--ROY RAYMOND!

YOU'RE KIDDING? YOU MEAN FROM THE "INCREDIBLE BUT TRUE" TV SHOW? USED TO COME ON RIGHT BEFORE "THE MUNSTERS"? PHHHHT.

THAT'S HIM, AND HE'S JUST DYING TO MEETCHA.

COME ON, MAN! WHAT WOULD SOME FAMOUS OLD GUY LIKE THAT WANT WITH

KOFF
KOF
KOFKOFKOF

WOOOAW! :KOFF:... KILLER WEED...

FREE HUEY DEWEY

3

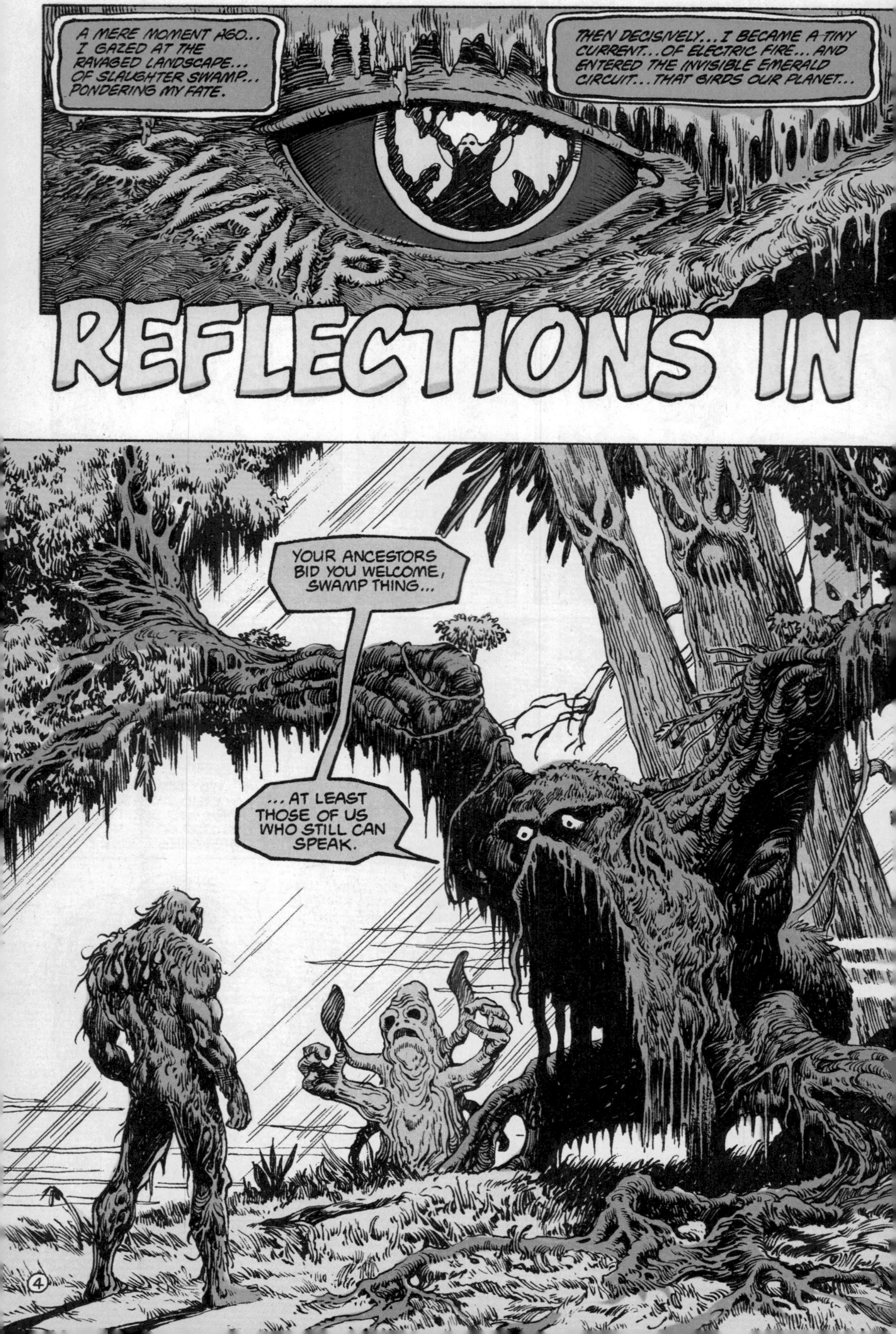
A MERE MOMENT AGO... I GAZED AT THE RAVAGED LANDSCAPE... OF SLAUGHTER SWAMP... PONDERING MY FATE.
THEN DECISIVELY... I BECAME A TINY CURRENT... OF ELECTRIC FIRE... AND ENTERED THE INVISIBLE EMERALD CIRCUIT... THAT GIRDS OUR PLANET...
SWAMP
REFLECTIONS IN
YOUR ANCESTORS BID YOU WELCOME, SWAMP THING...
...AT LEAST THOSE OF US WHO STILL CAN SPEAK.
4

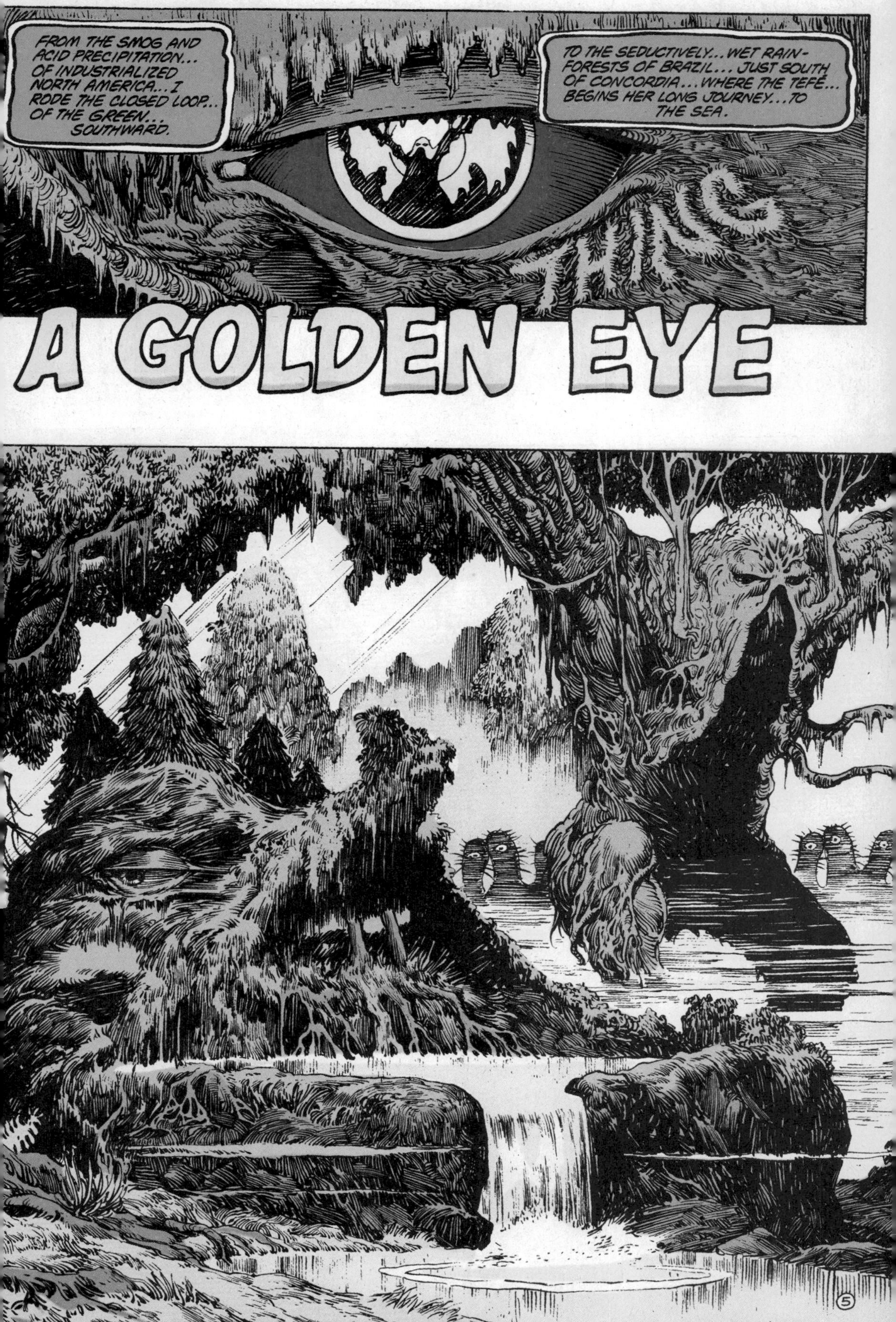
FROM THE SMOG AND ACID PRECIPITATION... OF INDUSTRIALIZED NORTH AMERICA... I RODE THE CLOSED LOOP... OF THE GREEN... SOUTHWARD.
TO THE SEDUCTIVELY...WET RAIN-FORESTS OF BRAZIL... JUST SOUTH OF CONCORDIA... WHERE THE TEFÉ... BEGINS HER LONG JOURNEY... TO THE SEA.
THING
A GOLDEN EYE
5

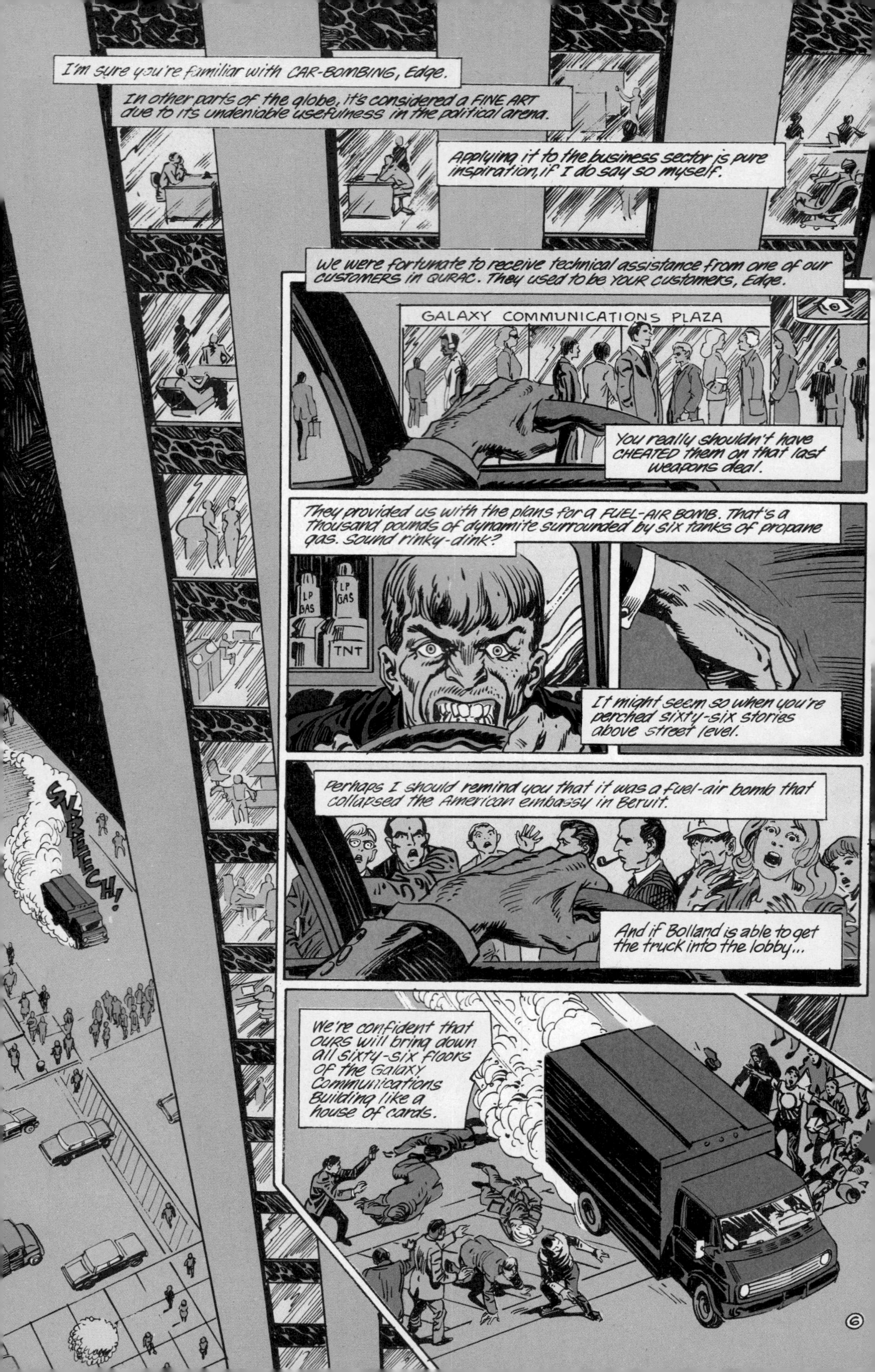

I'm sure you're familiar with CAR-BOMBING, Edge.
In other parts of the globe, it's considered a FINE ART due to its undeniable usefulness in the political arena.
Applying it to the business sector is pure inspiration, if I do say so myself.
We were fortunate to receive technical assistance from one of our CUSTOMERS in QURAC. They used to be YOUR customers, Edge.
GALAXY COMMUNICATIONS PLAZA
You really shouldn't have CHEATED them on that last weapons deal.
They provided us with the plans for a FUEL-AIR BOMB. That's a thousand pounds of dynamite surrounded by six tanks of propane gas. Sound rinky-dink?
LP GAS
LP GAS
TNT
It might seem so when you're perched sixty-six stories above street level.
SKREECH!
Perhaps I should remind you that it was a fuel-air bomb that collapsed the American embassy in Berut.
And if Bolland is able to get the truck into the lobby...
We're confident that OURS will bring down all sixty-six floors of the Galaxy Communications Building like a house of cards.

WHEN LIZ HAS A PANIC ATTACK ON MAIN STREET, HOUMA, I MAKE MATTERS WORSE BY LOSING MY PATIENCE. FOR SOME REASON I'M ANGRY TO SEE HER GIVE UP ALL THE GROUND SHE'S GAINED TO A FEW MEMORIES, NO MATTER HOW HORRIBLE. SHE BEGS TO GO RIGHT HOME BUT I SCOLD HER, INSISTING THAT WE CONTINUE ON TO THE POST OFFICE.

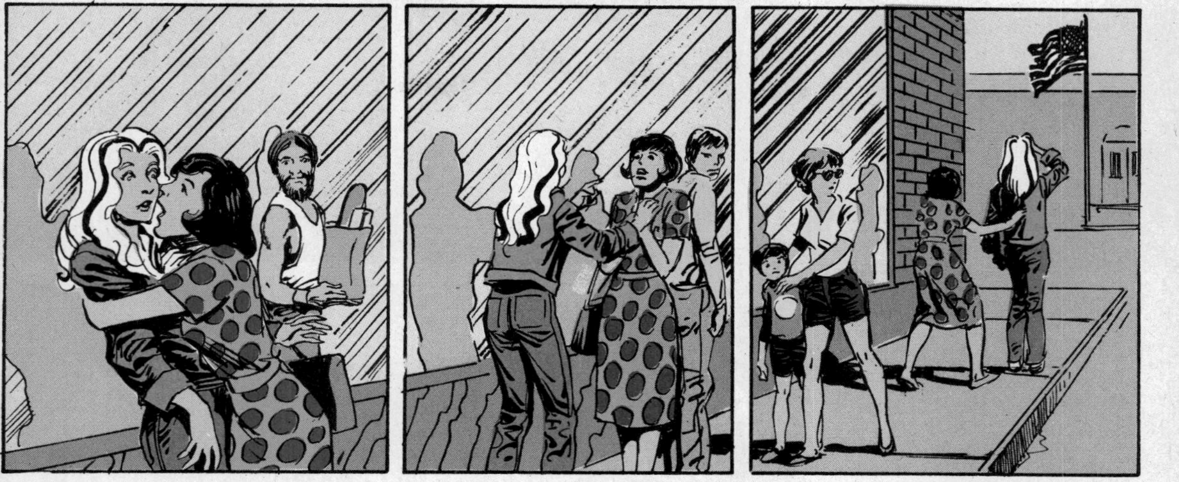

SHE'S SHIVERING AND HANGING ON TO ME RIGHT UP TO THE WINDOW WHERE THE CLERK RECOGNIZES ME FROM THE GOTHAM CITY AFFAIR (I WAS ON TV). HIS OBVIOUS NERVOUSNESS ADDS TO THE FEELING OF PARANOIA AS HE GINGERLY PUSHES MY MAIL ACROSS THE COUNTER.

ALONG WITH THE USUAL JUNKMAIL, THERE ARE SEVEN CHECKS FROM THE UNITED STATES TREASURY.

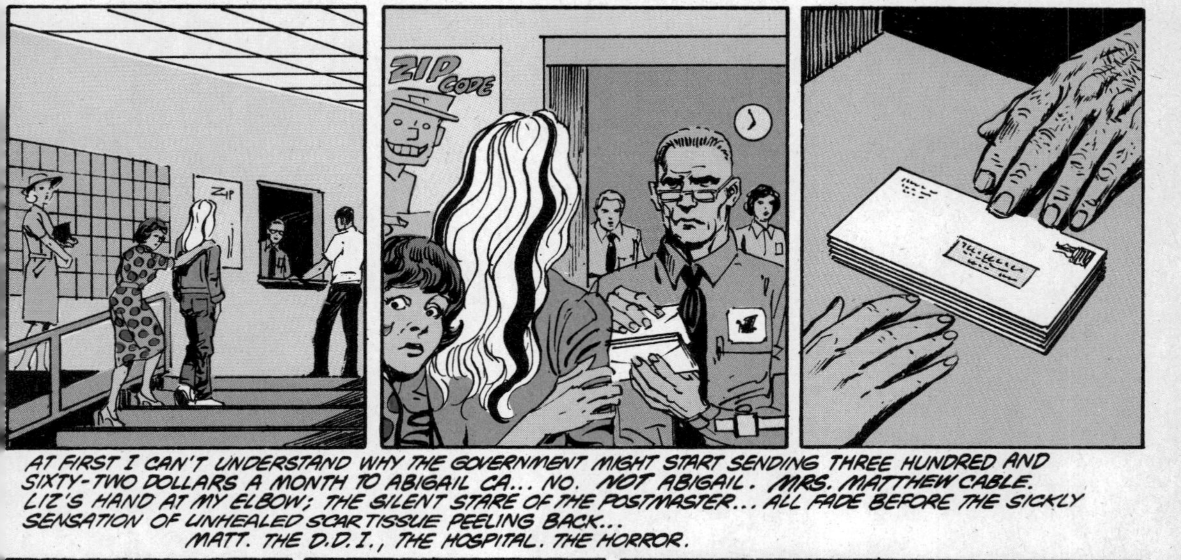
ZIP
ZIP CODE

AT FIRST I CAN'T UNDERSTAND WHY THE GOVERNMENT MIGHT START SENDING THREE HUNDRED AND SIXTY-TWO DOLLARS A MONTH TO ABIGAIL CA... NO. NOT ABIGAIL. MRS. MATTHEW CABLE.

LIZ'S HAND AT MY ELBOW; THE SILENT STARE OF THE POSTMASTER... ALL FADE BEFORE THE SICKLY SENSATION OF UNHEALED SCAR TISSUE PEELING BACK...

MATT. THE D.D.I., THE HOSPITAL. THE HORROR.

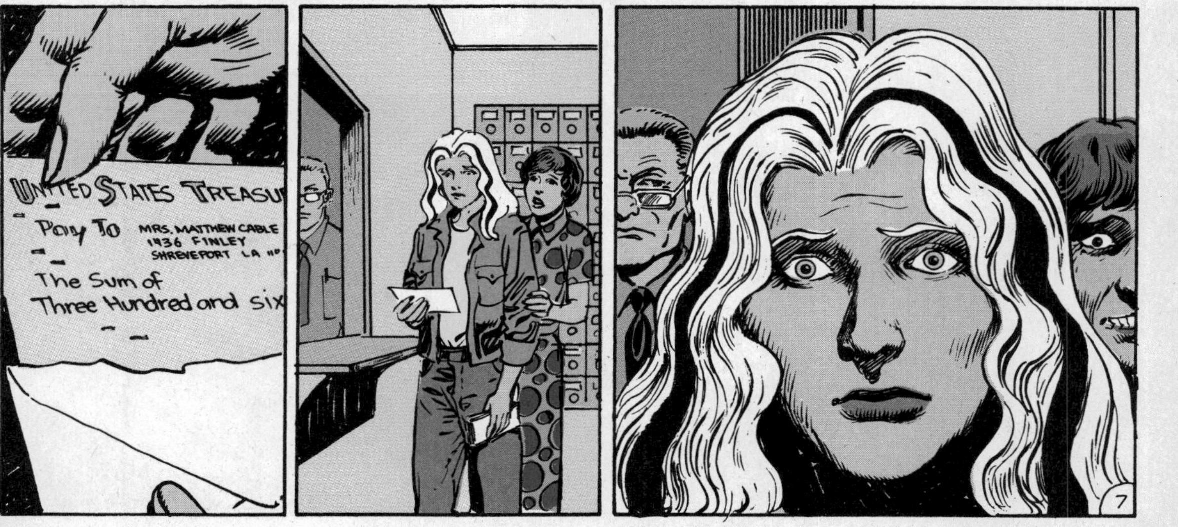
UNITED STATES TREASU
Pay To MRS. MATTHEW CABLE
1936 FINLEY
SHREVEPORT LA
The Sum of
Three Hundred and Six
7

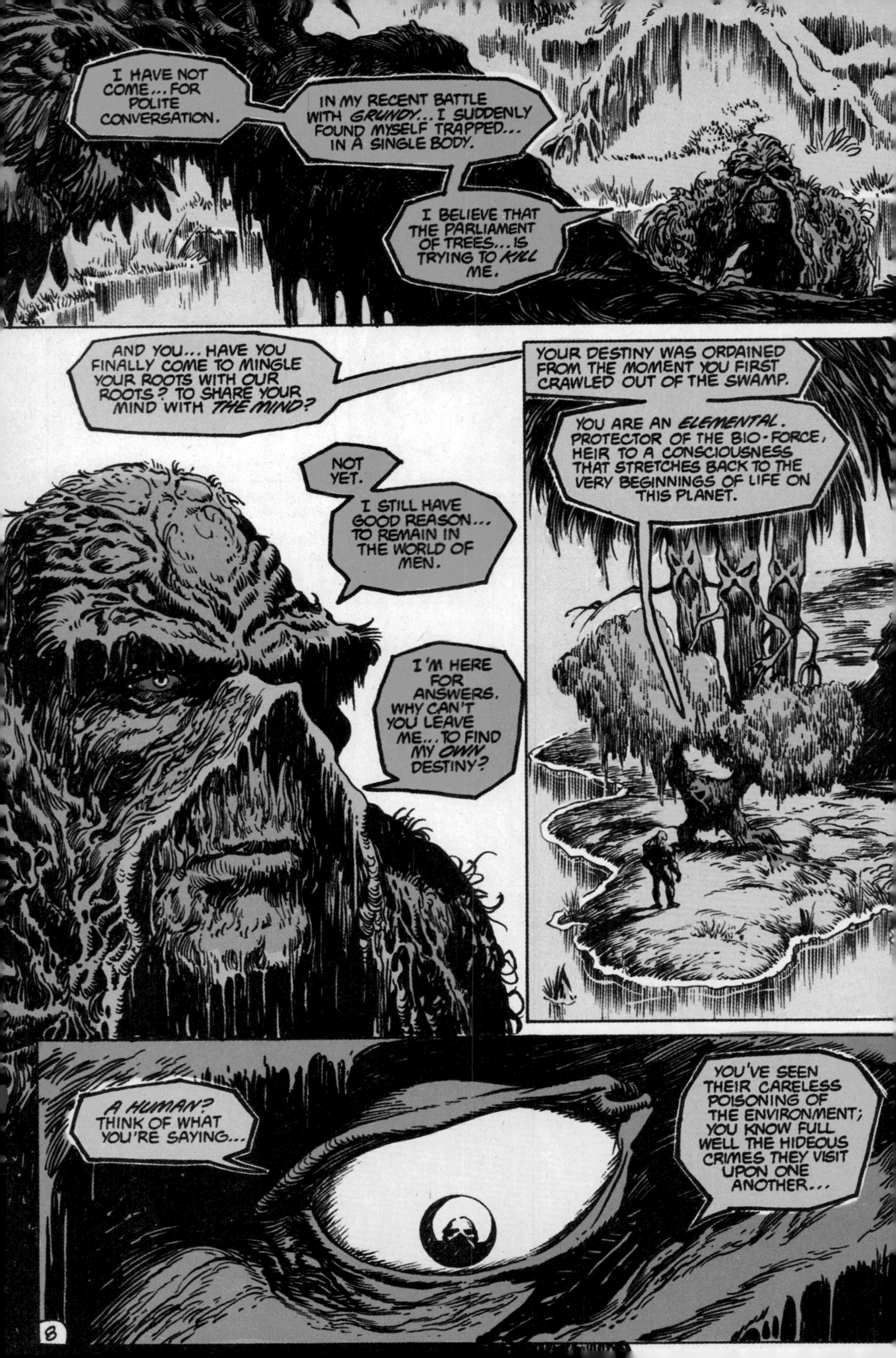
I HAVE NOT COME... FOR POLITE CONVERSATION.
IN MY RECENT BATTLE WITH GRUNDY... I SUDDENLY FOUND MYSELF TRAPPED... IN A SINGLE BODY.
I BELIEVE THAT THE PARLIAMENT OF TREES... IS TRYING TO KILL ME.
AND YOU... HAVE YOU FINALLY COME TO MINGLE YOUR ROOTS WITH OUR ROOTS? TO SHARE YOUR MIND WITH THE MIND?
NOT YET.
I STILL HAVE GOOD REASON... TO REMAIN IN THE WORLD OF MEN.
I'M HERE FOR ANSWERS. WHY CAN'T YOU LEAVE ME... TO FIND MY OWN DESTINY?
YOUR DESTINY WAS ORDAINED FROM THE MOMENT YOU FIRST CRAWLED OUT OF THE SWAMP.
YOU ARE AN ELEMENTAL. PROTECTOR OF THE BIO-FORCE, HEIR TO A CONSCIOUSNESS THAT STRETCHES BACK TO THE VERY BEGINNINGS OF LIFE ON THIS PLANET.
A HUMAN? THINK OF WHAT YOU'RE SAYING...
YOU'VE SEEN THEIR CARELESS POISONING OF THE ENVIRONMENT; YOU KNOW FULL WELL THE HIDEOUS CRIMES THEY VISIT UPON ONE ANOTHER...
8

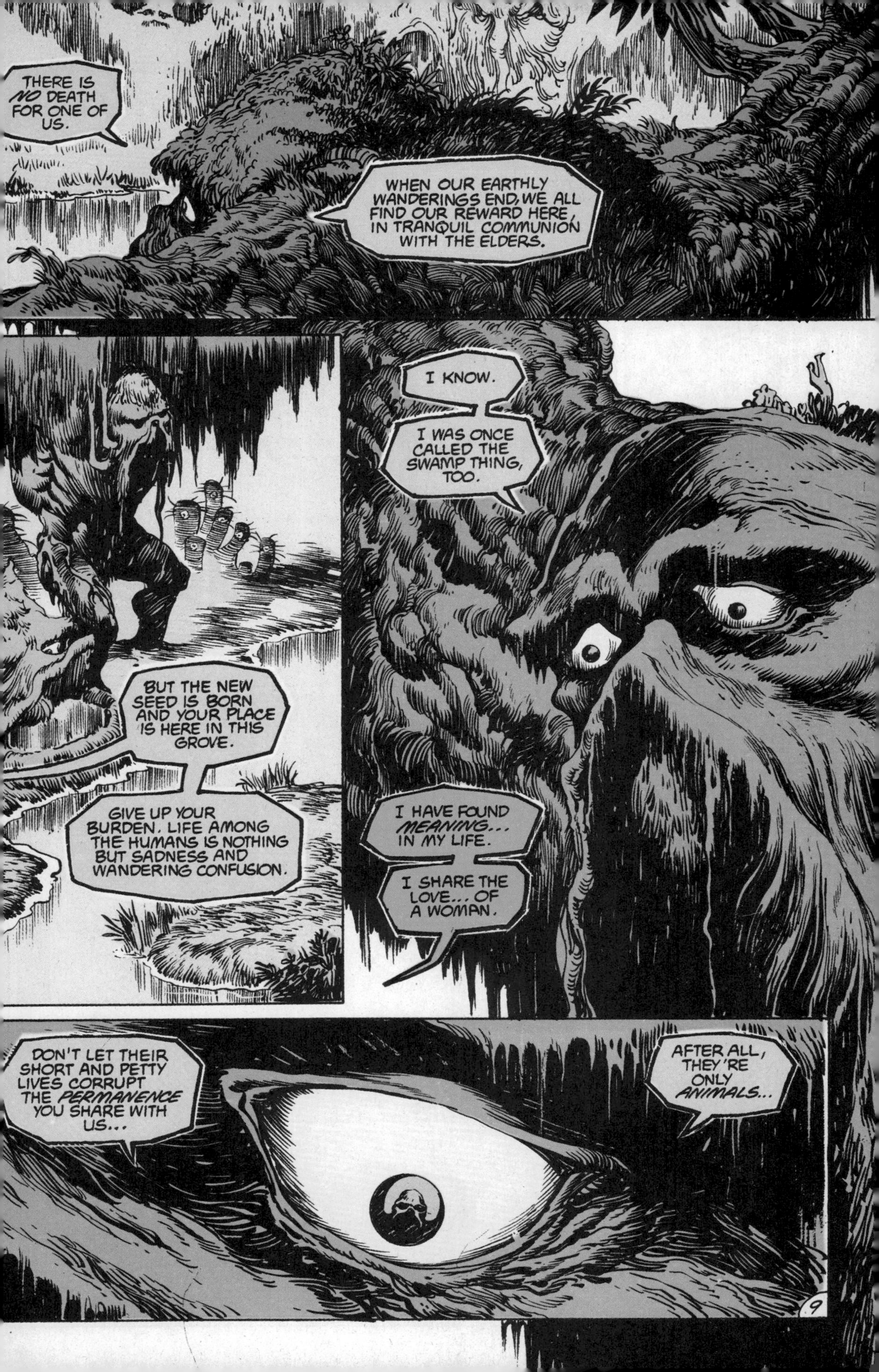
THERE IS NO DEATH FOR ONE OF US.
WHEN OUR EARTHLY WANDERINGS END, WE ALL FIND OUR REWARD HERE, IN TRANQUIL COMMUNION WITH THE ELDERS.
BUT THE NEW SEED IS BORN AND YOUR PLACE IS HERE IN THIS GROVE.
GIVE UP YOUR BURDEN. LIFE AMONG THE HUMANS IS NOTHING BUT SADNESS AND WANDERING CONFUSION.
I KNOW.
I WAS ONCE CALLED THE SWAMP THING, TOO.
I HAVE FOUND MEANING... IN MY LIFE.
I SHARE THE LOVE... OF A WOMAN.
DON'T LET THEIR SHORT AND PETTY LIVES CORRUPT THE PERMANENCE YOU SHARE WITH US...
AFTER ALL, THEY'RE ONLY ANIMALS...
9

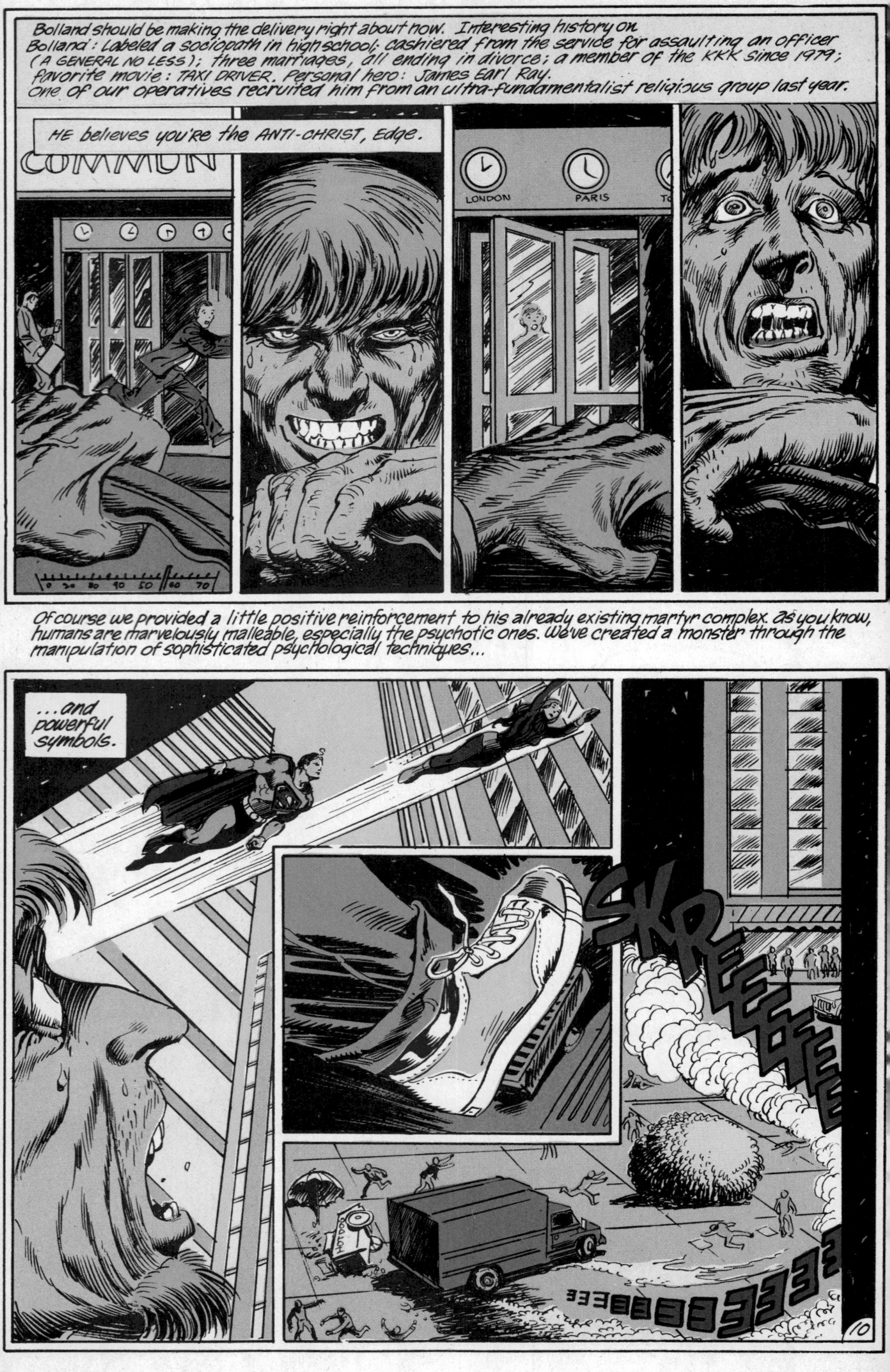
Bolland should be making the delivery right about now. Interesting history on Bolland: Labeled a sociopath in high school; cashiered from the service for assaulting an officer (A GENERAL NO LESS); three marriages, all ending in divorce; a member of the KKK since 1979; favorite movie: TAXI DRIVER. Personal hero: James Earl Ray. One of our operatives recruited him from an ultra-fundamentalist religious group last year.
HE believes you're the ANTI-CHRIST, Edge.
COMMUN
LONDON
PARIS
Of course we provided a little positive reinforcement to his already existing martyr complex. As you know, humans are marvelously malleable, especially the psychotic ones. We've created a monster through the manipulation of sophisticated psychological techniques...
...and powerful symbols.
10

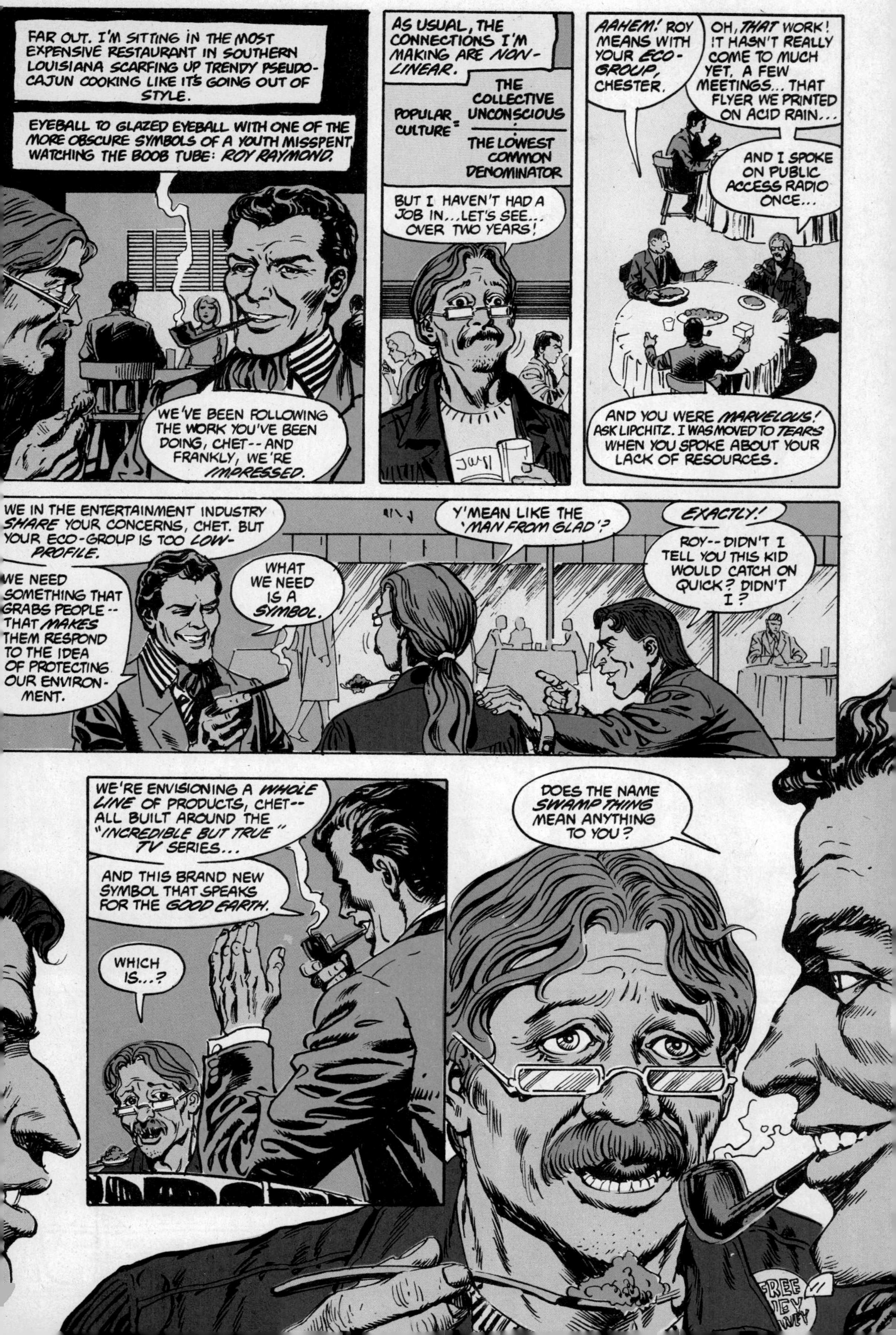
FAR OUT. I'M SITTING IN THE MOST EXPENSIVE RESTAURANT IN SOUTHERN LOUISIANA SCARFING UP TRENDY PSEUDO-CAJUN COOKING LIKE IT'S GOING OUT OF STYLE.
EYEBALL TO GLAZED EYEBALL WITH ONE OF THE MORE OBSCURE SYMBOLS OF A YOUTH MISSPENT WATCHING THE BOOB TUBE: ROY RAYMOND.
WE'VE BEEN FOLLOWING THE WORK YOU'VE BEEN DOING, CHET-- AND FRANKLY, WE'RE IMPRESSED.
AS USUAL, THE CONNECTIONS I'M MAKING ARE NON-LINEAR.
POPULAR CULTURE = THE COLLECTIVE UNCONSCIOUS / THE LOWEST COMMON DENOMINATOR
BUT I HAVEN'T HAD A JOB IN... LET'S SEE... OVER TWO YEARS!
AAHEM! ROY MEANS WITH YOUR ECO-GROUP, CHESTER.
OH, THAT WORK! IT HASN'T REALLY COME TO MUCH YET. A FEW MEETINGS... THAT FLYER WE PRINTED ON ACID RAIN...
AND I SPOKE ON PUBLIC ACCESS RADIO ONCE...
AND YOU WERE MARVELOUS! ASK LIPCHITZ. I WAS MOVED TO TEARS WHEN YOU SPOKE ABOUT YOUR LACK OF RESOURCES.
WE IN THE ENTERTAINMENT INDUSTRY SHARE YOUR CONCERNS, CHET. BUT YOUR ECO-GROUP IS TOO LOW-PROFILE.
WE NEED SOMETHING THAT GRABS PEOPLE-- THAT MAKES THEM RESPOND TO THE IDEA OF PROTECTING OUR ENVIRONMENT.
WHAT WE NEED IS A SYMBOL.
Y'MEAN LIKE THE 'MAN FROM GLAD'?
EXACTLY!
ROY-- DIDN'T I TELL YOU THIS KID WOULD CATCH ON QUICK? DIDN'T I?
WE'RE ENVISIONING A WHOLE LINE OF PRODUCTS, CHET-- ALL BUILT AROUND THE "INCREDIBLE BUT TRUE" TV SERIES...
AND THIS BRAND NEW SYMBOL THAT SPEAKS FOR THE GOOD EARTH.
WHICH IS...?
DOES THE NAME SWAMP THING MEAN ANYTHING TO YOU?

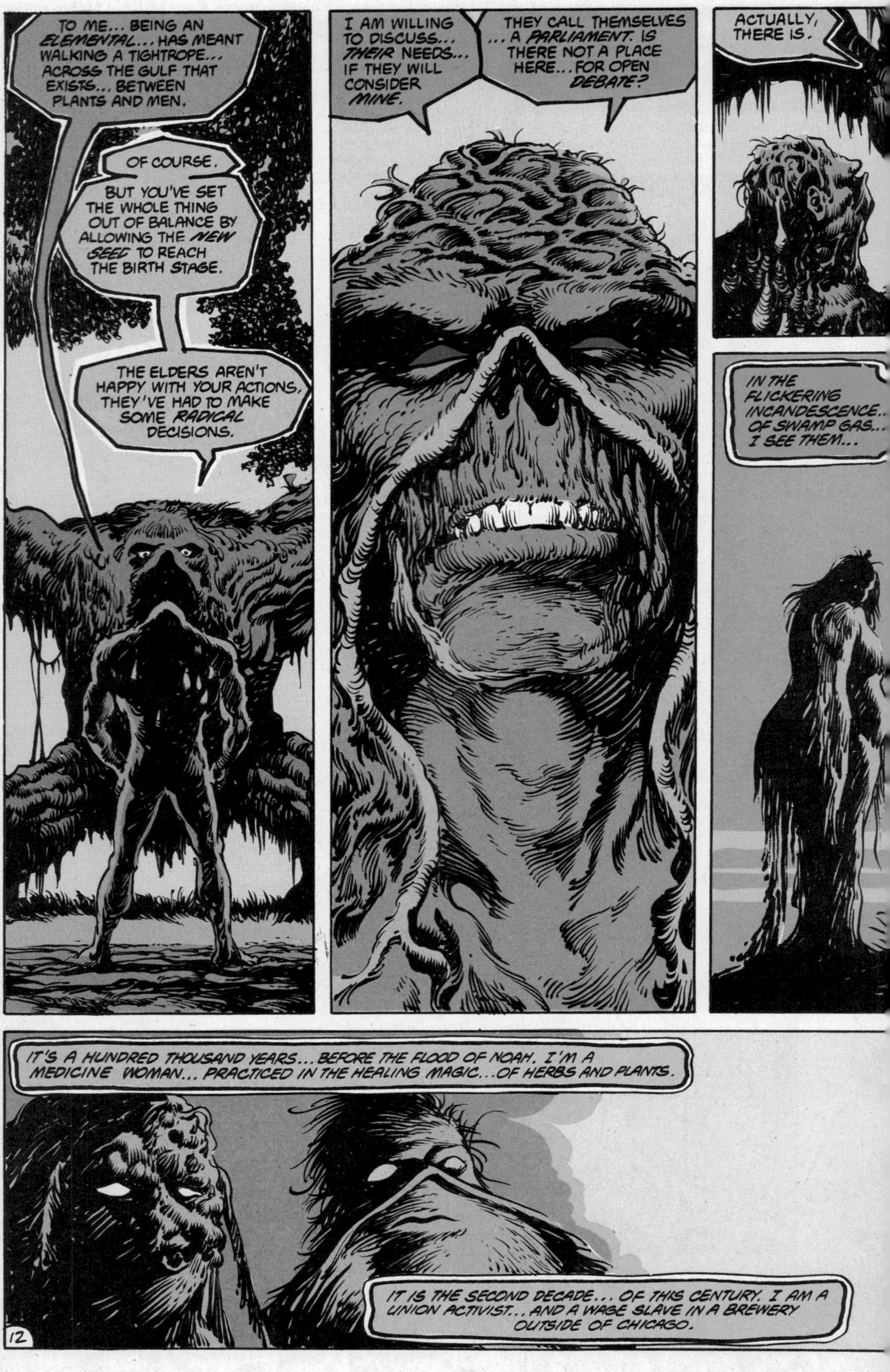
TO ME... BEING AN ELEMENTAL... HAS MEANT WALKING A TIGHTROPE... ACROSS THE GULF THAT EXISTS... BETWEEN PLANTS AND MEN.
OF COURSE.
BUT YOU'VE SET THE WHOLE THING OUT OF BALANCE BY ALLOWING THE NEW SEED TO REACH THE BIRTH STAGE.
THE ELDERS AREN'T HAPPY WITH YOUR ACTIONS. THEY'VE HAD TO MAKE SOME RADICAL DECISIONS.
I AM WILLING TO DISCUSS... THEIR NEEDS... IF THEY WILL CONSIDER MINE.
THEY CALL THEMSELVES ... A PARLIAMENT. IS THERE NOT A PLACE HERE... FOR OPEN DEBATE?
ACTUALLY, THERE IS.
IN THE FLICKERING INCANDESCENCE... OF SWAMP GAS... I SEE THEM...
IT'S A HUNDRED THOUSAND YEARS... BEFORE THE FLOOD OF NOAH. I'M A MEDICINE WOMAN... PRACTICED IN THE HEALING MAGIC... OF HERBS AND PLANTS.
IT IS THE SECOND DECADE... OF THIS CENTURY. I AM A UNION ACTIVIST... AND A WAGE SLAVE IN A BREWERY OUTSIDE OF CHICAGO.
12

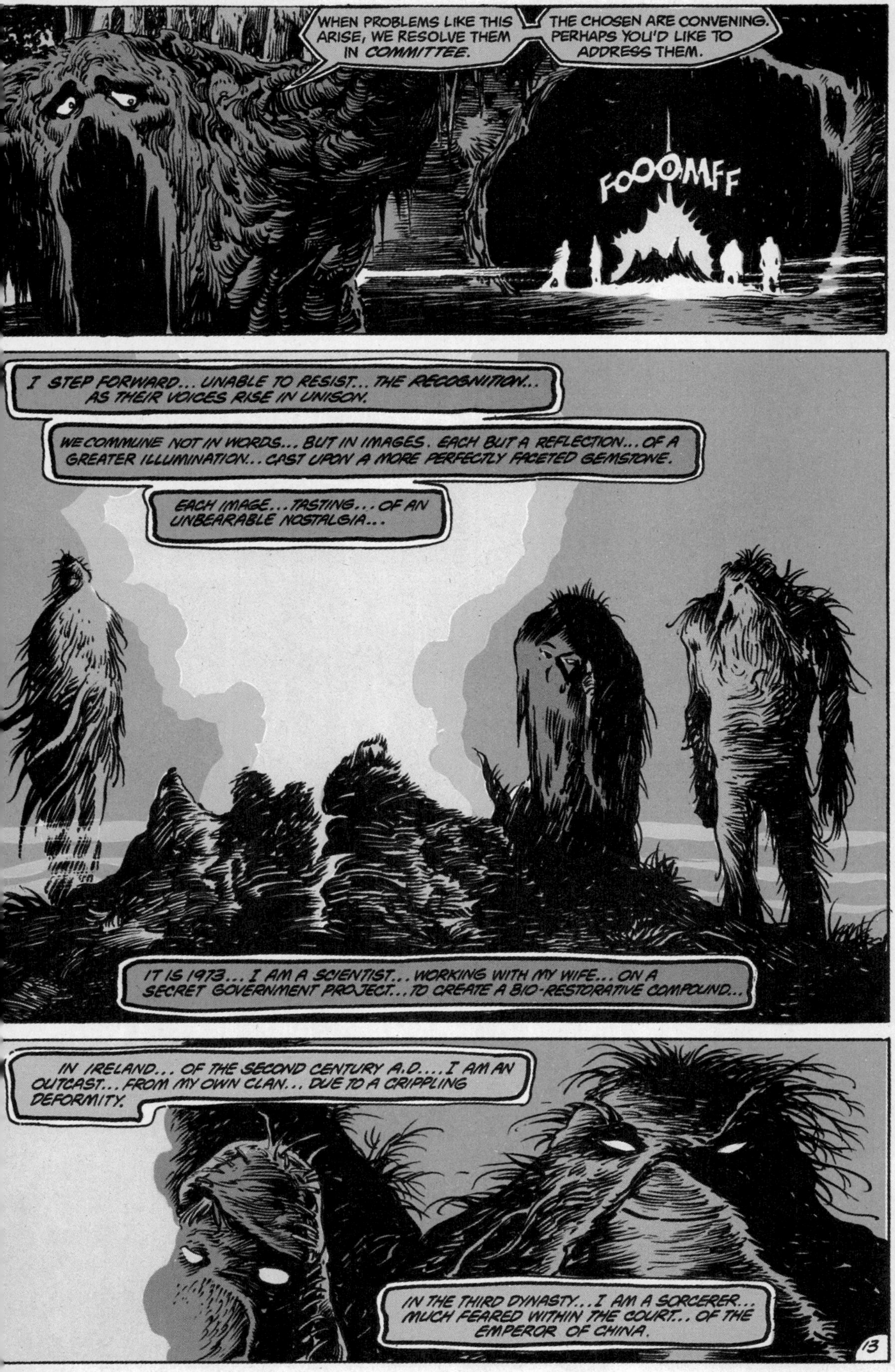
WHEN PROBLEMS LIKE THIS ARISE, WE RESOLVE THEM IN COMMITTEE.
THE CHOSEN ARE CONVENING. PERHAPS YOU'D LIKE TO ADDRESS THEM.
FOOOMFF
I STEP FORWARD... UNABLE TO RESIST... THE RECOGNITION... AS THEIR VOICES RISE IN UNISON.
WE COMMUNE NOT IN WORDS... BUT IN IMAGES. EACH BUT A REFLECTION... OF A GREATER ILLUMINATION... CAST UPON A MORE PERFECTLY FACETED GEMSTONE.
EACH IMAGE... TASTING... OF AN UNBEARABLE NOSTALGIA...
IT IS 1973... I AM A SCIENTIST... WORKING WITH MY WIFE... ON A SECRET GOVERNMENT PROJECT... TO CREATE A BIO-RESTORATIVE COMPOUND...
IN IRELAND... OF THE SECOND CENTURY A.D.... I AM AN OUTCAST... FROM MY OWN CLAN... DUE TO A CRIPPLING DEFORMITY.
IN THE THIRD DYNASTY... I AM A SORCERER... MUCH FEARED WITHIN THE COURT... OF THE EMPEROR OF CHINA.
13

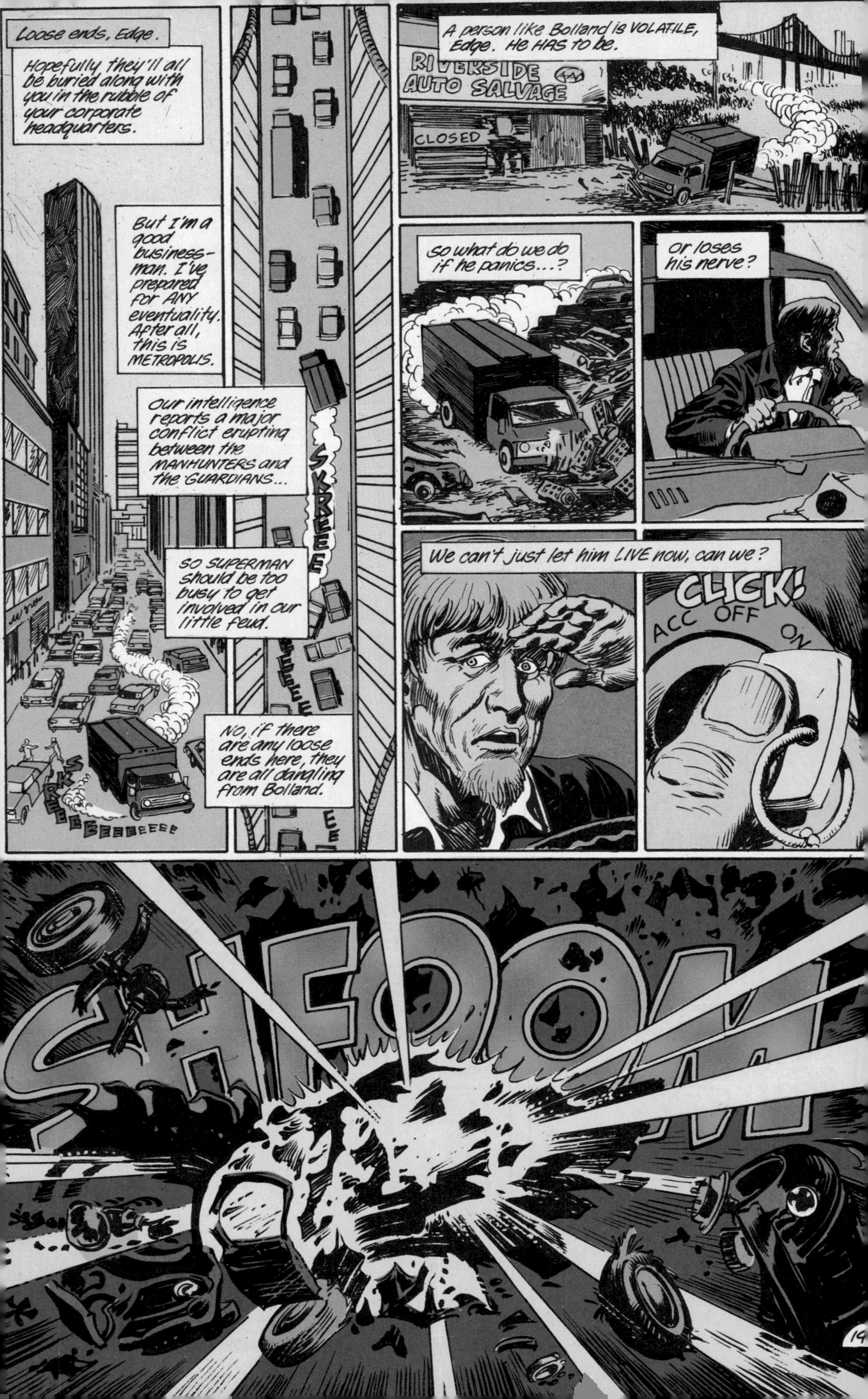
Loose ends, Edge.
Hopefully they'll all be buried along with you in the rubble of your corporate headquarters.
But I'm a good business-man. I've prepared for ANY eventuality. After all, this is METROPOLIS.
Our intelligence reports a major conflict erupting between the MANHUNTERS and the GUARDIANS...
SO SUPERMAN should be too busy to get involved in our little feud.
SKREEEEEEEEEE
No, if there are any loose ends here, they are all dangling from Bolland.
SKREEE
A person like Bolland is VOLATILE, Edge. He HAS to be.
RIVERSIDE AUTO SALVAGE
CLOSED
So what do we do if he panics...?
Or loses his nerve?
We can't just let him LIVE now, can we?
CLICK!
ACC OFF ON

THE ARRIVAL OF THE GOVERNMENT CHECKS HAS THE EFFECT OF A WRECKING BALL ON THE FORTRESS OF MY EMOTIONS. ONE BY ONE, THE LEVELS, SO SECURELY ANCHORED IN PLACE, BEGIN TO BUCKLE, THEN COLLAPSE UPON ONE ANOTHER, BURYING MY COMPOSURE IN A SMOKING RUIN OF MEMORIES, DREAMS AND REFLECTIONS. I STAGGER OUT OF THE POST OFFICE LIKE SOMEONE UNDER AN ANESTHETIC.

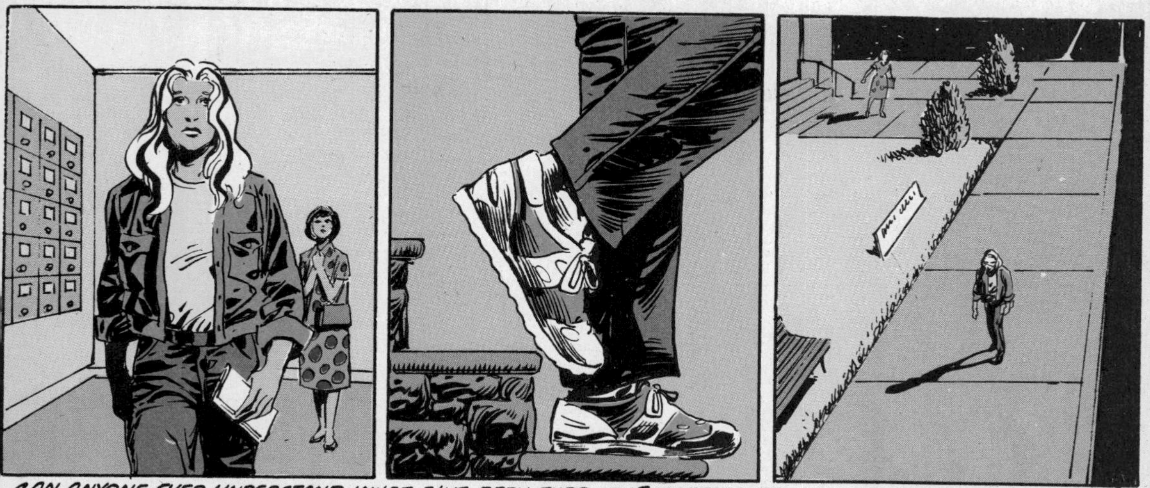

CAN ANYONE EVER UNDERSTAND WHAT I'VE BEEN THROUGH? DADDY'S DEATH... GROWING UP UNDER THE SHADOW OF CASTLE ARCANE... WHAT HAPPENED TO MATT. THANK GOD I WAS ABLE TO FIND ALEC. I DON'T EVEN KNOW WHERE I'VE FOUND THE STRENGTH I'VE NEEDED JUST TO SURVIVE. BUT WHEN I FEEL LIKE THIS, I'M CONVINCED THAT NO ONE CAN EVER UNDERSTAND THE DEPTH OF MY PAIN. NOT EVEN ALEC.

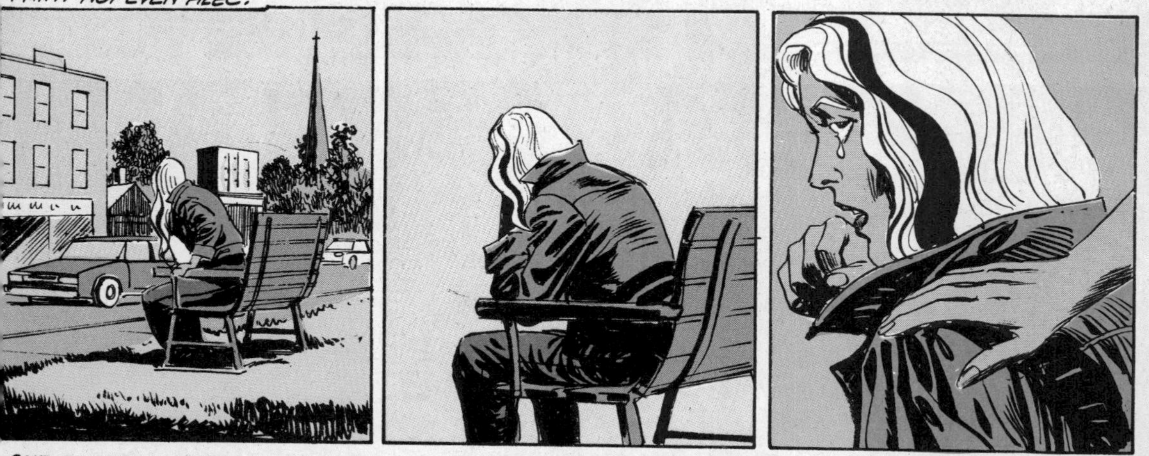

AND SUDDENLY THERE'S A HAND ON MY SHOULDER WHOSE TOUCH SPEAKS OF VIOLATION, HUMILIATION, AND A LONELY STRUGGLE FOR SIMPLE IDENTITY. AS THE HAND SLIPS NATURALLY INTO MY OWN A VOICE MURMURS WITH HARD-WON WISDOM: "ALL WE HAVE IN COMMON... IS THE HORROR," IT SAYS.

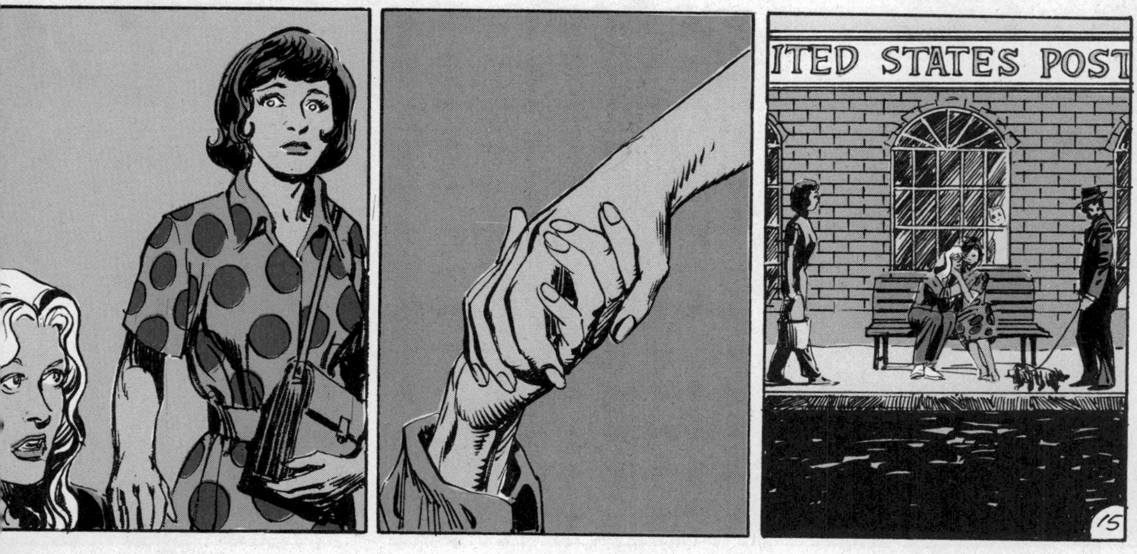
ITED STATES POST
15

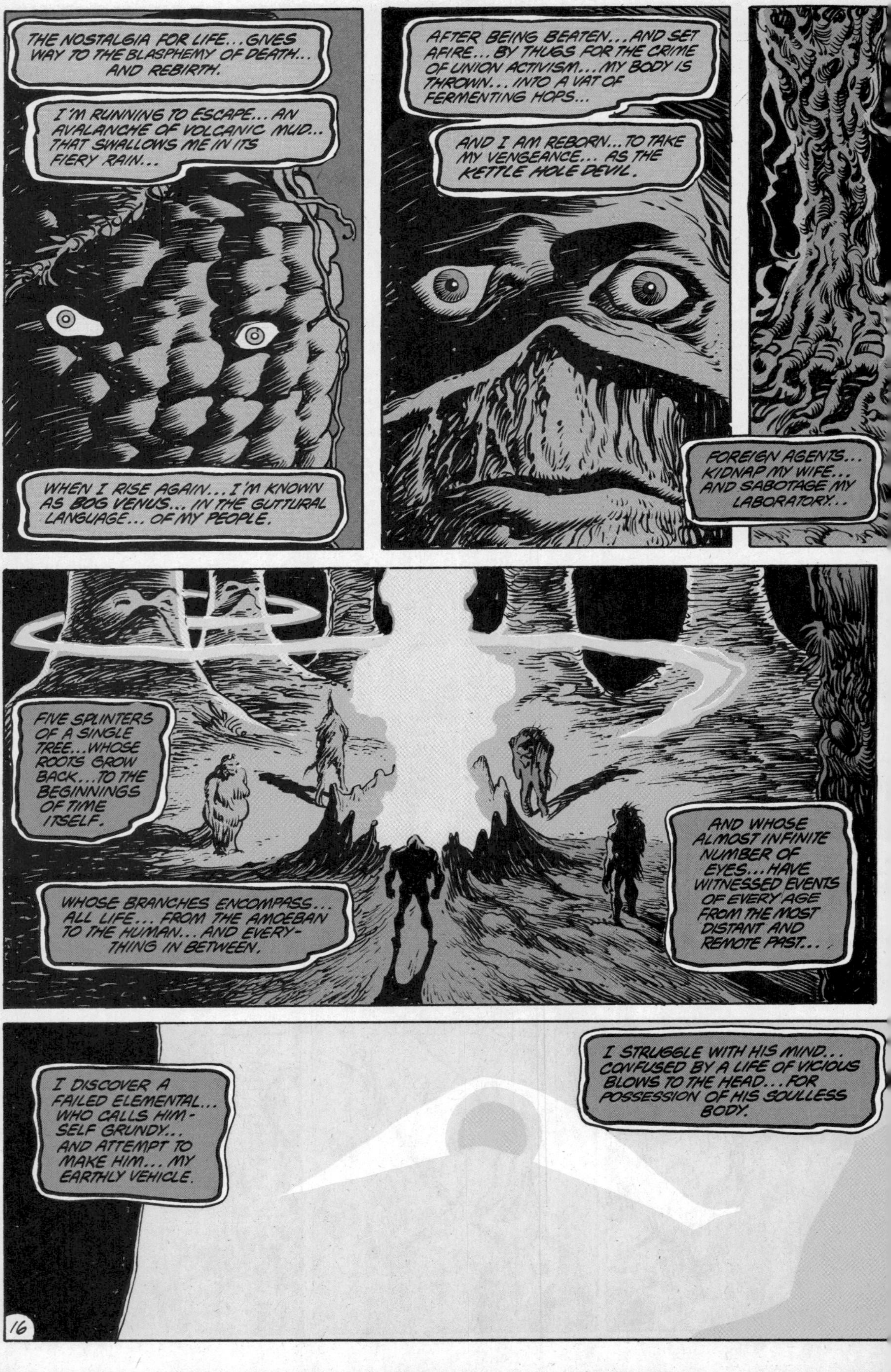
THE NOSTALGIA FOR LIFE... GIVES WAY TO THE BLASPHEMY OF DEATH... AND REBIRTH.
I'M RUNNING TO ESCAPE... AN AVALANCHE OF VOLCANIC MUD... THAT SWALLOWS ME IN ITS FIERY RAIN...
WHEN I RISE AGAIN... I'M KNOWN AS BOG VENUS... IN THE GUTTURAL LANGUAGE... OF MY PEOPLE.
AFTER BEING BEATEN... AND SET AFIRE... BY THUGS FOR THE CRIME OF UNION ACTIVISM... MY BODY IS THROWN... INTO A VAT OF FERMENTING HOPS...
AND I AM REBORN... TO TAKE MY VENGEANCE... AS THE KETTLE HOLE DEVIL.
FOREIGN AGENTS... KIDNAP MY WIFE... AND SABOTAGE MY LABORATORY...
FIVE SPLINTERS OF A SINGLE TREE... WHOSE ROOTS GROW BACK... TO THE BEGINNINGS OF TIME ITSELF.
WHOSE BRANCHES ENCOMPASS... ALL LIFE... FROM THE AMOEBAN TO THE HUMAN... AND EVERY-THING IN BETWEEN.
AND WHOSE ALMOST INFINITE NUMBER OF EYES... HAVE WITNESSED EVENTS OF EVERY AGE FROM THE MOST DISTANT AND REMOTE PAST...
I DISCOVER A FAILED ELEMENTAL... WHO CALLS HIM-SELF GRUNDY... AND ATTEMPT TO MAKE HIM... MY EARTHLY VEHICLE.
I STRUGGLE WITH HIS MIND... CONFUSED BY A LIFE OF VICIOUS BLOWS TO THE HEAD... FOR POSSESSION OF HIS SOULLESS BODY.
16

AFTER A LAST MEAL...OF BARLEY AND LINDSEED GRUEL...THEY HANG ME...AND THROW MY REMAINS INTO THE BOG...AS A SACRIFICE TO BEL, THE SUN GOD.

AGES LATER...WHEN I FINALLY ARISE FROM MY DARK CASKET OF PEAT...THERE IS A NEW GOD...AND HIS BELIEVERS NAME ME SAINT COLUMBA.

WHEN MY EXPERIMENTS...EXPLODE IN MY FACE...I BECOME A HUMAN TORCH...AND DIVE SCREAMING INTO THE SWAMP.

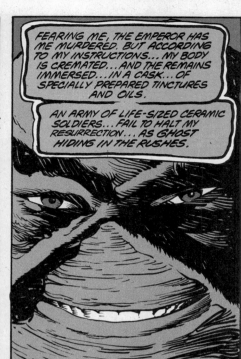

FEARING ME, THE EMPEROR HAS ME MURDERED. BUT ACCORDING TO MY INSTRUCTIONS...MY BODY IS CREMATED...AND THE REMAINS IMMERSED...IN A CASK...OF SPECIALLY PREPARED TINCTURES AND OILS.

AN ARMY OF LIFE-SIZED CERAMIC SOLDIERS...FAIL TO HALT MY RESURRECTION...AS GHOST HIDING IN THE RUSHES.

...TO THE IMMEDIATE PRESENT.

THE NEW ONE JOINS US...THE AGONIES OF BIRTH...ALREADY STAINING A MEMORY...THAT SHOULD BE PURE AND FRESH...

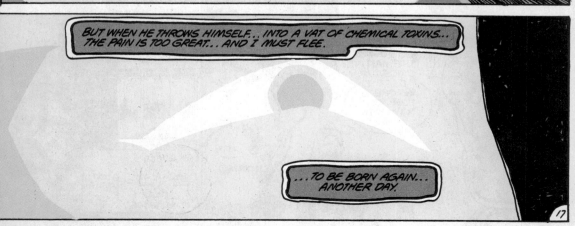

BUT WHEN HE THROWS HIMSELF...INTO A VAT OF CHEMICAL TOXINS...THE PAIN IS TOO GREAT...AND I MUST FLEE.

...TO BE BORN AGAIN...ANOTHER DAY.

17

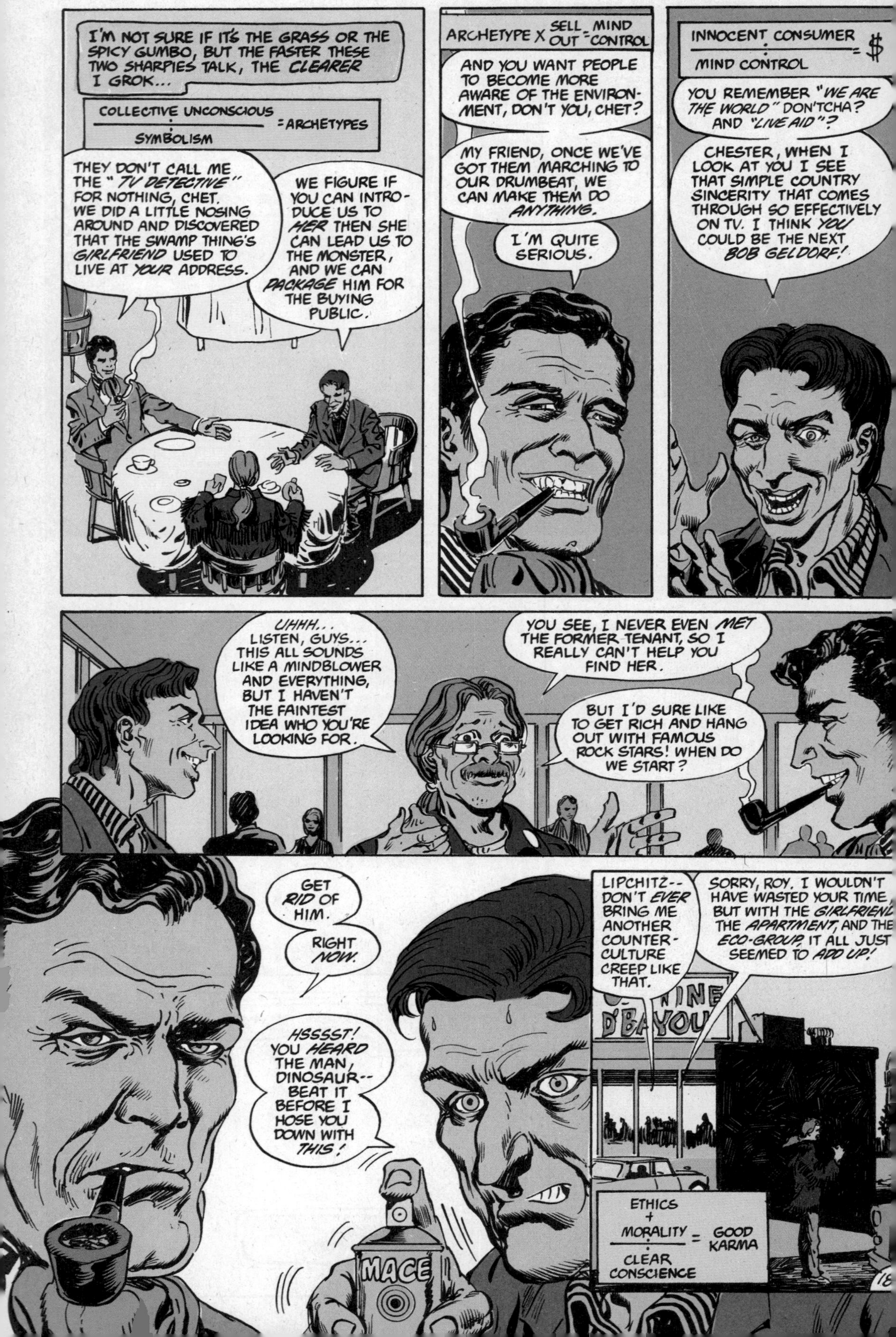
I'M NOT SURE IF IT'S THE GRASS OR THE SPICY GUMBO, BUT THE FASTER THESE TWO SHARPIES TALK, THE CLEARER I GROK...
COLLECTIVE UNCONSCIOUS ÷ SYMBOLISM = ARCHETYPES
THEY DON'T CALL ME THE "TV DETECTIVE" FOR NOTHING, CHET. WE DID A LITTLE NOSING AROUND AND DISCOVERED THAT THE SWAMP THING'S GIRLFRIEND USED TO LIVE AT YOUR ADDRESS.
WE FIGURE IF YOU CAN INTRODUCE US TO HER THEN SHE CAN LEAD US TO THE MONSTER, AND WE CAN PACKAGE HIM FOR THE BUYING PUBLIC.
ARCHETYPE X SELL OUT = MIND CONTROL
AND YOU WANT PEOPLE TO BECOME MORE AWARE OF THE ENVIRONMENT, DON'T YOU, CHET?
MY FRIEND, ONCE WE'VE GOT THEM MARCHING TO OUR DRUMBEAT, WE CAN MAKE THEM DO ANYTHING.
I'M QUITE SERIOUS.
INNOCENT CONSUMER ÷ MIND CONTROL = $
YOU REMEMBER "WE ARE THE WORLD" DON'TCHA? AND "LIVE AID"?
CHESTER, WHEN I LOOK AT YOU I SEE THAT SIMPLE COUNTRY SINCERITY THAT COMES THROUGH SO EFFECTIVELY ON TV. I THINK YOU COULD BE THE NEXT BOB GELDORF!
UHHH... LISTEN, GUYS... THIS ALL SOUNDS LIKE A MINDBLOWER AND EVERYTHING, BUT I HAVEN'T THE FAINTEST IDEA WHO YOU'RE LOOKING FOR.
YOU SEE, I NEVER EVEN MET THE FORMER TENANT, SO I REALLY CAN'T HELP YOU FIND HER.
BUT I'D SURE LIKE TO GET RICH AND HANG OUT WITH FAMOUS ROCK STARS! WHEN DO WE START?
GET RID OF HIM.
RIGHT NOW.
HSSSST! YOU HEARD THE MAN, DINOSAUR-- BEAT IT BEFORE I HOSE YOU DOWN WITH THIS!
MACE
LIPCHITZ-- DON'T EVER BRING ME ANOTHER COUNTER-CULTURE CREEP LIKE THAT.
SORRY, ROY. I WOULDN'T HAVE WASTED YOUR TIME, BUT WITH THE GIRLFRIEND, THE APARTMENT, AND THE ECO-GROUP, IT ALL JUST SEEMED TO ADD UP!
D'BAYOU
ETHICS + MORALITY ÷ CLEAR CONSCIENCE = GOOD KARMA

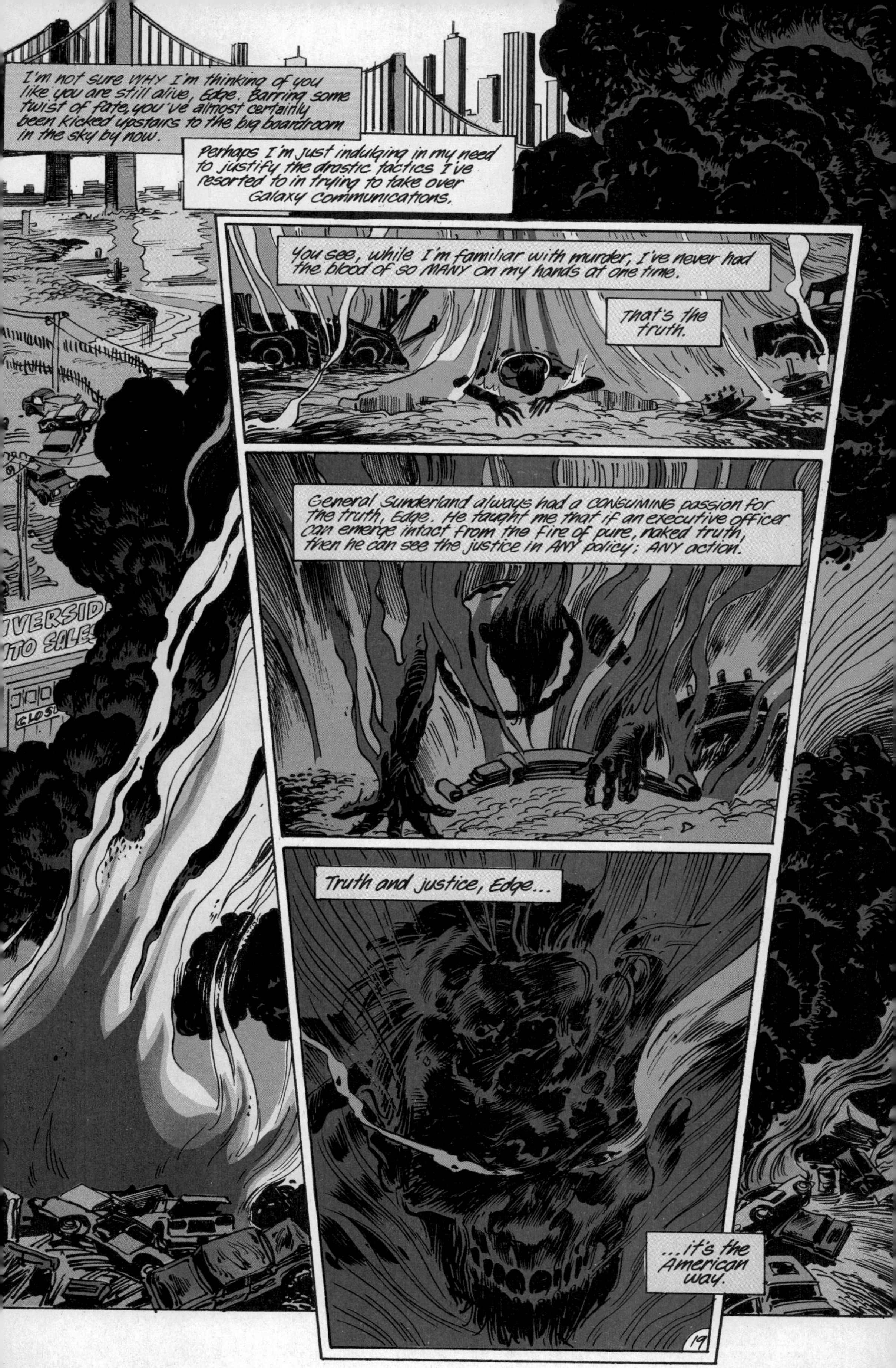

I'm not sure WHY I'm thinking of you like you are still alive, Edge. Barring some twist of fate, you've almost certainly been kicked upstairs to the big boardroom in the sky by now.
Perhaps I'm just indulging in my need to justify the drastic tactics I've resorted to in trying to take over Galaxy Communications.
You see, while I'm familiar with murder, I've never had the blood of so MANY on my hands at one time.
That's the truth.
General Sunderland always had a CONSUMING passion for the truth, Edge. He taught me that if an executive officer can emerge intact from the fire of pure, naked truth, then he can see the justice in ANY policy; ANY action.
Truth and justice, Edge...
...it's the American way.
19

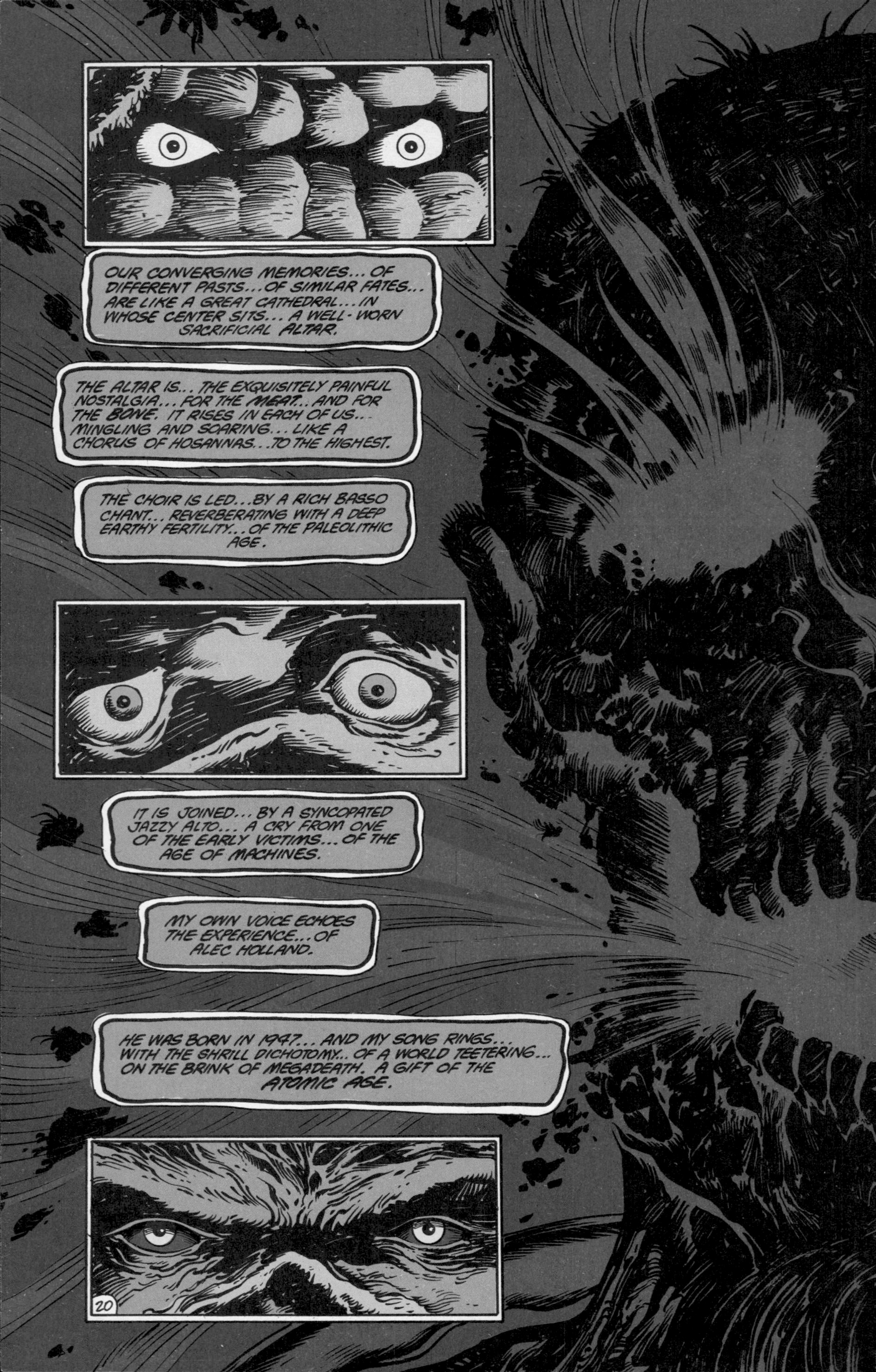
OUR CONVERGING MEMORIES... OF DIFFERENT PASTS...OF SIMILAR FATES... ARE LIKE A GREAT CATHEDRAL... IN WHOSE CENTER SITS... A WELL-WORN SACRIFICIAL ALTAR.
THE ALTAR IS... THE EXQUISITELY PAINFUL NOSTALGIA... FOR THE MEAT... AND FOR THE BONE. IT RISES IN EACH OF US... MINGLING AND SOARING... LIKE A CHORUS OF HOSANNAS...TO THE HIGHEST.
THE CHOIR IS LED...BY A RICH BASSO CHANT... REVERBERATING WITH A DEEP EARTHY FERTILITY...OF THE PALEOLITHIC AGE.
IT IS JOINED... BY A SYNCOPATED JAZZY ALTO... A CRY FROM ONE OF THE EARLY VICTIMS... OF THE AGE OF MACHINES.
MY OWN VOICE ECHOES THE EXPERIENCE...OF ALEC HOLLAND.
HE WAS BORN IN 1947... AND MY SONG RINGS... WITH THE SHRILL DICHOTOMY... OF A WORLD TEETERING... ON THE BRINK OF MEGADEATH. A GIFT OF THE ATOMIC AGE.
20

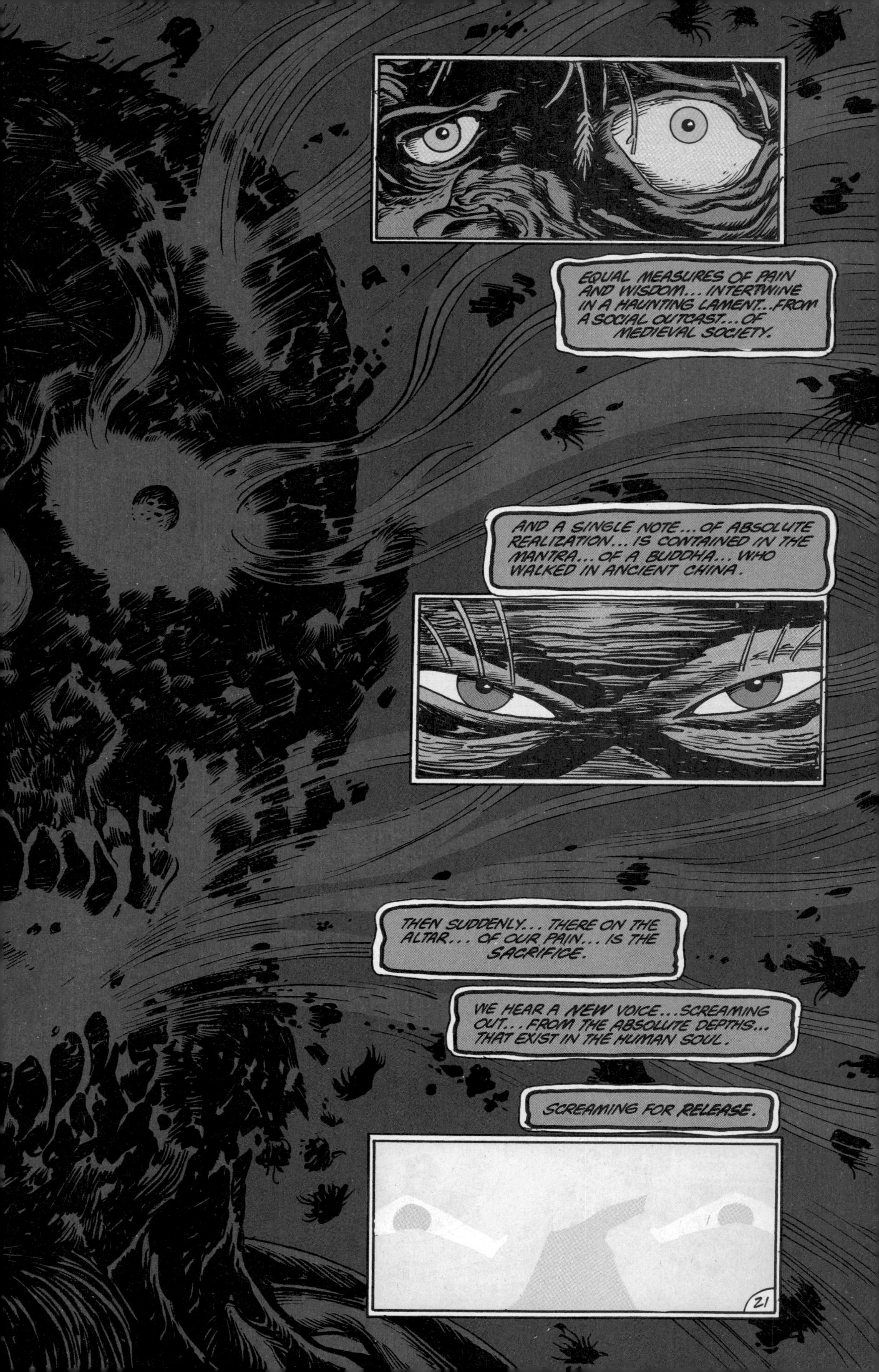
EQUAL MEASURES OF PAIN AND WISDOM... INTERTWINE IN A HAUNTING LAMENT...FROM A SOCIAL OUTCAST...OF MEDIEVAL SOCIETY.
AND A SINGLE NOTE... OF ABSOLUTE REALIZATION... IS CONTAINED IN THE MANTRA... OF A BUDDHA... WHO WALKED IN ANCIENT CHINA.
THEN SUDDENLY... THERE ON THE ALTAR... OF OUR PAIN... IS THE SACRIFICE.
WE HEAR A NEW VOICE...SCREAMING OUT...FROM THE ABSOLUTE DEPTHS... THAT EXIST IN THE HUMAN SOUL.
SCREAMING FOR RELEASE.
21

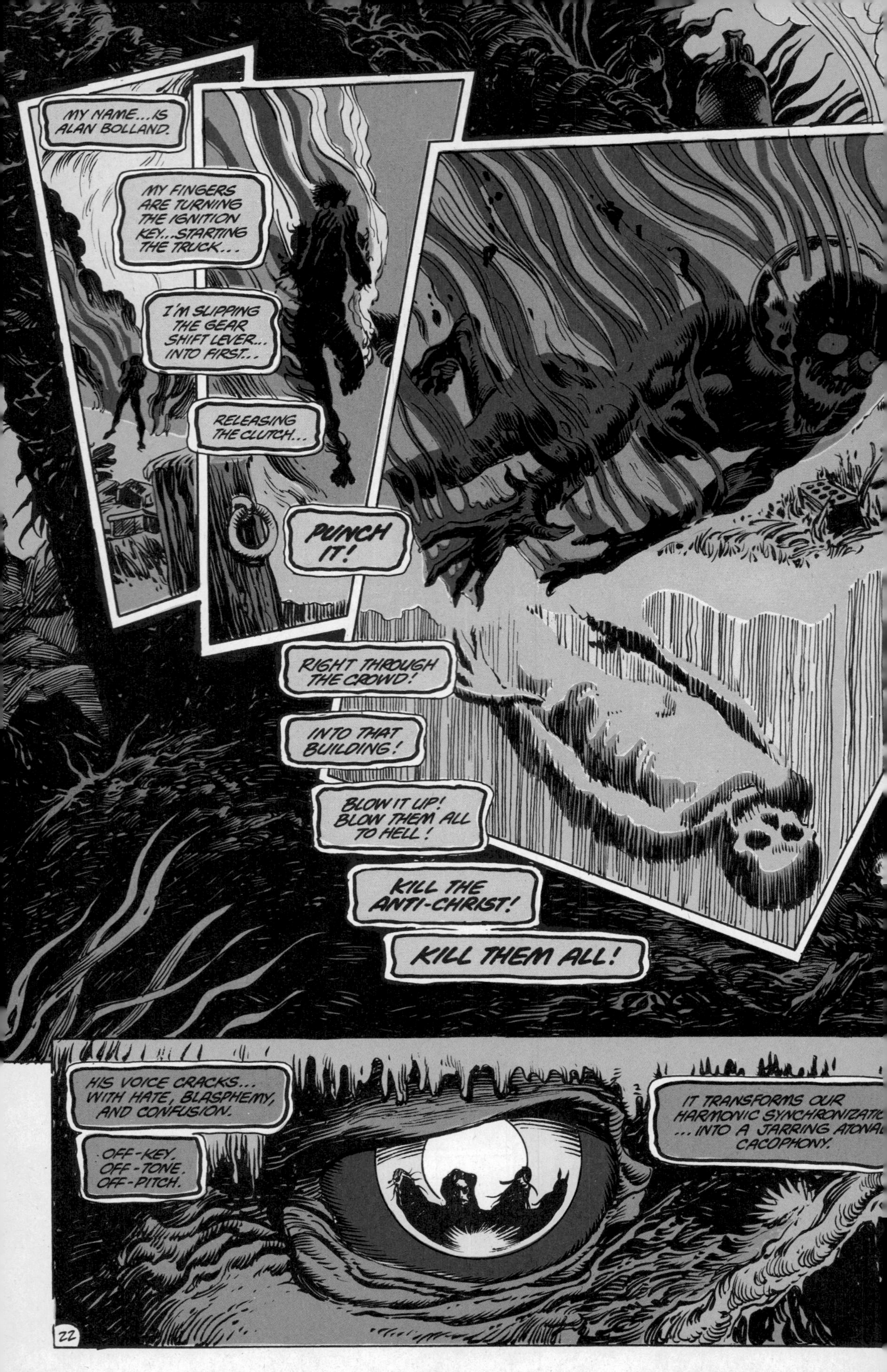
MY NAME...IS ALAN BOLLAND.
MY FINGERS ARE TURNING THE IGNITION KEY...STARTING THE TRUCK...
I'M SLIPPING THE GEAR SHIFT LEVER... INTO FIRST...
RELEASING THE CLUTCH...
PUNCH IT!
RIGHT THROUGH THE CROWD!
INTO THAT BUILDING!
BLOW IT UP! BLOW THEM ALL TO HELL!
KILL THE ANTI-CHRIST!
KILL THEM ALL!
HIS VOICE CRACKS... WITH HATE, BLASPHEMY, AND CONFUSION.
OFF-KEY. OFF-TONE. OFF-PITCH.
IT TRANSFORMS OUR HARMONIC SYNCHRONIZATI... INTO A JARRING ATONA CACOPHONY.

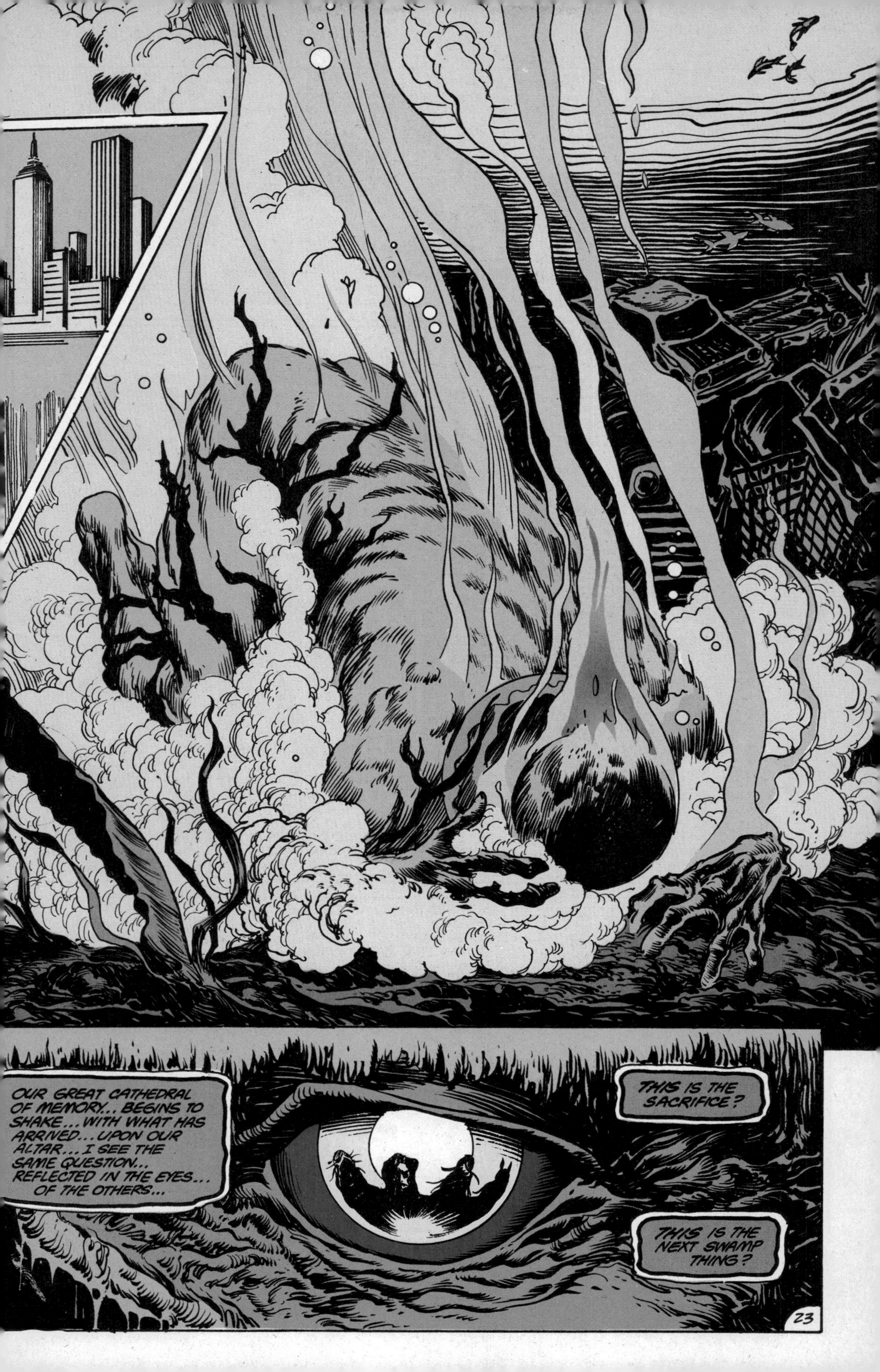
OUR GREAT CATHEDRAL OF MEMORY... BEGINS TO SHAKE... WITH WHAT HAS ARRIVED... UPON OUR ALTAR... I SEE THE SAME QUESTION... REFLECTED IN THE EYES... OF THE OTHERS...
THIS IS THE SACRIFICE?
THIS IS THE NEXT SWAMP THING?

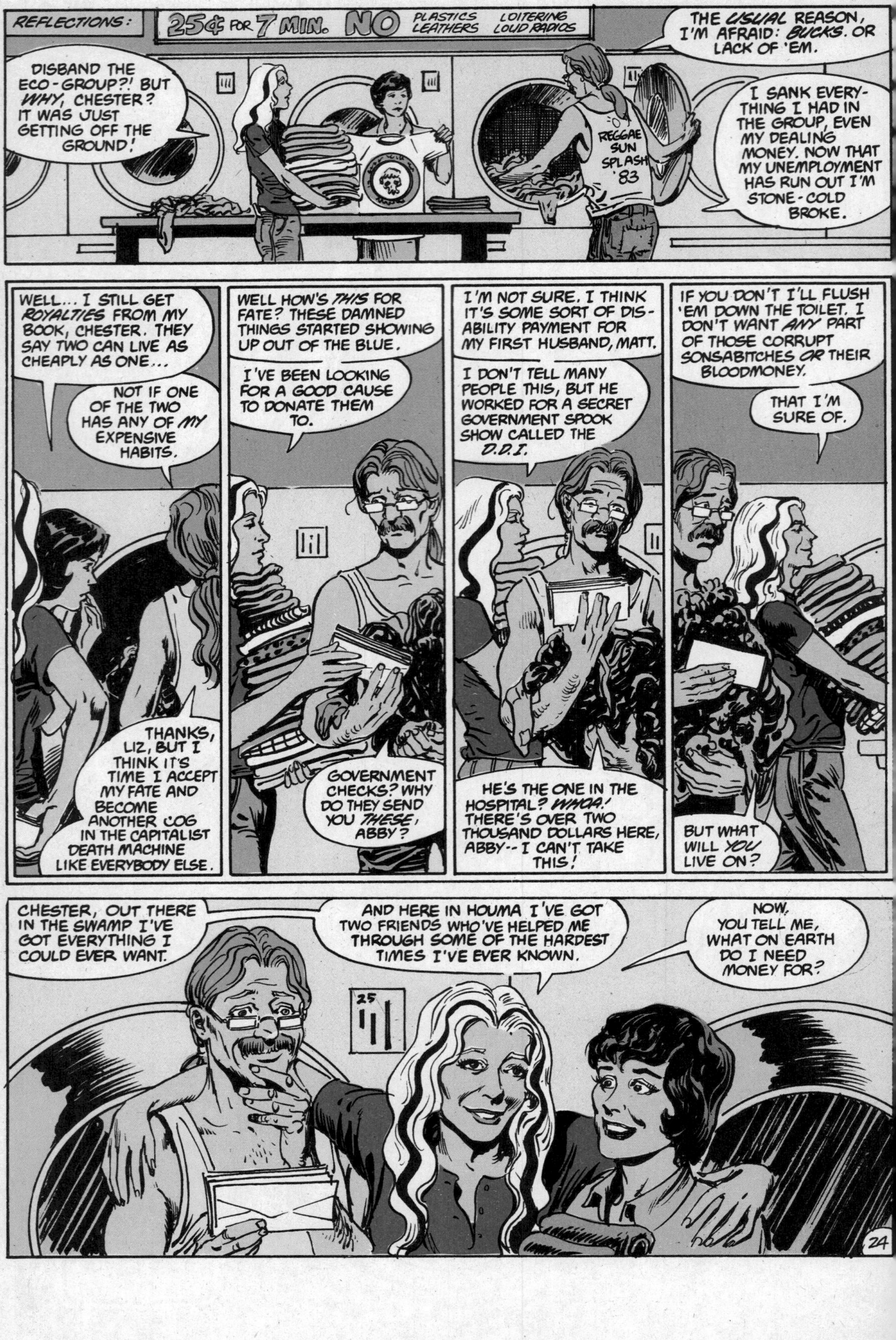
REFLECTIONS:
25¢ FOR 7 MIN.
NO PLASTICS LEATHERS LOITERING LOUD RADIOS
DISBAND THE ECO-GROUP?! BUT WHY, CHESTER? IT WAS JUST GETTING OFF THE GROUND!
THE USUAL REASON, I'M AFRAID: BUCKS. OR LACK OF 'EM.
I SANK EVERYTHING I HAD IN THE GROUP, EVEN MY DEALING MONEY. NOW THAT MY UNEMPLOYMENT HAS RUN OUT I'M STONE-COLD BROKE.
REGGAE SUN SPLASH '83
WELL... I STILL GET ROYALTIES FROM MY BOOK, CHESTER. THEY SAY TWO CAN LIVE AS CHEAPLY AS ONE...
NOT IF ONE OF THE TWO HAS ANY OF MY EXPENSIVE HABITS.
THANKS, LIZ, BUT I THINK IT'S TIME I ACCEPT MY FATE AND BECOME ANOTHER COG IN THE CAPITALIST DEATH MACHINE LIKE EVERYBODY ELSE.
WELL HOW'S THIS FOR FATE? THESE DAMNED THINGS STARTED SHOWING UP OUT OF THE BLUE.
I'VE BEEN LOOKING FOR A GOOD CAUSE TO DONATE THEM TO.
GOVERNMENT CHECKS? WHY DO THEY SEND YOU THESE, ABBY?
I'M NOT SURE. I THINK IT'S SOME SORT OF DISABILITY PAYMENT FOR MY FIRST HUSBAND, MATT.
I DON'T TELL MANY PEOPLE THIS, BUT HE WORKED FOR A SECRET GOVERNMENT SPOOK SHOW CALLED THE D.D.I.
HE'S THE ONE IN THE HOSPITAL? WHOA! THERE'S OVER TWO THOUSAND DOLLARS HERE, ABBY-- I CAN'T TAKE THIS!
IF YOU DON'T I'LL FLUSH 'EM DOWN THE TOILET. I DON'T WANT ANY PART OF THOSE CORRUPT SONSABITCHES OR THEIR BLOODMONEY.
THAT I'M SURE OF.
BUT WHAT WILL YOU LIVE ON?
CHESTER, OUT THERE IN THE SWAMP I'VE GOT EVERYTHING I COULD EVER WANT.
AND HERE IN HOUMA I'VE GOT TWO FRIENDS WHO'VE HELPED ME THROUGH SOME OF THE HARDEST TIMES I'VE EVER KNOWN.
NOW, YOU TELL ME, WHAT ON EARTH DO I NEED MONEY FOR?
24

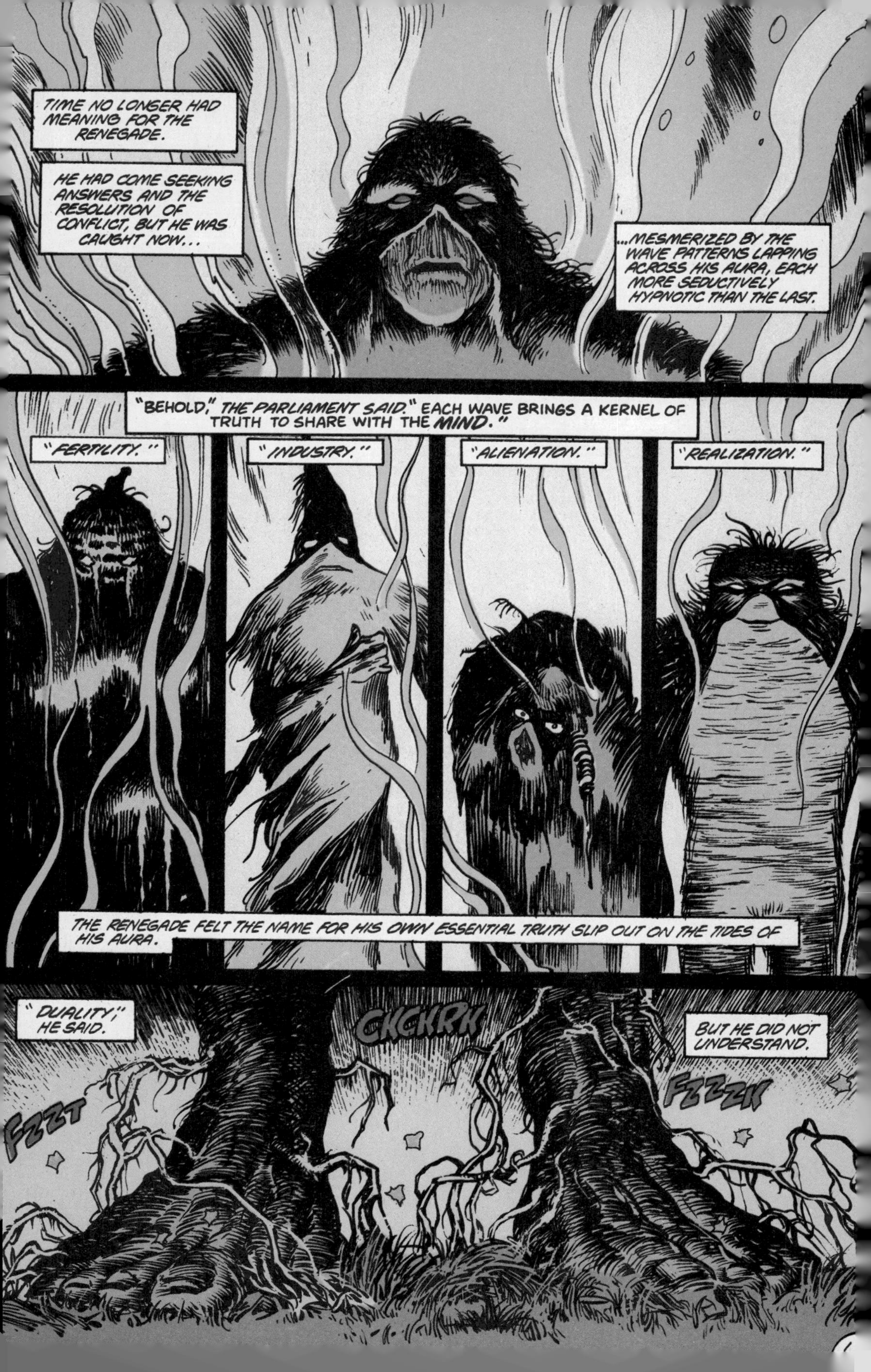

TIME NO LONGER HAD MEANING FOR THE RENEGADE.
HE HAD COME SEEKING ANSWERS AND THE RESOLUTION OF CONFLICT, BUT HE WAS CAUGHT NOW...
...MESMERIZED BY THE WAVE PATTERNS LAPPING ACROSS HIS AURA, EACH MORE SEDUCTIVELY HYPNOTIC THAN THE LAST.
"BEHOLD," THE PARLIAMENT SAID. "EACH WAVE BRINGS A KERNEL OF TRUTH TO SHARE WITH THE MIND."
"FERTILITY."
"INDUSTRY."
"ALIENATION."
"REALIZATION."
THE RENEGADE FELT THE NAME FOR HIS OWN ESSENTIAL TRUTH SLIP OUT ON THE TIDES OF HIS AURA.
"DUALITY," HE SAID.
CKCKRK
BUT HE DID NOT UNDERSTAND.
FZZT
FZZZK

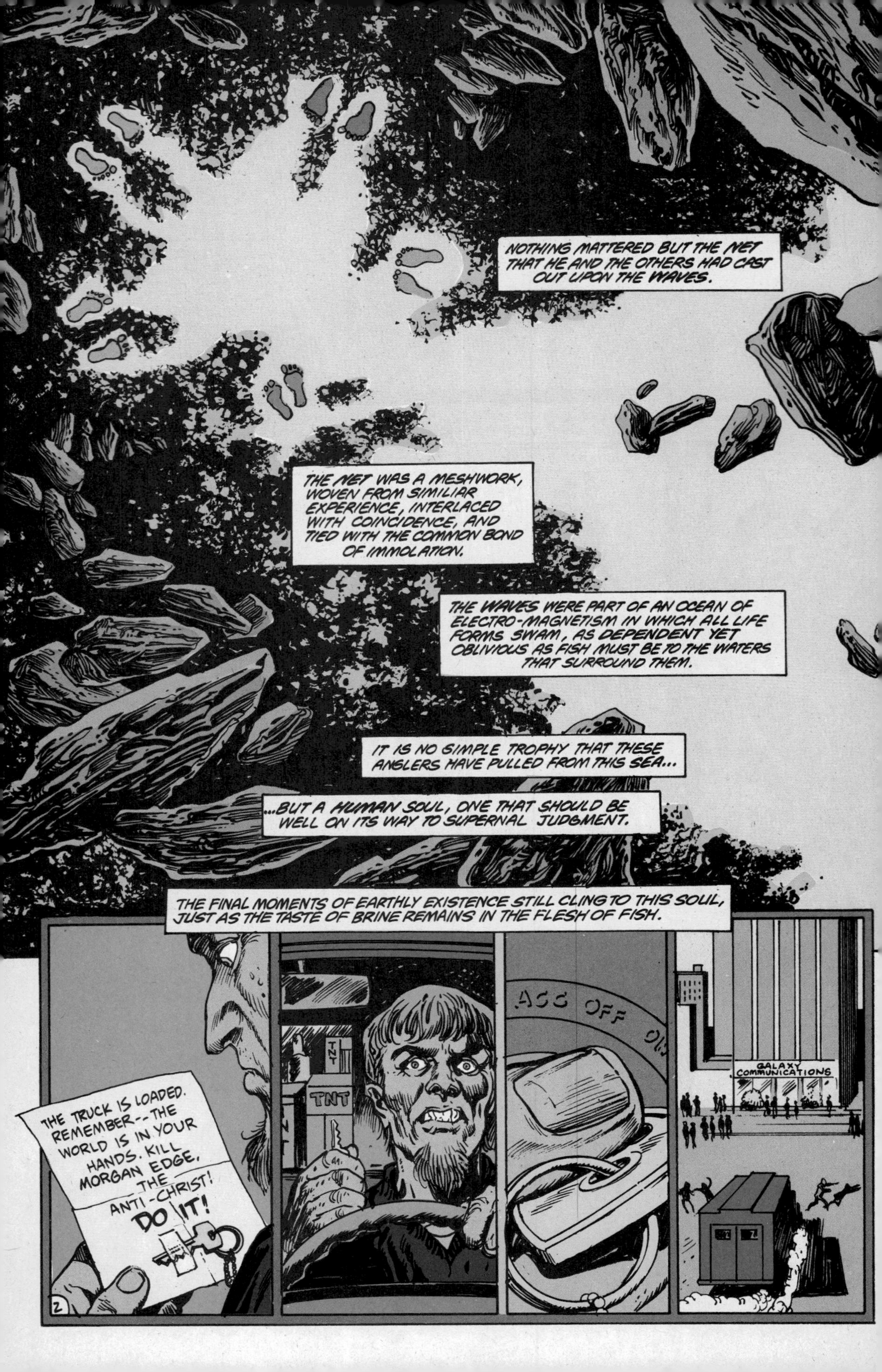
NOTHING MATTERED BUT THE NET THAT HE AND THE OTHERS HAD CAST OUT UPON THE WAVES.
THE NET WAS A MESHWORK, WOVEN FROM SIMILIAR EXPERIENCE, INTERLACED WITH COINCIDENCE, AND TIED WITH THE COMMON BOND OF IMMOLATION.
THE WAVES WERE PART OF AN OCEAN OF ELECTRO-MAGNETISM IN WHICH ALL LIFE FORMS SWAM, AS DEPENDENT YET OBLIVIOUS AS FISH MUST BE TO THE WATERS THAT SURROUND THEM.
IT IS NO SIMPLE TROPHY THAT THESE ANGLERS HAVE PULLED FROM THIS SEA...
...BUT A HUMAN SOUL, ONE THAT SHOULD BE WELL ON ITS WAY TO SUPERNAL JUDGMENT.
THE FINAL MOMENTS OF EARTHLY EXISTENCE STILL CLING TO THIS SOUL, JUST AS THE TASTE OF BRINE REMAINS IN THE FLESH OF FISH.
THE TRUCK IS LOADED. REMEMBER--THE WORLD IS IN YOUR HANDS. KILL MORGAN EDGE, THE ANTI-CHRIST! DO IT!
2
TNT
TNT
GALAXY COMMUNICATIONS

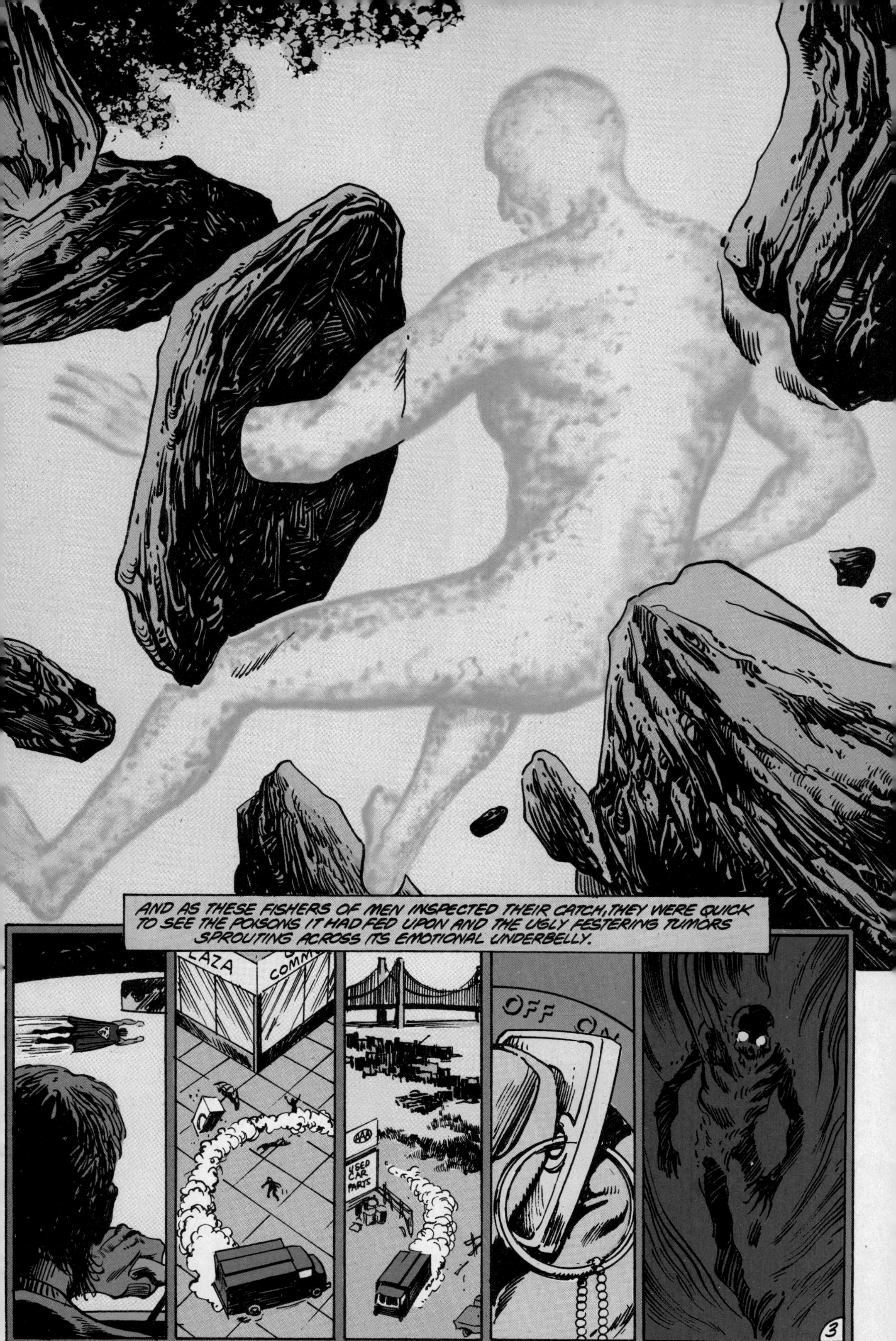
AND AS THESE FISHERS OF MEN INSPECTED THEIR CATCH, THEY WERE QUICK TO SEE THE POISONS IT HAD FED UPON AND THE UGLY FESTERING TUMORS SPROUTING ACROSS ITS EMOTIONAL UNDERBELLY.
LAZA
COMM
USED CAR PARTS
OFF
3

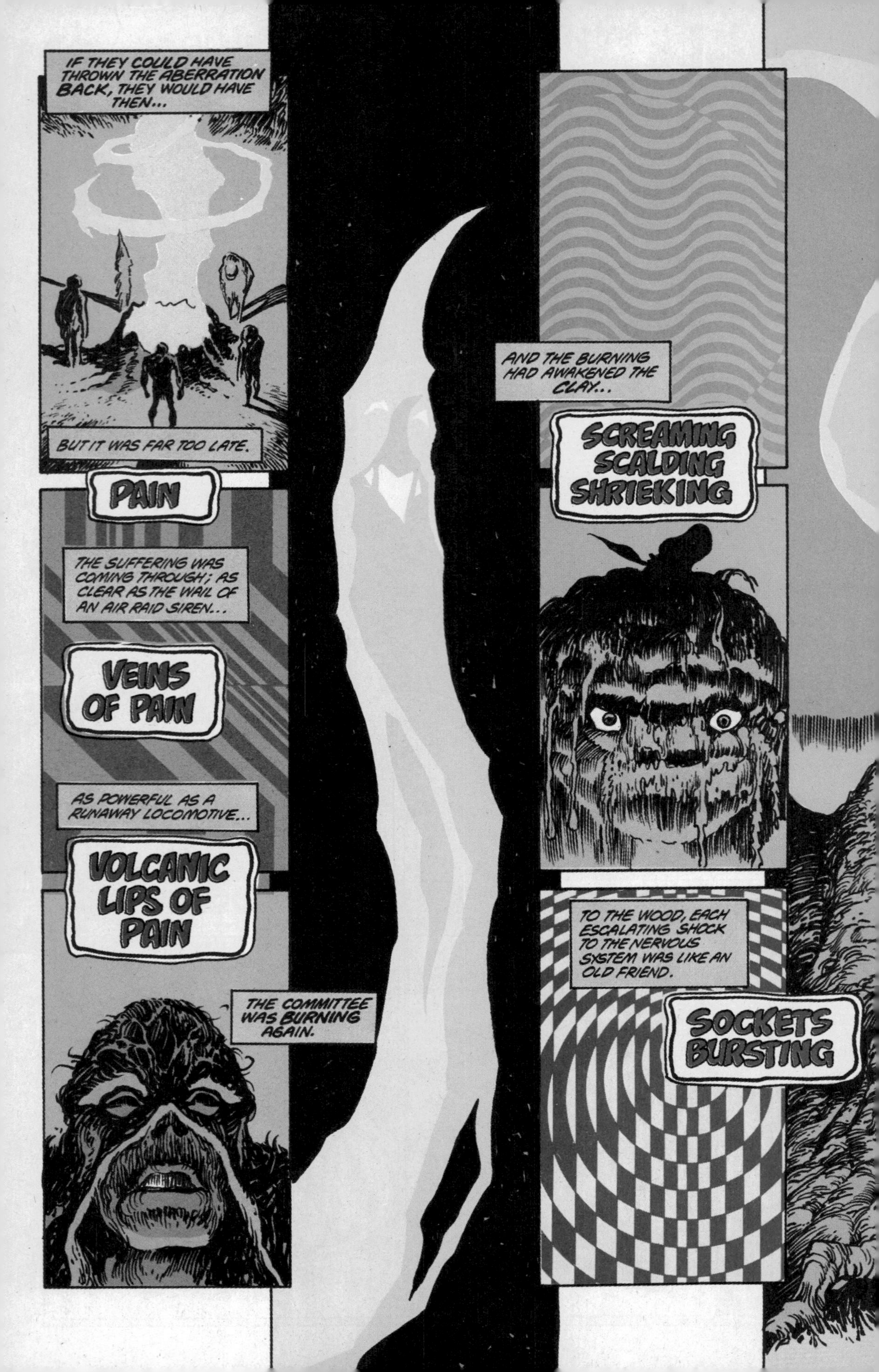

IF THEY COULD HAVE THROWN THE ABERRATION BACK, THEY WOULD HAVE THEN...
BUT IT WAS FAR TOO LATE.
PAIN
THE SUFFERING WAS COMING THROUGH; AS CLEAR AS THE WAIL OF AN AIR RAID SIREN...
VEINS OF PAIN
AS POWERFUL AS A RUNAWAY LOCOMOTIVE...
VOLCANIC LIPS OF PAIN
THE COMMITTEE WAS BURNING AGAIN.
AND THE BURNING HAD AWAKENED THE CLAY...
SCREAMING SCALDING SHRIEKING
TO THE WOOD, EACH ESCALATING SHOCK TO THE NERVOUS SYSTEM WAS LIKE AN OLD FRIEND.
SOCKETS BURSTING

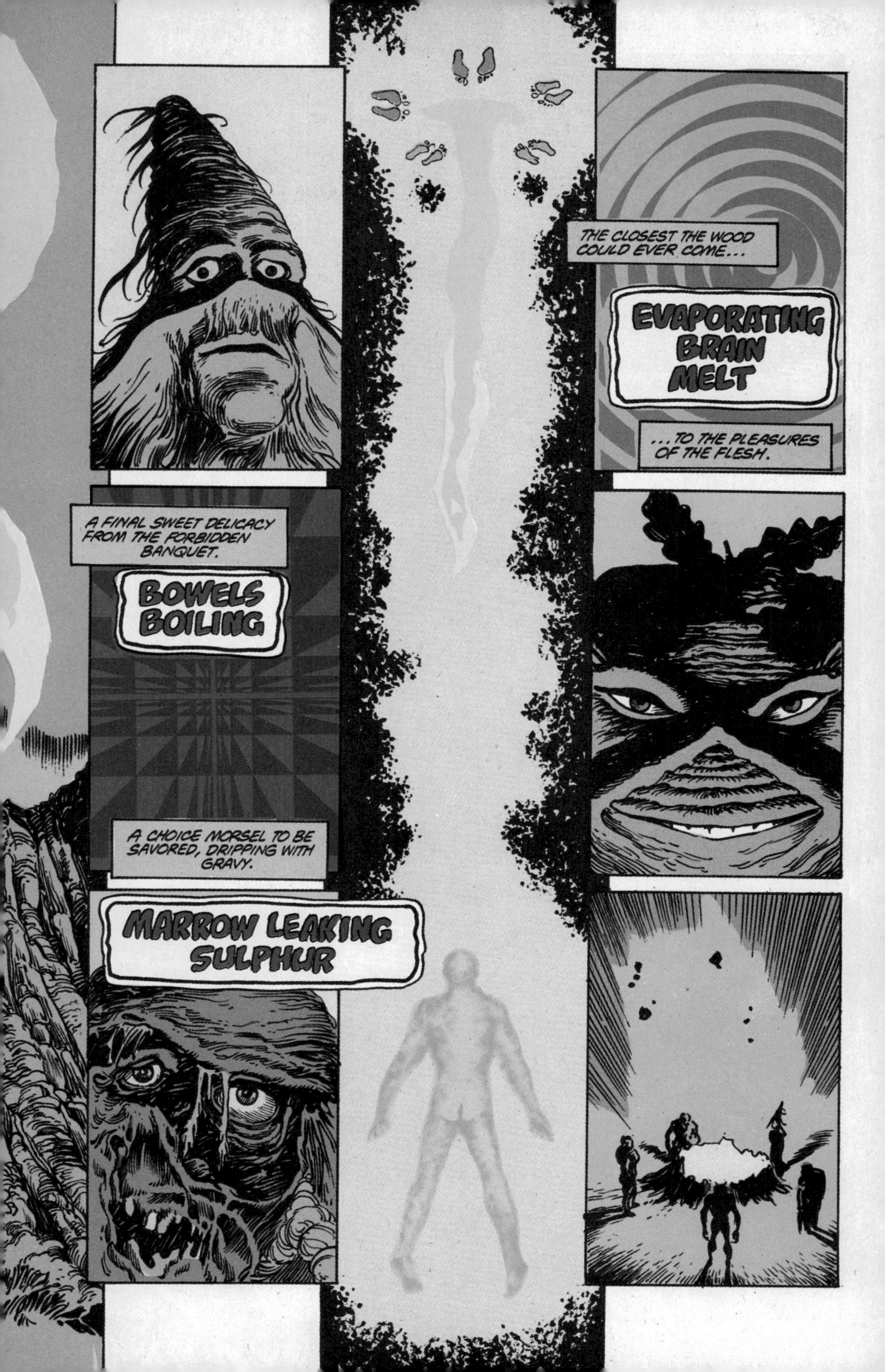
THE CLOSEST THE WOOD COULD EVER COME...
EVAPORATING BRAIN MELT
...TO THE PLEASURES OF THE FLESH.
A FINAL SWEET DELICACY FROM THE FORBIDDEN BANQUET.
BOWELS BOILING
A CHOICE MORSEL TO BE SAVORED, DRIPPING WITH GRAVY.
MARROW LEAKING SULPHUR

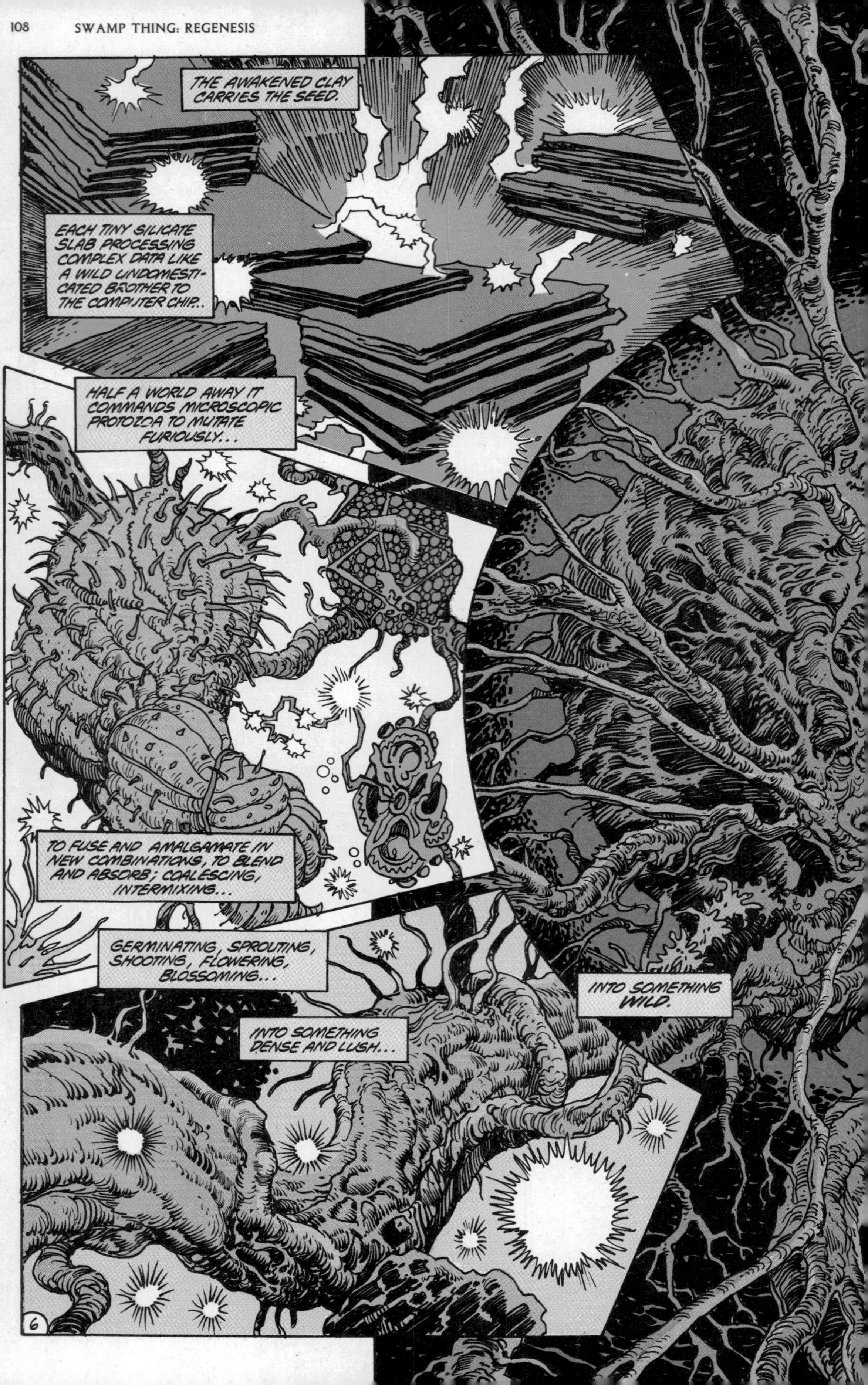
THE AWAKENED CLAY CARRIES THE SEED.
EACH TINY SILICATE SLAB PROCESSING COMPLEX DATA LIKE A WILD UNDOMESTICATED BROTHER TO THE COMPUTER CHIP...
HALF A WORLD AWAY IT COMMANDS MICROSCOPIC PROTOZOA TO MUTATE FURIOUSLY...
TO FUSE AND AMALGAMATE IN NEW COMBINATIONS, TO BLEND AND ABSORB; COALESCING, INTERMIXING...
GERMINATING, SPROUTING, SHOOTING, FLOWERING, BLOSSOMING...
INTO SOMETHING DENSE AND LUSH...
INTO SOMETHING WILD.
6

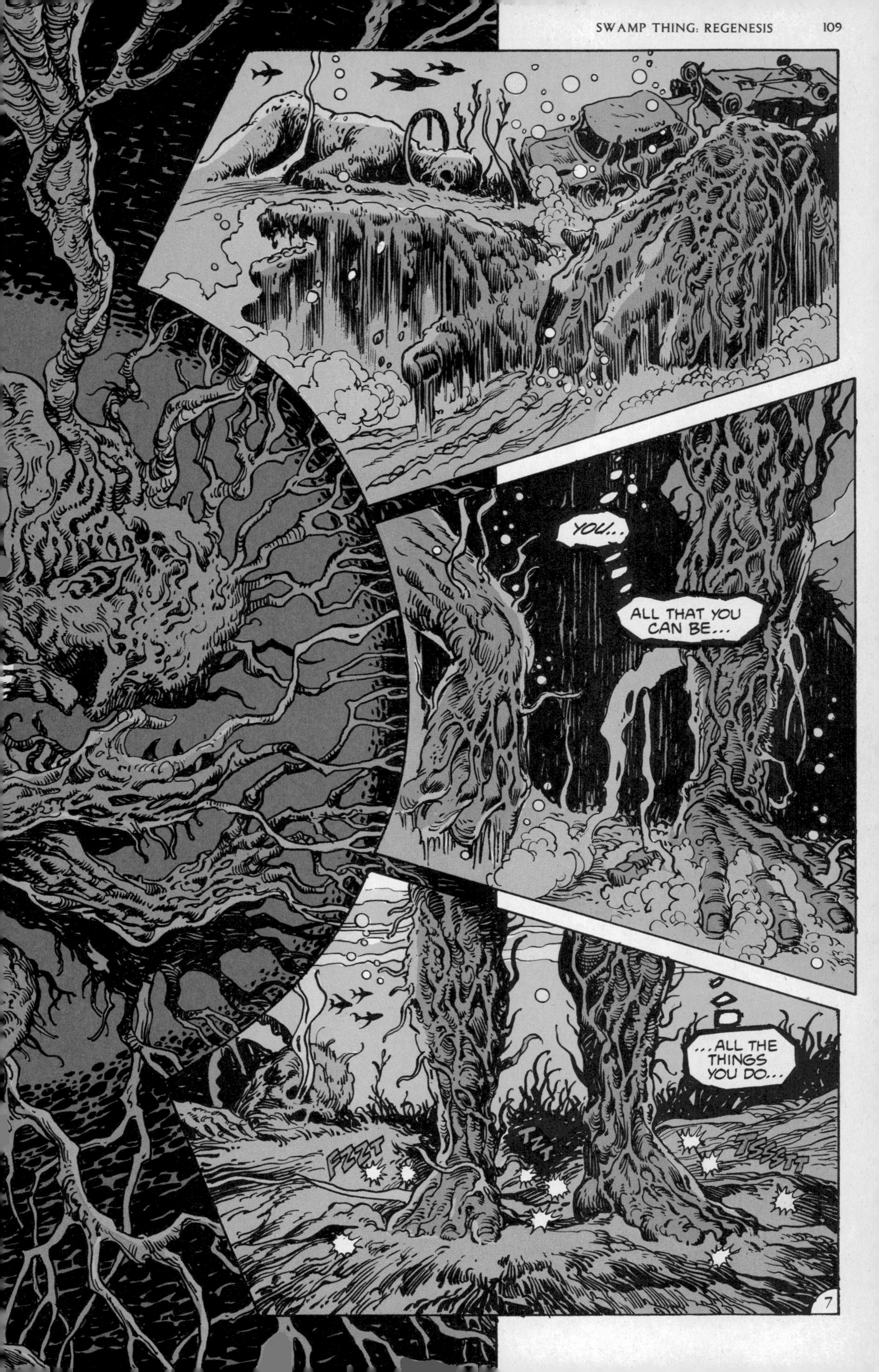
YOU...
ALL THAT YOU CAN BE...
...ALL THE THINGS YOU DO...
FZZT
TSSSTT
7

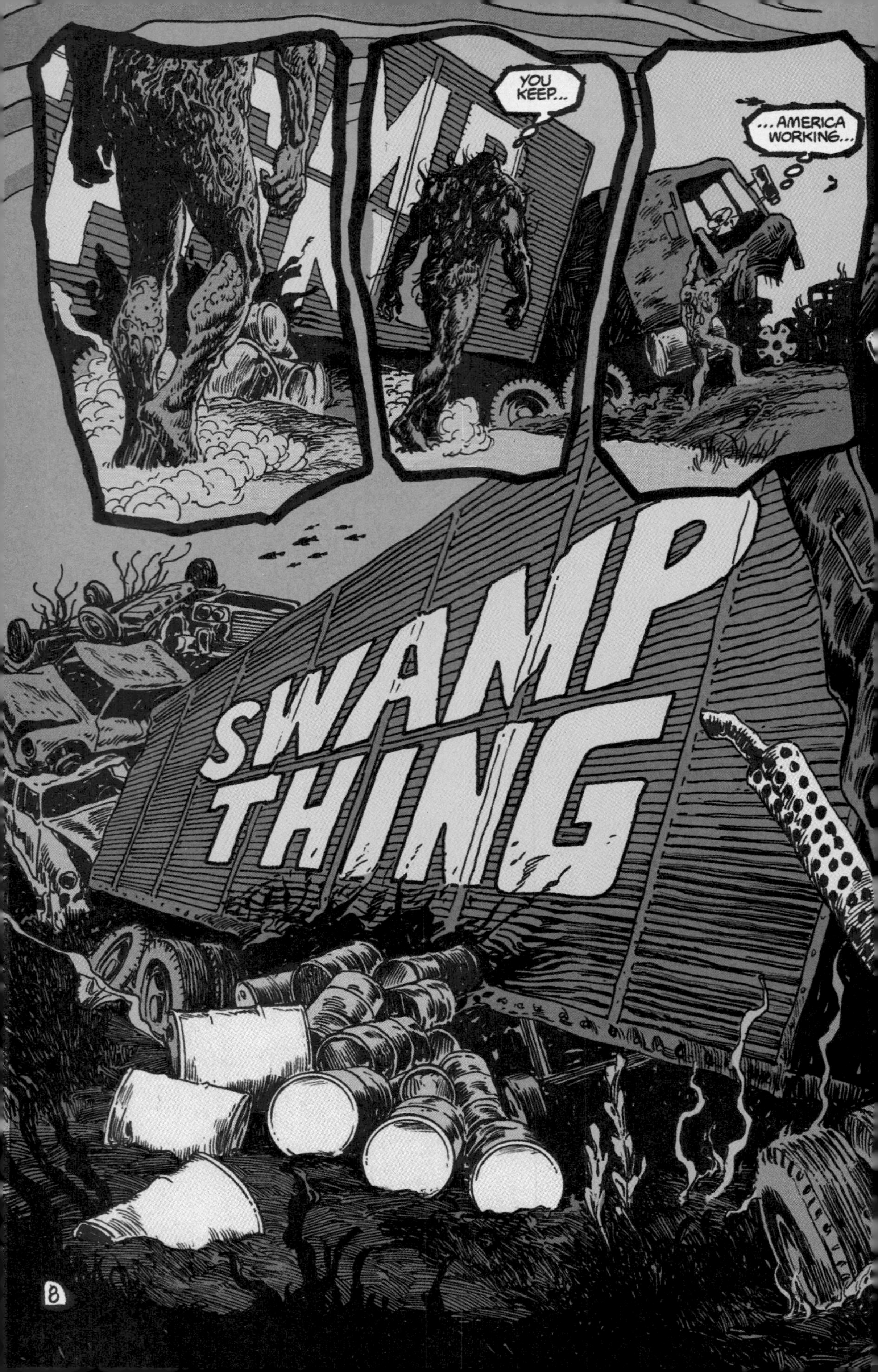
YOU KEEP...
...AMERICA WORKING...
SWAMP THING

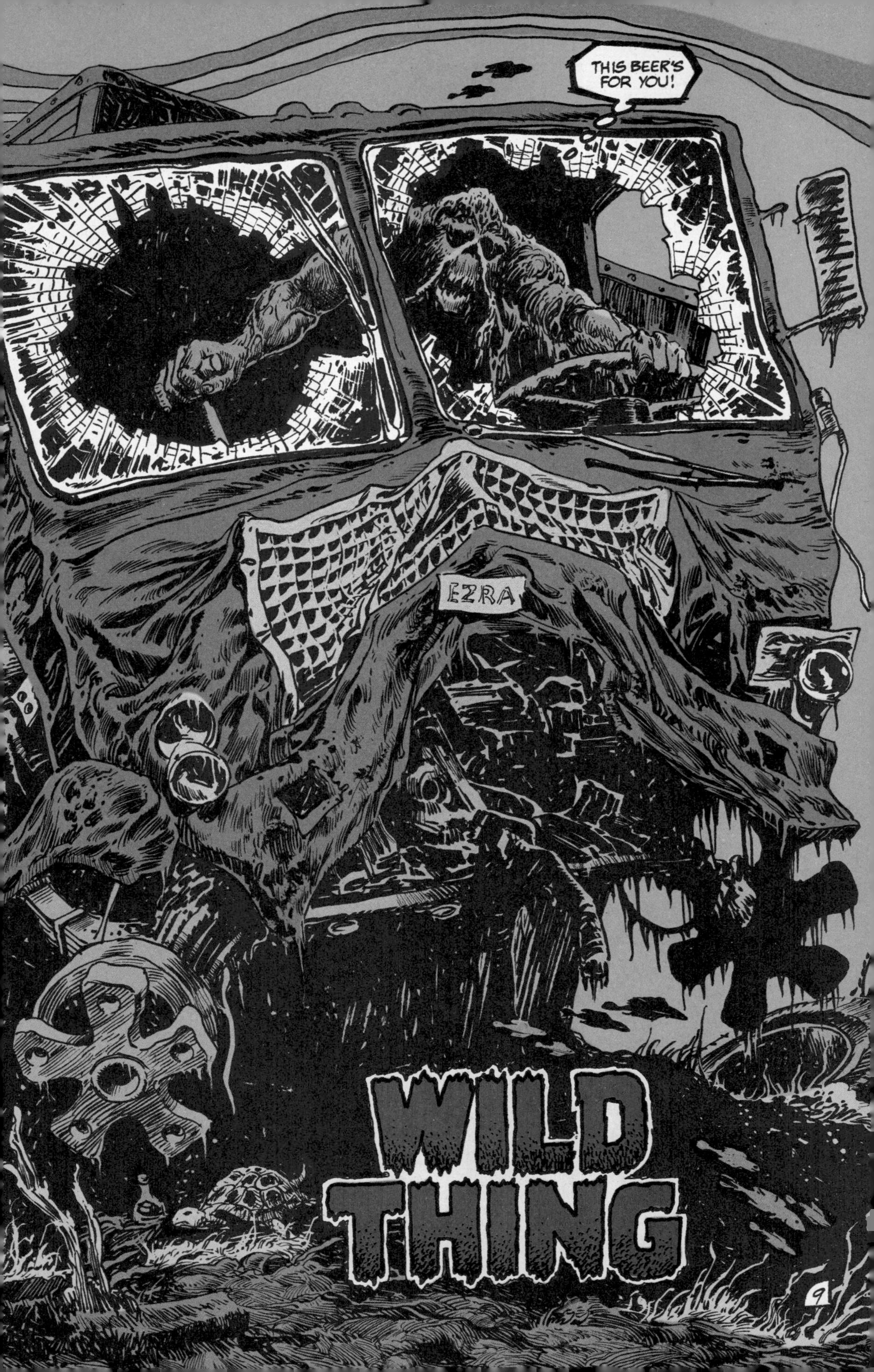

THIS BEER'S FOR YOU!
EZRA
WILD THING

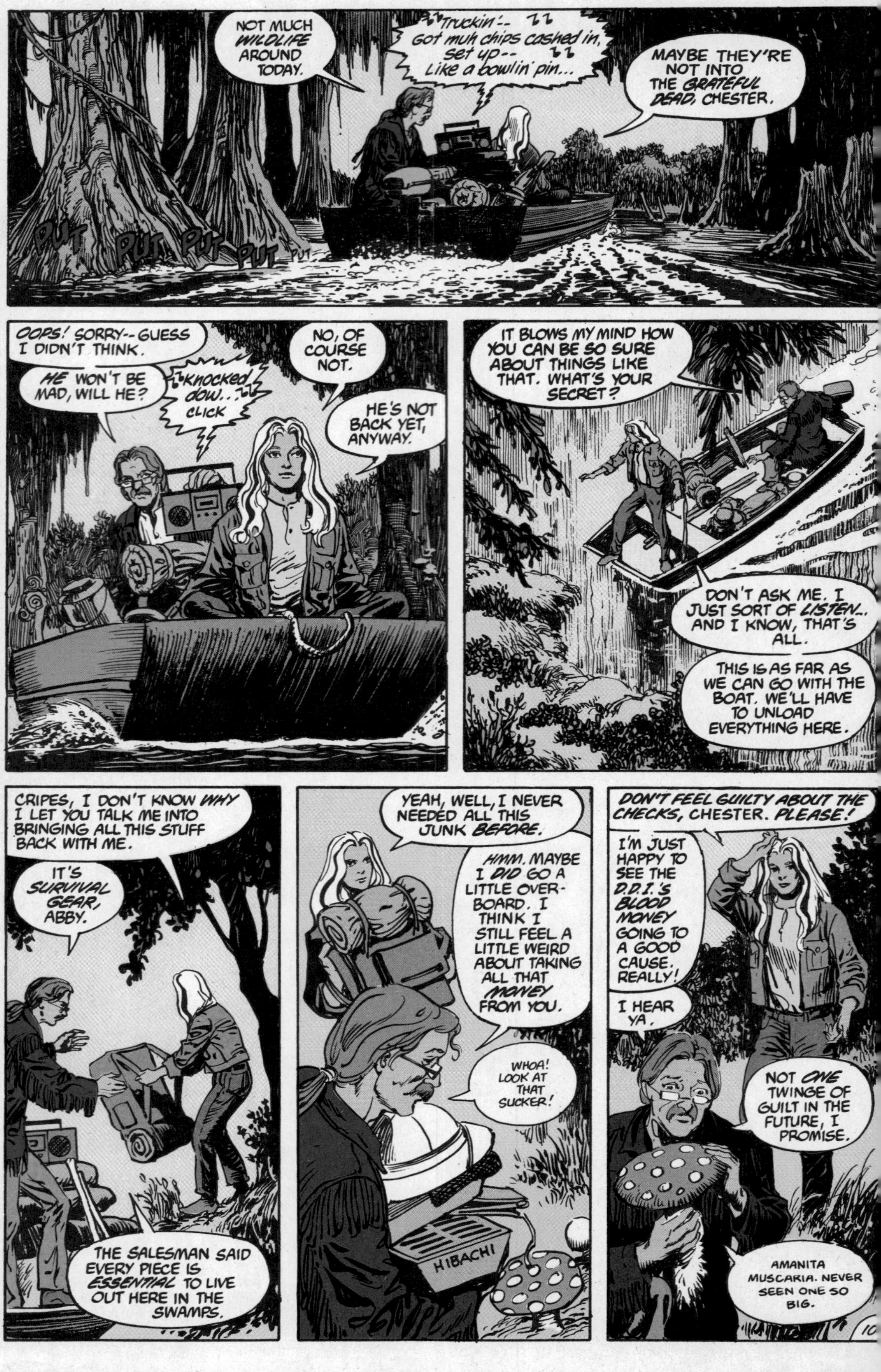
NOT MUCH WILDLIFE AROUND TODAY.
Truckin'-- Got muh chips cashed in, set up-- Like a bowlin' pin...
MAYBE THEY'RE NOT INTO THE GRATEFUL DEAD, CHESTER.
PUT PUT PUT PUT PUT
OOPS! SORRY--GUESS I DIDN'T THINK.
HE WON'T BE MAD, WILL HE?
Knocked dow... CLICK
NO, OF COURSE NOT.
HE'S NOT BACK YET, ANYWAY.
IT BLOWS MY MIND HOW YOU CAN BE SO SURE ABOUT THINGS LIKE THAT. WHAT'S YOUR SECRET?
DON'T ASK ME. I JUST SORT OF LISTEN... AND I KNOW, THAT'S ALL.
THIS IS AS FAR AS WE CAN GO WITH THE BOAT. WE'LL HAVE TO UNLOAD EVERYTHING HERE.
CRIPES, I DON'T KNOW WHY I LET YOU TALK ME INTO BRINGING ALL THIS STUFF BACK WITH ME.
IT'S SURVIVAL GEAR, ABBY.
THE SALESMAN SAID EVERY PIECE IS ESSENTIAL TO LIVE OUT HERE IN THE SWAMPS.
YEAH, WELL, I NEVER NEEDED ALL THIS JUNK BEFORE.
HMM. MAYBE I DID GO A LITTLE OVER-BOARD. I THINK I STILL FEEL A LITTLE WEIRD ABOUT TAKING ALL THAT MONEY FROM YOU.
WHOA! LOOK AT THAT SUCKER!
HIBACHI
DON'T FEEL GUILTY ABOUT THE CHECKS, CHESTER. PLEASE!
I'M JUST HAPPY TO SEE THE D.D.I.'S BLOOD MONEY GOING TO A GOOD CAUSE. REALLY!
I HEAR YA.
NOT ONE TWINGE OF GUILT IN THE FUTURE, I PROMISE.
AMANITA MUSCARIA. NEVER SEEN ONE SO BIG.
10

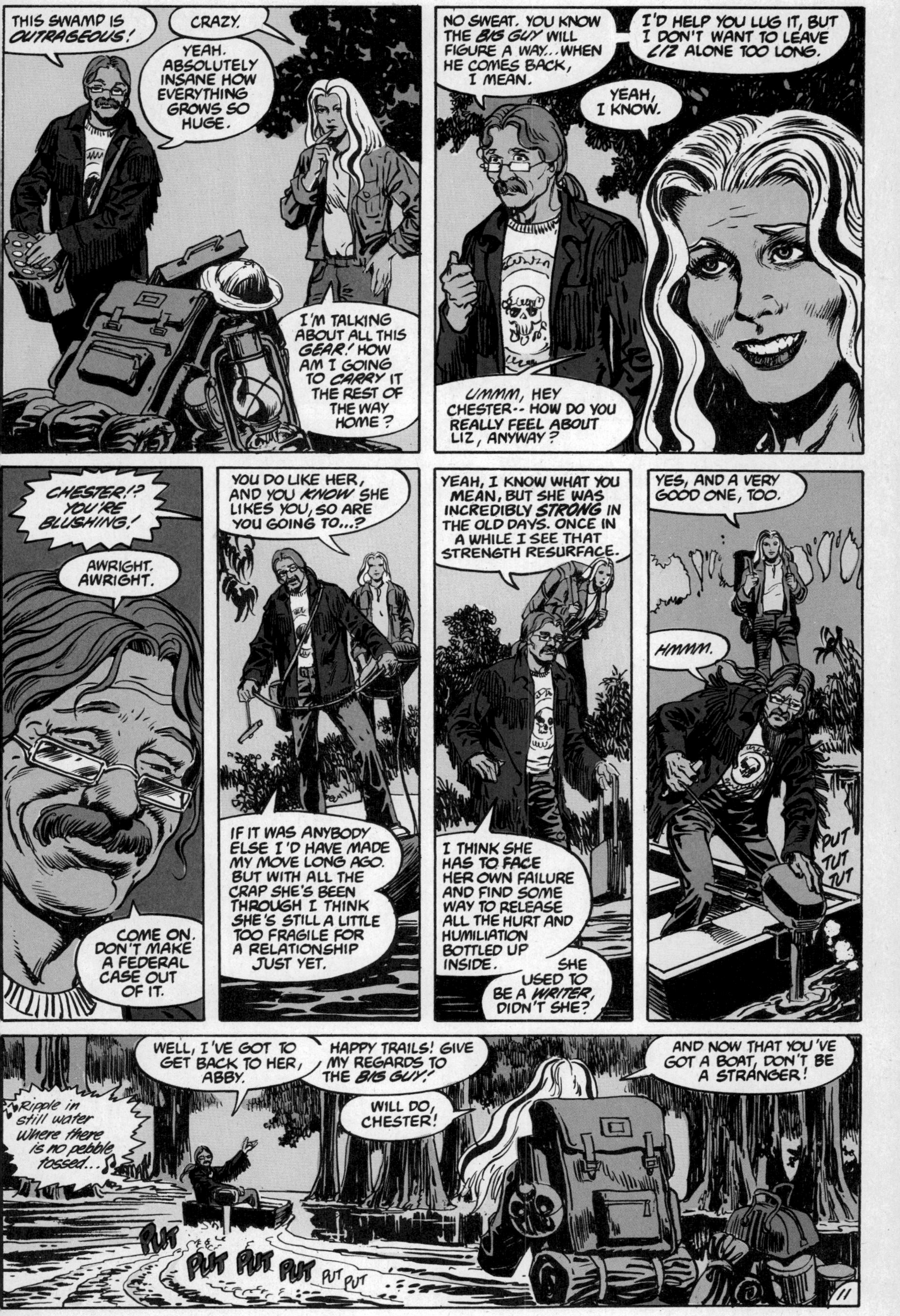
THIS SWAMP IS OUTRAGEOUS!
CRAZY.
YEAH. ABSOLUTELY INSANE HOW EVERYTHING GROWS SO HUGE.
I'M TALKING ABOUT ALL THIS GEAR! HOW AM I GOING TO CARRY IT THE REST OF THE WAY HOME?
NO SWEAT. YOU KNOW THE BIG GUY WILL FIGURE A WAY... WHEN HE COMES BACK, I MEAN.
I'D HELP YOU LUG IT, BUT I DON'T WANT TO LEAVE LIZ ALONE TOO LONG.
YEAH, I KNOW.
UMMM, HEY CHESTER-- HOW DO YOU REALLY FEEL ABOUT LIZ, ANYWAY?
CHESTER!? YOU'RE BLUSHING!
AWRIGHT. AWRIGHT.
COME ON. DON'T MAKE A FEDERAL CASE OUT OF IT.
YOU DO LIKE HER, AND YOU KNOW SHE LIKES YOU, SO ARE YOU GOING TO...?
IF IT WAS ANYBODY ELSE I'D HAVE MADE MY MOVE LONG AGO. BUT WITH ALL THE CRAP SHE'S BEEN THROUGH I THINK SHE'S STILL A LITTLE TOO FRAGILE FOR A RELATIONSHIP JUST YET.
YEAH, I KNOW WHAT YOU MEAN, BUT SHE WAS INCREDIBLY STRONG IN THE OLD DAYS. ONCE IN A WHILE I SEE THAT STRENGTH RESURFACE.
I THINK SHE HAS TO FACE HER OWN FAILURE AND FIND SOME WAY TO RELEASE ALL THE HURT AND HUMILIATION BOTTLED UP INSIDE.
SHE USED TO BE A WRITER, DIDN'T SHE?
YES, AND A VERY GOOD ONE, TOO.
HMMM.
PUT TUT TUT
WELL, I'VE GOT TO GET BACK TO HER, ABBY.
HAPPY TRAILS! GIVE MY REGARDS TO THE BIG GUY!
WILL DO, CHESTER!
AND NOW THAT YOU'VE GOT A BOAT, DON'T BE A STRANGER!
Ripple in still water Where there is no pebble tossed...
PUT PUT PUT PUT PUT PUT
11

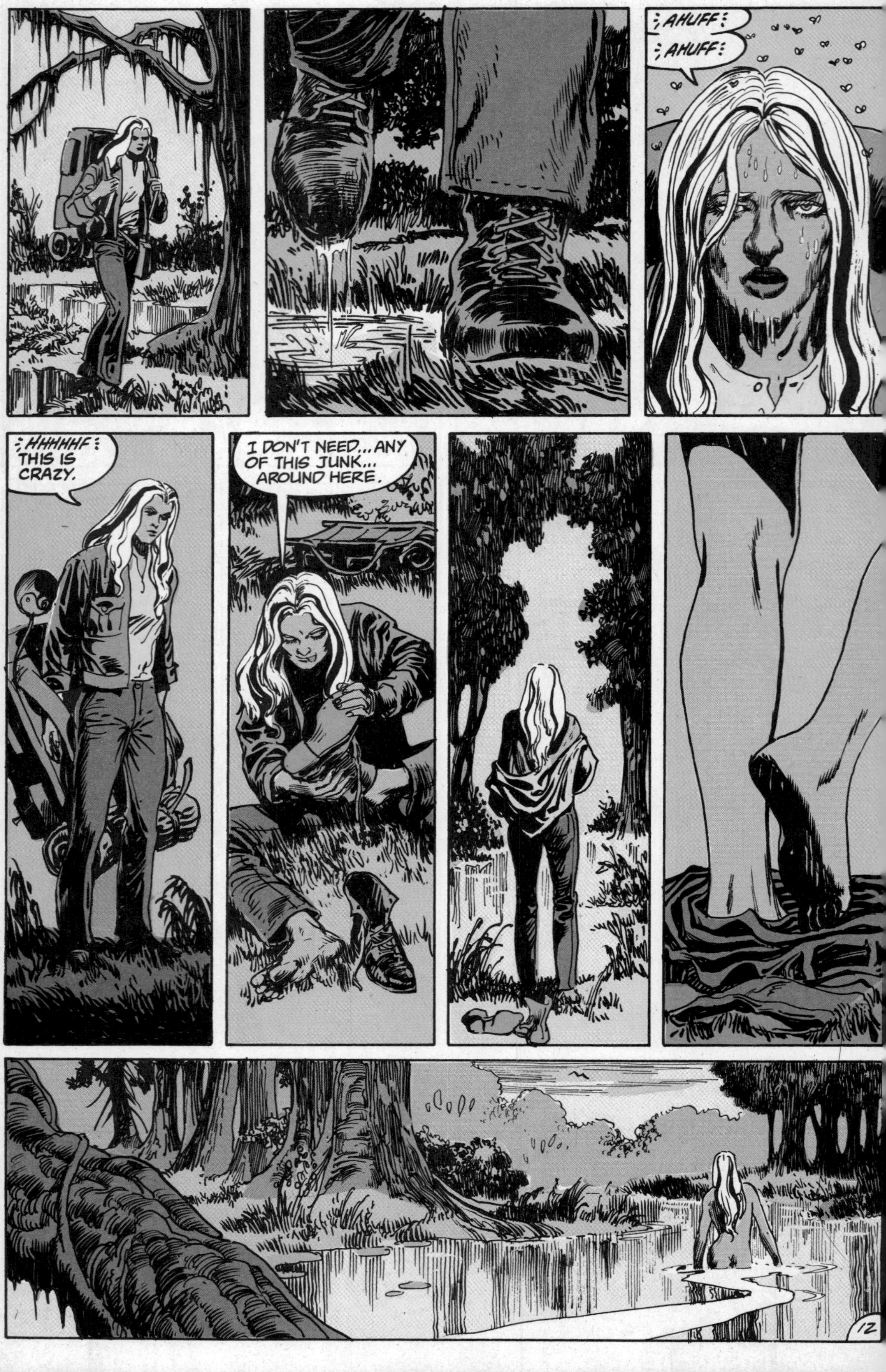
AHUFF
AHUFF
HHHHHF THIS IS CRAZY.
I DON'T NEED... ANY OF THIS JUNK... AROUND HERE.
12

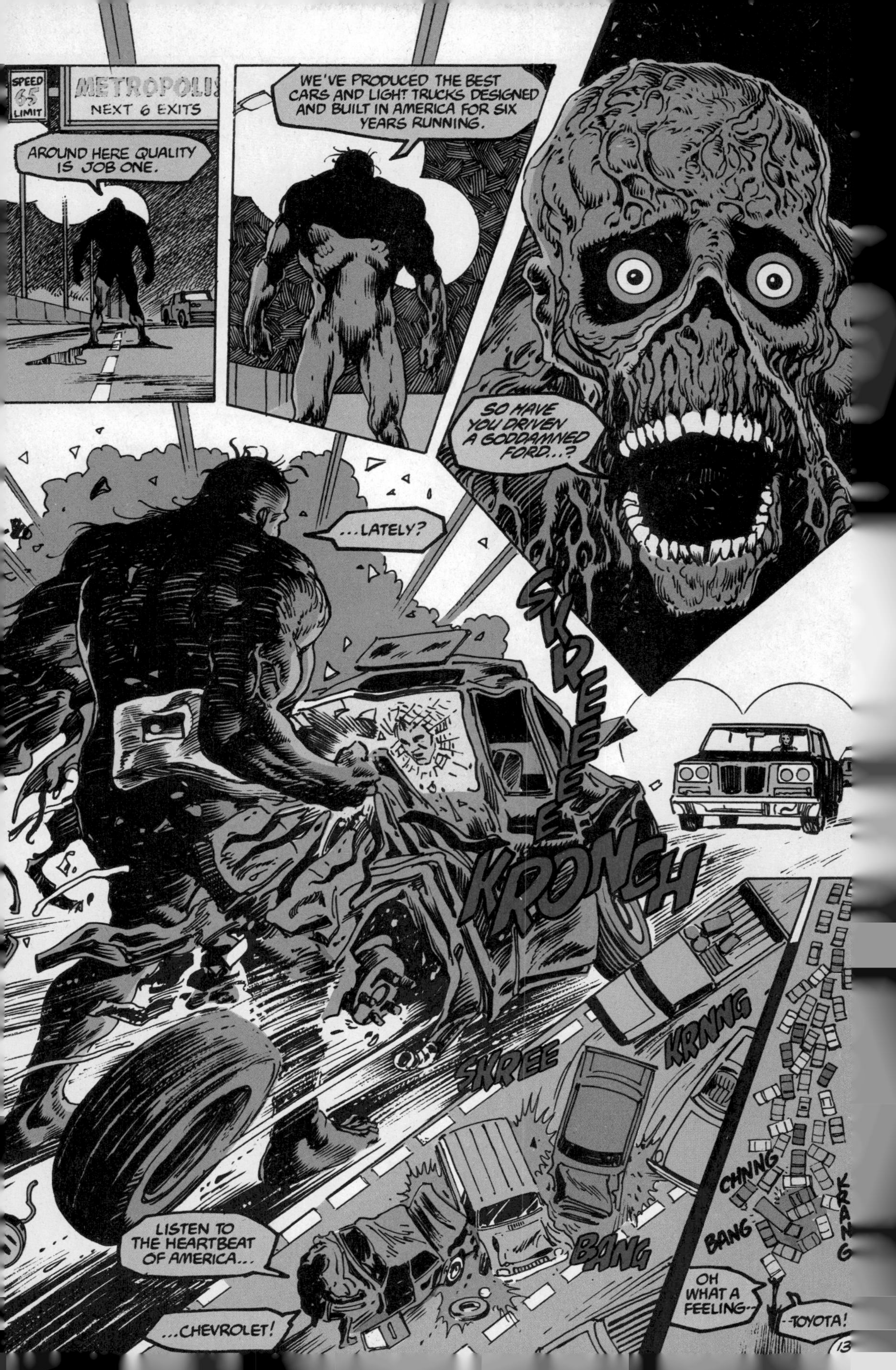
SPEED 65 LIMIT
METROPOLIS
NEXT 6 EXITS
AROUND HERE QUALITY IS JOB ONE.
WE'VE PRODUCED THE BEST CARS AND LIGHT TRUCKS DESIGNED AND BUILT IN AMERICA FOR SIX YEARS RUNNING.
SO HAVE YOU DRIVEN A GODDAMNED FORD...?
...LATELY?
SKREEEEEE
KRONCH
SKREE
KRNNG
CHNNG
KRANG
BANG
BANG
LISTEN TO THE HEARTBEAT OF AMERICA...
...CHEVROLET!
OH WHAT A FEELING--
--TOYOTA!

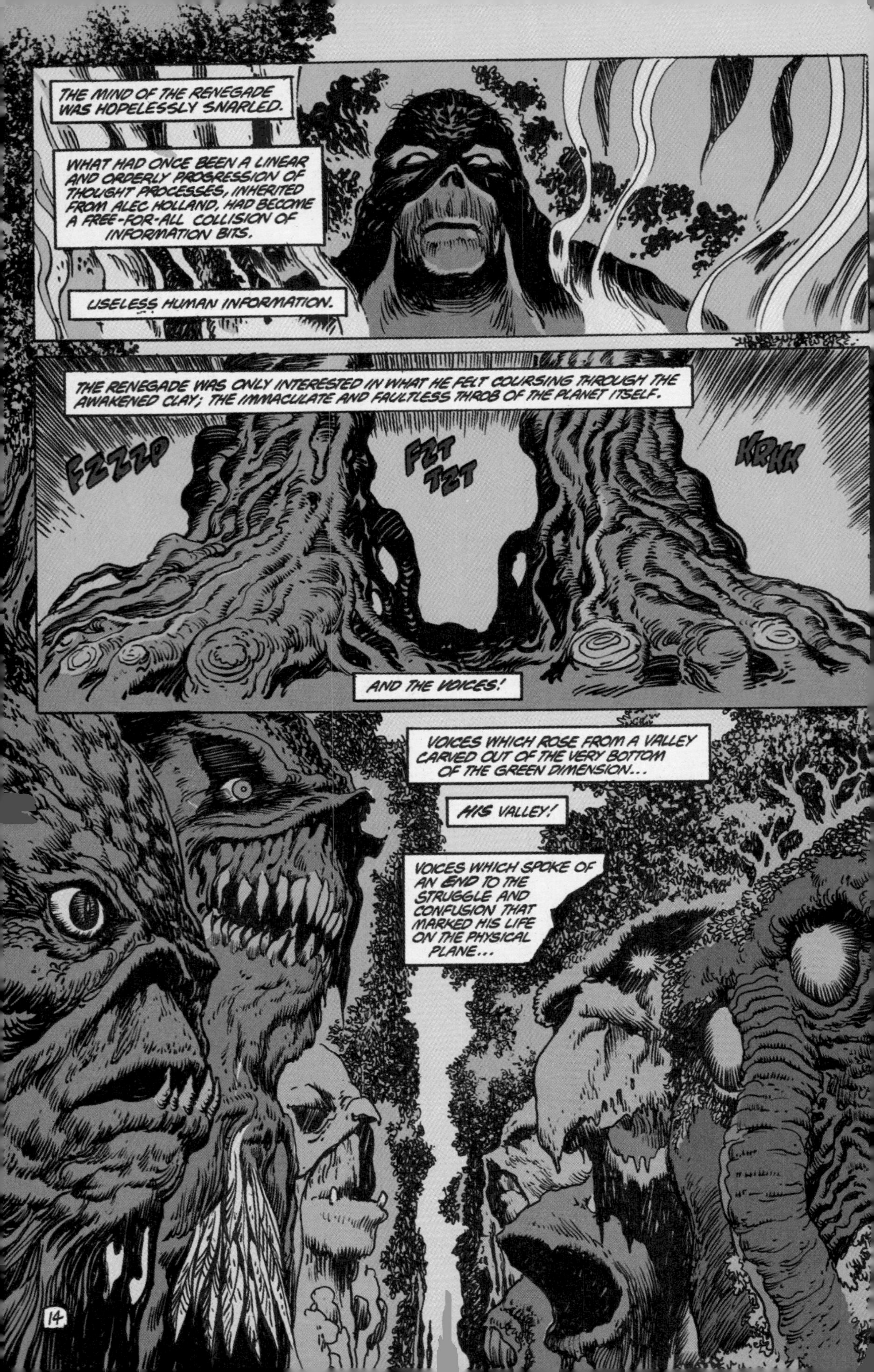
THE MIND OF THE RENEGADE WAS HOPELESSLY SNARLED.
WHAT HAD ONCE BEEN A LINEAR AND ORDERLY PROGRESSION OF THOUGHT PROCESSES, INHERITED FROM ALEC HOLLAND, HAD BECOME A FREE-FOR-ALL COLLISION OF INFORMATION BITS.
USELESS HUMAN INFORMATION.
THE RENEGADE WAS ONLY INTERESTED IN WHAT HE FELT COURSING THROUGH THE AWAKENED CLAY; THE IMMACULATE AND FAULTLESS THROB OF THE PLANET ITSELF.
FZZZZP
FZT TZT
KRKK
AND THE VOICES!
VOICES WHICH ROSE FROM A VALLEY CARVED OUT OF THE VERY BOTTOM OF THE GREEN DIMENSION...
HIS VALLEY!
VOICES WHICH SPOKE OF AN END TO THE STRUGGLE AND CONFUSION THAT MARKED HIS LIFE ON THE PHYSICAL PLANE...

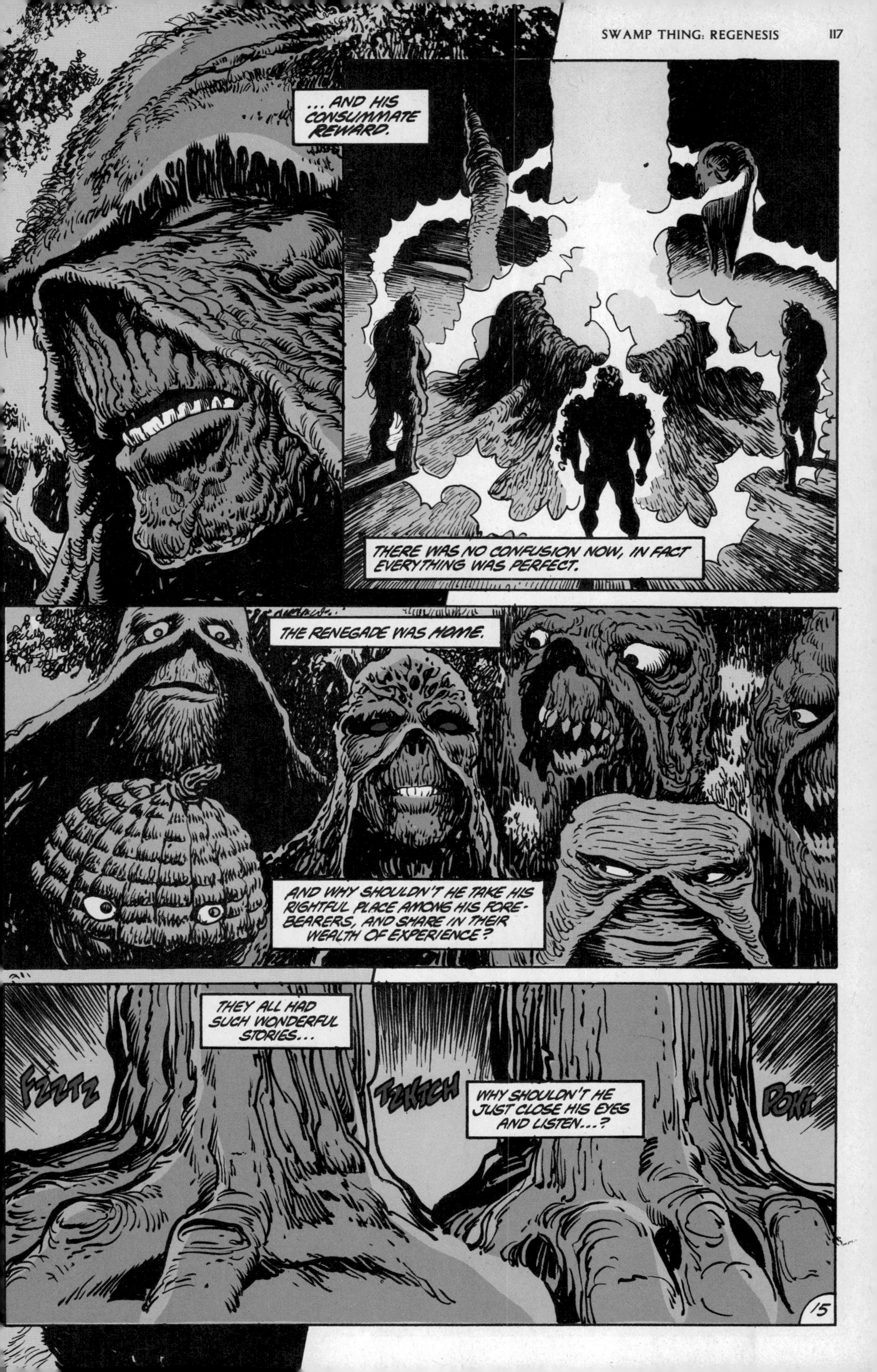
...AND HIS CONSUMMATE REWARD.
THERE WAS NO CONFUSION NOW, IN FACT EVERYTHING WAS PERFECT.
THE RENEGADE WAS HOME.
AND WHY SHOULDN'T HE TAKE HIS RIGHTFUL PLACE AMONG HIS FORE-BEARERS, AND SHARE IN THEIR WEALTH OF EXPERIENCE?
THEY ALL HAD SUCH WONDERFUL STORIES...
FZZZTZ
TZKTCH
WHY SHOULDN'T HE JUST CLOSE HIS EYES AND LISTEN...?
15

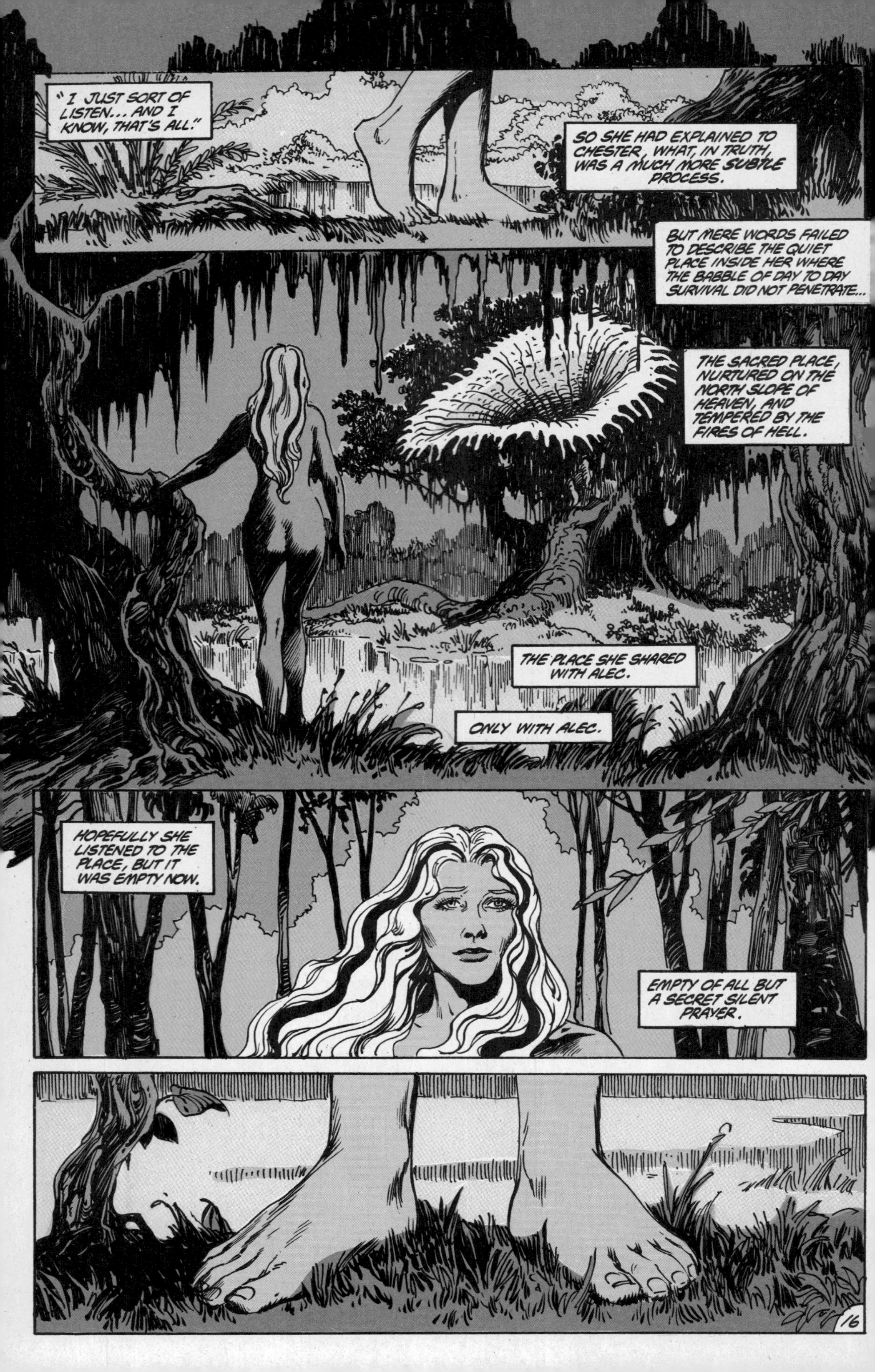
"I JUST SORT OF LISTEN... AND I KNOW, THAT'S ALL."
SO SHE HAD EXPLAINED TO CHESTER, WHAT, IN TRUTH, WAS A MUCH MORE SUBTLE PROCESS.
BUT MERE WORDS FAILED TO DESCRIBE THE QUIET PLACE INSIDE HER WHERE THE BABBLE OF DAY TO DAY SURVIVAL DID NOT PENETRATE...
THE SACRED PLACE, NURTURED ON THE NORTH SLOPE OF HEAVEN, AND TEMPERED BY THE FIRES OF HELL.
THE PLACE SHE SHARED WITH ALEC.
ONLY WITH ALEC.
HOPEFULLY SHE LISTENED TO THE PLACE, BUT IT WAS EMPTY NOW.
EMPTY OF ALL BUT A SECRET SILENT PRAYER.
16

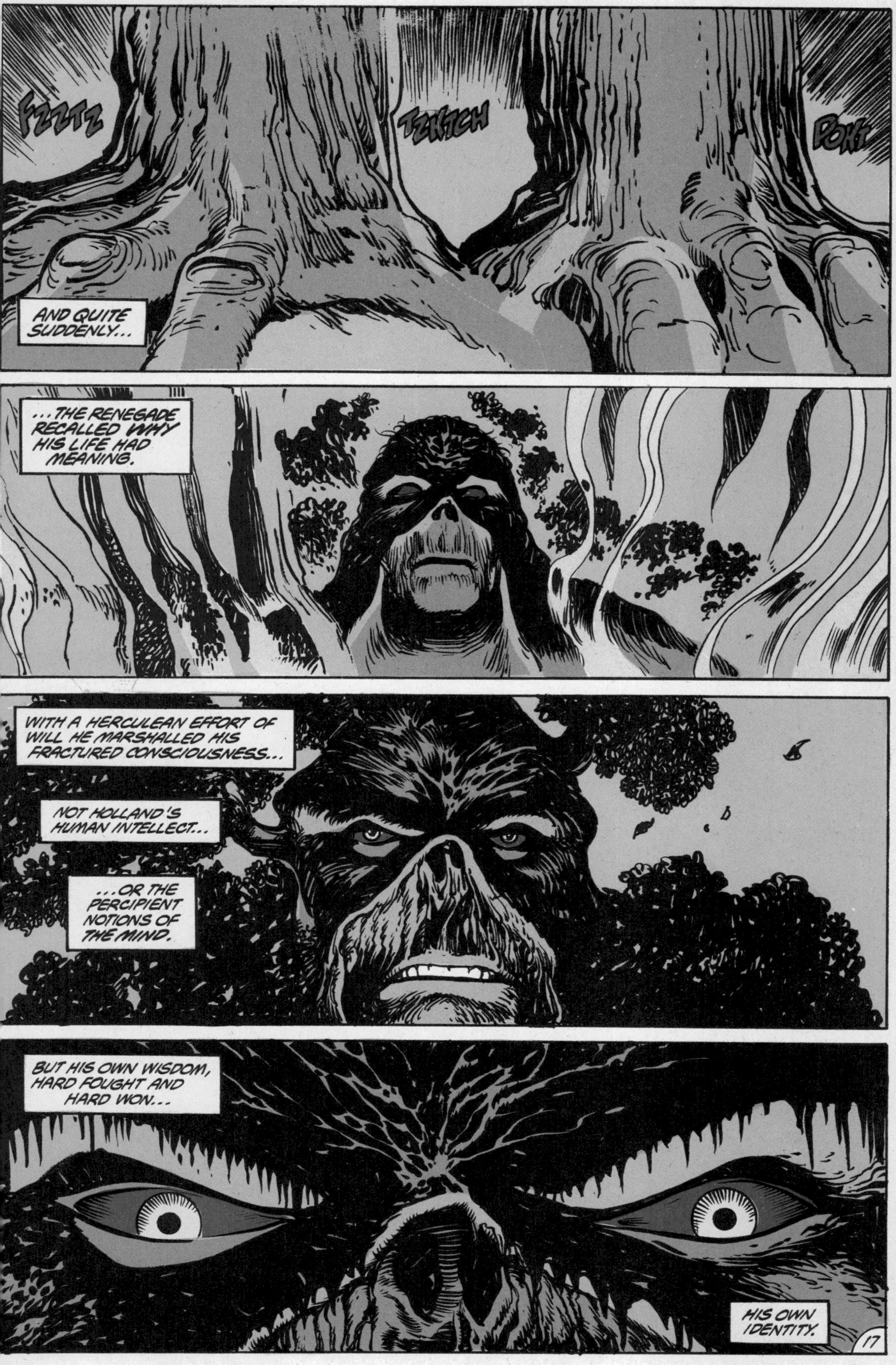
FZZZTZ
TZKTCH
POKT
AND QUITE SUDDENLY...
...THE RENEGADE RECALLED WHY HIS LIFE HAD MEANING.
WITH A HERCULEAN EFFORT OF WILL HE MARSHALLED HIS FRACTURED CONSCIOUSNESS...
NOT HOLLAND'S HUMAN INTELLECT...
...OR THE PERCIPIENT NOTIONS OF THE MIND.
BUT HIS OWN WISDOM, HARD FOUGHT AND HARD WON...
HIS OWN IDENTITY.
17

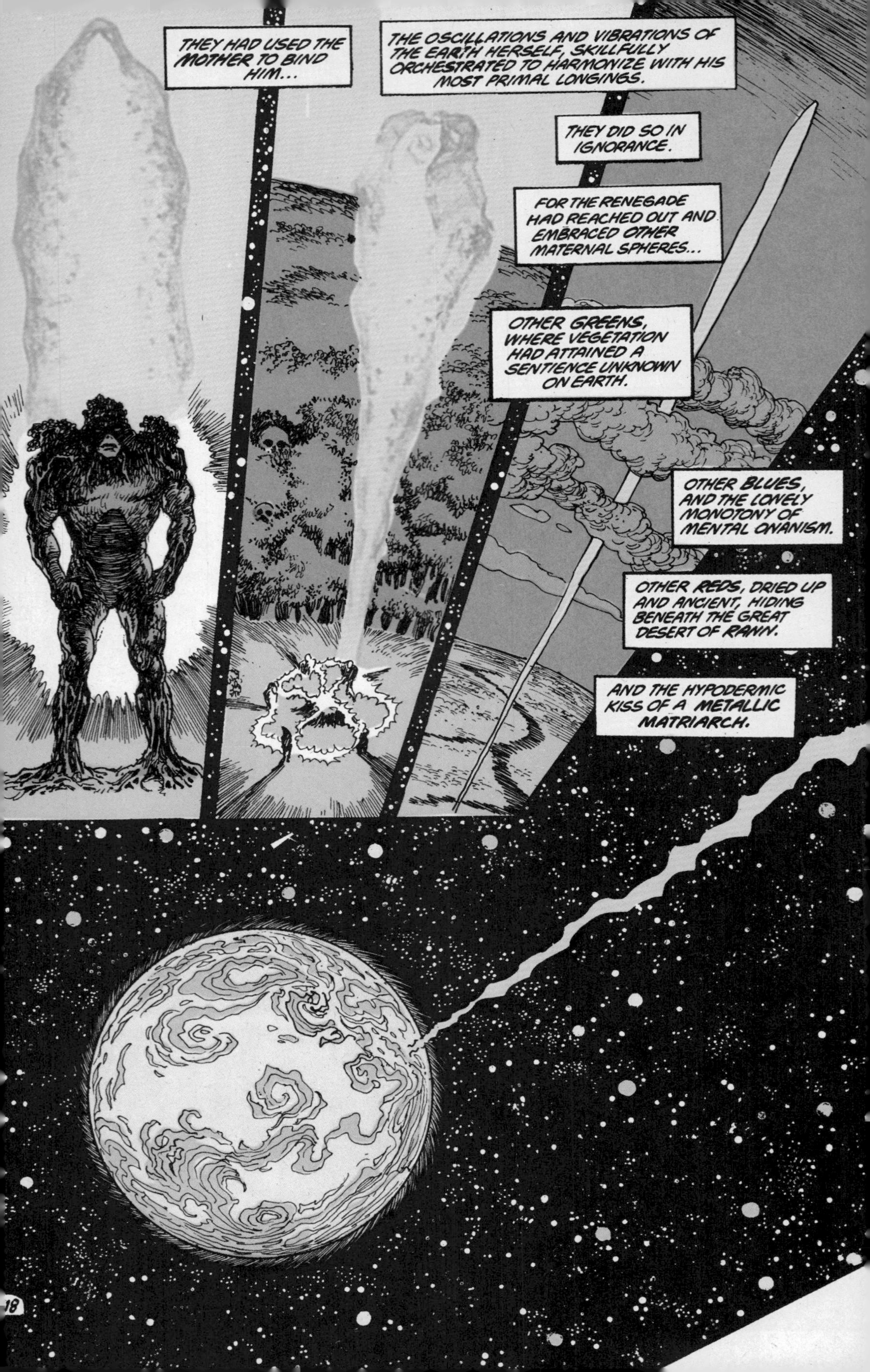
THEY HAD USED THE MOTHER TO BIND HIM...
THE OSCILLATIONS AND VIBRATIONS OF THE EARTH HERSELF, SKILLFULLY ORCHESTRATED TO HARMONIZE WITH HIS MOST PRIMAL LONGINGS.
THEY DID SO IN IGNORANCE.
FOR THE RENEGADE HAD REACHED OUT AND EMBRACED OTHER MATERNAL SPHERES...
OTHER GREENS, WHERE VEGETATION HAD ATTAINED A SENTIENCE UNKNOWN ON EARTH.
OTHER BLUES, AND THE LONELY MONOTONY OF MENTAL ONANISM.
OTHER REDS, DRIED UP AND ANCIENT, HIDING BENEATH THE GREAT DESERT OF RANN.
AND THE HYPODERMIC KISS OF A METALLIC MATRIARCH.

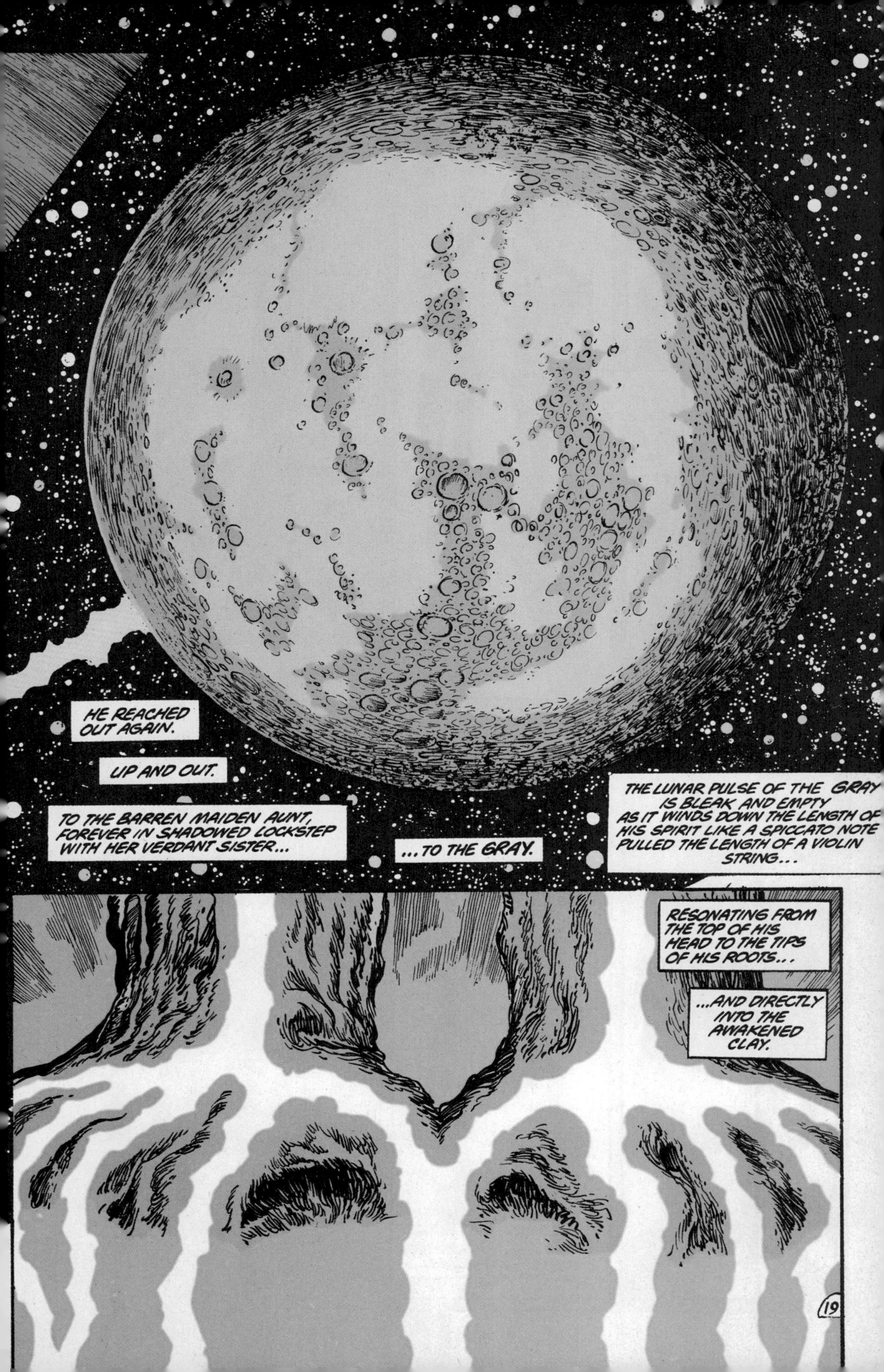
HE REACHED OUT AGAIN.
UP AND OUT.
TO THE BARREN MAIDEN AUNT, FOREVER IN SHADOWED LOCKSTEP WITH HER VERDANT SISTER...
...TO THE GRAY.
THE LUNAR PULSE OF THE GRAY IS BLEAK AND EMPTY AS IT WINDS DOWN THE LENGTH OF HIS SPIRIT LIKE A SPICCATO NOTE PULLED THE LENGTH OF A VIOLIN STRING...
RESONATING FROM THE TOP OF HIS HEAD TO THE TIPS OF HIS ROOTS...
...AND DIRECTLY INTO THE AWAKENED CLAY.
19

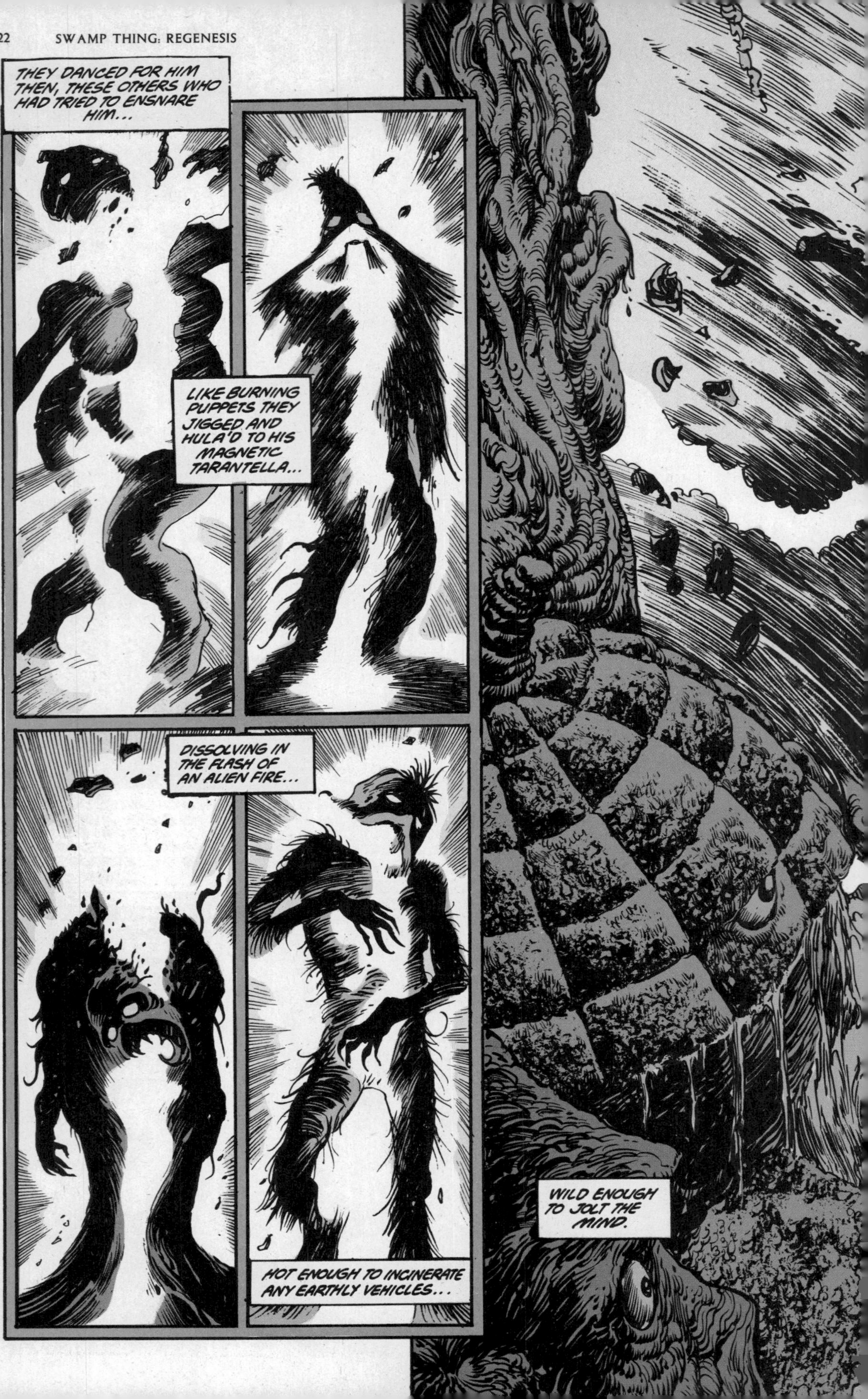
THEY DANCED FOR HIM THEN, THESE OTHERS WHO HAD TRIED TO ENSNARE HIM...
LIKE BURNING PUPPETS THEY JIGGED AND HULA'D TO HIS MAGNETIC TARANTELLA...
DISSOLVING IN THE FLASH OF AN ALIEN FIRE...
HOT ENOUGH TO INCINERATE ANY EARTHLY VEHICLES...
WILD ENOUGH TO JOLT THE MIND.

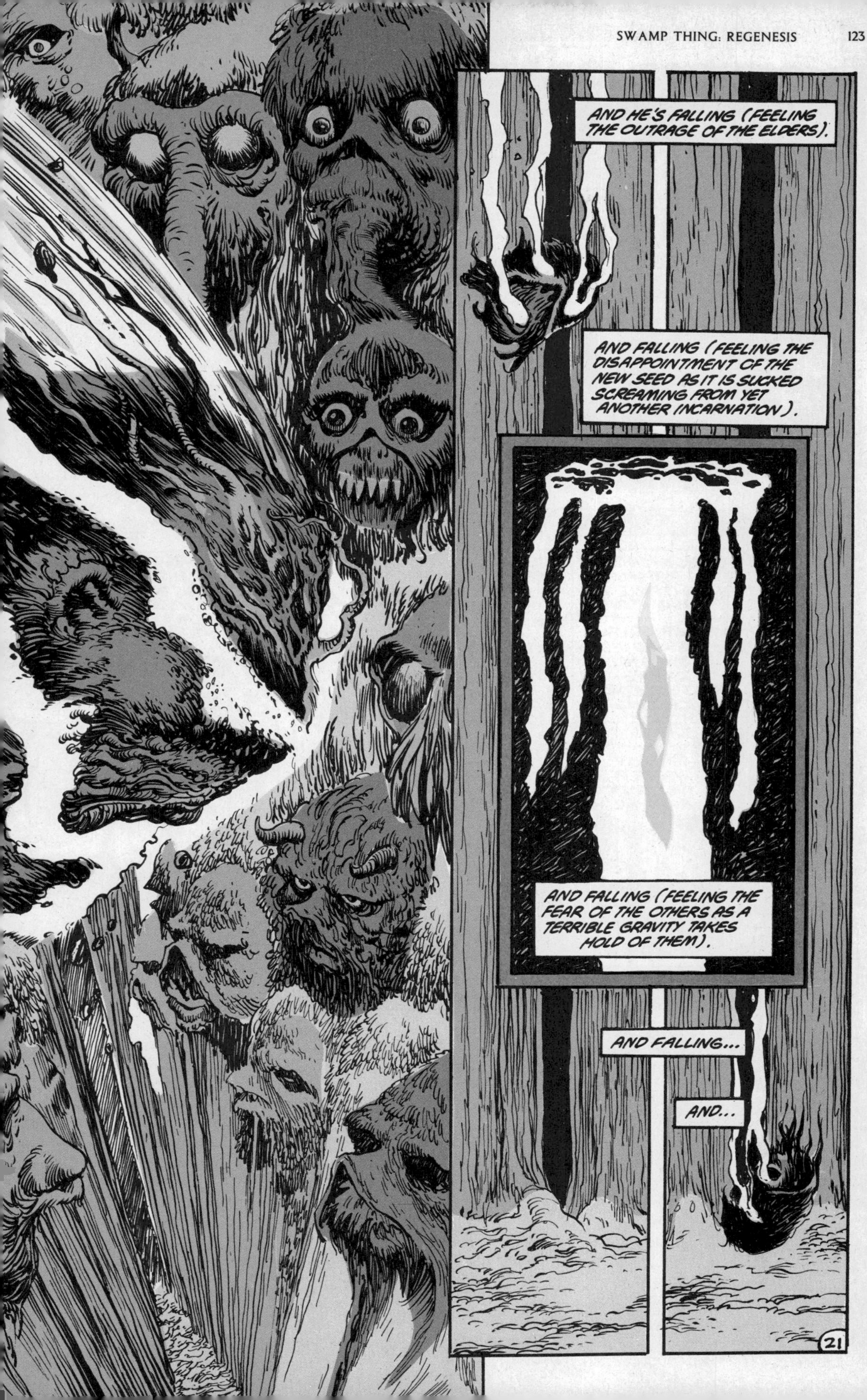
AND HE'S FALLING (FEELING THE OUTRAGE OF THE ELDERS).
AND FALLING (FEELING THE DISAPPOINTMENT OF THE NEW SEED AS IT IS SUCKED SCREAMING FROM YET ANOTHER INCARNATION).
AND FALLING (FEELING THE FEAR OF THE OTHERS AS A TERRIBLE GRAVITY TAKES HOLD OF THEM).
AND FALLING...
AND...
21

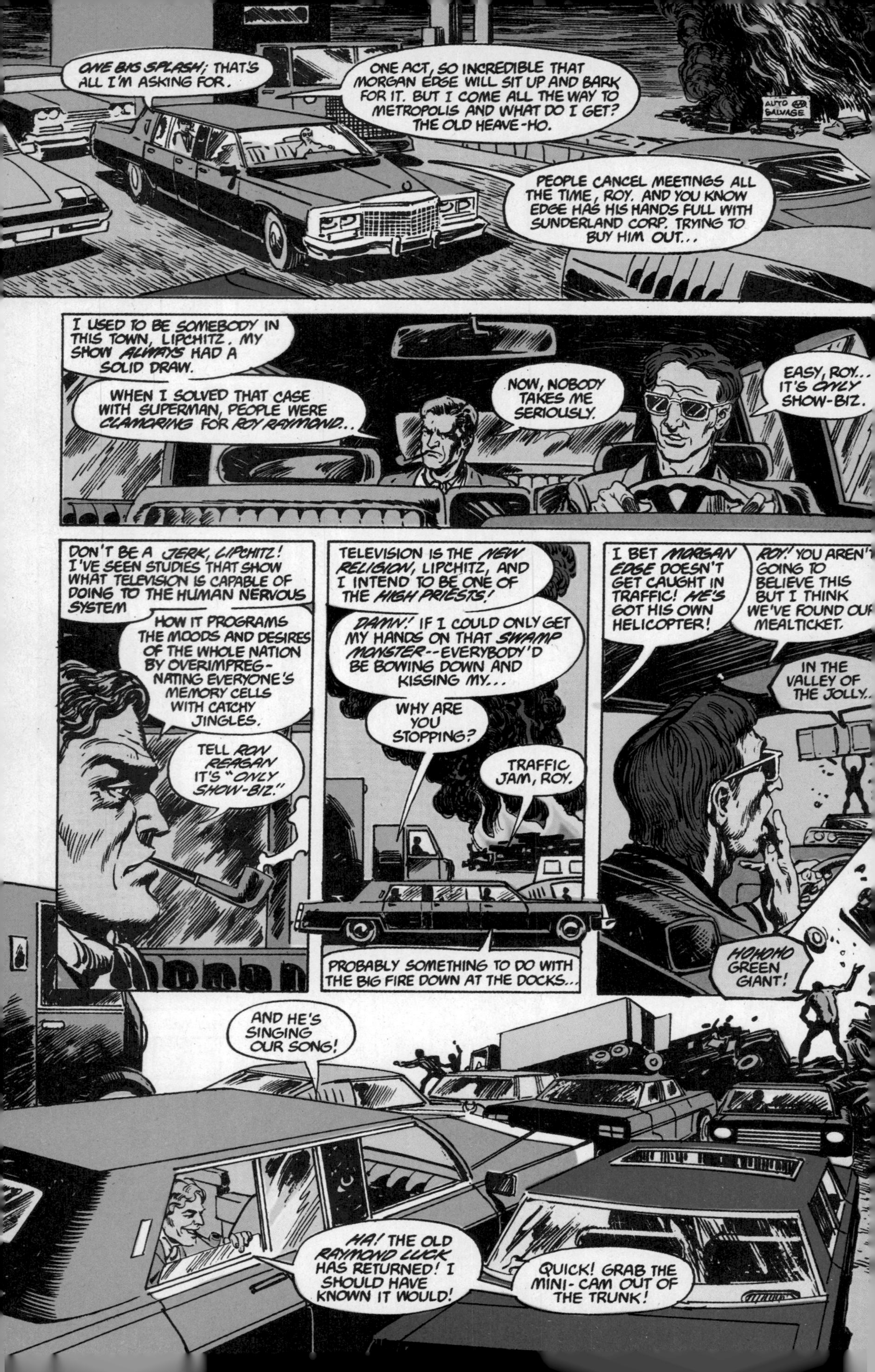
ONE BIG SPLASH; THAT'S ALL I'M ASKING FOR.
ONE ACT, SO INCREDIBLE THAT MORGAN EDGE WILL SIT UP AND BARK FOR IT. BUT I COME ALL THE WAY TO METROPOLIS AND WHAT DO I GET? THE OLD HEAVE-HO.
AUTO SALVAGE
PEOPLE CANCEL MEETINGS ALL THE TIME, ROY. AND YOU KNOW EDGE HAS HIS HANDS FULL WITH SUNDERLAND CORP. TRYING TO BUY HIM OUT...
I USED TO BE SOMEBODY IN THIS TOWN, LIPCHITZ. MY SHOW ALWAYS HAD A SOLID DRAW.
WHEN I SOLVED THAT CASE WITH SUPERMAN, PEOPLE WERE CLAMORING FOR ROY RAYMOND...
NOW, NOBODY TAKES ME SERIOUSLY.
EASY, ROY... IT'S ONLY SHOW-BIZ.
DON'T BE A JERK, LIPCHITZ! I'VE SEEN STUDIES THAT SHOW WHAT TELEVISION IS CAPABLE OF DOING TO THE HUMAN NERVOUS SYSTEM
HOW IT PROGRAMS THE MOODS AND DESIRES OF THE WHOLE NATION BY OVERIMPREG-NATING EVERYONE'S MEMORY CELLS WITH CATCHY JINGLES.
TELL RON REAGAN IT'S "ONLY SHOW-BIZ."
TELEVISION IS THE NEW RELIGION, LIPCHITZ, AND I INTEND TO BE ONE OF THE HIGH PRIESTS!
DAMN! IF I COULD ONLY GET MY HANDS ON THAT SWAMP MONSTER--EVERYBODY'D BE BOWING DOWN AND KISSING MY...
WHY ARE YOU STOPPING?
TRAFFIC JAM, ROY.
PROBABLY SOMETHING TO DO WITH THE BIG FIRE DOWN AT THE DOCKS...
I BET MORGAN EDGE DOESN'T GET CAUGHT IN TRAFFIC! HE'S GOT HIS OWN HELICOPTER!
ROY! YOU AREN'T GOING TO BELIEVE THIS BUT I THINK WE'VE FOUND OUR MEALTICKET.
IN THE VALLEY OF THE JOLLY...
HOHOHO GREEN GIANT!
AND HE'S SINGING OUR SONG!
HA! THE OLD RAYMOND LUCK HAS RETURNED! I SHOULD HAVE KNOWN IT WOULD!
QUICK! GRAB THE MINI-CAM OUT OF THE TRUNK!

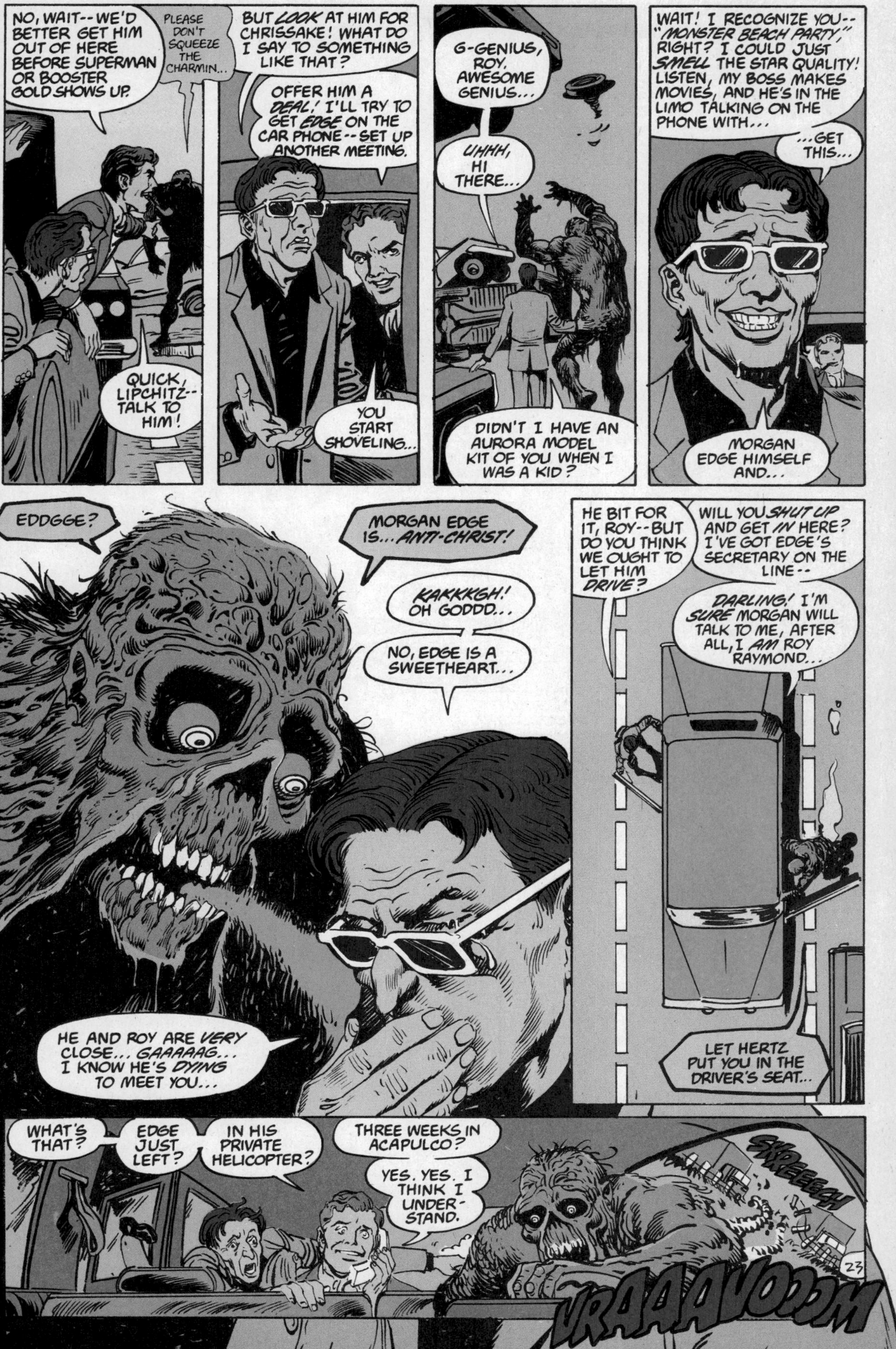
NO, WAIT--WE'D BETTER GET HIM OUT OF HERE BEFORE SUPERMAN OR BOOSTER GOLD SHOWS UP.
PLEASE DON'T SQUEEZE THE CHARMIN...
QUICK, LIPCHITZ--TALK TO HIM!
BUT LOOK AT HIM FOR CHRISSAKE! WHAT DO I SAY TO SOMETHING LIKE THAT?
OFFER HIM A DEAL! I'LL TRY TO GET EDGE ON THE CAR PHONE--SET UP ANOTHER MEETING.
YOU START SHOVELING...
G-GENIUS, ROY. AWESOME GENIUS...
UHHH, HI THERE...
DIDN'T I HAVE AN AURORA MODEL KIT OF YOU WHEN I WAS A KID?
WAIT! I RECOGNIZE YOU--"MONSTER BEACH PARTY," RIGHT? I COULD JUST SMELL THE STAR QUALITY! LISTEN, MY BOSS MAKES MOVIES, AND HE'S IN THE LIMO TALKING ON THE PHONE WITH...
...GET THIS...
MORGAN EDGE HIMSELF AND...
EDDGGE?
MORGAN EDGE IS...ANTI-CHRIST!
KAKKKGH! OH GODDD...
NO, EDGE IS A SWEETHEART...
HE AND ROY ARE VERY CLOSE... GAAAAAG... I KNOW HE'S DYING TO MEET YOU...
HE BIT FOR IT, ROY--BUT DO YOU THINK WE OUGHT TO LET HIM DRIVE?
WILL YOU SHUT UP AND GET IN HERE? I'VE GOT EDGE'S SECRETARY ON THE LINE--
DARLING! I'M SURE MORGAN WILL TALK TO ME, AFTER ALL, I AM ROY RAYMOND...
LET HERTZ PUT YOU IN THE DRIVER'S SEAT...
WHAT'S THAT?
EDGE JUST LEFT?
IN HIS PRIVATE HELICOPTER?
THREE WEEKS IN ACAPULCO?
YES. YES. I THINK I UNDERSTAND.
SKREEEECH
VRAAAAVOOOOM
23

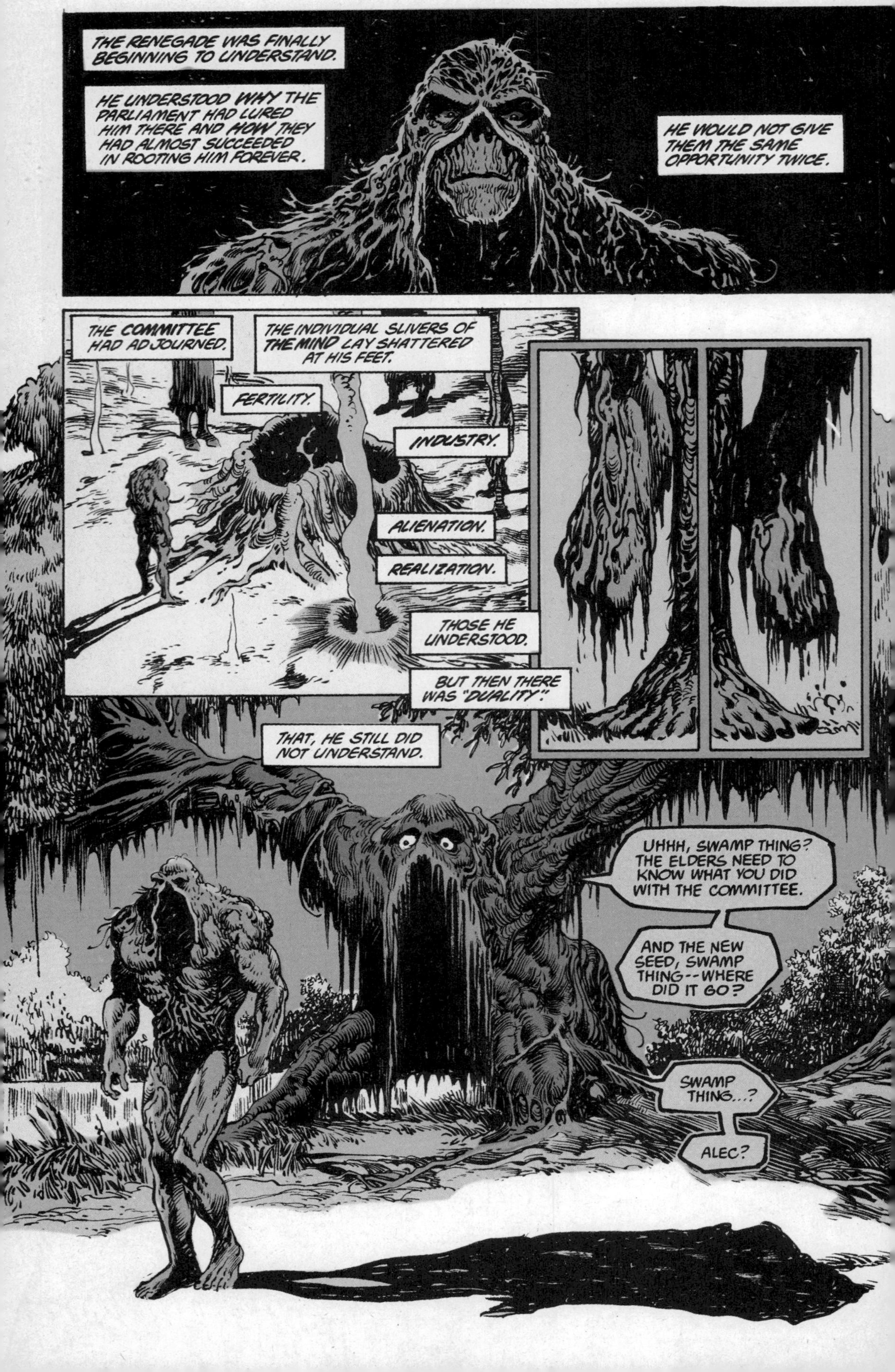
THE RENEGADE WAS FINALLY BEGINNING TO UNDERSTAND.
HE UNDERSTOOD WHY THE PARLIAMENT HAD LURED HIM THERE AND HOW THEY HAD ALMOST SUCCEEDED IN ROOTING HIM FOREVER.
HE WOULD NOT GIVE THEM THE SAME OPPORTUNITY TWICE.
THE COMMITTEE HAD ADJOURNED.
THE INDIVIDUAL SLIVERS OF THE MIND LAY SHATTERED AT HIS FEET.
FERTILITY.
INDUSTRY.
ALIENATION.
REALIZATION.
THOSE HE UNDERSTOOD.
BUT THEN THERE WAS "DUALITY".
THAT, HE STILL DID NOT UNDERSTAND.
UHHH, SWAMP THING? THE ELDERS NEED TO KNOW WHAT YOU DID WITH THE COMMITTEE.
AND THE NEW SEED, SWAMP THING--WHERE DID IT GO?
SWAMP THING...?
ALEC?

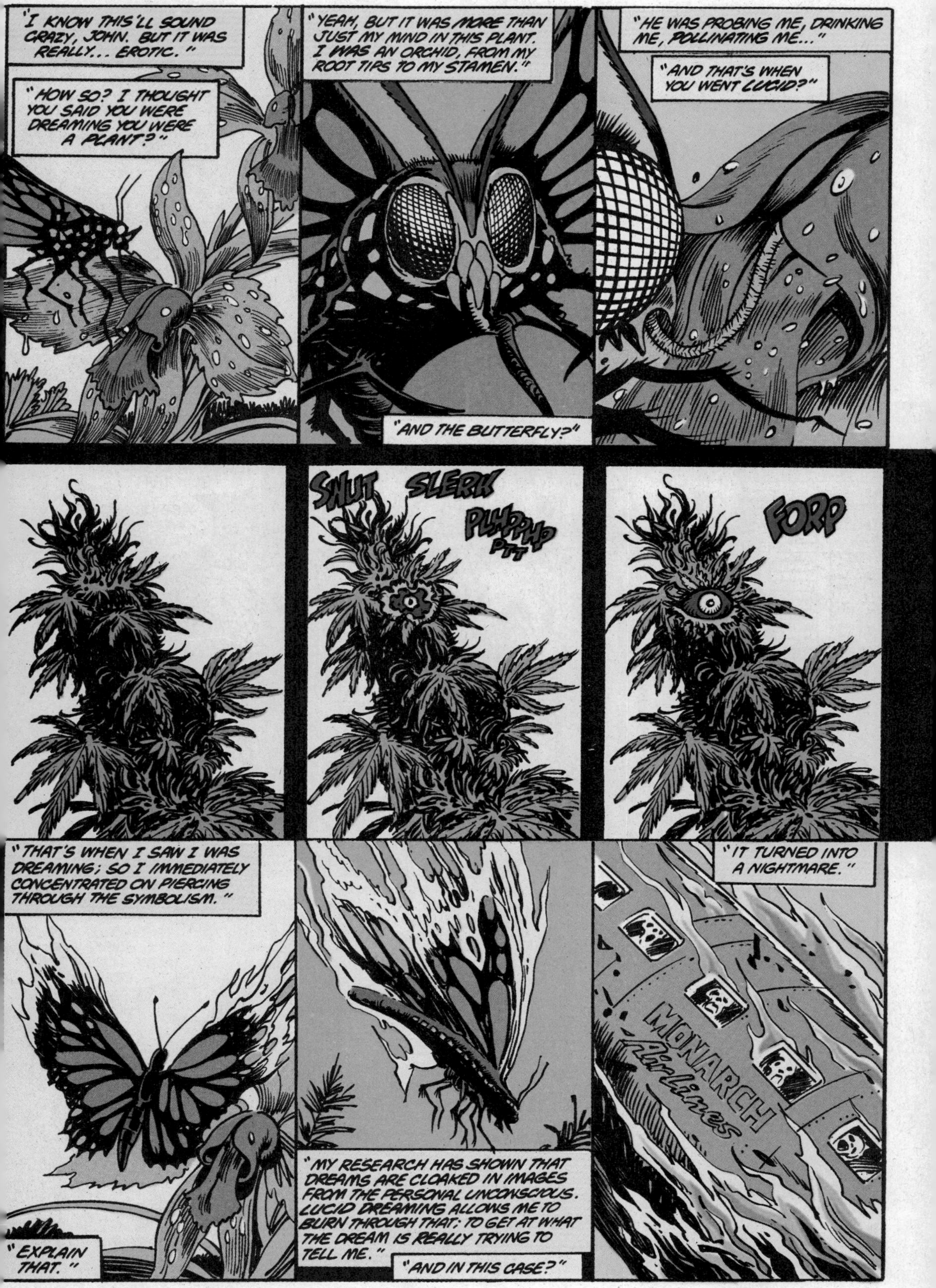
"I KNOW THIS'LL SOUND CRAZY, JOHN. BUT IT WAS REALLY... EROTIC."
"HOW SO? I THOUGHT YOU SAID YOU WERE DREAMING YOU WERE A PLANT?"
"YEAH, BUT IT WAS MORE THAN JUST MY MIND IN THIS PLANT. I WAS AN ORCHID, FROM MY ROOT TIPS TO MY STAMEN."
"AND THE BUTTERFLY?"
"HE WAS PROBING ME, DRINKING ME, POLLINATING ME..."
"AND THAT'S WHEN YOU WENT LUCID?"
SNUT
SLERK
PLHPPHP
PTT
FORP
"THAT'S WHEN I SAW I WAS DREAMING; SO I IMMEDIATELY CONCENTRATED ON PIERCING THROUGH THE SYMBOLISM."
"EXPLAIN THAT."
"MY RESEARCH HAS SHOWN THAT DREAMS ARE CLOAKED IN IMAGES FROM THE PERSONAL UNCONSCIOUS. LUCID DREAMING ALLOWS ME TO BURN THROUGH THAT: TO GET AT WHAT THE DREAM IS REALLY TRYING TO TELL ME."
"AND IN THIS CASE?"
"IT TURNED INTO A NIGHTMARE."
MONARCH
Air Lines

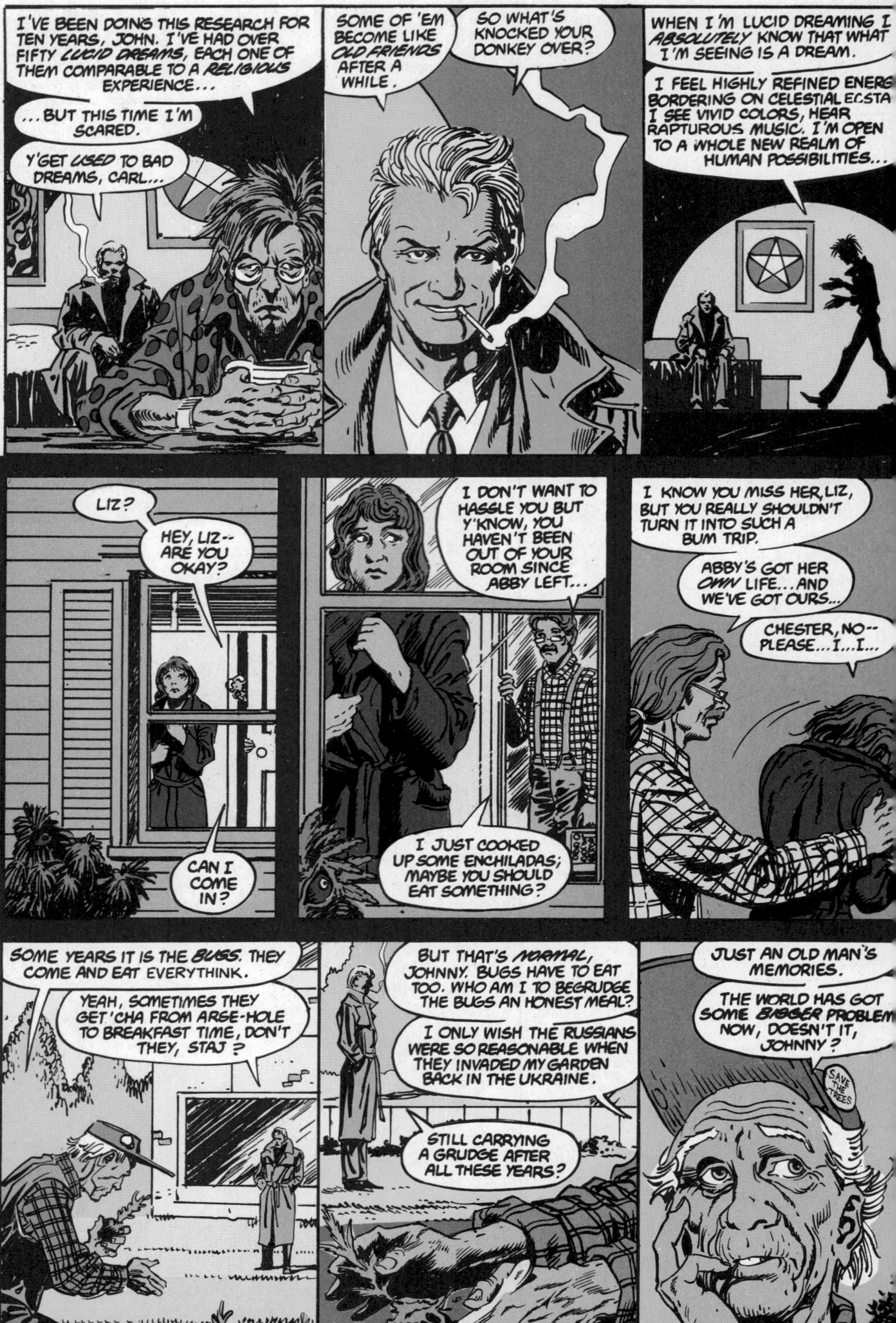
I'VE BEEN DOING THIS RESEARCH FOR TEN YEARS, JOHN. I'VE HAD OVER FIFTY LUCID DREAMS, EACH ONE OF THEM COMPARABLE TO A RELIGIOUS EXPERIENCE...
...BUT THIS TIME I'M SCARED.
Y'GET USED TO BAD DREAMS, CARL...
SOME OF 'EM BECOME LIKE OLD FRIENDS AFTER A WHILE.
SO WHAT'S KNOCKED YOUR DONKEY OVER?
WHEN I'M LUCID DREAMING I ABSOLUTELY KNOW THAT WHAT I'M SEEING IS A DREAM.
I FEEL HIGHLY REFINED ENERG BORDERING ON CELESTIAL ECSTA I SEE VIVID COLORS, HEAR RAPTUROUS MUSIC. I'M OPEN TO A WHOLE NEW REALM OF HUMAN POSSIBILITIES...
LIZ?
HEY, LIZ-- ARE YOU OKAY?
CAN I COME IN?
I DON'T WANT TO HASSLE YOU BUT Y'KNOW, YOU HAVEN'T BEEN OUT OF YOUR ROOM SINCE ABBY LEFT...
I JUST COOKED UP SOME ENCHILADAS; MAYBE YOU SHOULD EAT SOMETHING?
I KNOW YOU MISS HER, LIZ, BUT YOU REALLY SHOULDN'T TURN IT INTO SUCH A BUM TRIP.
ABBY'S GOT HER OWN LIFE... AND WE'VE GOT OURS...
CHESTER, NO-- PLEASE... I... I...
SOME YEARS IT IS THE BUGS. THEY COME AND EAT EVERYTHINK.
YEAH, SOMETIMES THEY GET 'CHA FROM ARSE-HOLE TO BREAKFAST TIME, DON'T THEY, STAJ?
2
BUT THAT'S NORMAL, JOHNNY. BUGS HAVE TO EAT TOO. WHO AM I TO BEGRUDGE THE BUGS AN HONEST MEAL?
I ONLY WISH THE RUSSIANS WERE SO REASONABLE WHEN THEY INVADED MY GARDEN BACK IN THE UKRAINE.
STILL CARRYING A GRUDGE AFTER ALL THESE YEARS?
JUST AN OLD MAN'S MEMORIES.
THE WORLD HAS GOT SOME BIGGER PROBLEM NOW, DOESN'T IT, JOHNNY?
SAVE THE TREES

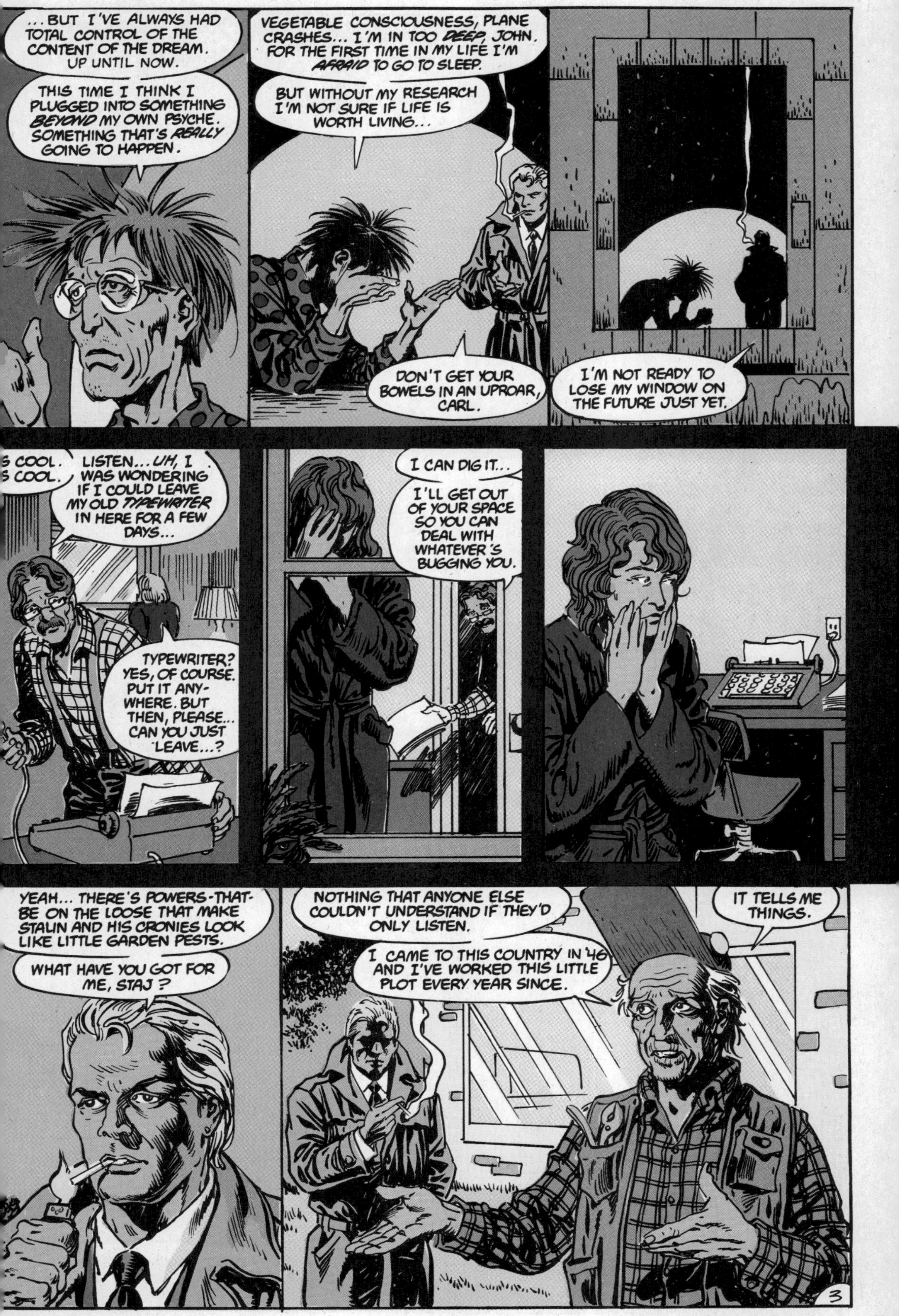
...BUT I'VE ALWAYS HAD TOTAL CONTROL OF THE CONTENT OF THE DREAM. UP UNTIL NOW.
THIS TIME I THINK I PLUGGED INTO SOMETHING BEYOND MY OWN PSYCHE. SOMETHING THAT'S REALLY GOING TO HAPPEN.
VEGETABLE CONSCIOUSNESS, PLANE CRASHES... I'M IN TOO DEEP, JOHN. FOR THE FIRST TIME IN MY LIFE I'M AFRAID TO GO TO SLEEP.
BUT WITHOUT MY RESEARCH I'M NOT SURE IF LIFE IS WORTH LIVING...
DON'T GET YOUR BOWELS IN AN UPROAR, CARL.
I'M NOT READY TO LOSE MY WINDOW ON THE FUTURE JUST YET.
S COOL.
S COOL.
LISTEN... UH, I WAS WONDERING IF I COULD LEAVE MY OLD TYPEWRITER IN HERE FOR A FEW DAYS...
TYPEWRITER? YES, OF COURSE. PUT IT ANYWHERE. BUT THEN, PLEASE... CAN YOU JUST LEAVE...?
I CAN DIG IT...
I'LL GET OUT OF YOUR SPACE SO YOU CAN DEAL WITH WHATEVER'S BUGGING YOU.
YEAH... THERE'S POWERS-THAT-BE ON THE LOOSE THAT MAKE STALIN AND HIS CRONIES LOOK LIKE LITTLE GARDEN PESTS.
WHAT HAVE YOU GOT FOR ME, STAJ?
NOTHING THAT ANYONE ELSE COULDN'T UNDERSTAND IF THEY'D ONLY LISTEN.
I CAME TO THIS COUNTRY IN '46 AND I'VE WORKED THIS LITTLE PLOT EVERY YEAR SINCE.
IT TELLS ME THINGS.
3

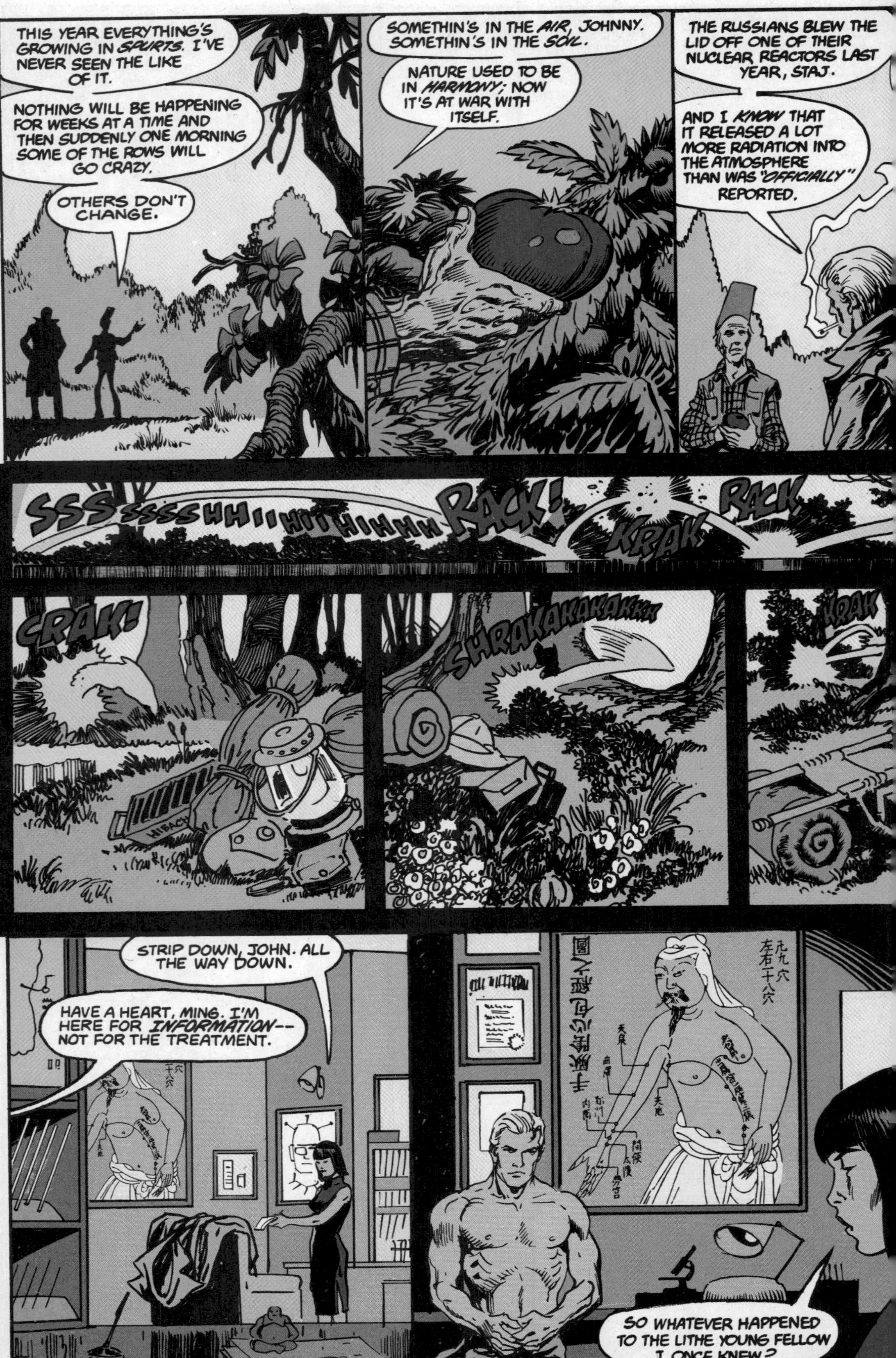

THIS YEAR EVERYTHING'S GROWING IN SPURTS. I'VE NEVER SEEN THE LIKE OF IT.
NOTHING WILL BE HAPPENING FOR WEEKS AT A TIME AND THEN SUDDENLY ONE MORNING SOME OF THE ROWS WILL GO CRAZY.
OTHERS DON'T CHANGE.
SOMETHIN'S IN THE AIR, JOHNNY. SOMETHIN'S IN THE SOIL.
NATURE USED TO BE IN HARMONY; NOW IT'S AT WAR WITH ITSELF.
THE RUSSIANS BLEW THE LID OFF ONE OF THEIR NUCLEAR REACTORS LAST YEAR, STAJ.
AND I KNOW THAT IT RELEASED A LOT MORE RADIATION INTO THE ATMOSPHERE THAN WAS "OFFICIALLY" REPORTED.
SSSSSSSHHIIHIIHIHHHRACK!
KRAK
RACK
CRAK!
HIBACHI
SHRAKAKAKAKAKKK
KRAK
STRIP DOWN, JOHN. ALL THE WAY DOWN.
HAVE A HEART, MING. I'M HERE FOR INFORMATION--NOT FOR THE TREATMENT.
SO WHATEVER HAPPENED TO THE LITHE YOUNG FELLOW I ONCE KNEW?
4

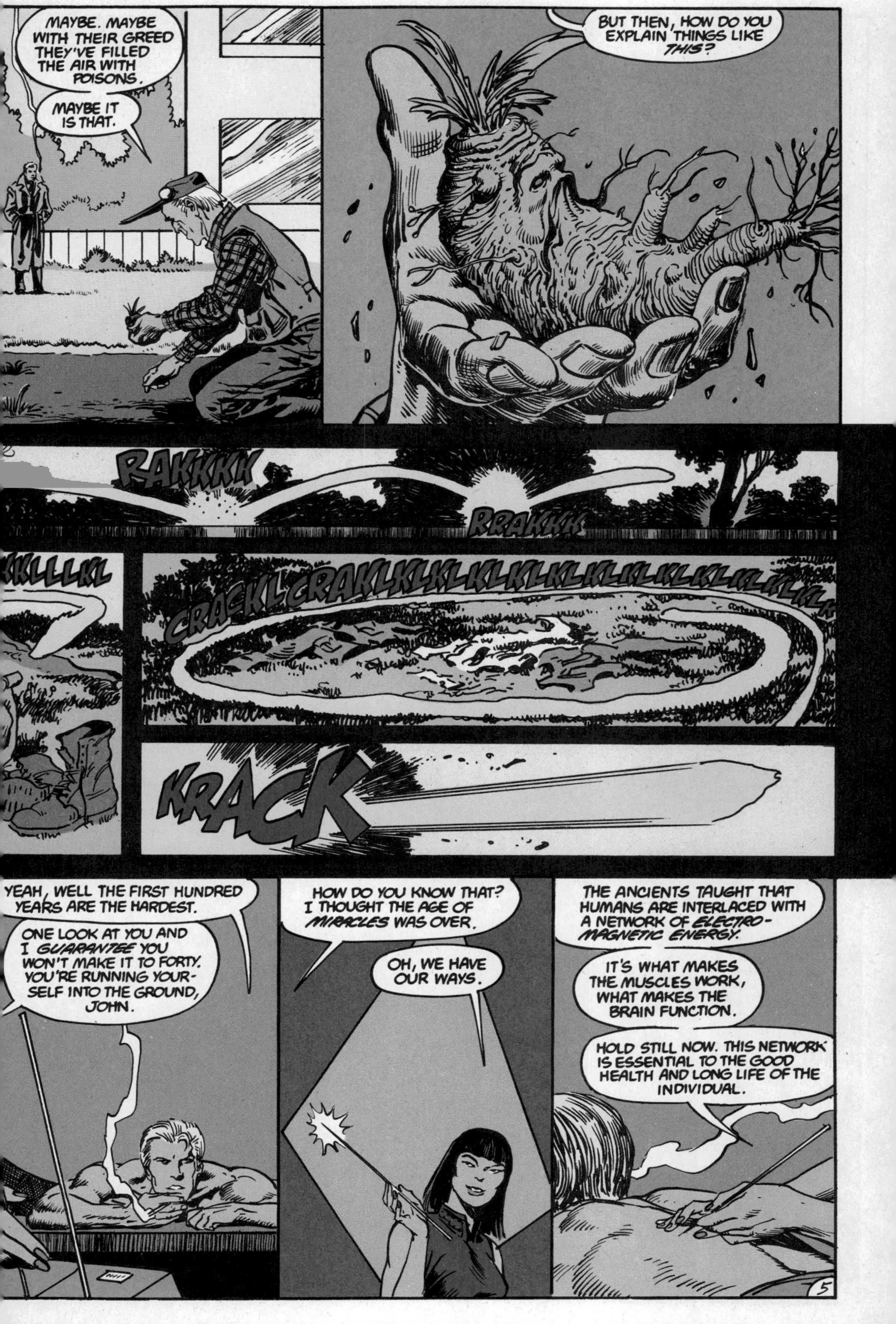
MAYBE. MAYBE WITH THEIR GREED THEY'VE FILLED THE AIR WITH POISONS.
MAYBE IT IS THAT.
BUT THEN, HOW DO YOU EXPLAIN THINGS LIKE THIS?
RAKKKK
RRAKKKK
KLLLLKL
CRACKL CRAKLKLKLKLKLKLKLKLKLKLKLKLKLK
KRACK
YEAH, WELL THE FIRST HUNDRED YEARS ARE THE HARDEST.
ONE LOOK AT YOU AND I GUARANTEE YOU WON'T MAKE IT TO FORTY. YOU'RE RUNNING YOURSELF INTO THE GROUND, JOHN.
HOW DO YOU KNOW THAT? I THOUGHT THE AGE OF MIRACLES WAS OVER.
OH, WE HAVE OUR WAYS.
THE ANCIENTS TAUGHT THAT HUMANS ARE INTERLACED WITH A NETWORK OF ELECTRO-MAGNETIC ENERGY.
IT'S WHAT MAKES THE MUSCLES WORK, WHAT MAKES THE BRAIN FUNCTION.
HOLD STILL NOW. THIS NETWORK IS ESSENTIAL TO THE GOOD HEALTH AND LONG LIFE OF THE INDIVIDUAL.
5

THE ANCIENTS, IN THEIR WISDOM, FOUND A WAY TO *MANIPULATE* THIS NETWORK, TO PUT IT BACK IN HARMONY WITH NATURE.

TODAY WE CALL THIS SCIENCE *ACUPUNCTURE*.

HEY NOW, I'M *NOT* FROM WIGAN.

I'M QUITE FAMILIAR WITH THE BASICS, THANK YOU. WHAT I *NEED* TO KNOW IS WHAT WOULD HAPPEN IN A *SPECIALIZED* CASE.

SAY SOMEONE'S ELECTRO-MAGNETIC SPECTRUM WAS BEING ALTERED BY *HIDDEN* MEANS; COULD YOU TELL?

HMM. THAT'S A TOUGH ONE.

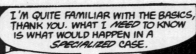

I'M PRETTY GOOD AT SPOTTING DISEASES AND SICKNESS, BUT ANYTHING BEYOND THAT YOU'LL NEED SOMEONE WITH THE *GIFT.*

THERE USED TO BE AN OLD WINO IN GOTHAM THEY SAID HAD THE TALENT. HIS NAME IS DOGBUM.

SWUT PLEP LEP

CRAK
CRAK
CRAK

FWIT

"THE SECRET

SKREK

6

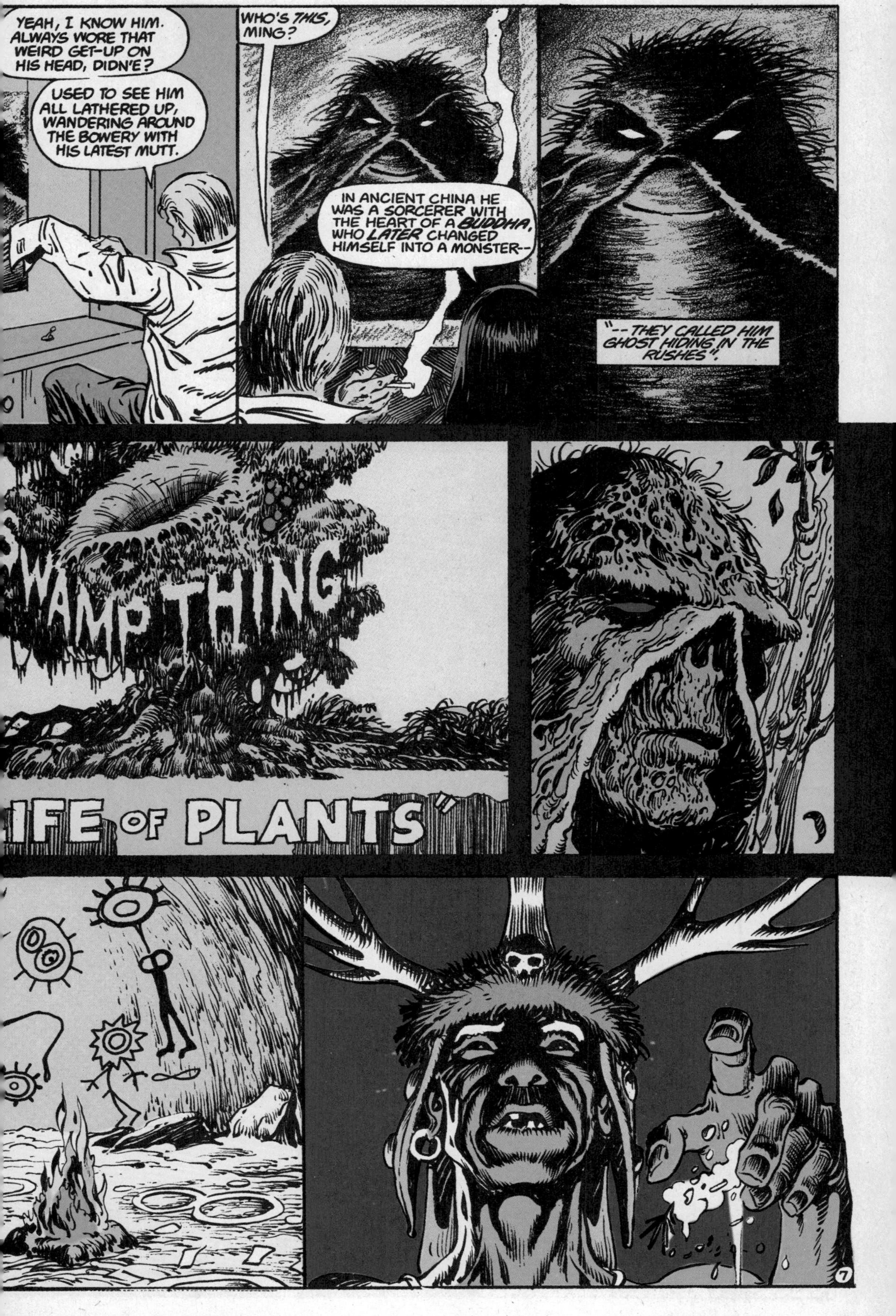
YEAH, I KNOW HIM. ALWAYS WORE THAT WEIRD GET-UP ON HIS HEAD, DIDN'E?
USED TO SEE HIM ALL LATHERED UP, WANDERING AROUND THE BOWERY WITH HIS LATEST MUTT.
WHO'S THIS, MING?
IN ANCIENT CHINA HE WAS A SORCERER WITH THE HEART OF A BUDDHA, WHO LATER CHANGED HIMSELF INTO A MONSTER--
"--THEY CALLED HIM GHOST HIDING IN THE RUSHES".
SWAMP THING
IFE OF PLANTS"
7

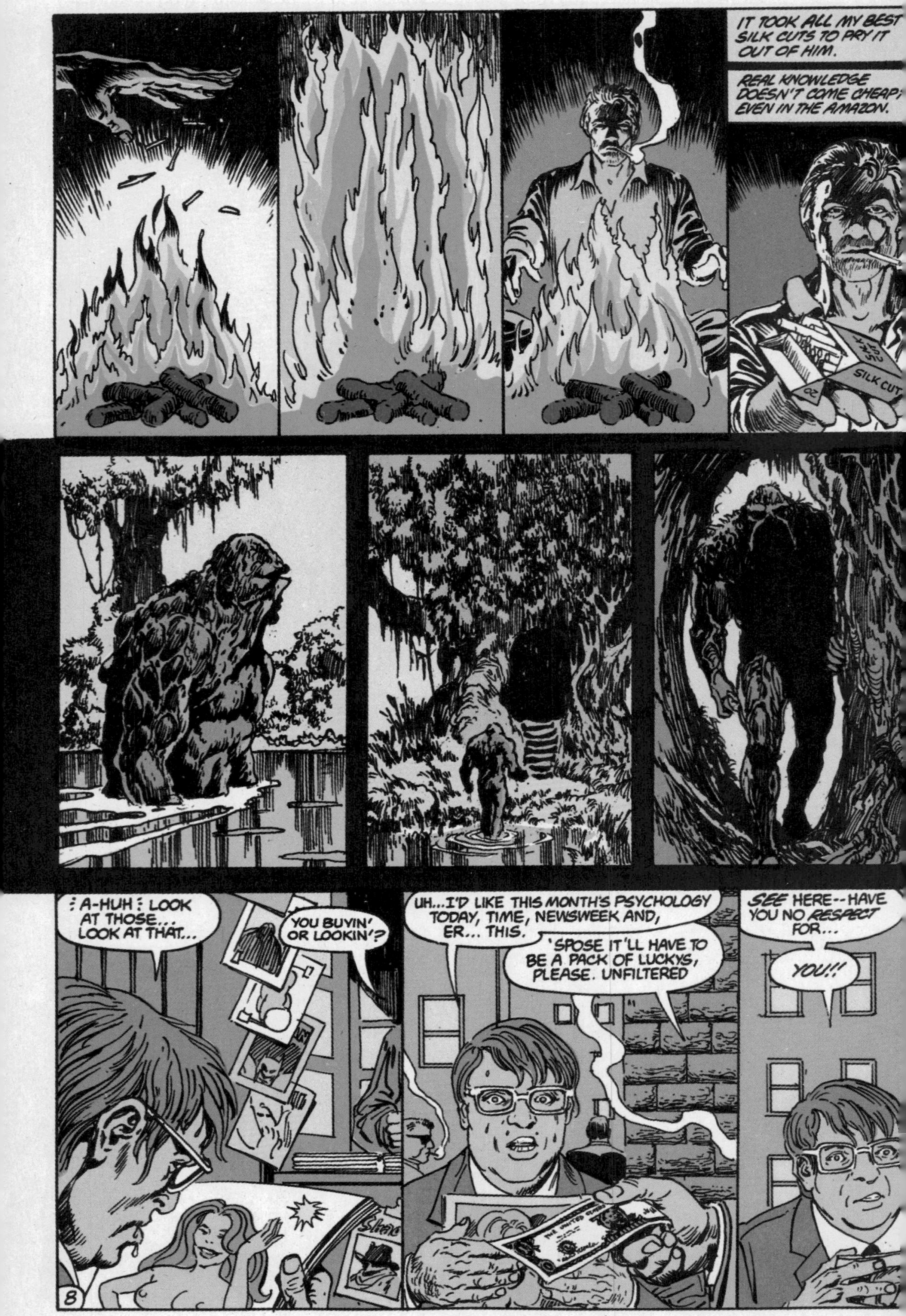
IT TOOK ALL MY BEST SILK CUTS TO PRY IT OUT OF HIM.
REAL KNOWLEDGE DOESN'T COME CHEAP: EVEN IN THE AMAZON.
SILK CUT
A-HUH LOOK AT THOSE... LOOK AT THAT...
YOU BUYIN' OR LOOKIN'?
UH...I'D LIKE THIS MONTH'S PSYCHOLOGY TODAY, TIME, NEWSWEEK AND, ER... THIS.
'SPOSE IT'LL HAVE TO BE A PACK OF LUCKYS, PLEASE. UNFILTERED
SEE HERE--HAVE YOU NO RESPECT FOR...
YOU!!
8

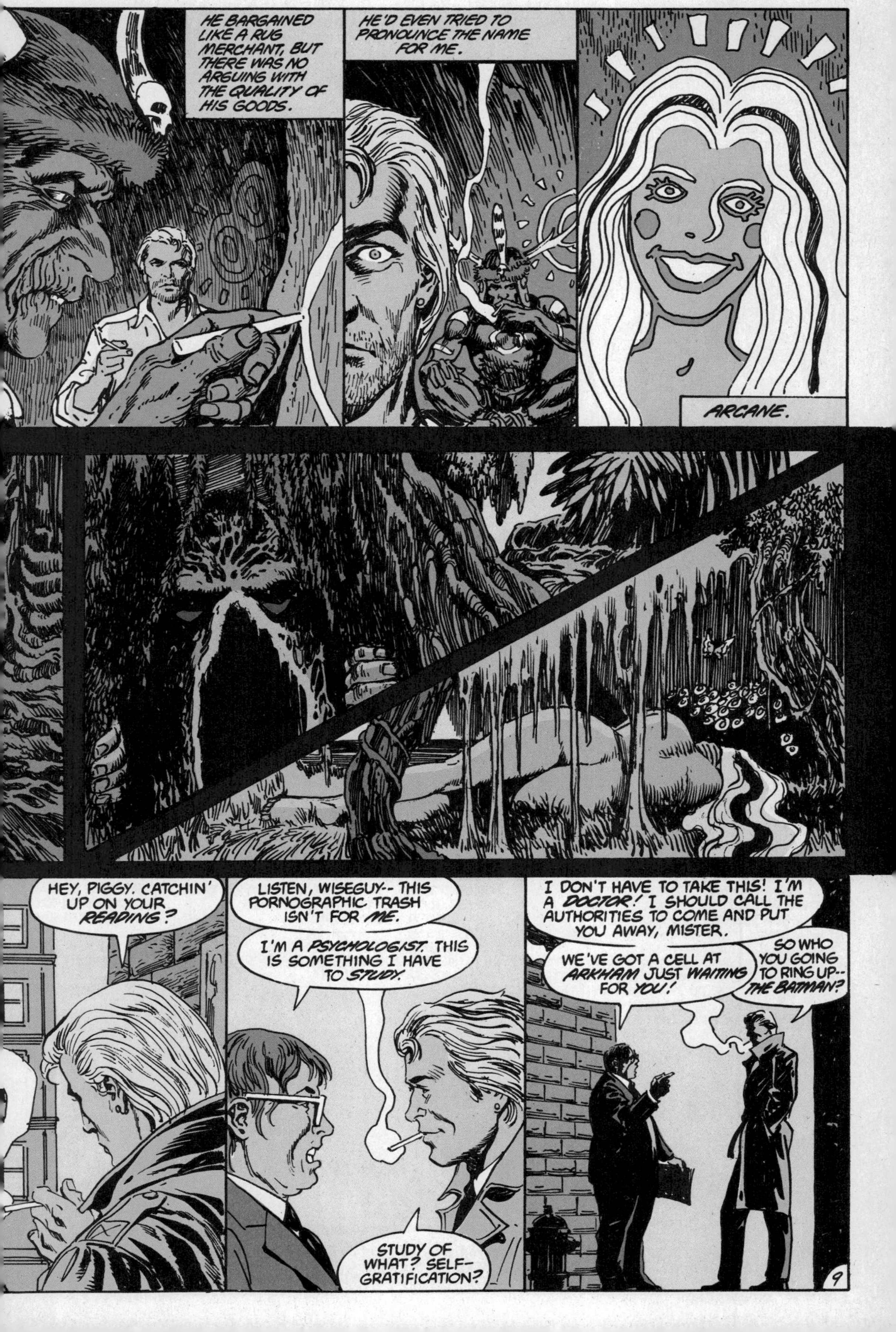
HE BARGAINED LIKE A RUG MERCHANT, BUT THERE WAS NO ARGUING WITH THE QUALITY OF HIS GOODS.
HE'D EVEN TRIED TO PRONOUNCE THE NAME FOR ME.
ARCANE.
HEY, PIGGY. CATCHIN' UP ON YOUR READING?
LISTEN, WISEGUY-- THIS PORNOGRAPHIC TRASH ISN'T FOR ME.
I'M A PSYCHOLOGIST. THIS IS SOMETHING I HAVE TO STUDY.
STUDY OF WHAT? SELF-GRATIFICATION?
I DON'T HAVE TO TAKE THIS! I'M A DOCTOR! I SHOULD CALL THE AUTHORITIES TO COME AND PUT YOU AWAY, MISTER.
WE'VE GOT A CELL AT ARKHAM JUST WAITING FOR YOU!
SO WHO YOU GOING TO RING UP-- THE BATMAN?
9

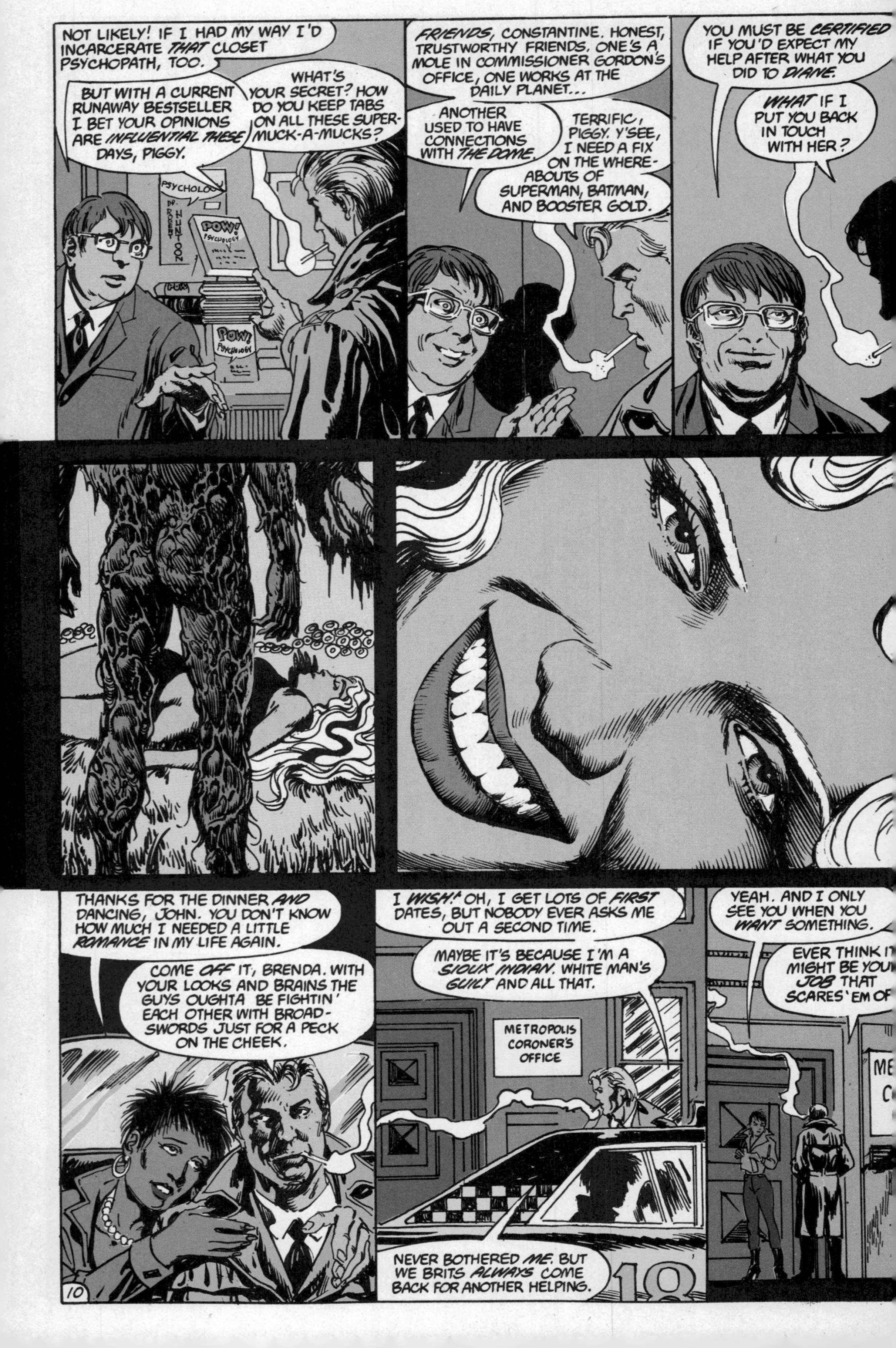
NOT LIKELY! IF I HAD MY WAY I'D INCARCERATE THAT CLOSET PSYCHOPATH, TOO.
BUT WITH A CURRENT RUNAWAY BESTSELLER I BET YOUR OPINIONS ARE INFLUENTIAL THESE DAYS, PIGGY.
WHAT'S YOUR SECRET? HOW DO YOU KEEP TABS ON ALL THESE SUPER-MUCK-A-MUCKS?
PSYCHOLO
DR. ROBERT HUNTOON
POW! PSYCHOLOGY
POW! PSYCHOLOGY
FRIENDS, CONSTANTINE. HONEST, TRUSTWORTHY FRIENDS. ONE'S A MOLE IN COMMISSIONER GORDON'S OFFICE, ONE WORKS AT THE DAILY PLANET...
ANOTHER USED TO HAVE CONNECTIONS WITH THE DOME.
TERRIFIC, PIGGY. Y'SEE, I NEED A FIX ON THE WHERE-ABOUTS OF SUPERMAN, BATMAN, AND BOOSTER GOLD.
YOU MUST BE CERTIFIED IF YOU'D EXPECT MY HELP AFTER WHAT YOU DID TO DIANE.
WHAT IF I PUT YOU BACK IN TOUCH WITH HER?
THANKS FOR THE DINNER AND DANCING, JOHN. YOU DON'T KNOW HOW MUCH I NEEDED A LITTLE ROMANCE IN MY LIFE AGAIN.
COME OFF IT, BRENDA. WITH YOUR LOOKS AND BRAINS THE GUYS OUGHTA BE FIGHTIN' EACH OTHER WITH BROAD-SWORDS JUST FOR A PECK ON THE CHEEK.
10
I WISH! OH, I GET LOTS OF FIRST DATES, BUT NOBODY EVER ASKS ME OUT A SECOND TIME.
MAYBE IT'S BECAUSE I'M A SIOUX INDIAN. WHITE MAN'S GUILT AND ALL THAT.
METROPOLIS CORONER'S OFFICE
NEVER BOTHERED ME. BUT WE BRITS ALWAYS COME BACK FOR ANOTHER HELPING.
18
YEAH. AND I ONLY SEE YOU WHEN YOU WANT SOMETHING.
EVER THINK IT MIGHT BE YOU JOB THAT SCARES 'EM OF

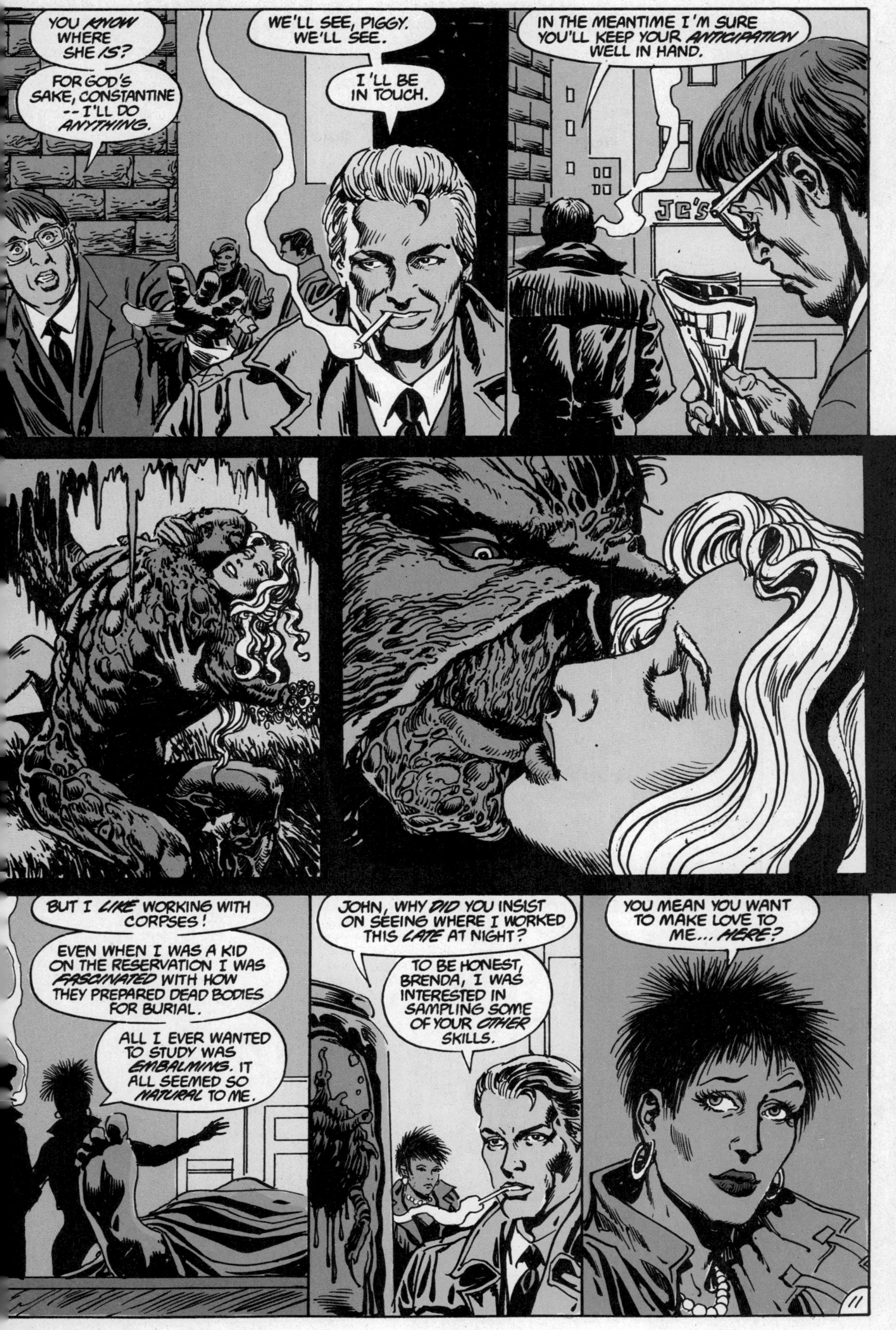
YOU KNOW WHERE SHE IS?
FOR GOD'S SAKE, CONSTANTINE -- I'LL DO ANYTHING.
WE'LL SEE, PIGGY. WE'LL SEE.
I'LL BE IN TOUCH.
IN THE MEANTIME I'M SURE YOU'LL KEEP YOUR ANTICIPATION WELL IN HAND.
JC'S
BUT I LIKE WORKING WITH CORPSES!
EVEN WHEN I WAS A KID ON THE RESERVATION I WAS FASCINATED WITH HOW THEY PREPARED DEAD BODIES FOR BURIAL.
ALL I EVER WANTED TO STUDY WAS EMBALMING. IT ALL SEEMED SO NATURAL TO ME.
JOHN, WHY DID YOU INSIST ON SEEING WHERE I WORKED THIS LATE AT NIGHT?
TO BE HONEST, BRENDA, I WAS INTERESTED IN SAMPLING SOME OF YOUR OTHER SKILLS.
YOU MEAN YOU WANT TO MAKE LOVE TO ME... HERE?
11

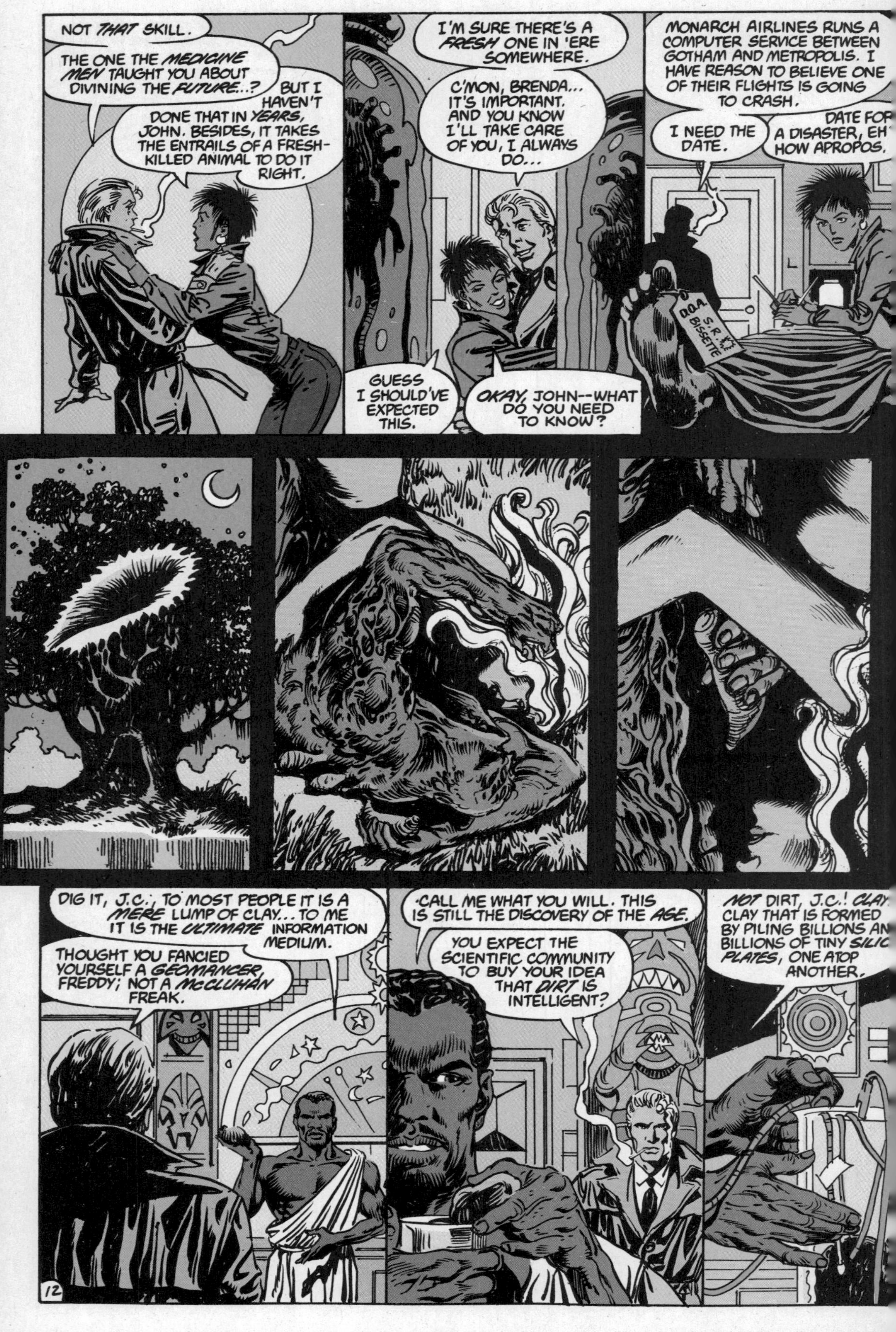
NOT THAT SKILL.
THE ONE THE MEDICINE MEN TAUGHT YOU ABOUT DIVINING THE FUTURE...?
BUT I HAVEN'T DONE THAT IN YEARS, JOHN. BESIDES, IT TAKES THE ENTRAILS OF A FRESH-KILLED ANIMAL TO DO IT RIGHT.
I'M SURE THERE'S A FRESH ONE IN 'ERE SOMEWHERE.
C'MON, BRENDA... IT'S IMPORTANT. AND YOU KNOW I'LL TAKE CARE OF YOU, I ALWAYS DO...
GUESS I SHOULD'VE EXPECTED THIS.
OKAY, JOHN--WHAT DO YOU NEED TO KNOW?
MONARCH AIRLINES RUNS A COMPUTER SERVICE BETWEEN GOTHAM AND METROPOLIS. I HAVE REASON TO BELIEVE ONE OF THEIR FLIGHTS IS GOING TO CRASH.
I NEED THE DATE.
DATE FOR A DISASTER, EH HOW APROPOS.
D.O.A. S.R. BISSETTE
DIG IT, J.C., TO MOST PEOPLE IT IS A MERE LUMP OF CLAY... TO ME IT IS THE ULTIMATE INFORMATION MEDIUM.
THOUGHT YOU FANCIED YOURSELF A GEOMANCER, FREDDY; NOT A McCLUHAN FREAK.
CALL ME WHAT YOU WILL. THIS IS STILL THE DISCOVERY OF THE AGE.
YOU EXPECT THE SCIENTIFIC COMMUNITY TO BUY YOUR IDEA THAT DIRT IS INTELLIGENT?
NOT DIRT, J.C.! CLAY CLAY THAT IS FORMED BY PILING BILLIONS AN BILLIONS OF TINY SILIC PLATES, ONE ATOP ANOTHER.
12

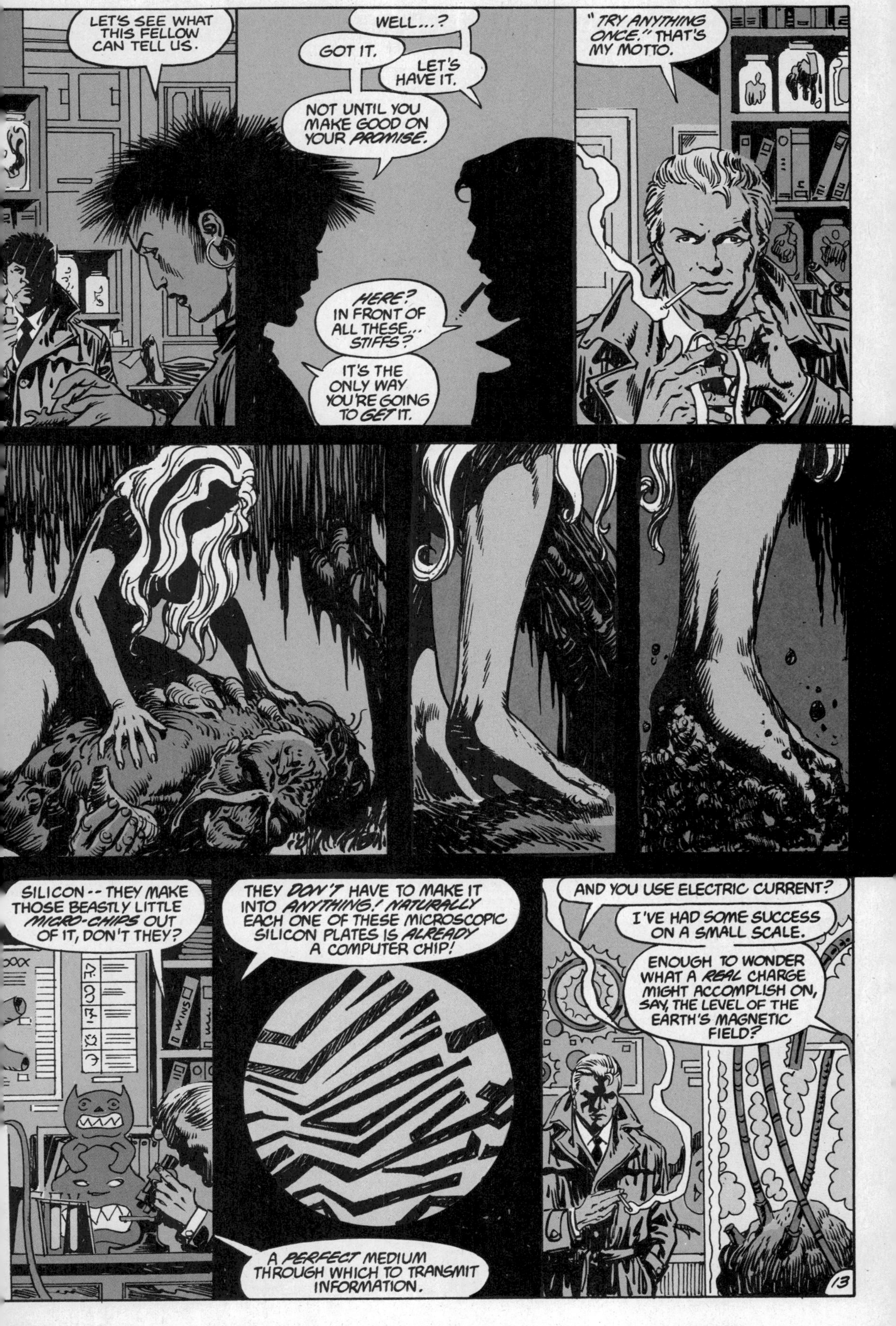
LET'S SEE WHAT THIS FELLOW CAN TELL US.
WELL...?
GOT IT.
LET'S HAVE IT.
NOT UNTIL YOU MAKE GOOD ON YOUR PROMISE.
HERE? IN FRONT OF ALL THESE... STIFFS?
IT'S THE ONLY WAY YOU'RE GOING TO GET IT.
"TRY ANYTHING ONCE." THAT'S MY MOTTO.
SILICON -- THEY MAKE THOSE BEASTLY LITTLE MICRO-CHIPS OUT OF IT, DON'T THEY?
THEY DON'T HAVE TO MAKE IT INTO ANYTHING! NATURALLY EACH ONE OF THESE MICROSCOPIC SILICON PLATES IS ALREADY A COMPUTER CHIP!
A PERFECT MEDIUM THROUGH WHICH TO TRANSMIT INFORMATION.
AND YOU USE ELECTRIC CURRENT?
I'VE HAD SOME SUCCESS ON A SMALL SCALE.
ENOUGH TO WONDER WHAT A REAL CHARGE MIGHT ACCOMPLISH ON, SAY, THE LEVEL OF THE EARTH'S MAGNETIC FIELD?
13

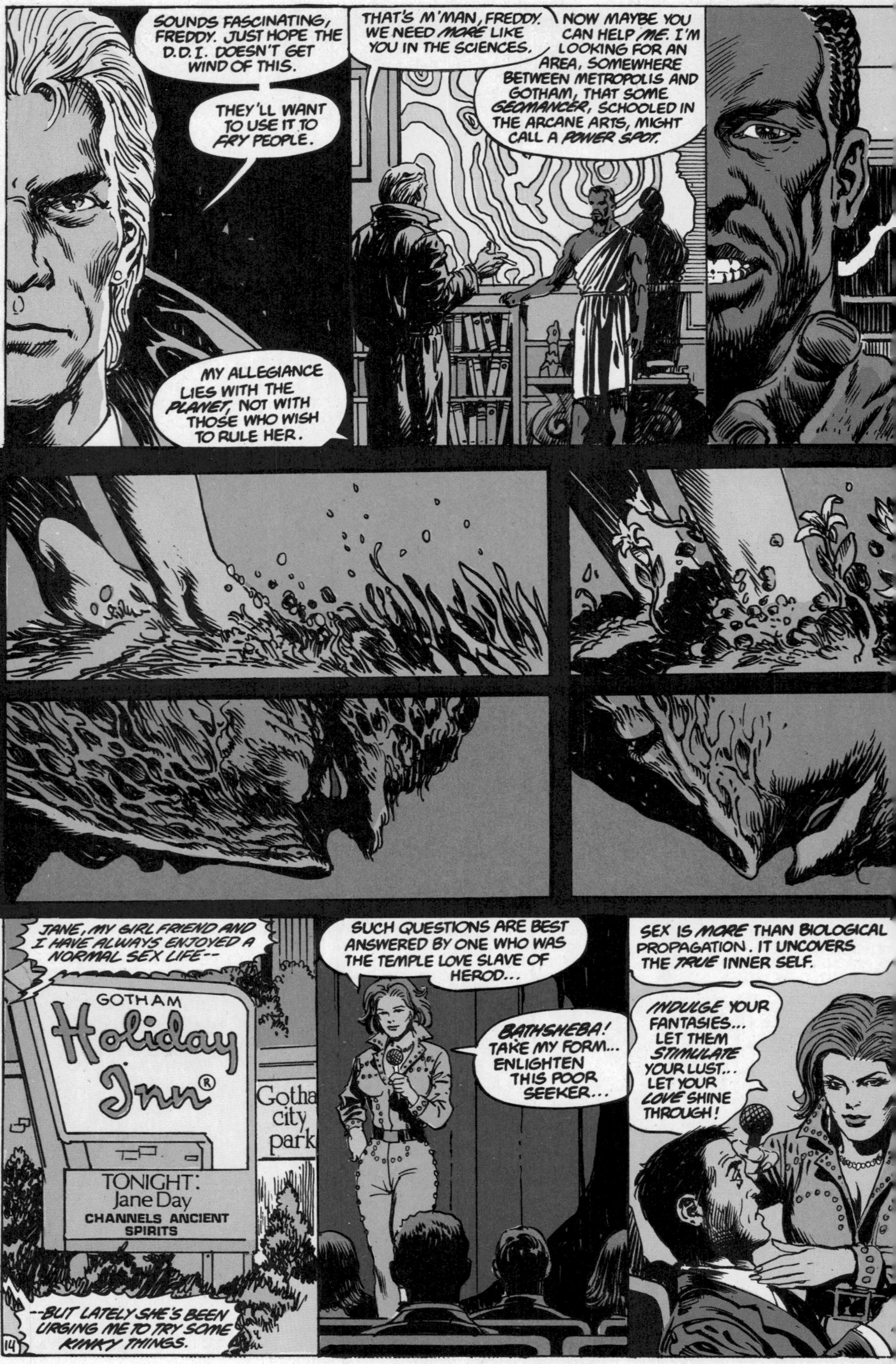
SOUNDS FASCINATING, FREDDY. JUST HOPE THE D.D.I. DOESN'T GET WIND OF THIS.
THEY'LL WANT TO USE IT TO FRY PEOPLE.
MY ALLEGIANCE LIES WITH THE PLANET, NOT WITH THOSE WHO WISH TO RULE HER.
THAT'S M'MAN, FREDDY. WE NEED MORE LIKE YOU IN THE SCIENCES.
NOW MAYBE YOU CAN HELP ME. I'M LOOKING FOR AN AREA, SOMEWHERE BETWEEN METROPOLIS AND GOTHAM, THAT SOME GEOMANCER, SCHOOLED IN THE ARCANE ARTS, MIGHT CALL A POWER SPOT.
JANE, MY GIRL FRIEND AND I HAVE ALWAYS ENJOYED A NORMAL SEX LIFE--
GOTHAM
Holiday Inn®
TONIGHT:
Jane Day
CHANNELS ANCIENT SPIRITS
Gotha
city
park
--BUT LATELY SHE'S BEEN URGING ME TO TRY SOME KINKY THINGS.
14
SUCH QUESTIONS ARE BEST ANSWERED BY ONE WHO WAS THE TEMPLE LOVE SLAVE OF HEROD...
BATHSHEBA! TAKE MY FORM... ENLIGHTEN THIS POOR SEEKER...
SEX IS MORE THAN BIOLOGICAL PROPAGATION. IT UNCOVERS THE TRUE INNER SELF.
INDULGE YOUR FANTASIES... LET THEM STIMULATE YOUR LUST... LET YOUR LOVE SHINE THROUGH!

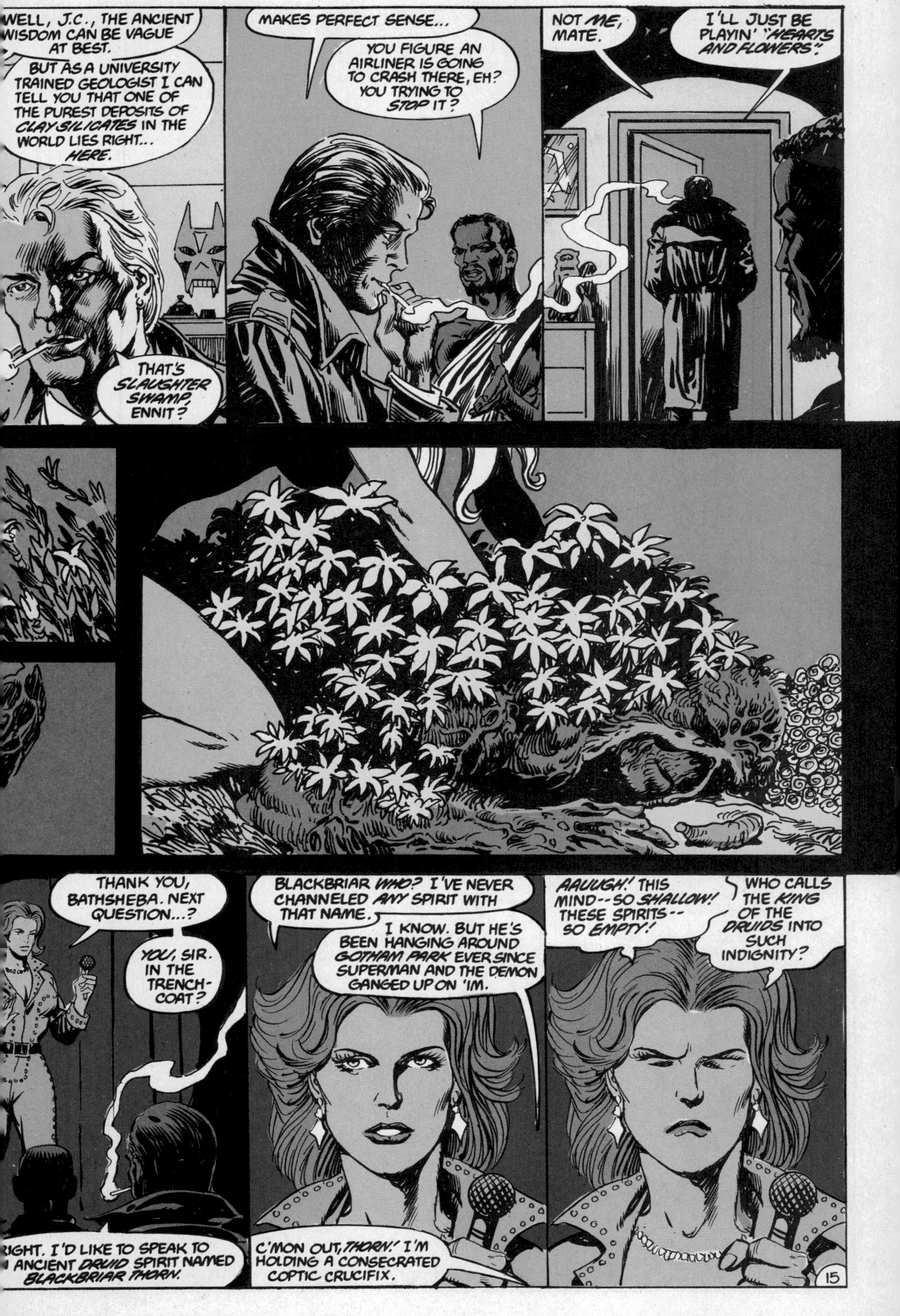
WELL, J.C., THE ANCIENT WISDOM CAN BE VAGUE AT BEST.
BUT AS A UNIVERSITY TRAINED GEOLOGIST I CAN TELL YOU THAT ONE OF THE PUREST DEPOSITS OF CLAY SILICATES IN THE WORLD LIES RIGHT... HERE.
THAT'S SLAUGHTER SWAMP, ENNIT?
MAKES PERFECT SENSE...
YOU FIGURE AN AIRLINER IS GOING TO CRASH THERE, EH? YOU TRYING TO STOP IT?
NOT ME, MATE.
I'LL JUST BE PLAYIN' "HEARTS AND FLOWERS."
THANK YOU, BATHSHEBA. NEXT QUESTION...?
YOU, SIR. IN THE TRENCH-COAT?
RIGHT. I'D LIKE TO SPEAK TO AN ANCIENT DRUID SPIRIT NAMED BLACKBRIAR THORN.
BLACKBRIAR WHO? I'VE NEVER CHANNELED ANY SPIRIT WITH THAT NAME.
I KNOW. BUT HE'S BEEN HANGING AROUND GOTHAM PARK EVER SINCE SUPERMAN AND THE DEMON GANGED UP ON 'IM.
C'MON OUT, THORN! I'M HOLDING A CONSECRATED COPTIC CRUCIFIX.
AAUUGH! THIS MIND--SO SHALLOW! THESE SPIRITS--SO EMPTY!
WHO CALLS THE KING OF THE DRUIDS INTO SUCH INDIGNITY?
15

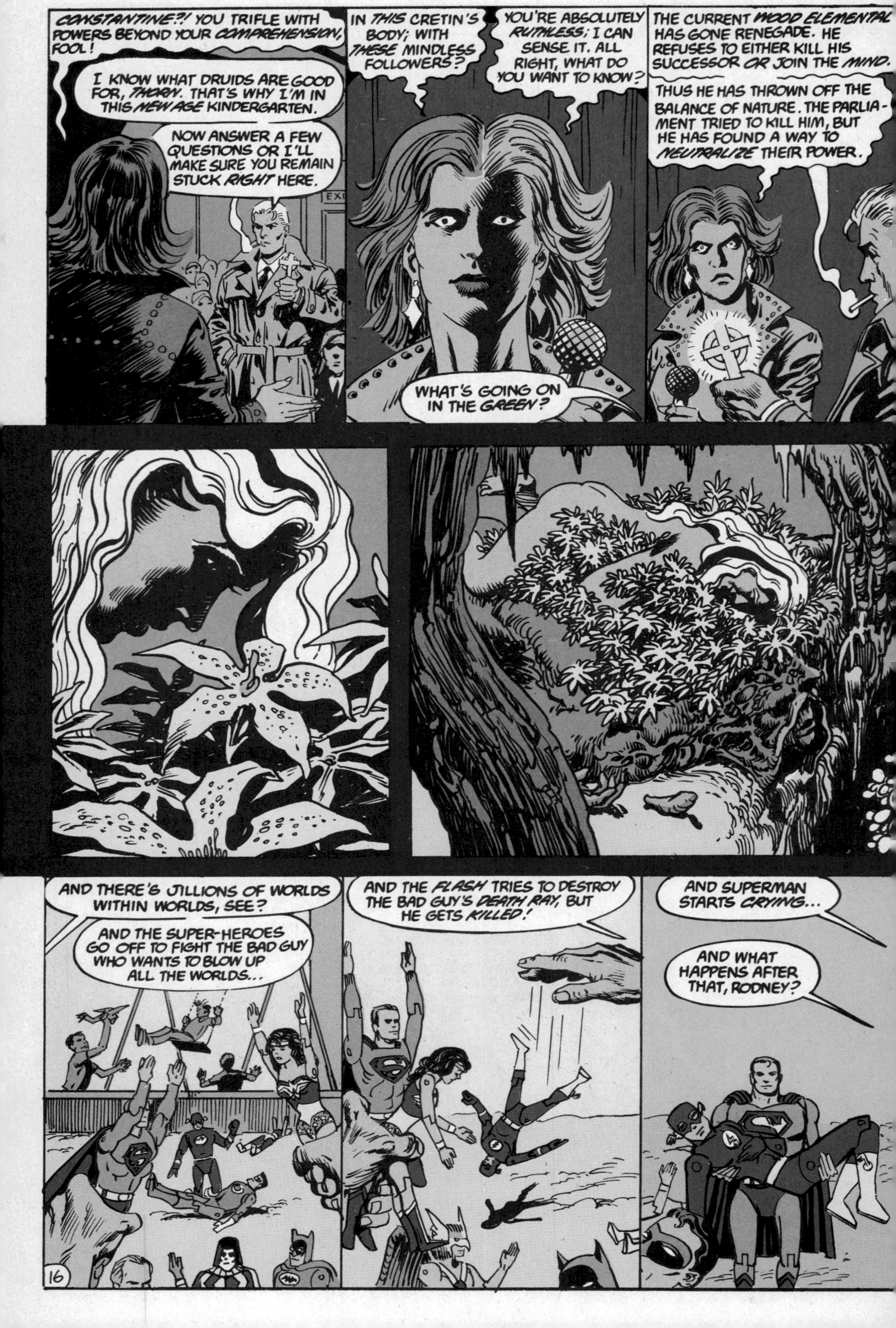
CONSTANTINE?! YOU TRIFLE WITH POWERS BEYOND YOUR COMPREHENSION, FOOL!
I KNOW WHAT DRUIDS ARE GOOD FOR, THORN. THAT'S WHY I'M IN THIS NEW AGE KINDERGARTEN.
NOW ANSWER A FEW QUESTIONS OR I'LL MAKE SURE YOU REMAIN STUCK RIGHT HERE.
IN THIS CRETIN'S BODY; WITH THESE MINDLESS FOLLOWERS?
YOU'RE ABSOLUTELY RUTHLESS; I CAN SENSE IT. ALL RIGHT, WHAT DO YOU WANT TO KNOW?
WHAT'S GOING ON IN THE GREEN?
THE CURRENT WOOD ELEMENTAL HAS GONE RENEGADE. HE REFUSES TO EITHER KILL HIS SUCCESSOR OR JOIN THE MIND.
THUS HE HAS THROWN OFF THE BALANCE OF NATURE. THE PARLIAMENT TRIED TO KILL HIM, BUT HE HAS FOUND A WAY TO NEUTRALIZE THEIR POWER.
AND THERE'S JILLIONS OF WORLDS WITHIN WORLDS, SEE?
AND THE SUPER-HEROES GO OFF TO FIGHT THE BAD GUY WHO WANTS TO BLOW UP ALL THE WORLDS...
AND THE FLASH TRIES TO DESTROY THE BAD GUY'S DEATH RAY, BUT HE GETS KILLED!
AND SUPERMAN STARTS CRYING...
AND WHAT HAPPENS AFTER THAT, RODNEY?
16

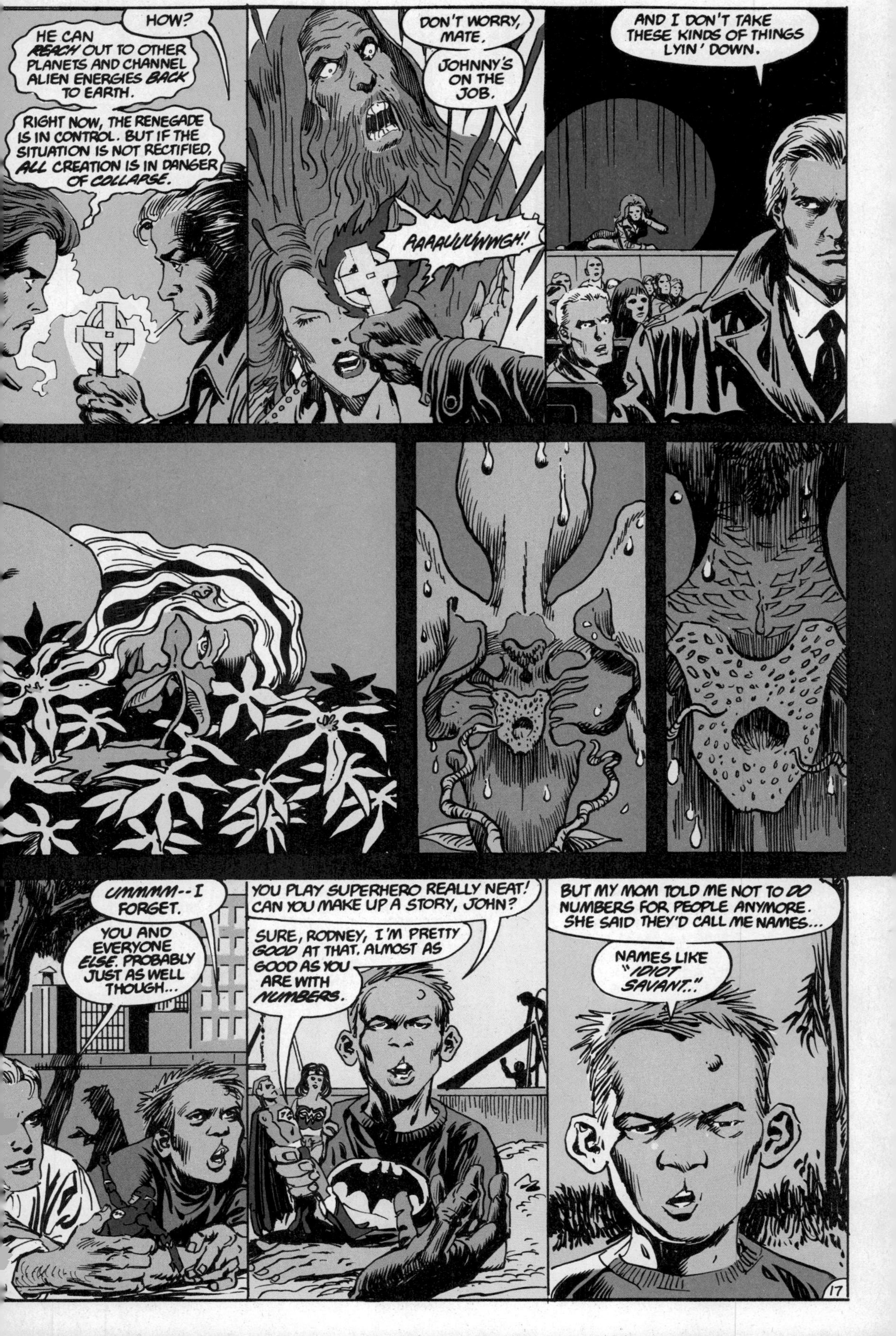
HOW?
HE CAN REACH OUT TO OTHER PLANETS AND CHANNEL ALIEN ENERGIES BACK TO EARTH.
RIGHT NOW, THE RENEGADE IS IN CONTROL. BUT IF THE SITUATION IS NOT RECTIFIED, ALL CREATION IS IN DANGER OF COLLAPSE.
DON'T WORRY, MATE.
JOHNNY'S ON THE JOB.
AAAAUUUWWGH!
AND I DON'T TAKE THESE KINDS OF THINGS LYIN' DOWN.
UMMMM--I FORGET.
YOU AND EVERYONE ELSE. PROBABLY JUST AS WELL THOUGH...
YOU PLAY SUPERHERO REALLY NEAT! CAN YOU MAKE UP A STORY, JOHN?
SURE, RODNEY, I'M PRETTY GOOD AT THAT. ALMOST AS GOOD AS YOU ARE WITH NUMBERS.
BUT MY MOM TOLD ME NOT TO DO NUMBERS FOR PEOPLE ANYMORE. SHE SAID THEY'D CALL ME NAMES...
NAMES LIKE "IDIOT SAVANT..."
17

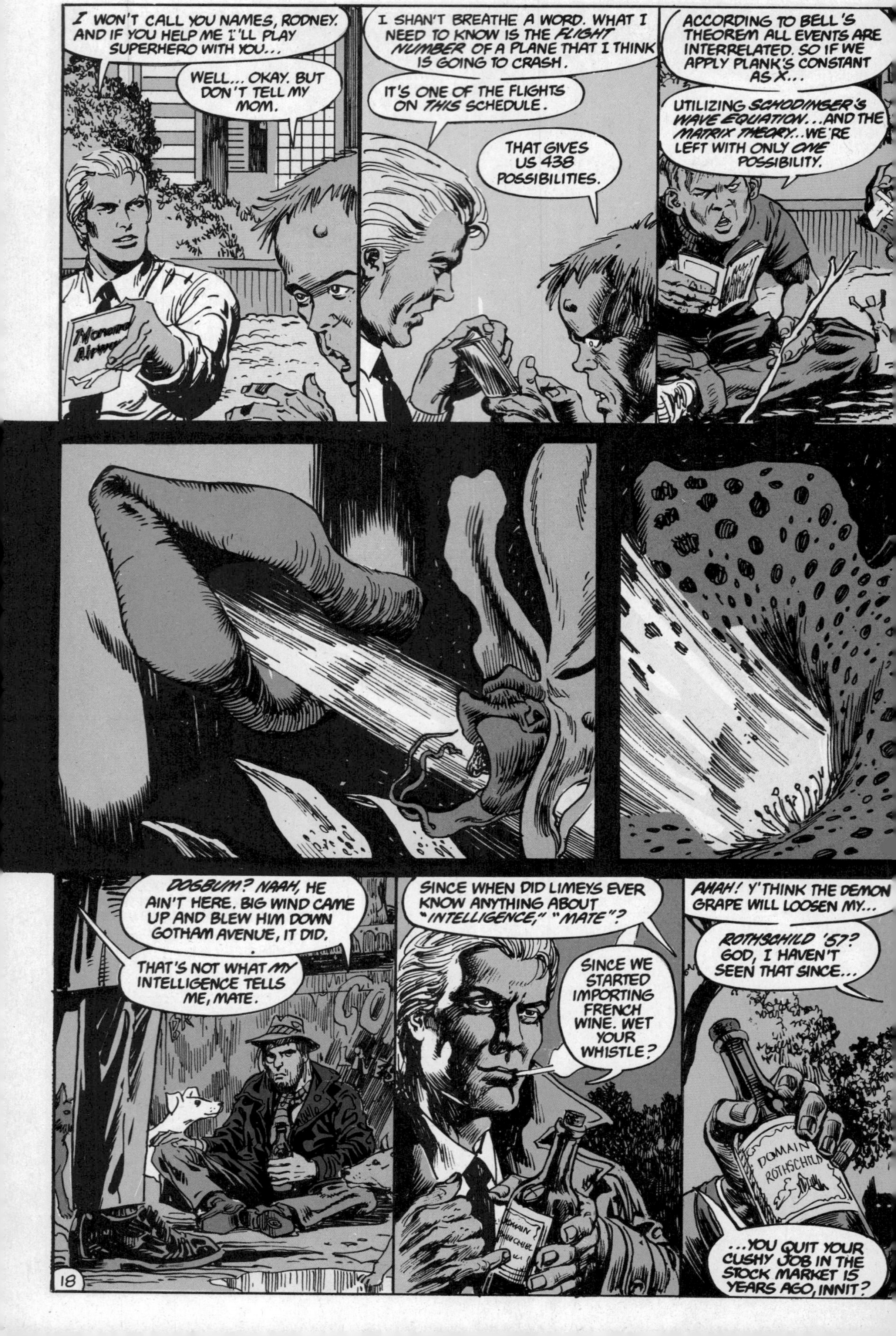
I WON'T CALL YOU NAMES, RODNEY. AND IF YOU HELP ME I'LL PLAY SUPERHERO WITH YOU...
WELL... OKAY. BUT DON'T TELL MY MOM.
I SHAN'T BREATHE A WORD. WHAT I NEED TO KNOW IS THE *FLIGHT NUMBER* OF A PLANE THAT I THINK IS GOING TO CRASH.
IT'S ONE OF THE FLIGHTS ON *THIS* SCHEDULE.
THAT GIVES US 438 POSSIBILITIES.
ACCORDING TO BELL'S THEOREM ALL EVENTS ARE INTERRELATED. SO IF WE APPLY PLANK'S CONSTANT AS X...
UTILIZING *SCHODINGER'S WAVE EQUATION*... AND THE *MATRIX THEORY*... WE'RE LEFT WITH ONLY *ONE* POSSIBILITY.
DOGBUM? NAAH, HE AIN'T HERE. BIG WIND CAME UP AND BLEW HIM DOWN GOTHAM AVENUE, IT DID.
THAT'S NOT WHAT *MY* INTELLIGENCE TELLS ME, MATE.
SINCE WHEN DID LIMEYS EVER KNOW ANYTHING ABOUT *"INTELLIGENCE," "MATE"*?
SINCE WE STARTED IMPORTING FRENCH WINE. WET YOUR WHISTLE?
AHAH! Y'THINK THE DEMON GRAPE WILL LOOSEN MY...
ROTHSCHILD '57? GOD, I HAVEN'T SEEN THAT SINCE...
DOMAIN ROTHSCHILD
...YOU QUIT YOUR CUSHY JOB IN THE STOCK MARKET IS YEARS AGO, INNIT?
18

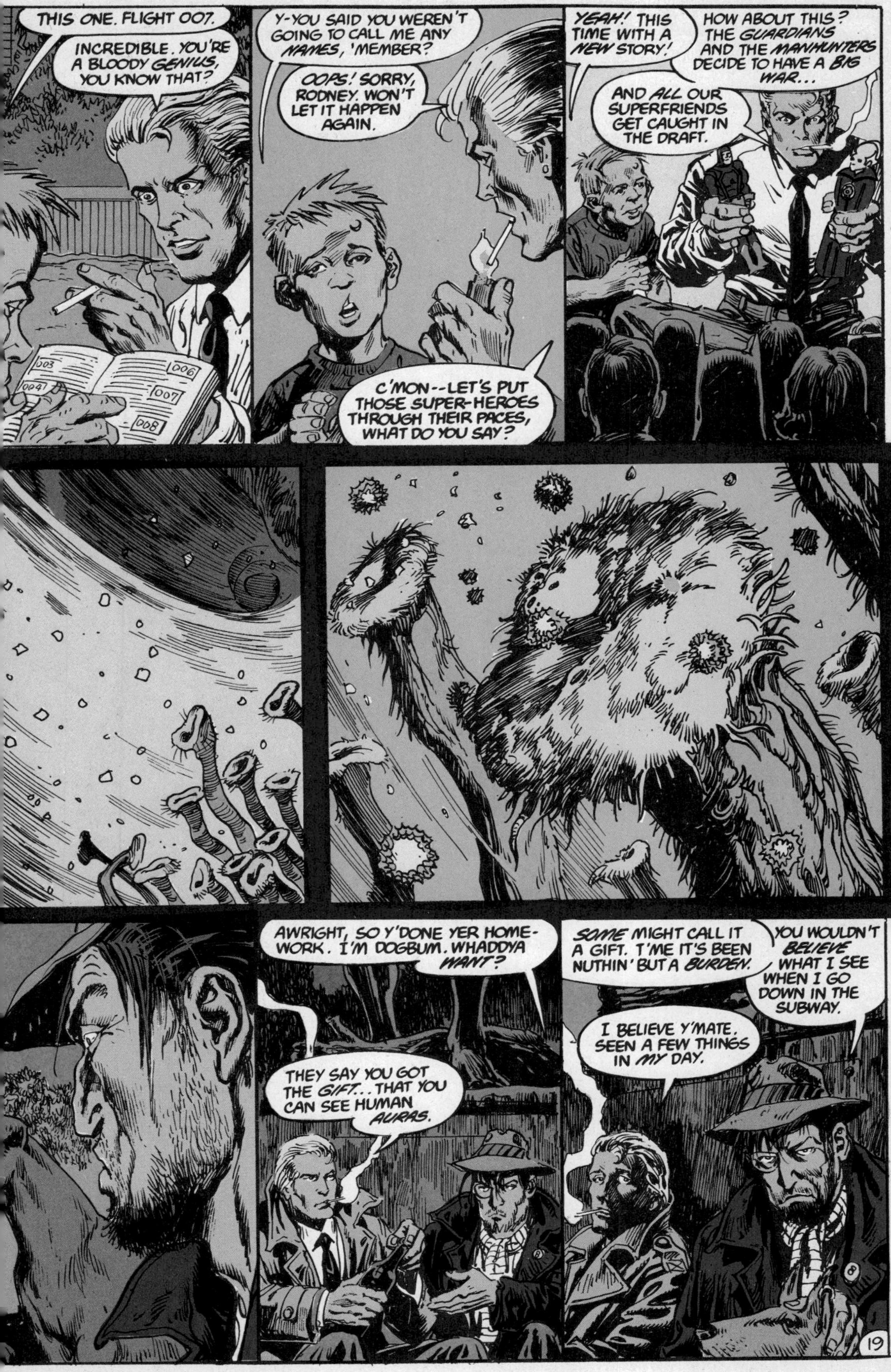
THIS ONE. FLIGHT 007.
INCREDIBLE. YOU'RE A BLOODY GENIUS, YOU KNOW THAT?
Y-YOU SAID YOU WEREN'T GOING TO CALL ME ANY NAMES, 'MEMBER?
OOPS! SORRY, RODNEY. WON'T LET IT HAPPEN AGAIN.
C'MON--LET'S PUT THOSE SUPER-HEROES THROUGH THEIR PACES, WHAT DO YOU SAY?
YEAH! THIS TIME WITH A NEW STORY!
HOW ABOUT THIS? THE GUARDIANS AND THE MANHUNTERS DECIDE TO HAVE A BIG WAR...
AND ALL OUR SUPERFRIENDS GET CAUGHT IN THE DRAFT.
AWRIGHT, SO Y'DONE YER HOME-WORK. I'M DOGBUM. WHADDYA WANT?
THEY SAY YOU GOT THE GIFT... THAT YOU CAN SEE HUMAN AURAS.
SOME MIGHT CALL IT A GIFT. T'ME IT'S BEEN NUTHIN' BUT A BURDEN.
YOU WOULDN'T BELIEVE WHAT I SEE WHEN I GO DOWN IN THE SUBWAY.
I BELIEVE Y'MATE. SEEN A FEW THINGS IN MY DAY.
19

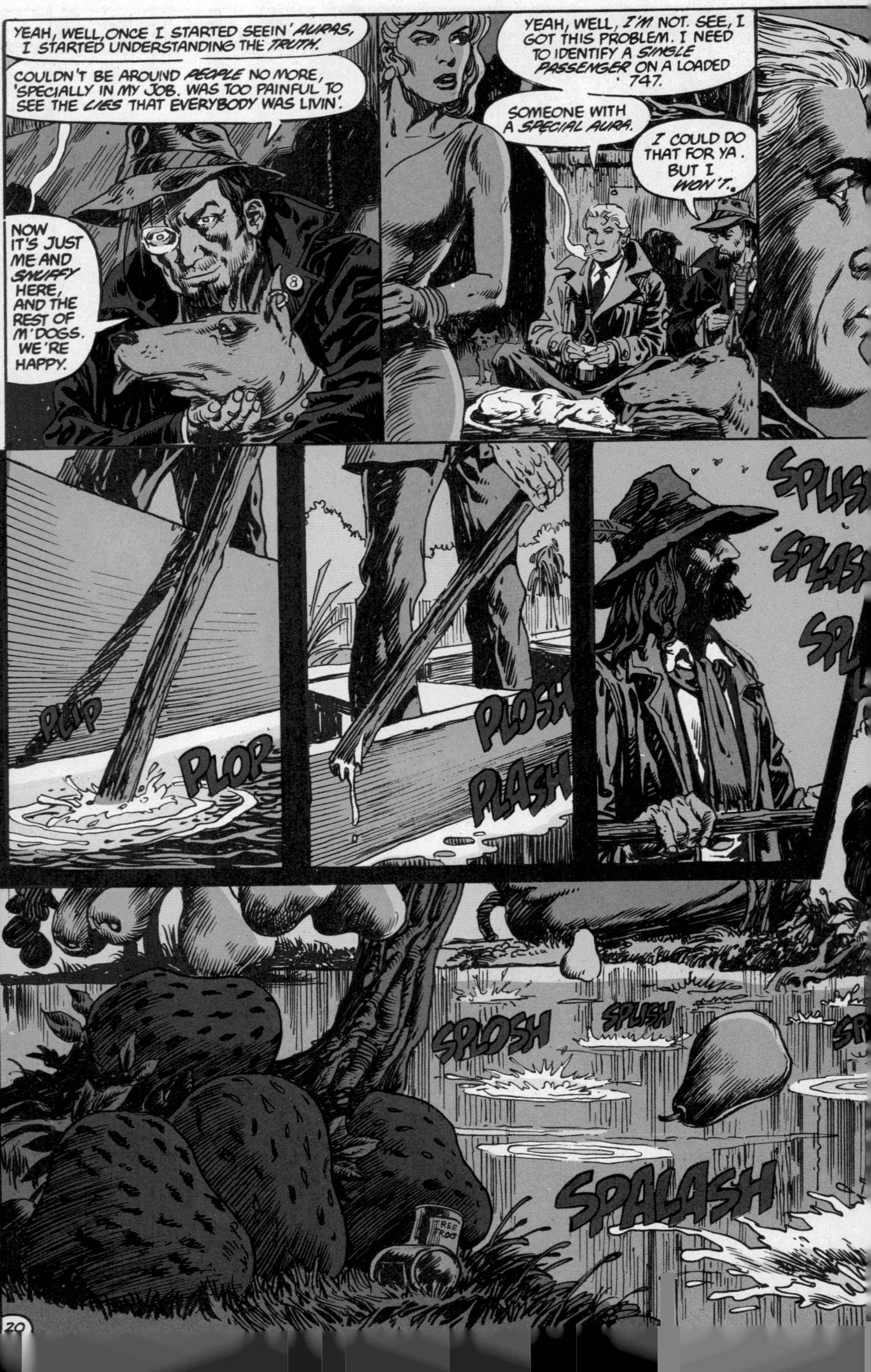
YEAH, WELL, ONCE I STARTED SEEIN' AURAS, I STARTED UNDERSTANDING THE TRUTH.
COULDN'T BE AROUND PEOPLE NO MORE, 'SPECIALLY IN MY JOB. WAS TOO PAINFUL TO SEE THE LIES THAT EVERYBODY WAS LIVIN'.
NOW IT'S JUST ME AND SNUFFY HERE, AND THE REST OF M' DOGS. WE'RE HAPPY.
YEAH, WELL, I'M NOT. SEE, I GOT THIS PROBLEM. I NEED TO IDENTIFY A SINGLE PASSENGER ON A LOADED 747.
SOMEONE WITH A SPECIAL AURA.
I COULD DO THAT FOR YA. BUT I WON'T.
PLIP
PLOP
PLOSH
PLASH
SPLISH
SPLASH
SPLOSH
SPLISH
SPALASH
TREE FROG

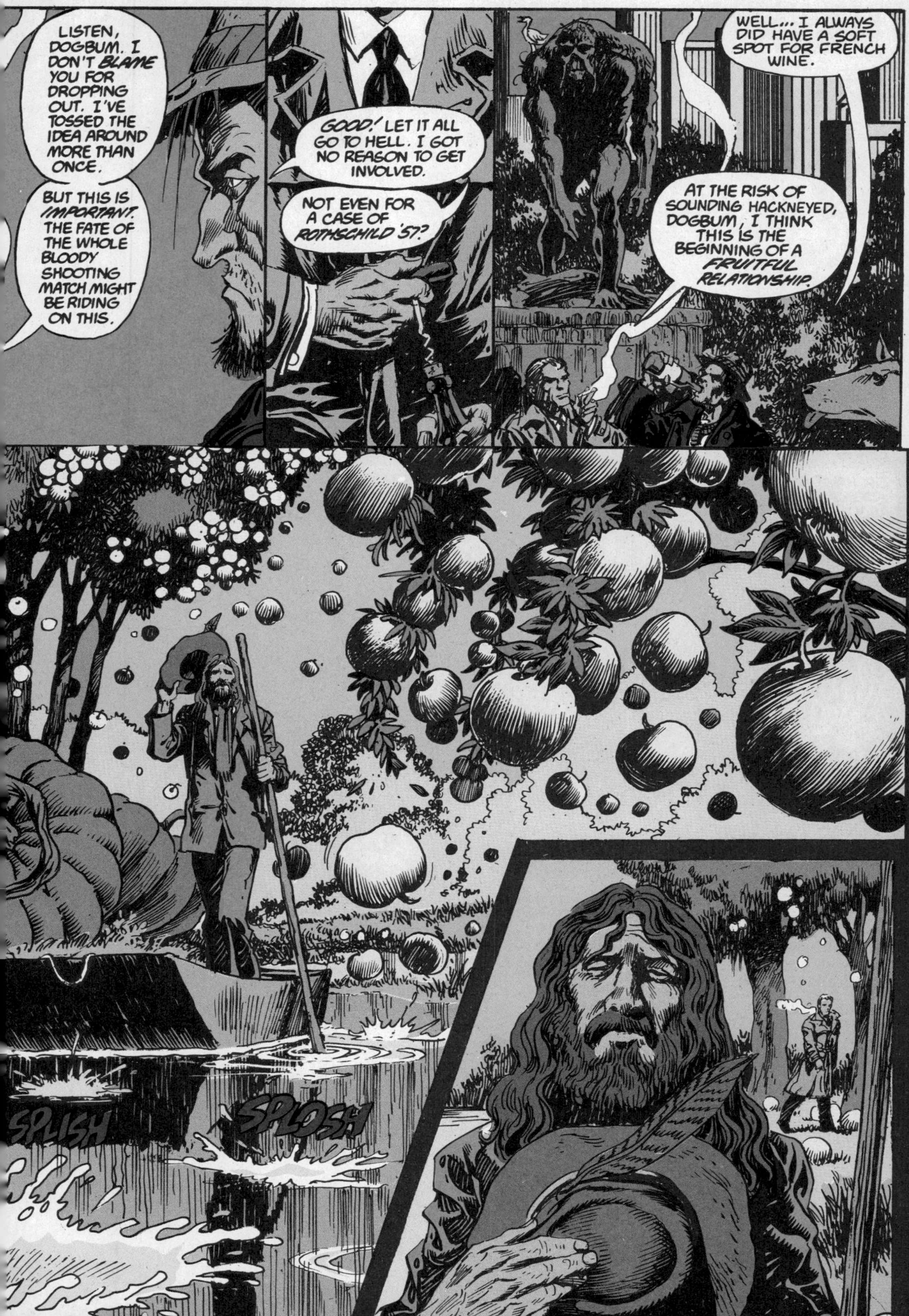
LISTEN, DOGBUM. I DON'T BLAME YOU FOR DROPPING OUT. I'VE TOSSED THE IDEA AROUND MORE THAN ONCE.
BUT THIS IS IMPORTANT. THE FATE OF THE WHOLE BLOODY SHOOTING MATCH MIGHT BE RIDING ON THIS.
GOOD! LET IT ALL GO TO HELL. I GOT NO REASON TO GET INVOLVED.
NOT EVEN FOR A CASE OF ROTHSCHILD '57?
WELL... I ALWAYS DID HAVE A SOFT SPOT FOR FRENCH WINE.
AT THE RISK OF SOUNDING HACKNEYED, DOGBUM, I THINK THIS IS THE BEGINNING OF A FRUITFUL RELATIONSHIP.
SPLISH
SPLOSH
21

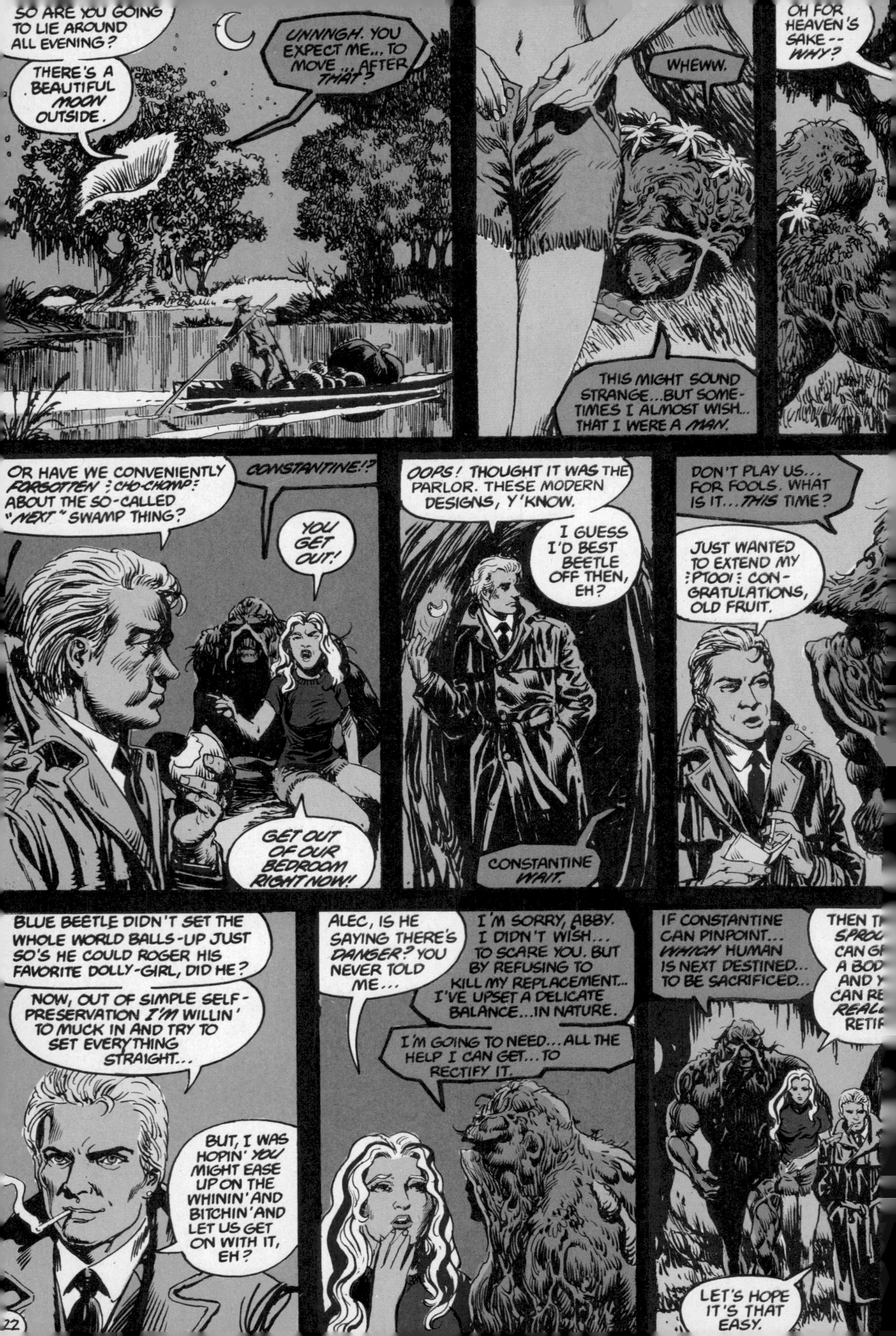

SO ARE YOU GOING TO LIE AROUND ALL EVENING?
THERE'S A BEAUTIFUL MOON OUTSIDE.
UNNNGH. YOU EXPECT ME... TO MOVE... AFTER THAT?
WHEWW.
THIS MIGHT SOUND STRANGE... BUT SOMETIMES I ALMOST WISH... THAT I WERE A MAN.
OH FOR HEAVEN'S SAKE -- WHY?
OR HAVE WE CONVENIENTLY FORGOTTEN :CHO-CHOMP: ABOUT THE SO-CALLED "NEXT" SWAMP THING?
CONSTANTINE!?
YOU GET OUT!
GET OUT OF OUR BEDROOM RIGHT NOW!
OOPS! THOUGHT IT WAS THE PARLOR. THESE MODERN DESIGNS, Y'KNOW.
I GUESS I'D BEST BEETLE OFF THEN, EH?
CONSTANTINE WAIT.
DON'T PLAY US... FOR FOOLS. WHAT IS IT... THIS TIME?
JUST WANTED TO EXTEND MY :PTOOI: CONGRATULATIONS, OLD FRUIT.
BLUE BEETLE DIDN'T SET THE WHOLE WORLD BALLS-UP JUST SO'S HE COULD ROGER HIS FAVORITE DOLLY-GIRL, DID HE?
NOW, OUT OF SIMPLE SELF-PRESERVATION I'M WILLIN' TO MUCK IN AND TRY TO SET EVERYTHING STRAIGHT...
BUT, I WAS HOPIN' YOU MIGHT EASE UP ON THE WHININ' AND BITCHIN' AND LET US GET ON WITH IT, EH?
ALEC, IS HE SAYING THERE'S DANGER? YOU NEVER TOLD ME...
I'M SORRY, ABBY. I DIDN'T WISH... TO SCARE YOU. BUT BY REFUSING TO KILL MY REPLACEMENT... I'VE UPSET A DELICATE BALANCE... IN NATURE.
I'M GOING TO NEED... ALL THE HELP I CAN GET... TO RECTIFY IT.
IF CONSTANTINE CAN PINPOINT... WHICH HUMAN IS NEXT DESTINED... TO BE SACRIFICED...
LET'S HOPE IT'S THAT EASY.

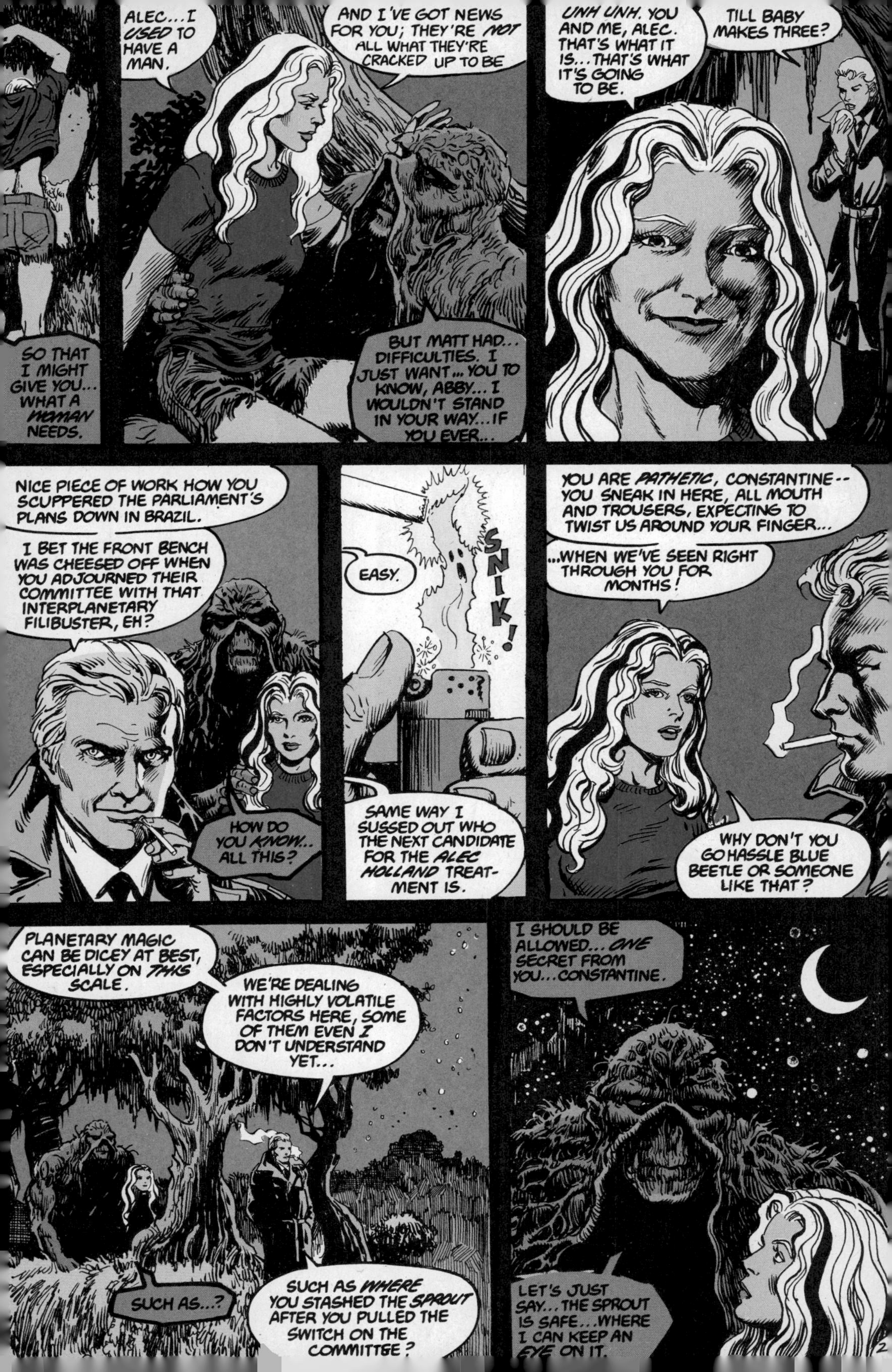
SO THAT I MIGHT GIVE YOU... WHAT A WOMAN NEEDS.
ALEC...I USED TO HAVE A MAN.
AND I'VE GOT NEWS FOR YOU; THEY'RE NOT ALL WHAT THEY'RE CRACKED UP TO BE
BUT MATT HAD... DIFFICULTIES. I JUST WANT... YOU TO KNOW, ABBY... I WOULDN'T STAND IN YOUR WAY...IF YOU EVER...
UNH UNH. YOU AND ME, ALEC. THAT'S WHAT IT IS...THAT'S WHAT IT'S GOING TO BE.
TILL BABY MAKES THREE?
NICE PIECE OF WORK HOW YOU SCUPPERED THE PARLIAMENT'S PLANS DOWN IN BRAZIL.
I BET THE FRONT BENCH WAS CHEESED OFF WHEN YOU ADJOURNED THEIR COMMITTEE WITH THAT INTERPLANETARY FILIBUSTER, EH?
HOW DO YOU KNOW... ALL THIS?
EASY.
SNIK!
SAME WAY I SUSSED OUT WHO THE NEXT CANDIDATE FOR THE ALEC HOLLAND TREATMENT IS.
YOU ARE PATHETIC, CONSTANTINE-- YOU SNEAK IN HERE, ALL MOUTH AND TROUSERS, EXPECTING TO TWIST US AROUND YOUR FINGER...
...WHEN WE'VE SEEN RIGHT THROUGH YOU FOR MONTHS!
WHY DON'T YOU GO HASSLE BLUE BEETLE OR SOMEONE LIKE THAT?
PLANETARY MAGIC CAN BE DICEY AT BEST, ESPECIALLY ON THIS SCALE.
WE'RE DEALING WITH HIGHLY VOLATILE FACTORS HERE, SOME OF THEM EVEN I DON'T UNDERSTAND YET...
SUCH AS...?
SUCH AS WHERE YOU STASHED THE SPROUT AFTER YOU PULLED THE SWITCH ON THE COMMITTEE?
I SHOULD BE ALLOWED... ONE SECRET FROM YOU...CONSTANTINE.
LET'S JUST SAY... THE SPROUT IS SAFE...WHERE I CAN KEEP AN EYE ON IT.

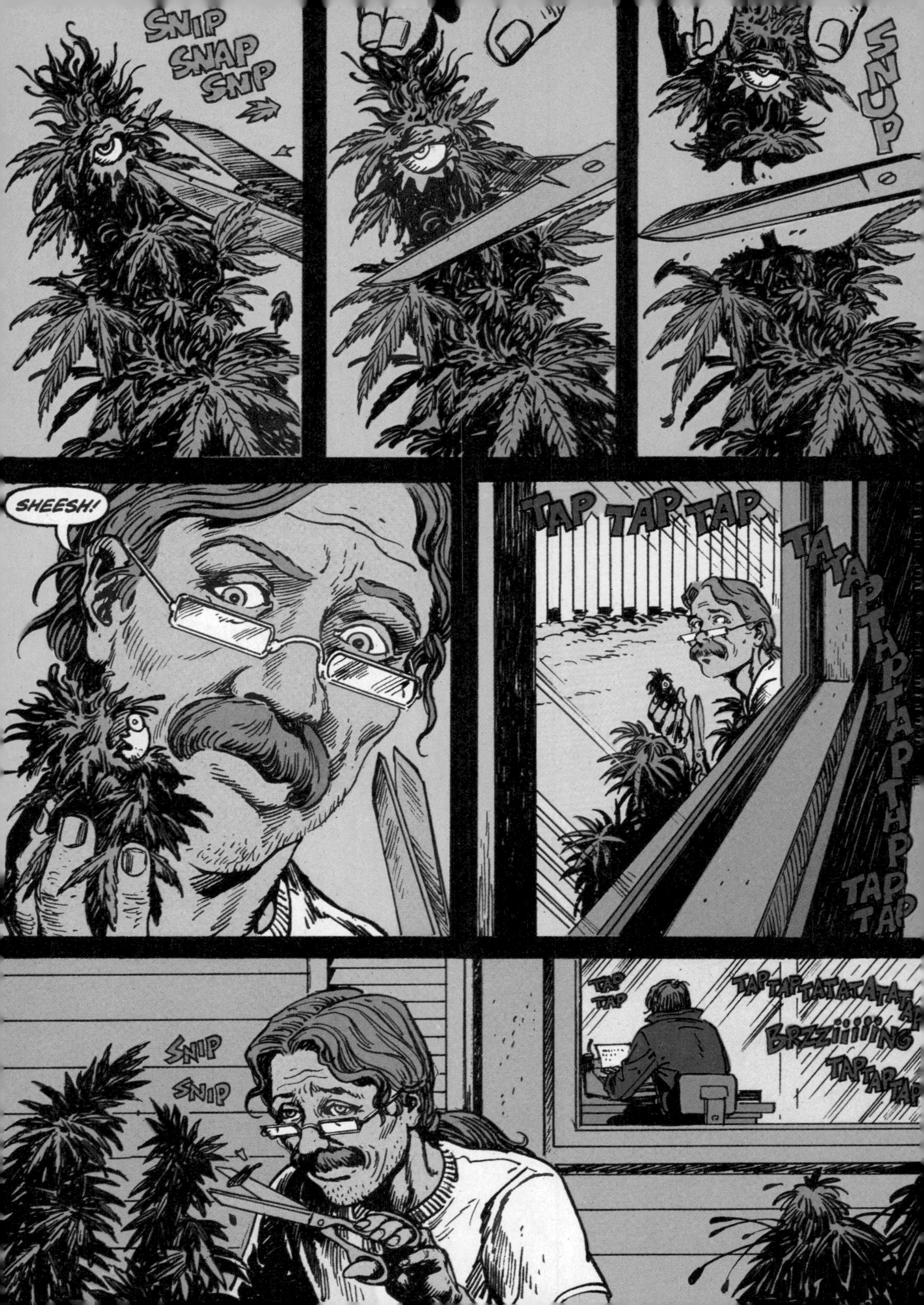
SNIP
SNAP
SNP
SNUP
SHEESH!
TAP TAP TAP
TATAPTAPTAPTAPTAPTAP
TAP
TAP
SNIP
SNIP
TAP
TAP
TAPTAPTATATATATA
BRZZiiiiiNG
TAPTAPTA

SWAMP THING
cover gallery

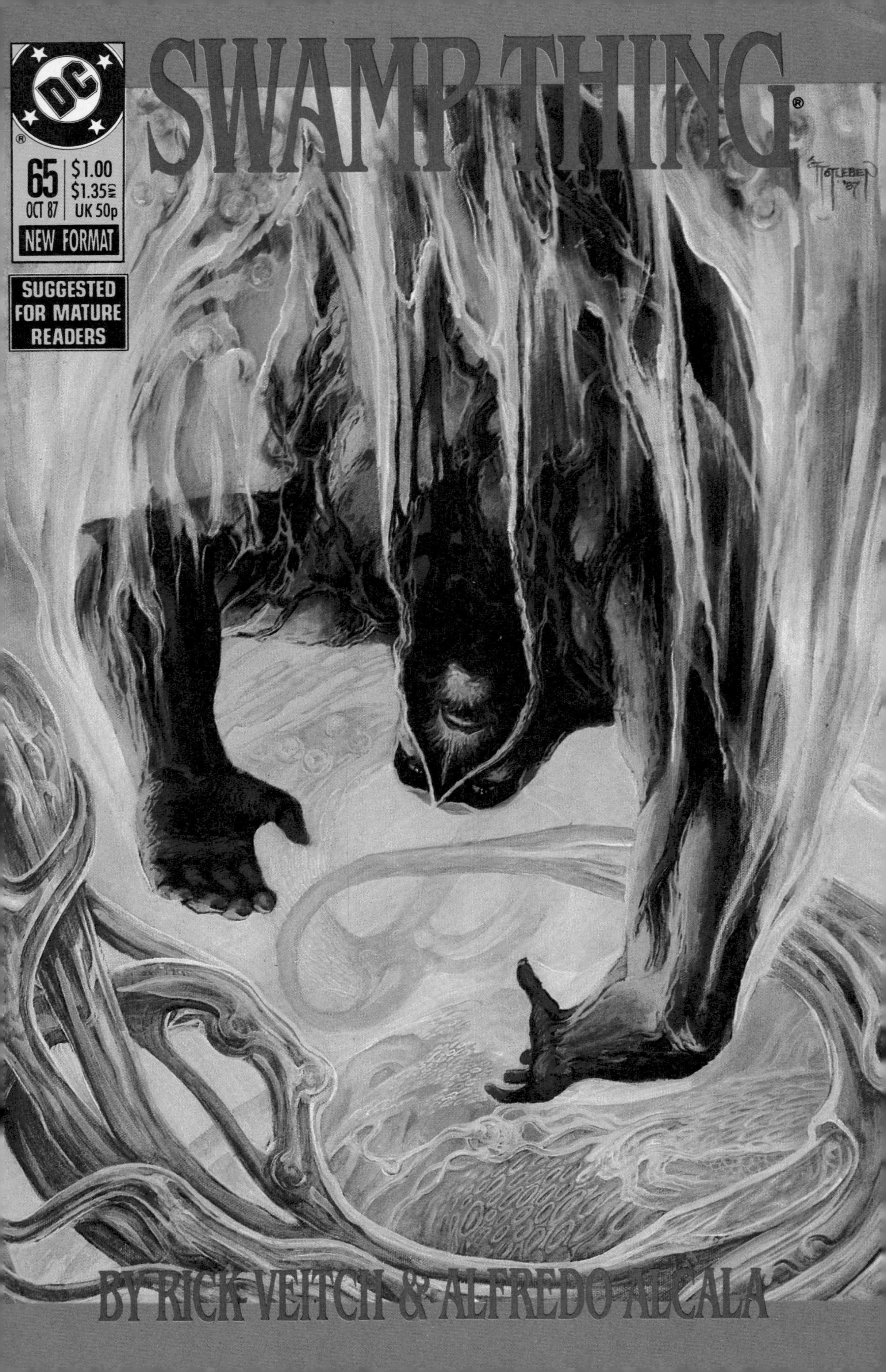
SWAMP THING
65
$1.00
$1.35 CAN
OCT 87
UK 50p
NEW FORMAT
SUGGESTED FOR MATURE READERS
TOTLEBEN '87
BY RICK VEITCH & ALFREDO ALCALA

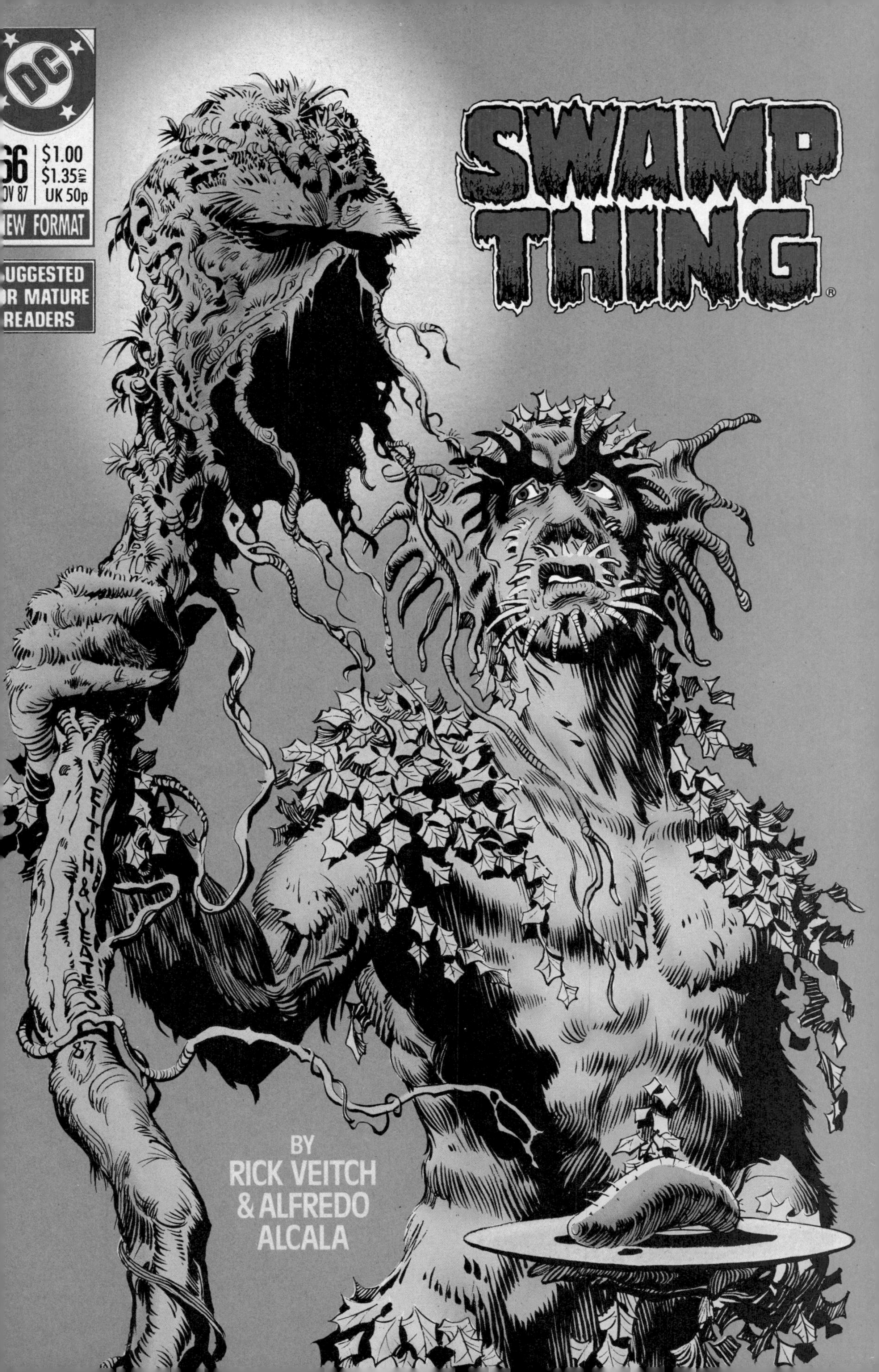

DC
66 NOV 87
$1.00
$1.35 CAN
UK 50p
NEW FORMAT
SUGGESTED FOR MATURE READERS
SWAMP THING®
VEITCH & YEATES 87
BY
RICK VEITCH
& ALFREDO
ALCALA

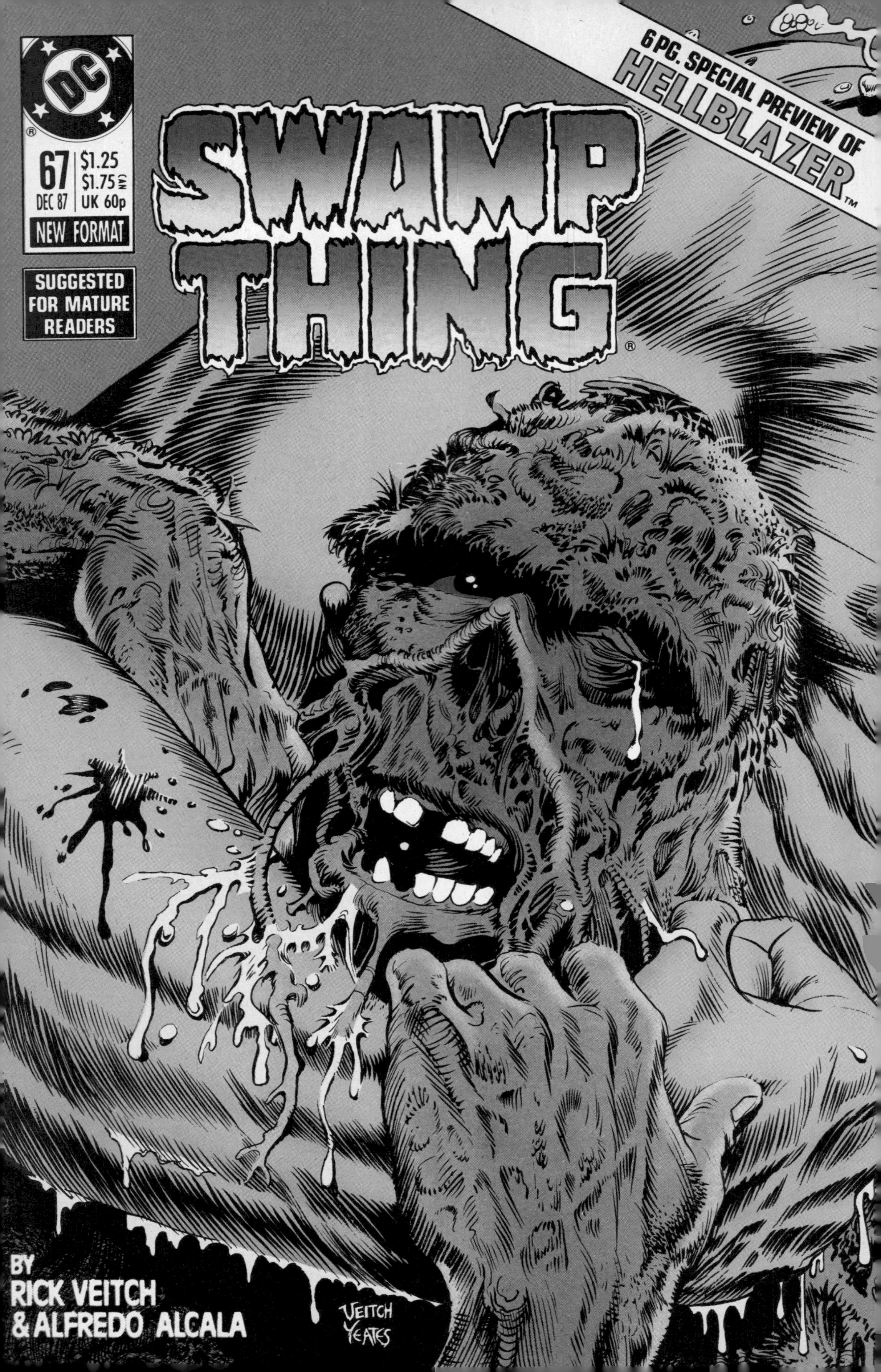
DC
67
DEC 87
$1.25
$1.75 CAN
UK 60p
NEW FORMAT
SUGGESTED FOR MATURE READERS
SWAMP THING
6 PG. SPECIAL PREVIEW OF HELLBLAZER
BY
RICK VEITCH
& ALFREDO ALCALA
VEITCH
YEATES

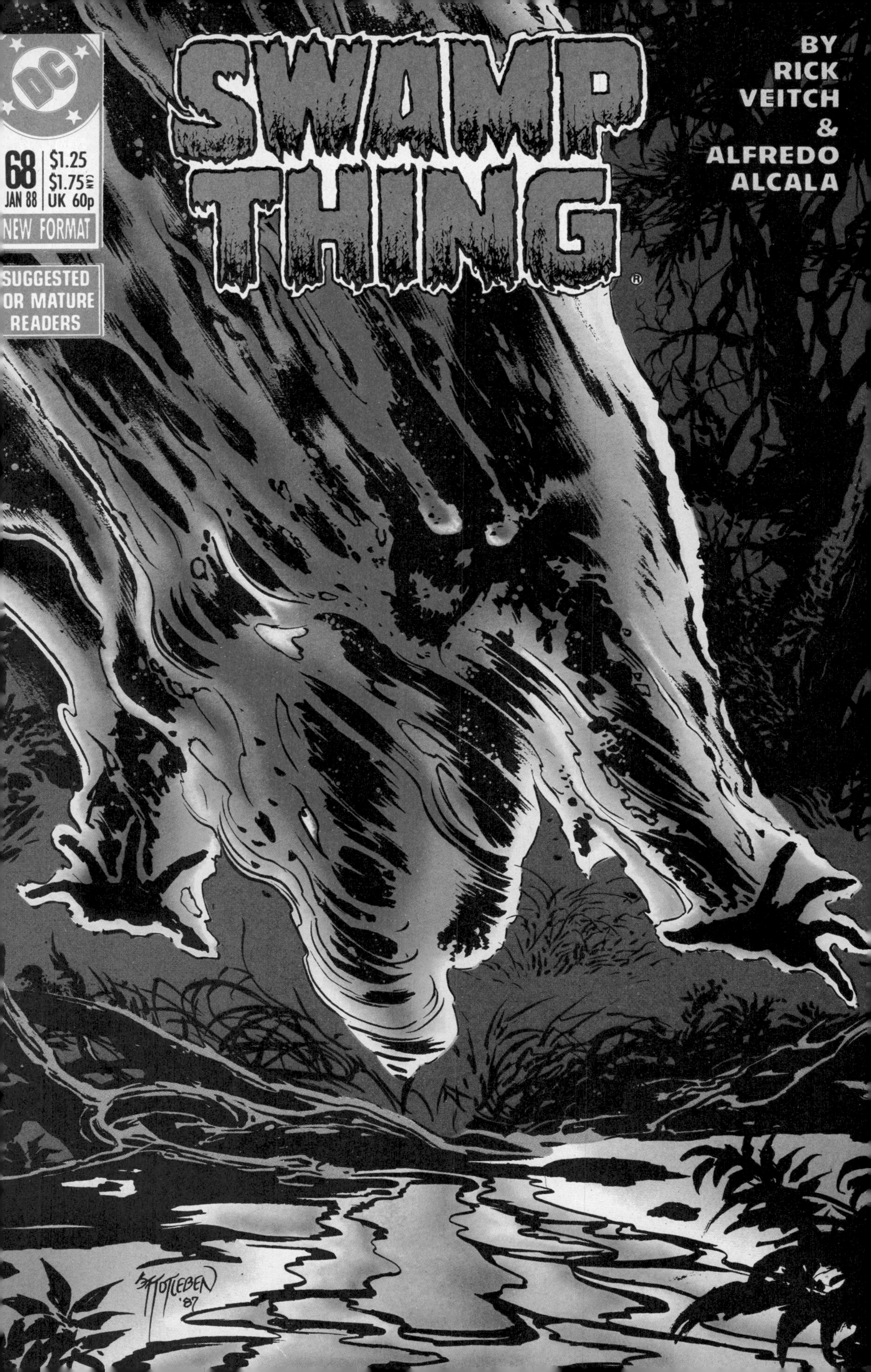

SWAMP THING
BY RICK VEITCH & ALFREDO ALCALA
68
JAN 88
$1.25
$1.75 CAN
UK 60p
NEW FORMAT
SUGGESTED FOR MATURE READERS

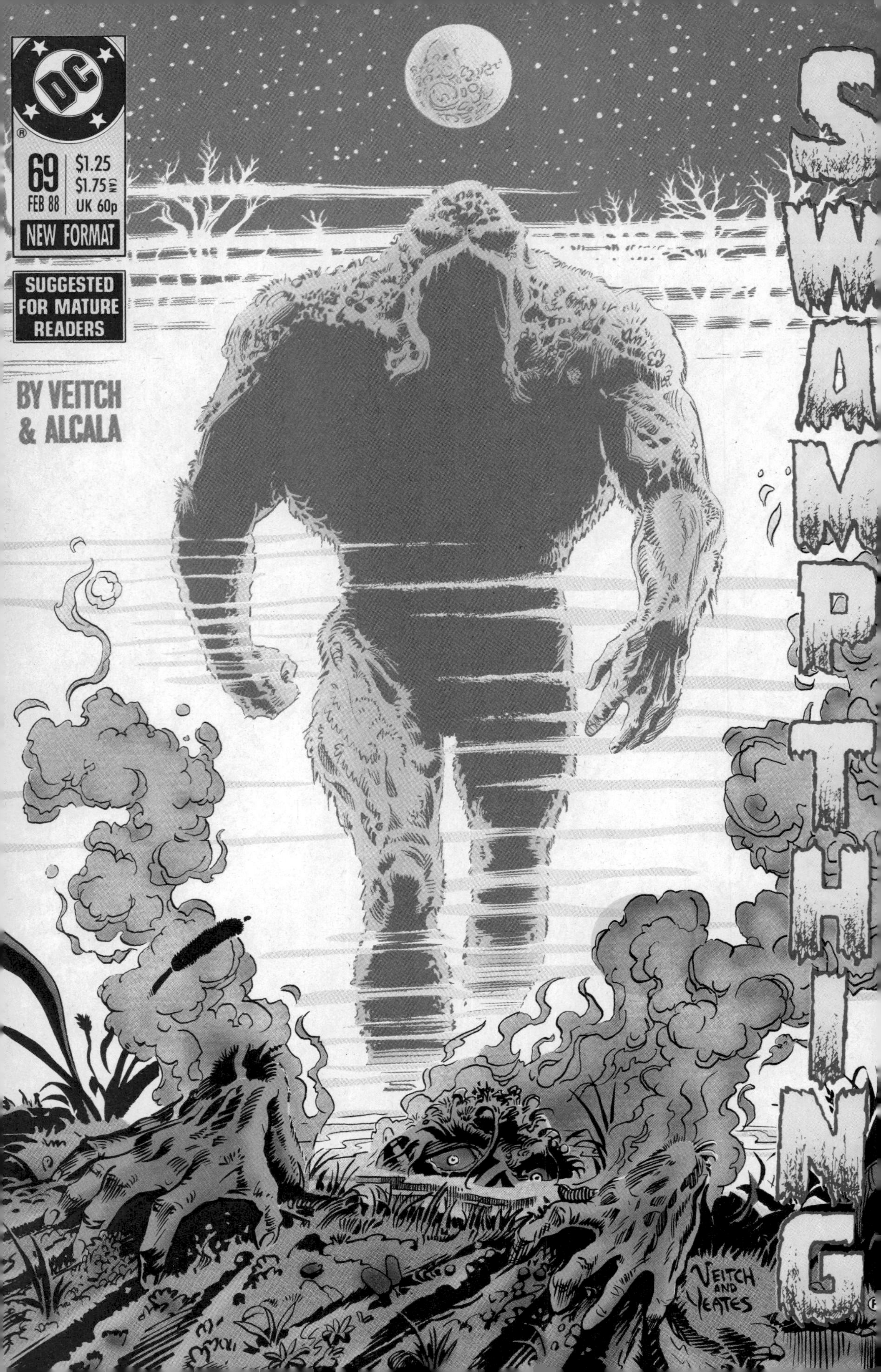
DC
69
FEB 88
$1.25
$1.75 CAN
UK 60p
NEW FORMAT
SUGGESTED FOR MATURE READERS
BY VEITCH & ALCALA
SWAMP THING
VEITCH AND YEATES

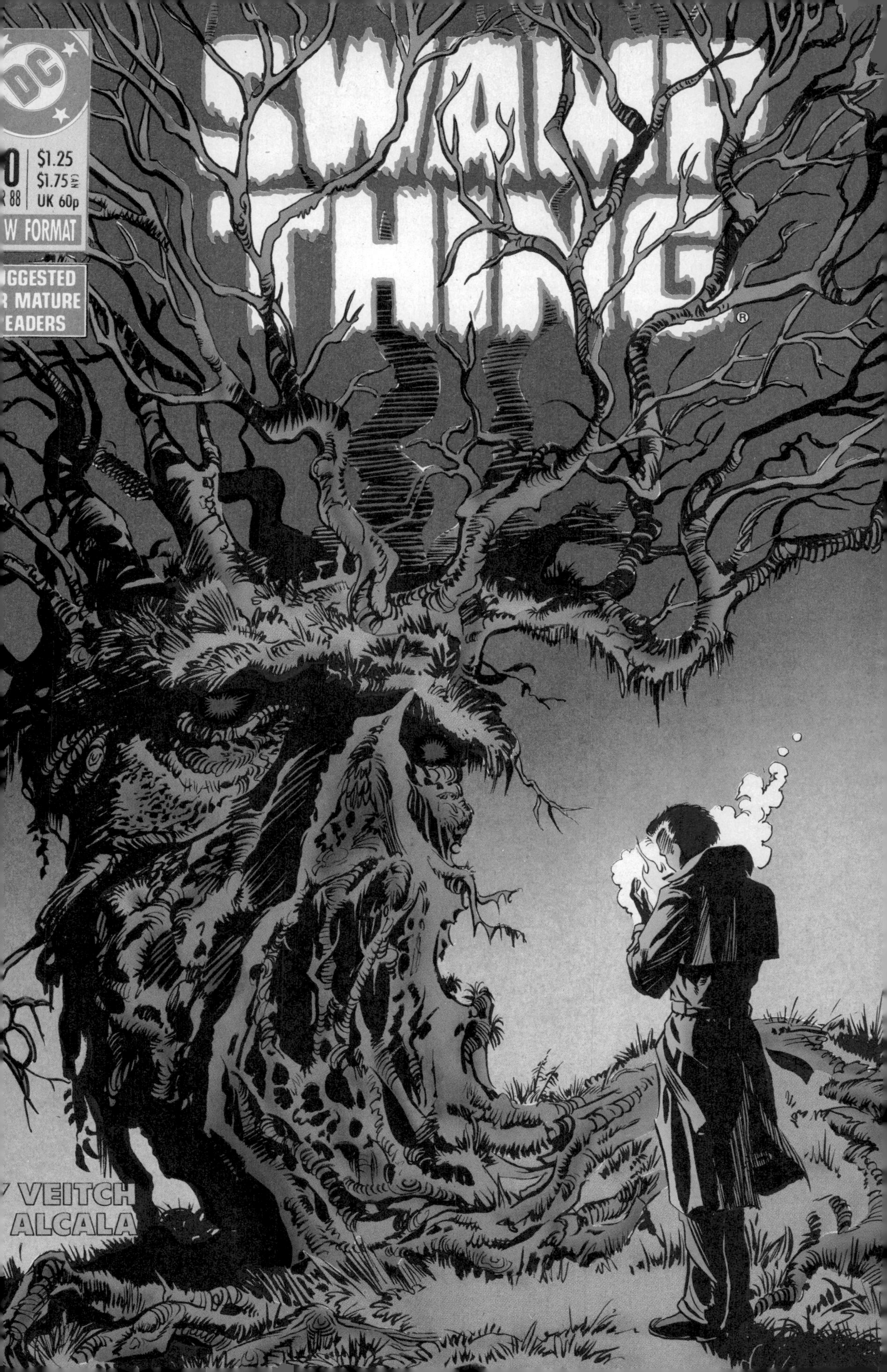

SWAMP THING
$1.25
$1.75 CAN
UK 60p
R 88
W FORMAT
UGGESTED
R MATURE
EADERS
VEITCH
ALCALA

Biographies

Rick Veitch

Rick Veitch worked in the underground comics scene before attending the Joe Kubert School of Cartoon and Graphic Art. After graduating, he worked with Stephen Bissette on *Bizarre Adventures* before creating and illustrating *The One*, the innovative epic comics miniseries. In addition to writing and drawing an acclaimed run on *Swamp Thing*, he is the creator/cartoonist of *Brat Pack*, *Maximortal*, and the dream-based *Rare Bit Fiends*, and a contributing artist on *1963*. He is also the writer and artist of the miniseries *Greyshirt: Indigo Sunset* from America's Best Comics, and is currently at work on *Can't Get No* from Vertigo.

Alfredo Alcala

Alfredo Alcala's graceful, moody inks helped maintain the style on *Swamp Thing* through many penciller changes. DC first employed Alcala's talents in its horror and war comics such as *Ghosts*, *Unexpected*, and *Weird War Tales*. Later he moved on to titles including *All-Star Squadron*, *Savage Sword of Conan*, *Batman*, *Swamp Thing* and countless others for both DC and Marvel. After a long battle with cancer, Alcala passed away in April, 2000.

Brett Ewins

After making his debut in the weekly U.K. magazine *2000 AD*, artist Brett Ewins has gone on to a long and successful career in the British comics world, contributing to a host of stories in *2000 AD* and co-creating the magazine's *Bad Company* storyline. Ewins was also a co-founding editor of *Deadline* magazine, and created the acclaimed *Skreemer* series for Vertigo with writer Peter Milligan.

John Totleben

After a childhood in Erie, Pennsylvania spent consuming a steady diet of comics, monster magazines, and monster movies, John Totleben went to the Joe Kubert School of Cartoon and Graphic Art where he met Steve Bissette. Together they worked on *Bizarre Adventures* followed by *Swamp Thing*, which they drew for almost three years. A finely detailed artist, Totleben is best known for his illustrative work on Alan Moore's *Miracleman*. His other credits include *1963*, *Vermillion* and *The Dreaming*.

Tom Yeates

Born in 1955, Tom Yeates was one of the first graduates of the Joe Kubert School of Cartoon and Graphic Art (along with classmates Rick Veitch, Stephen Bissette, and John Totleben). Influenced primarily by classic adventure illustrators like Alex Raymond and Hal Foster, Yeates has contributed artwork to a host of titles and publishers, and has served as an editor for Eclipse Comics as well as illustrating a newspaper strip revival of *Zorro* from 1999 to 2000.

Tatjana Wood

Tatjana Wood switched careers from dressmaking to comics coloring in the late 1960s and quickly established herself as one of the top colorists in the field, winning two Shazam Awards in the early 1970s. Wood continues to color for DC Comics.

John Costanza

John Costanza entered the comics field in the late 1960s, lettering such groundbreaking series as Dennis O'Neil and Neal Adams's *Green Lantern/Green Arrow* and Jack Kirby's *New Gods*. In addition to his lettering work, John is also an accomplished cartoonist.

Beginning with a gothic nightmare brought to life, this revolutionary series evolves into a masterpiece of lyrical fantasy, telling the horrifying yet poignant story of a man transformed into a monster, and from there into the living avatar of all the green life on Earth.

SWAMP THING: DARK GENESIS
LEN WEIN/BERNI WRIGHTSON

**SWAMP THING VOLUME 1:
SAGA OF THE SWAMP THING**
ALAN MOORE/STEPHEN BISSETTE/
JOHN TOTLEBEN

**SWAMP THING VOLUME 2:
LOVE & DEATH**
ALAN MOORE/STEPHEN BISSETTE/
JOHN TOTLEBEN/SHAWN MCMANUS

**SWAMP THING VOLUME 3:
THE CURSE**
ALAN MOORE/STEPHEN BISSETTE/
JOHN TOTLEBEN

**SWAMP THING VOLUME 4:
A MURDER OF CROWS**
ALAN MOORE/VARIOUS

**SWAMP THING VOLUME 5:
EARTH TO EARTH**
ALAN MOORE/JOHN TOTLEBEN/
RICK VEITCH/ALFREDO ALCALA

**SWAMP THING VOLUME 6:
REUNION**
ALAN MOORE/RICK VEITCH/STEPHEN
BISSETTE/ALFREDO ALCALA /JOHN TOTLEBEN

**SWAMP THING VOLUME 7:
REGENESIS**
RICK VEITCH/ALFREDO ALCALA/BRETT EWINS

Look for these other VERTIGO books:
All Vertigo titles are Suggested for Mature Readers